Contemporary Entrepreneurship

Jerry W. Moorman
Professor of Business Administration
Mesa State College
Grand Junction, Colorado

James W. Halloran
Entrepreneur-in-Residence
Business and Accounting Department
Muhlenberg College
Allentown, Pennsylvania

SOUTH-WESTERN EDUCATIONAL PUBLISHING

Cover design by Cindy Beckmeyer, Bruce Design
Cover Illustration: David Tillinghast

Page 77 photo: Ralph Cowan/Tony Stone Worldwide/Click Chicago, LTD

Vice-President/Editor-in-Chief: Dennis M. Kokoruda
Developmental Editor: Willis S. Vincent
Production Coordinator: Carol Sturzenberger
Marketing Manager: Larry Qualls
Production Editor: Mark Cheatham
Internal Design: Elaine St. John-Lagenaur
Photo Editors: Alix Roughen
                Fred M. Middendorf
Production, Art, and Prepress: PC&F, Inc.

Copyright © 1996
by South-Western Educational Publishing
Cincinnati, Ohio

All Rights Reserved

The text of this publication, or any part thereof, may not be reproduced or transmitted in any form or by any means, electronic or mechanical, including photocopying, recording, storage in an information retrieval system, or otherwise, without the prior written permission of the publisher.

ISBN: 0-538-71261-9

Library of Congress Catalog Card Number: 95-069636

   1 2 3 4 5 6 7 8 9 PR 99 98 97 96 95

Printed in the United States of America

I(T)P
International Thomson Publishing

South-Western Educational Publishing is a division of International Thomson Publishing Inc. The ITP trademark is used under license.

PREFACE

What an exciting time it is for college students to begin their study of business. At no time in recent history has the world market been in such a state of flux. Eastern Europe and the states of the former Soviet Union have made drastic changes in the way they conduct business. They have begun to embrace capitalism with vigor and anticipation. At the heart of that anticipation is the belief that individuals can own and operate their own businesses with success. This interest and belief in entrepreneurship is sweeping the world.

In the course of America's history, we can trace the country's phenomenal success to the spirit of individual entrepreneurs who were not afraid to strike out on their own in pursuit of business dreams. Large companies such as Xerox and Apple Computer began as dreams of individuals. From those small dreams grew large, successful corporations.

Entrepreneurs will mold the future business success of America just as they have in the past. As we race toward the year 2000, entrepreneurs will blaze the trail through business innovation and creativity.

A BOOK FOR ENTREPRENEURS

Contemporary Entrepreneurship is a postsecondary level textbook designed with entrepreneurs in mind. It is written in simple and understandable language. All topics were carefully chosen with an eye toward presenting practical material for use in real entrepreneurial situations.

To assist the instructor, an annotated edition of *Contemporary Entrepreneurship* is available. The annotated version has teaching suggestions included in the margins, alongside the student text, for the instructor's convenience. Margin notes were developed by teachers for teachers. They were written and organized so that even teachers not experienced in entrepreneurship can deliver the material in a clear and professional manner.

Both authors have extensive experience as small business consultants and are full-time postsecondary faculty members. Dr. Moorman is a tenured Professor of Business at Mesa State College in Grand Junction, Colorado, and Mr. Halloran serves as Entrepreneur-in-Residence at Muhlenberg College in Allentown, Pennsylvania. The expertise that they have developed as a result of working with and advising hundreds of clients, as well as their years of teaching experience, are reflected throughout the book. That experience and expertise have been combined with the latest learning theory to create a text that is both technically accurate and educationally sound.

TEXT ORGANIZATION

Contemporary Entrepreneurship is divided into six units. The topics are arranged so that readers encounter the steps to successful entrepreneurship in a logical order.

- Unit 1 is an introduction to and overview of entrepreneurship. It deals with the individual as an entrepreneur and presents an overview of the process necessary to plan a small business. Purchasing an existing business and a franchise are also covered.
- Unit 2 begins with getting to know your customers and competition. An examination of location and facilities is followed by a detailed explanation of how to develop the marketing plan. This unit includes a discussion of pricing and sales planning and ends with a chapter on promotional strategies.
- Unit 3 is devoted to financing a small business. Topics include initial capitalization and financial resources.
- Unit 4 moves into the management of a new business. Chapters in this unit cover forms of ownership, human resource management, management control tools, computer applications, and sources of assistance for entrepreneurs.
- Unit 5, perhaps the most technical in nature, outlines the legal requirements of entrepreneurship. This unit presents issues of business law that are most important for entrepreneurs to understand. Topics include special regulations, contracts and agreements, buying and selling, and real property and insurance. A discussion of ethics and social responsibility in entrepreneurship concludes the unit.
- Unit 6 examines both international and environmental entrepreneurship, two rapidly growing areas of business that provide today's entrepreneur with numerous opportunities for success.

Each chapter opens with chapter objectives followed by the text that includes an ongoing case entitled *The Fashion Attic* which tracks the growth of a new business. In this section, Laura Watson, a fictional entrepreneur, applies the concepts presented in that specific chapter to her business. Sometimes she is successful and sometimes she makes mistakes—each situation provides a new opportunity to discuss chapter content.

End-of-chapter features include a *Summary, Vocabulary Builder, Review Questions, Discussion Questions,* a *Critical Thinking* exercise, a *Short Case*, and a *Project Challenge. Project Challenges* are designed to allow each student to apply chapter concepts to the building of a hypothetical entrepreneurial venture of his or her own choice.

To complement the text, the authors have developed a *Student Workbook* that reinforces the material presented. Also available is an *Instructor's Manual*, which includes chapter outlines, transparency masters, and solutions to student text, *Student Workbook,* and *Test Bank* questions and activities. A *Test Bank* includes questions for each chapter as well as a pretest and post-test. A *MicroExam* is also available, providing another method to check comprehension.

CONTENTS

UNIT 1 ENTREPRENEURSHIP AND YOU

1 You as an Entrepreneur   2

What Is an Entrepreneur?, 2; Characteristics of Successful Entrepreneurs, 4; Working in the Right Environment, 7; Setting Personal Goals, 10; The Fashion Attic, 18; Creative Entrepreneurship, 19; Summary, 21; Vocabulary Builder, 21; Review Questions, 21; Discussion Questions, 22; Critical Thinking, 22; Short Case: Airplanes Versus Yogurt, 22; Project Challenge, 23

2 Planning the Small Business   24

Getting Started, 24; Planning, 25; The Business Plan, 25; Formulating a Business Plan, 26; Deciding Whether or Not To Go Into Business, 34; Sources for Planning Assistance, 35; The Fashion Attic, 36; Summary, 37; Vocabulary Builder, 37; Review Questions, 37; Discussion Questions, 38; Critical Thinking, 38; Short Case: To Loan or Not to Loan, 38; Project Challenge, 39

3 Purchasing An Existing Business   40

Purchasing an Existing Business, 40; How to Purchase a Business, 45; Evaluating Business For Sale Opportunity, 48; The Fashion Attic, 52; Summary, 53; Vocabulary Builder, 53; Review Questions, 54; Discussion Questions, 54; Critical Thinking, 54; Short Case: A Business For Sale Opportunity, 55; Project Challenge, 55

4 Purchasing a Franchise   56

Definition, 57; Classifications, 57; Advantages, 58; Disadvantages, 60; Legal Aspects of Franchising, 60; Questions to Ask, 65; The Fashion Attic, 68; Summary, 69; Vocabulary Builder, 70; Review Questions, 70; Discussion Questions, 70; Critical Thinking, 71; Short Case: Career Decision, 71; Project Challenge, 72

Unit 1 Case   The Wrong Business Plan, 73

UNIT 2 MARKETING THE SMALL BUSINESS

5 Getting to Know Your Customers — 78

What Are Customers?, 78; Where Are the Customers?, 79; The Fashion Attic, 90; Summary, 91; Vocabulary Builder, 92; Review Questions, 92; Discussion Questions, 92; Critical Thinking, 93; Short Case: Not Enough Information, 93; Project Challenge, 94

6 Getting to Know Your Competition — 95

The Impact of Competition, 96; Competition and Private Enterprise, 96; Types of Competition, 98; Geographic Distribution of Customers, 100; Analyzing Competitive Strengths and Weaknesses, 102; The Fashion Attic, 105; Summary, 107; Vocabulary Builder, 108; Review Questions, 108; Discussion Questions, 108; Critical Thinking, 108; Short Case: "A Good Job" for the Competition, 109; Project Challenge, 110

7 Deciding on a Location and Facilities — 111

The Importance of Convenience, 111; Classifying Consumer Goods, 112; Choosing a Location, 113; Leasing, 120; Evaluating a Facility, 121; The Fashion Attic, 122; Summary, 124; Vocabulary Builder, 125; Review Questions, 125; Discussion Questions, 126; Critical Thinking, 126; Short Case: The Wrong Side of the Street, 126; Project Challenge, 127

8 Developing the Marketing Plan — 129

The Marketing Concept, 129; Market Segmentation and Target Marketing, 129; Target Marketing Questions, 130; Marketing Research, 131; Marketing Mix, 135; Marketing Strategies, 140; The Fashion Attic, 142; Summary, 145; Vocabulary Builder, 145; Review Questions, 146; Discussion Questions, 146; Critical Thinking, 146; Short Case: Selecting a Personal Shopper, 147; Project Challenge, 147

9 Pricing and Sales Planning — 148

Understanding Supply and Demand, 148; Determining Price, 150; The Sales Plan, 156; The Fashion Attic, 160; Summary, 162; Vocabulary Builder, 162; Review Questions, 162; Discussion Questions, 163; Critical Thinking, 163; Short Case: The Sales "Deal", 164; Project Challenge, 165

10 Promotional Strategies   166

Advertising, 167; Advertising Vehicles That Work for Small Businesses, 169; Creating Copy, 174; Evaluating Advertising Results, 175; Staging a Promotional Event, 177; The Dynamics of Selling, 178; The Fashion Attic, 181; Summary, 184; Vocabulary Builder, 184; Review Questions, 184; Discussion Questions, 185; Critical Thinking, 185; Short Case: Creating an Advertisement, 185; Project Challenge, 186

Unit 2 Case   Marketing from Scratch, 187

UNIT 3   FINANCING THE SMALL BUSINESS

11 Personal Finances   192

Personal Resumé, 192; Financial Contribution, 196; The Fashion Attic, 202; Summary, 204; Vocabulary Builder, 205; Review Questions, 205; Discussion Questions, 205; Critical Thinking, 206; Short Case: Too Soon to Expand, 206; Project Challenge, 206

12 Analysis of Financial Sources   207

Financing a New Business, 207; Debt Capital, 207; Equity Capital, 215; Other Sources of Funds, 217; Matching Financial Sources to Business Needs, 217; How the Lending/Investing Decision Is Made, 218; The Fashion Attic, 218; Summary, 220; Vocabulary Builder, 221; Review Questions, 221; Discussion Questions, 221; Critical Thinking, 221; Short Case: To Buy Or Not To Buy, 222; Project Challenge, 223

13 Initial Capitalization and Financial Planning   224

Putting Together a Financial Plan, 224; Computing Initial Capital Needs, 225; Financial Statements, 227; Maintaining Financial Records, 235; The Fashion Attic, 241; Summary, 247; Vocabulary Builder, 247; Review Questions, 247; Discussion Questions, 248; Critical Thinking, 248; Short Case: Capitalization—A Capital Idea, 248; Project Challenge, 250

Unit 3 Case   The Banker, 251

viii Contents

UNIT 4 MANAGING THE SMALL BUSINESS

14 Forms of Ownership — 258

Questions of Ownership, 258; Sole Proprietorship, 258; Partnership, 261; Corporations, 265; Comparing Forms of Ownership, 270; The Fashion Attic, 271; Summary, 272; Vocabulary Builder, 273; Review Questions, 273; Discussion Questions, 273; Critical Thinking, 273; Short Case: Ownership—Safety in Numbers, 274; Project Challenge, 275

15 Human Resources Management — 276

Staffing, 276; Directing, 283; Controlling, 286; Labor Laws, 289; The Fashion Attic, 291; Summary, 293; Vocabulary Builder, 294; Review Questions, 294; Discussion Questions, 295; Critical Thinking, 295; Short Case: Inconsistent Management, 295; Project Challenge, 296

16 Management Control Tools — 297

Management By Objectives, 297; Controlling Revenues, 299; Controlling Inventory, 299; Inventory and Sales Fluctuations, 307; Effects of Inventory and Sales Fluctuations on Other Business Operations, 310; Using Computers as a Control, 314; The Fashion Attic, 316; Summary, 317; Vocabulary Builder, 318; Review Questions, 318; Discussion Questions, 318; Critical Thinking, 319; Short Case: Too Many Suppliers, 319; Project Challenge, 320

17 Computer Applications — 321

Computer Basics, 322; Computer Hardware, 322; Computer Software, 325; Telecommunications, 330; The Fashion Attic, 334; Summary, 336; Vocabulary Builder, 336; Review Questions, 336; Discussion Questions, 337; Critical Thinking, 337; Short Case: Business is Booming, 338; Project Challenge, 339

18 Small Business Assistance — 340

Federal Agencies, 340; Federal/State Cooperatives, 346; State Agencies, 347; Community Resources, 350; Professional Services, 351; The Fashion Attic, 353; Summary, 354; Vocabulary Builder, 354; Review Questions, 354; Discussion Questions, 355; Critical Thinking, 355; Short Case: Ready or Not, 355; Project Challenge, 356

Unit 4 Case   Partnership with a Handshake, 357

UNIT 5   LEGAL AND ETHICAL CONSIDERATIONS

19 Special Regulations — 362

Federal Trade Commission, 362; State and Local Regulations, 370; Consumer Protection, 370; The Fashion Attic, 373; Summary, 374; Vocabulary Builder, 375; Review Questions, 375; Discussion Questions, 375; Critical Thinking, 376; Short Case: The Haberdashery Hoax, 376; Project Challenge, 377

20 Contracts and Agreements — 378

Contractual Requirements, 378; Contract Classifications, 386; Breach of Contract, 387; Assignment of Contract, 389; The Fashion Attic, 390; Summary, 391; Vocabulary Builder, 392; Review Questions, 392; Discussion Questions, 392; Critical Thinking, 393; Short Case: Assign and Breach—Are They the Same?, 393; Project Challenge, 394

21 Buying and Selling — 395

Sale of Goods, 396; Sales Contracts, 396; Transfer of Ownership and Risk of Loss, 402; Obligations and Performance, 405; The Fashion Attic, 406; Summary, 407; Vocabulary Builder, 407; Review Questions, 408; Discussion Questions, 408; Critical Thinking, 408; Short Case: Mini-Golf, Anyone?, 408; Project Challenge, 409

22 Real Property and Insurance — 410

Property Ownership, 410; Leasing Real Property, 417; Insurance, 419; The Fashion Attic, 421; Summary, 422; Vocabulary Builder, 423; Review Questions, 423; Discussion Questions, 423; Critical Thinking, 424; Short Case: Insurance Information Wanted, 424; Project Challenge, 424

23 Ethics and Social Responsibility in Entrepreneurship — 425

A Code of Ethics, 425; Treatment of Consumers, 427; Treatment of the Competition, 430; Treatment of Employees, 431; Treatment of the Environment, 432; Use of Computer Technology, 433; Establishing a Code of Ethics, 435; The Fashion Attic, 436; Summary, 437; Vocabulary Builder, 438; Review Questions, 438; Discussion Questions, 438; Critical Thinking, 439; Short Case: Kemp Computer Services, 439; Project Challenge, 440

Unit 5 Case   Salvaging the Salvage Company, 441

UNIT 6   CAREERS IN ENTREPRENEURSHIP

24 International Entrepreneurship — 444

The International Market, 444; The International Trade Administration, 445; Overseas Marketing, 447; Overseas Financing Sources, 450; Methods of Payment, 452; Economic Integration and Trade Agreements, 452; NAFTA, 455; GATT, 456; Opportunities in International Trade, 457; Getting Started, 457; The Fashion Attic, 458; Summary, 459; Vocabulary Builder, 460; Review Questions, 460; Discussion Questions, 461; Critical Thinking, 461; Short Case: Don't Be Afraid to Ask, 461; Project Challenge, 462

25 Environmental Entrepreneurship — 463

Environmental Issues, 464; Environmental Legislation, 466; Entrepreneurial Opportunities, 468; The Need for Environmentally Friendly Businesses, 473; The Fashion Attic, 474; Summary, 475; Vocabulary Builder, 475; Review Questions, 475; Discussion Questions, 476; Critical Thinking, 476; Short Case: Pick Up and Recycle, 476; Project Challenge, 477

Unit 6 Case   The Search, 479

GLOSSARY — 481

INDEX — 491

UNIT 1
ENTREPRENEURSHIP AND YOU

1. You as an Entrepreneur
2. Planning the Small Business
3. Purchasing an Existing Business
4. Purchasing a Franchise

1
You as an Entrepreneur

After mastering the information contained in this chapter, you should be able to:

1-1 Describe the nature of entrepreneurship.

1-2 Define what it takes to be a successful entrepreneur.

1-3 Explain why individuals decide to become entrepreneurs.

1-4 Explain the importance of choosing the right environment in which to work.

1-5 Describe how to explore possibilities that might lead to becoming an entrepreneur.

entrepreneurship, the act of managing an enterprise that has the potential to make a profit or incur a loss

entrepreneur, an individual who is willing to take the risk of investing time and money in a business that has the potential to make a profit or incur a loss

WHAT IS AN ENTREPRENEUR?

Did you know that if you operated a lemonade stand as a child you were an entrepreneur? You took the risk that you could sell enough servings to pay for the lemons, cups, and sugar and generate additional income to compensate yourself for the time you spent setting up the stand and selling the product. Whether one is selling lemonade or starting a company that will research the cure for the common cold, the act of managing that enterprise is **entrepreneurship** and the individual is acting as an **entrepreneur**.

Illus. 1-1 If you operated a lemonade stand as a child, you were an entrepreneur.

© *Lew Long/The Stock Market*

2

An entrepreneur is very simply an individual who is willing to risk investing time and money in a business activity that has the potential to make a profit or incur a loss. Entrepreneurs sense the needs of the marketplace and take risks to reach the goals that are important to them. Whether they start a business or create a new direction for a large organization, they are the innovators. Entrepreneurs make things happen.

Contribution to Our Economy

Entrepreneurs come from all types of backgrounds. There are no age barriers or educational requirements. The types of business that entrepreneurs create come in all shapes and sizes. They range from craft shops to consulting firms to construction companies.

Entrepreneurs are active in all classifications of business activity. Figure 1-1 illustrates the percentage of small businesses that exist in different categories. Entrepreneurs are the foundation of the small business sector of our country's economy. This sector accounts for more than half of the jobs in America and the majority of new product

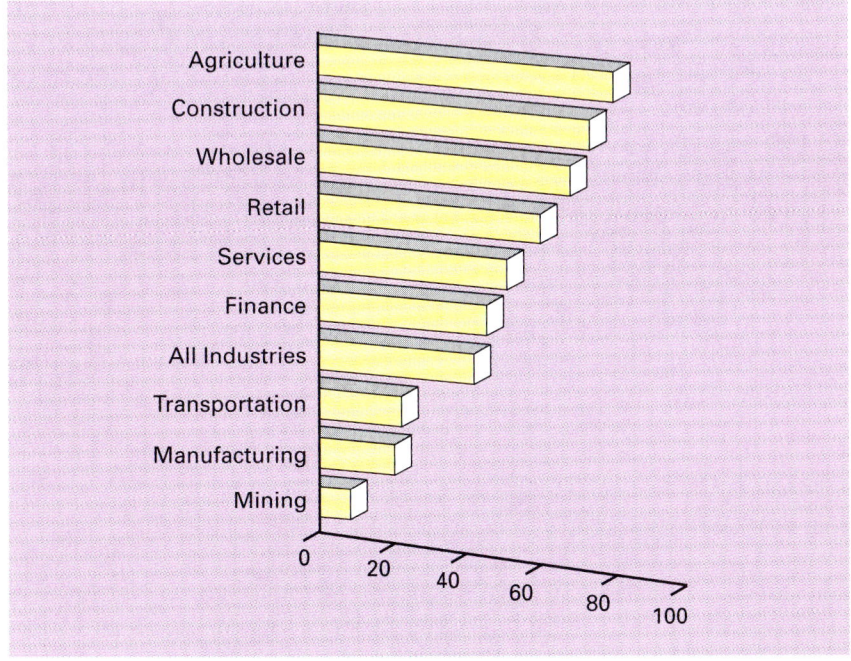

Figure 1-1 Small Businesses in Different Categories

Office of the President, State of Small Business

innovations. These small business owners are essential to the economic strength of our country. It is important for us to understand these risk takers and what makes them successful.

Why Become an Entrepreneur?

Individuals who venture out on their own into the marketplace as entrepreneurs do so for a combination of three reasons:

1. They desire to control their own destinies. This desire brings about the greatest benefits and is often the greatest motivator. As small business owners, individuals control how they wish to run their personal lives. Entrepreneurs plan their own business activities. They schedule their professional responsibilities and duties around their personal priorities. Entrepreneurs are not told that they must go to meetings at the expense of missing important events in their personal lives, such as a child's school play or a family reunion. Entrepreneurs make these types of decisions based on how important they feel a business activity is and not how important anyone else believes it is. This right is the greatest reward of entrepreneurship.
2. They desire to achieve freedom from direct supervision of a boss. Entrepreneurs still must answer to those on whom they depend, such as bankers, landlords, suppliers, or possibly franchisors; however, these relationships are on an equal basis and not a subordinate one.
3. They strive for the potential to achieve profits greater than a salary earned from working for someone else. This is the hardest objective to achieve and usually takes the longest to accomplish. If the determination to succeed is present, greater profits can be a reachable goal.

Unfortunately, more new small businesses fail than succeed in our very competitive marketplace. It is important for us to understand why some succeed while others fail. (See Figure 1-2.)

CHARACTERISTICS OF SUCCESSFUL ENTREPRENEURS

Small Business Administration, a federal agency created to assist the development of the country's small business sector

The **Small Business Administration** (SBA), a federal agency created to assist the development of the country's small business sector, reports that 24 out of every 100 businesses starting out today will be closed in two years. An additional 27 will close within four years.

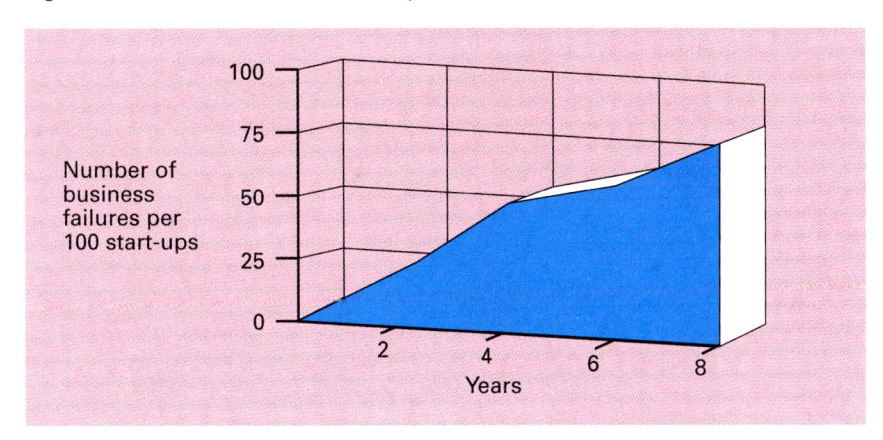

Figure 1-2 Small Business Start-ups and Failures

Source: Small Business Administration

Within six years, more than 60 will shut down. It is very difficult to succeed as a small business owner. Those who do should be commended for beating the odds. The entrepreneurs who head these businesses have succeeded because they probably had good business plans, and because they possess the unique individual characteristics needed to overcome the obstacles encountered along the way.

A business plan is a written description of all the steps necessary to ensure success in opening and operating a business. Creating a business plan will be discussed at length as you proceed through the textbook.

Necessary Characteristics

The necessary personal characteristics of successful entrepreneurs are as follows:

1. Entrepreneurs must possess the confidence to make decisions. Small business owners cannot "pass the buck." They make the decisions that will determine success or failure. Decisions are usually made without the advantage of a professional research staff or the numerous committees that are part of large corporations. Decision makers must be confident in their abilities. When a decision turns out to be wrong, entrepreneurs need the confidence to bounce back, because they will immediately face another decision to make.
2. Entrepreneurs need to have determination and perseverance. Unfortunately, there will be times when things will look quite

APPLY • Discuss how written plans are important in students' everyday lives. Ask students why a list of things to accomplish on a daily, weekly, or longer basis is needed to keep priorities in order.

TEACHING WITH VISUALS • Use TM 1-3, *Questions to Ponder*, to engage students in a discussion of entrepreneurial characteristics. Conclude the discussion by describing how individuals working for large organizations can act as entrepreneurs by assuming responsibility for product or service innovations.

Illus. 1-2   When customers are few, running a business takes perseverance and determination.

Photo by Alan Brown/Photonics

bleak. Entrepreneurs must be willing to persist until the objective is achieved. Too many businesses fail prematurely because the owner grows tired of the struggle. Running a business is not easy and only the determined succeed.

3. Successful entrepreneurs should possess creativity. Why do some businesses selling the same product or service succeed while others do not? The successful entrepreneur is doing something better then the competition. A very competitive marketplace is dominated by those who can think and move quickly to attract customers.

4. Successful entrepreneurs have a need to achieve. They are constantly setting new goals. The challenge of attaining those goals is fun for them. Very wealthy entrepreneurs do not need to continue to expand their business or earn more money for financial reasons—they get most of their satisfaction from achieving goals they have set.

Questions to Ponder

To determine if the ingredients previously described are part of his or her character, an aspiring entrepreneur can do a self-analysis by answering the following questions.

1. Do you give up on your favorite football team when it is two touchdowns behind with five minutes left to play? Determined entrepreneurs do not give up easily.

2. If you see a stream, are you curious as to where it started and where it ends? Entrepreneurs are constantly looking for answers and information. Entrepreneurs are curious and ask questions. It is part of the creative process.
3. Do people look to you for leadership in critical times? As a small business owner, the entrepreneur is the captain, leader, and motivator at all times. These responsibilities require self-confidence.
4. Are you constantly resetting your goals in building toward a long-term objective? Always reaching for new heights means achieving goals and striving for others.
5. Do you consult others for most decisions? Successful entrepreneurs must have the confidence to make decisions on their own.
6. Do you tend to be a daydreamer? Entrepreneurs are dreamers. Their dreams motivate them and produce creative energy. However, dreams must be based on a sense of reality.
7. Do routine chores cause you to be restless? Entrepreneurs are action-oriented goal seekers. Sometimes it is difficult for them to do the necessary, routine aspects of their jobs.
8. Are you stubborn? A certain amount of stubbornness comes from determination. Be stubborn, but also be sensible.
9. Do you like yourself? Confidence comes from within the individual. Good leadership stems from self-assuredness.
10. Is making money your only goal in starting a business? The satisfaction of doing things on your own should rank higher than making money.

WORKING IN THE RIGHT ENVIRONMENT

Success as an entrepreneur requires being committed to a business or an idea. Commitment involves long hours and an abundance of energy. If entrepreneurs work in the wrong field, they will not be able to make the necessary commitment over the long haul. As individuals, we strive to reach our potential. Since self-employed people are working toward their own goals, as opposed to someone else's goals, they are more likely to reach their potential.

Goal setting in an environment you enjoy is stimulating and exciting. Since the choice of a vocation represents a great commitment on the part of the entrepreneur, it must be in a field of interest and enjoyment. The choice of a vocation should not be made without considering past experiences that were meaningful and fulfilling. An administrator who was restless while working behind a desk, but enjoyed working with people, needs to think about that reality before considering opening a business that would confine his or her activities to an office. Analyzing past experiences gives the entrepreneur an idea of the experiences that will most likely bring personal satisfaction.

Career Anchors

Dr. Edgar Schein of M.I.T. University has identified five **career anchors**—technical, managerial, security, creativity, and autonomy. Within these five anchors, he identified vocational choices. Anchors refer to the important motivator within us. These anchors help us to make choices, determine directions, pursue ambitions, and measure success. They help determine business choices and also influence job changes.

An individual with a **technical anchor** gains satisfaction from being able to do a specific job correctly. People with technical anchors might be technicians, surgeons, or any kind of specialist. Such individuals are not as concerned with titles and promotions as much as with being considered experts in their fields. These people should seek self-employment in areas that allow them to concentrate on a specific mission. Automobile mechanics, computer-repair shop

career anchor, essential satisfiers we wish to achieve from our work

technical anchor, trait that allows individuals to derive satisfaction from doing a specific job correctly

TEACHING WITH VISUALS • Ask students to help you fill in the blanks of TM 1-4, *Career Anchors*. Discuss each anchor separately and how it applies to each business listed.

Illus. 1-3

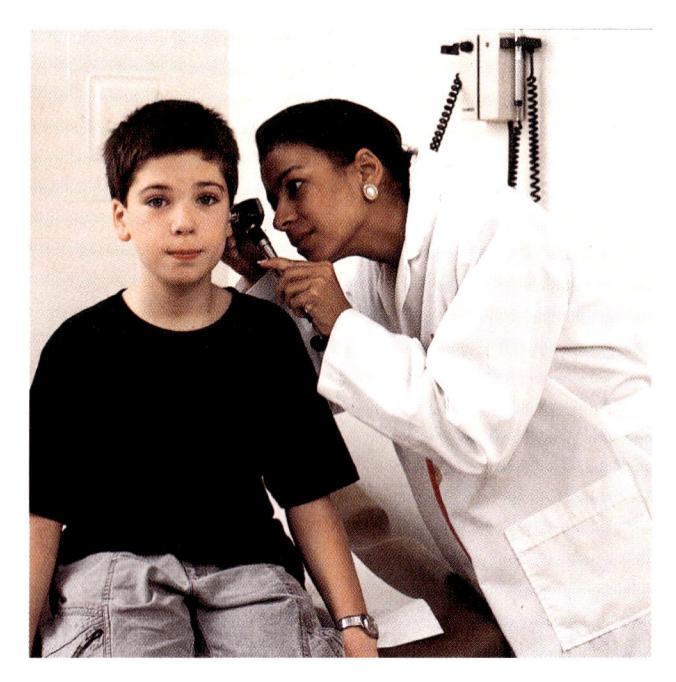

An individual with a technical anchor gains satisfaction from doing a specific job correctly.

owners, hobby shop owners, and small technology manufacturers are examples of entrepreneurs who work at specific job pursuits.

Individuals with a **managerial anchor** are generalists as opposed to specialists. They enjoy working with people. They are able to handle many duties and responsibilities. As entrepreneurs, they do well in businesses with multiple outlets, or in businesses producing and selling many products. Chain store owners and manufacturers who produce many types of products are examples of entrepreneurs with managerial anchors.

People with a **security anchor** are generally not equipped to handle the risks of self-employment. They are content to work in large organizational environments that offer regular paychecks, company benefit programs, and the assurance of long-term employment. Purchasing and managing a well-established franchise, such as McDonald's or Pizza Hut, or an existing successful business might appeal to a person with this type of anchor; however, these types of firms are expensive to acquire because they have proven to be successful. The initial risk was taken by someone else who is entitled to additional compensation for successfully developing the franchise or business. When establishing a new business, there is little in the way of security.

Individuals with a **creativity anchor** enjoy coming up with unique ideas. They do not like routine tasks and are constantly looking for new ways of doing things. They are often successful as small business owners because they are able to devise better ways to sell products or services. People with creativity anchors should be wary of business opportunities that depend principally on administrative talents. These types of people excel in promotion-minded business, such as advertising agencies, and also in retail merchandising.

People with an **autonomy anchor** are free thinkers and individualists. They are seldom concerned with security. They have a natural aptitude for starting small businesses; however, they sometimes do not have the patience and endurance needed to stick with it. Individuals with autonomy anchors like to do things their own way with little interference from others. Inventors, writers, and artists are examples of this anchor classification.

Sample Career Anchor Questions

To help you determine what your career anchors are, a list of questions follows. Answering these questions truthfully and realistically can help lead you to the work environment that is right for you.

---

managerial anchor, trait that allows individuals to be satisfied by working with and through people and by assuming many duties and responsibilities

security anchor, trait that allows individuals to be satisfied by working in a large organization with the assurance of long-term employment

creativity anchor, trait that allows individuals to derive satisfaction from coming up with unique ideas

autonomy anchor, trait that allows individuals to be satisfied by being free thinkers and individualists

1. What are your greatest career aspirations?
2. What kinds of changes in your work responsibilities do you enjoy the most?
3. When have you particularly enjoyed your work?
4. What do you dislike about your work?
5. Is it important for you to receive recognition?
6. When do you feel the most fulfillment from your work?
7. How would you describe your career ambitions?
8. What is most important to you when you seek your first job after graduation?
9. What strategy will you see in attaining job progression?
10. What characteristics of a career are most important to you?

Values, Attitudes, Needs, Expectations

The ultimate goal of all entrepreneurs should be to match their values, attitudes, needs, and expectations with a business opportunity. This process is referred to by the acronym **VANE,** which is derived from the initial letter of each term—values, attitudes, needs, expectations.

Values are the intangible beliefs and inner convictions that we hold dear. Attitudes refer to how we feel about something. Needs are the tangibles (the things we see) and intangibles (the things we feel) that we must have to live an acceptable lifestyle. Expectations are the minimum goals that we attempt to achieve.

Aspiring entrepreneurs who have given thoughtful analysis to their values, attitudes, needs, and expectations will feel confident that they are personally prepared for the challenge ahead of them. If equipped with a proper business plan, they have greatly enhanced their chances for a successful business.

margin note: **VANE,** acronym for values, attitudes, needs, expectations

SETTING PERSONAL GOALS

Once career values, attitudes, needs, and expectations are determined, aspiring entrepreneurs need to look specifically at what business they should enter. Having acknowledged that goal-oriented individuals make successful entrepreneurs, it is important that the goal setting starts with stating the priorities in their personal lives.

Making Choices

An aspiring entrepreneur must establish personal goals with respect to income, personal satisfaction, and status.

Income. In setting realistic goals concerning income level, the new business owner must be aware that there is initially a direct correlation between how much money and time is invested and how much potential profit there is. Over a period of time, the experience, perseverance, and creativity of the owner will determine profits. For instance, in most retail and service businesses, the owner will do well to make a profit of 20 percent of total, or gross, sales. To make a profit of $40,000 per year, the business must generate annual sales of $200,000. If $40,000 is the profit goal, enough money must be invested in inventory, fixtures, and equipment to guarantee sales of $200,000. If some of the initial money is borrowed, the interest and principal to be paid back must come from the $40,000 profit.

Quite often you hear that it takes five years to get a business on its feet. Five years is the most commonly used payoff period on a new business loan. Until the initial debt is paid, there is seldom much extra income available for the owner. For example, an entrepreneur starts a business that requires an investment of $100,000. The owner has $50,000 and borrows $50,000 from the bank and promises to pay the loan back over five years. The first year, the business may sell $200,000 in goods and make a profit of $40,000. The owner must pay the bank out of profits earned each year until the loan is paid off. The business's finances look like this after the first year:

Total investment	$100,000
Borrowed funds	50,000
Sales	200,000
Profit	40,000
Less principal and interest	–13,000
Available to owner (before taxes)	27,000

Because the owner is forced to borrow, he or she will not be able to realize the goal of a $40,000 personal profit until there is growth in sales or the debt is paid. In reality, the owner has invested $50,000 cash and given up a salary to make a risky $27,000 per year. Before a business can be declared a success, not only will the original debt have to be paid, but the owner should also have regained the original $50,000 investment. However, once the initial debt is paid and sales have increased, the profits can be generous enough to pay an attractive salary and show healthy retained earnings. **Retained earnings** are profits that remain in the business for either future use for business expansion or for distribution to the owner(s) as an investment payback. The investment payback is termed **return on investment.**

retained earnings, profits that remain in a business for future use

return on investment, the payback of the money invested in a business operation

In this case, the owner is to be paid back the $50,000 which was initially invested in the business. The same business five years later might look as follows:

Sales	$350,000
Profit	70,000
Less principal and interest	–0
Available to owner	55,000
Retained earnings	15,000

Goal setting with respect to income needs and expectations must be realistic concerning amount invested, returned, and future potential return. For example, business owners should not expect a 100 percent payback on their investment within one year. Entrepreneurs must realize they will have to make some financial sacrifices in their own lives and, as a result, may have to adjust their goals because of unexpected changes in the business's earnings.

Personal Satisfaction. When setting goals for personal satisfaction, entrepreneurs must state the goals they wish to attain in addition to making a profit. These goals are usually intangible and include such things as what they wish to contribute to society or family. People need to feel satisfied with what they do in this world. Working in a career that is personally rewarding greatly enhances the ability of a person to achieve satisfaction.

Status. Declaring a status goal is an important process in determining the best business to enter. In the context of entrepreneurship, status refers to the respect a business owner receives based on how others feel about his or her business or vocation. The noted psychologist Dr. Abraham Maslow includes status, the need for respect from others, as a need we all share. Since businesses require so much personal input from entrepreneurs, it is important that they take great pride in their efforts. Recognition of accomplishments is an important motivation for many individuals.

Type of Work

After declaring personal goals, individuals should match the type of work that really excites them to their goals. These preferences might include working with numbers, selling, office work, working with one's hands, working outdoors, or other preferences. A decision about work content dictates what an individual's main occupation will be for the many hours required to operate a successful business.

Illus. 1-4 This farmer likely chose his vocation because of a decision about work goals.

Photo courtesy of New Idea, Coldwater, Ohio

Another consideration is how a person feels about working with people. Would the individual rather work alone? How does the person feel about selling? Profits are generated by the exchange or sale of goods and services; therefore selling is an important business function. Some entrepreneurs engage in direct, face-to-face selling with customers. Others assign this responsibility to someone else or choose a business in which selling can be handled in an impersonal manner, such as through the mail or over the telephone. In any selling situation, there will be interaction with employees, suppliers, and customers. Some businesses place more emphasis on one group than another. New business owners must decide on the selling environment in which they feel most comfortable.

The entrepreneur will have to decide the amount of time and involvement required in running a business. Is it to be a full-time endeavor, a part-time project, or possibly a business that will start small with the goal of growing into a full-time business? Small businesses offer all forms of arrangements, ranging from weekend or off-hours involvement to full-time management. Many operate under **absentee management** in which the owner oversees the business but is not present. Sometimes timing and the nature of the situation dictate the decision, as it did for Mary Lawrence.

APPLY • Have students discuss the following statement: Not everyone has to be a super salesperson to succeed; however, interaction with people is a common aspect of most occupations.

absentee management, when a business owner oversees the business but is not present at the location

During Mary's maternity leave from her job as a schoolteacher, she had more time available to work on her favorite hobby, making custom jewelry for friends and acquaintances. Her creations were imaginative and were received very enthusiastically. The husband of one of her friends was a manufacturer's representative for some fashion clothing and accessory companies. After seeing Mary's work, he offered to take some samples with him to the fall fashion show at the Atlanta Apparel Mart to display to retailers. He returned with orders totaling more than $25,000. Mary had the start of a very prosperous full-time business, and eventually hired her husband on a full-time basis as well.

Many successful businesses start as part-time operations until sufficient demand for a product or service requires the owner to quit his or her regular employment.

Life-style

The life-style preferred by the entrepreneur should have a bearing on the type of business to open. Does the owner like to travel, work at night, entertain clients, or be entertained? As stated, small businesses come in all sizes and forms. Their owners can decide how they want to live. To many, the idea of controlling one's life-style is the greatest advantage and appeal of small business ownership. Starting a business is a declaration of independence.

Capabilities

The abilities and characteristics that the entrepreneur has developed are an important part of the decision-making process. Thought needs to be given to both the physical and psychological demands of any venture. A list should be made of the abilities that have been developed through education, career, hobbies, and interests.

Finally, what are the entrepreneur's financial capabilities? This question is usually the toughest to answer and represents the biggest obstacle to entrepreneurs. Care must be taken in determining how much money is available and how much the individual is willing to invest in a business. The degree of confidence in the business idea and how much risk the individual is willing to take will help determine the amount of investment required. Individuals should not risk everything in a new business venture. They also need to consider personal living expenses for themselves and their families. Tables 1-1 and 1-2 can serve as guides for aspiring entrepreneurs in evaluating business opportunities.

Table 1-1

GUIDE FOR SETTING PERSONAL GOALS

GOALS	**Income Needed** $_____ 1st year $_____ 2nd year $_____ 3rd year	**Personal Satisfaction Objective** *(Rank from 1 to 6)* ____ Recognition by others ____ Fame ____ Helping others ____ Expressing creativity ____ Expertise ____ Other	**Status Considerations** *(Rank from 1 to 4)* ____ Status in community ____ Feeling challenged ____ Personal growth potential ____ Expertise ____ Other
TYPE OF WORK DESIRED	**Type of Activity** *(Rank from 1 to 6)* ____ Sales ____ Clerical ____ Working with hands ____ Working outdoors ____ Freedom of movement ____ Technology	**People Contact** *(Rank from 1 to 5)* ____ Direct contact with customers ____ Indirect contact with customers ____ Frequent contact with suppliers ____ Close contact with personnel ____ Work alone	**Business Involvement** *(Rank from 1 to 5)* ____ Part-time ____ 8 hours per day, 5 days per week ____ 10 to 12 hours per day, 5 to 7 days per week ____ Weekends and off-time hours only ____ Absentee management
LIFE-STYLE	**Travel Desired** Example: 1 day a week? 1 week a month? _____ _____ _____	**Amount of Entertaining Involved** _____ _____ _____	**Community Involvement Desired** _____ _____ _____

(Table 1-1 continued)

PHYSICAL AND PSYCHOLOGICAL CAPABILITIES	Example: Age and Stamina
LEARNED ABILITIES	Example: Specialist, Generalist
FINANCIAL CAPABILITIES	Example: How much money can you invest? Do you need matching funds?
RISK FACTOR CONSIDERATIONS	*(Circle One)* 1. High-risk, high profit potential 2. Moderate risk factor, moderate profit potential 3. Lower risk factor, slower profit growth potential

Table 1-2 Determining Capital Available

ASSETS		LIABILITIES	
Cash on hand and in bank	$_____	Notes payable to bank	$_____
Government securities	$_____	Notes payable to others	$_____
Stocks and/or bonds	$_____	Accounts and bills due	$_____
Accounts and notes receivable	$_____		
Real estate owned		Real estate mortgage	
Home	$_____	Home	$_____
Auto	$_____	Other	$_____
Other	$_____	Other debts	$_____
Cash surrender value	$_____		
Life insurance	$_____		
TOTAL ASSETS	$_____	TOTAL LIABILITIES	$_____

NET WORTH CALCULATIONS

Total assets	$_____
Less total liabilities	$_____
Equals capital surplus	$_____
Amount of capital willing to risk	$_____

THE FASHION ATTIC

To illustrate how a successful business is established, you will follow Laura Watson through every chapter of this text. You will learn the lessons that she learned in building a retail fashion boutique.

After six years of flying the friendly skies, Laura had seen enough of the world as a stewardess for a major airline. She had served enough dinners to last a lifetime. She often thought of returning home to settle down into a more normal life-style. But what would she do?

She carefully reviewed her past to gain a better look into her future. There were parts of her job she enjoyed entirely. Helping customers and spending time in large cities stood out in her mind. On the other hand, she resented being on call at a moment's notice to go to work. She had no control over her own time. Furthermore, she did not always see eye to eye with her supervisors, particularly when they did not listen to her suggestions to improve service. As time went on she realized that she did not fit the company mold and that this should not be her long-term career.

Laura had some long talks with her childhood friend Paula about the future. Both she and Paula had majored in fashion design at State U. Except for college, Paula had never left Johnson City, and she married her boyfriend from high school. Paula worked as a merchandise buyer for a furniture store chain and enjoyed retailing.

It was actually Paula who came up with the initial suggestion. "Laura, why don't you investigate opening a fashion boutique here in Johnson City? You know the town and you studied fashion merchandising. I've learned about the area retail market at my job, and I think there might be a need for a high-quality ladies apparel store. You like to travel to cities, which you could do on buying trips, and you would be marvelous at helping customers make their selections."

Laura realized what a great idea this was, but she was concerned about the risk involved with investing her savings in a small business. However, the more she thought about it, the bolder she became. "Why not?" she thought. "I'm 28 years old, I have no immediate overburdening financial commitments, and I want to control my own life and not work for someone else. If it works, there could be some great financial rewards, and I could have a career built around my own talents. Plus, it would be great to go home and become part of the community."

She called Paula. "I want to do it, Paula. I'm excited. I'm hoping you can help me do some research and maybe even become a partner or investor. I'll be home next month to get started."

We will get to know Laura as she proceeds step-by-step through creating a business plan. For now, we have identified her motivation. She has a strong desire to control her own destiny and not work for someone else. She wants to work for her own goals and not those of a large organization. She has chosen the retail environment, which fits her background and personal characteristics. Laura seems to have a creative orientation and a desire to feel part of a community, two characteristics that fit well with the choice of retailing. This choice will allow her to use creativity in product display, buying, and advertising. It will also require managerial talents in controlling inventory, supervising personnel, and budgeting. Laura does not appear to have a strong security anchor prohibiting taking risks; however, her choice of a well-established field that requires working closely with the public is conservative enough that total autonomy is not a goal.

Laura has started down the path of entrepreneurship. We will catch up with her in the next chapter as she begins to write out a plan of action.

CREATIVE ENTREPRENEURSHIP

To be an entrepreneur, we have learned that there are no requirements of age, education, or certification. Anyone with an idea, self-confidence, determination, creativity, and the need to achieve can be an entrepreneur. Sometimes special hobbies, skills, or talents give people ideas. Have you ever had an idea for a business or an invention that you wish you had investigated? Next time, don't stop with the idea—explore the possibilities as Tim Holton did.

Tim was 16 years old and a baseball card collector. His hobby was sometimes an annoyance to his mother, who often threatened to throw away his cards if he continued to leave them spread out on his bedroom floor. He shuddered to think of this possibility, since he owned some cards that he knew would be great value in the future.

So, he took a poster-size sheet of green cardboard, drew a baseball diamond on it, and attached his cards to the positions on the diamond that the players had played. He made a number of these and proudly displayed them on his bedroom walls. Soon his friends were copying his idea. He wondered if he had stumbled on an idea that, if produced, would sell.

Tim and his father, with the help of a design engineer at his father's plant, produced a thousand units for resale. The first production run cost $1,500. They purchased the necessary materials and proceeded to try to sell them through mail-order advertising.

The first advertisement was a small 1 × 3 inch mail order advertisement in a national weekly sports publication, the *Sporting News*. The cost of the advertisement, $480, added to the production cost, meant that they had almost $2,000 invested in the idea. Tim very nervously awaited the results. The day after the ad ran, Tim hurried to their rented post office box and was elated to find more than $600 in receipts and orders. More orders followed, and although the receipts were not enough to recover the total initial investment, he earned enough money to proceed with the idea. Other advertising media were used, and ideas such as wholesaling to retail collectors' stores were tried. Tim and his dad even visited a major league team in an unsuccessful effort to sell them on the idea of using the plaque as a promotional item at one of their games. Some ideas were successful and some were not. The product did eventually make some money, but the real value was the excitement it gave Tim. Through his initiative, he was able to conceive, develop, and market a product. His research showed that there were twenty million baseball card collectors in the United States alone. He dreamed of being able to sell to ten percent of that market and make huge profits. A simple idea devised to get Tim out of the doghouse with his mom resulted in a moneymaking venture. Whether the profits were great or small, Tim Holton experienced the challenge and the excitement of entrepreneurship. You can, too![1]

---

[1]Reprinted, with permission, from book #30049 *The Entrepreneur's Guide to Starting a Successful Business* by James W. Halloran. Copyright 1987 by Liberty Hall Press/TAB Books, a division of McGraw-Hill, Blue Ridge Summit, PA 17294 (1-800-233-1128 or 1-717-794-2191).

SUMMARY

Entrepreneurs are risk takers who are able to sense the needs of the marketplace. They are often small business owners who are willing to invest their money, time, and abilities in pursuit of achieving profits at the risk of incurring losses. Entrepreneurs are also found in large organizations and businesses as the innovators of ideas. They possess the personal characteristics of self-confidence, determination, creativity, and the need to achieve.

It is important that these individuals work in environments that are personally satisfying to them so they work to their utmost potential. Their values, attitudes, needs, and expectations must match the goals they set out to accomplish.

It is mandatory that aspiring entrepreneurs write out a good business plan. The business plan will act as a guide to achieving objectives. The business plan must take into consideration personal goals with respect to income, personal satisfaction, status, work content, and life-style.

Entrepreneurship is available to anyone with the necessary personal characteristics to succeed in building a business.

RETEACH • Use the end-of-chapter activities so students can review the chapter content. Activities can be completed individually or in small groups. Use them to reteach difficult concepts or to review prior to testing.

VOCABULARY BUILDER

On a separate sheet of paper, write a brief definition of each word or phrase based on your reading of the chapter.

1. Entrepreneurship
2. Entrepreneur
3. Small Business Administration
4. Career anchor
5. Technical anchor
6. Managerial anchor
7. Security anchor
8. Creativity anchor
9. Autonomy anchor
10. VANE
11. Retained earnings
12. Return on investment
13. Absentee management

REVIEW QUESTIONS

1. Define the term *entrepreneur*.
2. Why do individuals become entrepreneurs?
3. What is the purpose of a business plan?
4. Recall the necessary characteristics of successful entrepreneurs.
5. Identify the five career anchors.

6. How does determining an individual's career anchor(s) help in deciding on a business endeavor?
7. Why is a security anchor not a good career anchor for an aspiring entrepreneur?
8. What is meant by values, attitudes, needs, and expectations as applied to entrepreneurship?
9. What personal goals should be addressed by individuals before opening a business?
10. Why does it normally take five years for a business to become successful?
11. Why is it important to calculate the return on investment of a business opportunity?
12. What determines how much money an entrepreneur should invest in a business opportunity?

DISCUSSION QUESTIONS

1. Why are entrepreneurs so vital to the economic well-being of our country?
2. How do the four essential characteristics of successful entrepreneurs relate to the reasons individuals open small businesses?
3. What is the importance of being in the right work environment?
4. Apply VANE analysis to choosing a business.
5. What is the danger of not considering return on investment in deciding on a business opportunity?

CRITICAL THINKING

Using an idea of your own, develop a scenario depicting yourself as an entrepreneur. What are the risks of the enterprise? What needs does the enterprise serve? What contribution to society would it make? What are its economic implications?

SHORT CASE: AIRPLANES VERSUS YOGURT

Woody Harmon had spent his entire career of 22 years as an airline pilot for a major commercial airline. Labor and management problems threatened to close the airline in 1989. He was too old to be a prime candidate for the position with another airline, and too young to retire. Woody knew he must prepare for a new career in case the company collapsed. One of his friends, Isabel Lopez, was the owner of a local frozen yogurt store chain. "Great business, great profit potential, Woody, as long as you work hard and keep an eye on it." It sounded perfect to Woody. He spent a Saturday helping Isabel at one of the stores and excitedly reported to his wife, Ann, that he had found what he wanted to do. Ann worried about Woody's lack of business experience, but Woody insisted that it was right for him. She kept her fingers crossed that the airline would continue to fly.

It didn't, and Woody signed a three-year lease within two weeks of his final flight. He borrowed $75,000 on his house, and, with Isabel's help and advice, ordered all the equipment and frozen yogurt mix needed to open the store.

He absolutely hated the frozen yogurt business. Working seven days a week, confined to a small store, and supervising sales clerks was far from what he was interested in doing. Business started slowly, which further depressed him. He was making poor business decisions, was irritable at home, and couldn't sleep because he kept thinking of his large, sinking investment. He looked to the sky with every passing airplane. Why, he thought, had he ever thought he could be a retailer? He belonged in an airplane, not in a frozen yogurt store.[2]

Questions

1. What could have been done to prevent this situation?
2. What should Woody do now?

PROJECT CHALLENGE

As you proceed through the textbook you can start to write out a business plan for a hypothetical business of your choice. As you proceed, each chapter will give recommendations on each step. The challenge from this chapter is to determine what type of business you wish to investigate. Once you decide, write a paragraph describing why you have chosen that particular type of business.

---

[2] Case study entitled "Airplanes versus Yogurt" reprinted, with permission, from book #3511 *Why Entrepreneurs Fail: Avoid the 20 Pitfalls of Running Your Own Business* by James W. Halloran. Copyright 1991 by Liberty Hall Press/TAB Books, a division of McGraw-Hill, Blue Ridge Summit, PA 17294 (1-800-233-1128 or 1-717-794-2191).

2
Planning the Small Business

After mastering the information contained in this chapter, you should be able to:

2-1 Define the term *business plan*.

2-2 Describe the importance of planning to the small business.

2-3 List the components of a business plan.

2-4 Describe the components of a business plan.

2-5 Describe how the business plan can be used to decide whether or not to go into business.

2-6 List the sources for assistance in planning a small business.

2-7 Explain the importance of working with an accountant and an attorney in the planning process.

GETTING STARTED

Getting into business is much like going on a long journey. Both undertakings require time, effort, know-how, and a sense of adventure. Both are more enjoyable and rewarding if you know how to go, what to take along, how long it will last, and what to expect along the way. You may still encounter some surprises, but chances are you will be prepared to deal with them.

Illus. 2-1 Starting a business is much like taking a long journey.

PLANNING

Once aspiring entrepreneurs have identified a business idea that seems promising, they must begin preparing for the journey that will transform the idea into a business success. The key step in the preparations is planning. Planning is the systematic process of developing an outline for the accomplishment of a goal or set of goals. A well-prepared outline serves as a road map that guides the traveler to the desired destination.

Planning is one of the most important skills needed for starting a business. Whether the entrepreneur is going to start a new business, buy an established business, or purchase a franchise, good planning is the key to business success.

THE BUSINESS PLAN

A **business plan** serves as a manual to help the entrepreneur during the design and start-up phases of the business. It also states the entrepreneur's expectations, which serve as criteria by which business performance can be periodically evaluated. A good business plan is an ever-evolving resource that grows and changes with the business. As such, it should be consulted regularly and updated annually.

Many an entrepreneur has stumbled upon an idea that seems certain to be a success. It is tempting to skip the planning phase and jump right into business. After all, a day spent planning is a day without profit.

The considerations involved in starting and maintaining even the smallest business can be overwhelming. Neglecting even a minor detail may cause unnecessary aggravation and expense. Overlooking a major detail may ultimately lead to business failure.

Writing a comprehensive business plan ensures that all of the details of the proposed business are addressed. It helps the entrepreneur avoid many of the pitfalls that can delay or prevent business success.

Many entrepreneurs have plenty of ideas but very little capital with which to start a business. Most of them have to go to a bank or other financial institution for a loan.

A majority of all banks require a written business plan before they will consider loaning money for a small business. Nine out of ten banks will probably require that the entrepreneur provide some form

business plan, a written description of all steps necessary to ensure success in owning and operating a business

Illus. 2-2   More than one-third of all banks require a written business plan.

Photo by Jay Bachemin

of written information about the new business venture.[1] A comprehensive and detailed business plan shows the bank that the entrepreneur has invested considerable time and effort in planning what will be a successful business. Such a proposal is more likely to win the bank's support than one that presents only sketchy details.

FORMULATING A BUSINESS PLAN

Below is an outline of a typical business plan. Several of the headings on the outline may not be applicable to certain types of businesses. In these cases the headings may be omitted from the business plan. Also, the amount of information required under each heading will vary from business to business.

1. Concept History and Background
    A. Description of Product or Service
    B. Idea History
    C. Summary of Experience

---

[1]Moorman, Jerry, "What Bankers Have to Say About Business Planning," *IDEAS For Marketing Educators,* March 1990, pp. 7–8.

2. Goals and Objectives
3. Marketing Plan
   A. Consumers and Demand
   B. Competition
   C. Geographic Market
   D. Pricing Policy
4. Legal Requirements
5. Form of Ownership
6. Financial Plan
   A. Initial Capitalization Plan
   B. Projected Income Statement
   C. Projected Operating Statement
   D. Cash Flow Projection
7. Organization, Management, and Staffing Plan
   A. Organization Chart
   B. Employee Requirements
   C. Resumés
   D. Personal Financial Statements
   E. References
8. Special Considerations
   A. Production and Manufacturing Needs
   B. Facility Needs
   C. Education and Training Needs
   D. Land and Utility Needs
   E. Research and Development
   F. Other

The individual components of a business plan and how they are developed will be described in greater detail in later chapters. For the purpose of discussing the general principles of business planning, however, a brief description of each component and its importance in the planning process are covered here.

Concept History and Background

The first part of the business plan describes the business concept, how it was developed, and what qualifications the potential entrepreneur has for the intended business.

Description of Product or Service. In the business plan the potential entrepreneur should describe in very specific terms the product or service that the business is going to offer. The description should

Illus. 2-3   A business plan should describe the business concept, how it was developed, and the potential entrepreneur's qualifications.

Photo by Alan Brown/Photonics

point out how the product or service is different from or better than existing products or services. Such description aids in determining the feasibility of the proposed business.

Idea History. An idea history summarizes when, how, and why the potential entrepreneur developed the idea for the business. This component is important primarily during the loan application process. At least half of all bank loan officers require entrepreneurs to include an idea history in their business plans.[2]

Summary of Experience. Most banks consider a written summary of the entrepreneur's experience an essential component of the business plan. The summary should highlight practical exposure to the intended business. Relevant volunteer work and leisure pursuits, as well as paid employment, may have provided valuable experience

---

[2]Moorman, Jerry, "What Bankers Have to Say About Business Planning," *IDEAS For Marketing Educators,* March 1990, pp. 7–8.

that could be helpful in running the business. Such experience may greatly increase the business owner's chances of success both at the bank and in the marketplace.

Goals and Objectives

A goal can be defined as the overall end toward which one directs one's efforts. An objective is a specific result that is desired. For example, a well-defined goal should answer the question, "What do I want to achieve?" An objective must state what specific results one wishes to accomplish that will ultimately aid in reaching one's goal.

Goals and objectives are important because they provide direction and focus for your activities. How will you know where you are going unless you identify where you want to go? A college football team might set a goal of becoming conference champions this season. One of the objectives may be to win eight out of eight games. By setting the goal and several objectives, the team has established the direction it will take.

Goals and objectives work in much the same way for entrepreneurs by keeping business owners focused on what they are trying to achieve. Many entrepreneurial goals deal with profitability. Goals and objectives are also useful to banks because the lender must know the entrepreneur's intentions. More than two-thirds of banks require written goals and objectives for at least the first year.[3] For this reason, entrepreneurs should be insightful, realistic, and concise when writing goals and objectives for the business plan.

Short-Term and Long-Term Goals

Entrepreneurs need to set both short- and long-term goals. A short-term goal is one that can be achieved in a short period of time, perhaps within several months or a year. A long-term goal is one that is to be achieved over a long period of time, such as a number of years. The entrepreneur should set short- and long-term goals concerning both financial and personal interests, always focusing on the ultimate goal of the business.

As an example, a short-term personal goal might sound like this: Work part-time while planning a new business, then, at the end of

---

[3]Moorman, Jerry, "What Bankers Have to Say About Business Planning," *IDEAS For Marketing Educators,* March 1990, pp. 7–8.

one year, quit my other job and devote all of my efforts to opening and managing the new business. A long-term financial goal might sound like this: Pay back my $20,000 start-up loan within six years.

Using Goals and Objectives to Measure Success

Success can be measured by how close entrepreneurs come to reaching their goals and objectives. Certainly one of the most satisfying feelings for entrepreneurs comes from achieving the goals and objectives they established—personal as well as financial. If they accomplish this, they should consider themselves successful.

If, after some period of time, goals or objectives are not being met, they may have been unrealistic in the first place. The entrepreneur should re-evaluate the business and try to determine what went wrong. The important thing to remember is to review, re-evaluate, and, if appropriate, re-establish goals and objectives at least once a year to make sure that the business venture is on the path to success.

Marketing Plan

Just speculating that many people will want to buy a product or service is not enough. Entrepreneurs need to quantify information about their potential markets.

The **marketing plan** defines and quantifies consumers, demand, competition, geographic market, and pricing policy for a specific small business. Most business experts consider the marketing plan a key component of the planning process. Drawing an accurate picture of the potential market for a product or service helps the entrepreneur to set realistic goals and objectives for the business. Successful entrepreneurs will devote considerable attention to the marketing plan, as will bank loan officers.

marketing plan, defines and qualifies consumers, demand, competition, geographic market, and pricing policy for a specific small business

Consumers and Demand. The first part of the marketing plan describes the consumers and demand for the product or service. It may profile a typical customer in terms of age, sex, income, occupation, family status, or other characteristics that make that person likely to frequent the business. It may also estimate how often a typical customer will want to buy the product or service and at what price.

Competition. The second part of the marketing plan deals with competition. Suppose you decide that a shoe store is a good venture. We all know that everybody in town is already wearing shoes. In other words, they are shopping at your competitors' stores. The only way for you to bring customers into your new store is to lure them away from the competition. One way you can do this is by making your store different from others in terms of location, selection, quality, price, or service. But in order to make your store different, you need to know about the competition. In addition you need to consider what the competition's reaction will be to your business. What will you do, then, to counteract their responses?

As you plan your business, you should learn as much as possible about the competition. In particular, you should determine how the competition is different from the business you have in mind. All of this information should be summarized in your marketing plan.

Do banks think you should be concerned with your competition? You bet they do! One of the first questions many loan officers ask is, "What can you tell us about your competition?" If your answer is "Nothing," their next statement may well be "Goodbye!"

Geographic Market. This part of the marketing plan describes the geographic area from which the business will draw its customers. The entrepreneur must project how far people will be willing to travel to frequent the business, and from which areas they will come. Correctly identifying the geographic market makes setting realistic sales goals easier. Thus, identifying the geographic market is a crucial step in planning a business.

Pricing Policy. The last part of the marketing plan consists of the pricing policy, which determines how you will set prices for the product or service. The prices set have a direct impact on the number of customers the entrepreneur will have and the profits accumulated. A carefully considered pricing policy can help you achieve your sales and profit goals.

Legal Requirements

As aspiring entrepreneurs consider opening their new businesses, legal problems are the last thing on their minds. But if they do not devote time and attention to the legal aspects of a new business, legal problems may soon be the *only* thing on their minds. Entrepreneurs must consider potential legal problems before they actually go into business.

The legal requirements for conducting almost any business today can be extensive and complicated. The planning phase is the proper time to consider what these requirements are and how they will be met.

Illus. 2-4 Entrepreneurs should determine what patents, copyrights, agreements, contracts, or other legal arrangements will be needed to carry out day-to-day business.

Entrepreneurs should determine what patents, copyrights, agreements, contracts, or other legal arrangements will be needed to carry out day-to-day business. All of these items should be included in the business plan. Indeed, 94 percent of the banks doing business with entrepreneurs in new small business ventures require that the legal aspects of the ventures be addressed in the planning process.[4]

Form of Ownership

When you seek financial assistance, you must have decided upon a form of ownership for your business. If you are going it alone, this part of the plan is easy. If you are starting the new business with one or more other people, however, choosing the form of ownership becomes a very critical decision. Form of ownership has ramifications for business management, division of profits, division of labor, liability, and many other issues.

The most common forms of ownership are sole proprietorship, partnership, and corporation. Each of these will be discussed in detail in Chapter 14. Entrepreneurs must decide during the planning phase which form of ownership best suits the needs of the business and the people involved.

---

[4]Moorman, Jerry, "What Bankers Have to Say About Business Planning," *IDEAS For Marketing Educators,* March 1990, pp. 7–8.

Financial Plan

Along with the marketing plan, the financial section of the business plan is a key component in the overall planning process. A basic **financial plan** contains the entrepreneur's estimates for the following categories:

1. cost of starting the business and maintaining it for a specified period of time (initial capitalization plan)
2. projected income
3. projected operating expenses
4. projected cash flow

financial plan, portion of a business plan that projects start-up costs, income, operating expenses, and cash flow

Starting Point? Some small business experts say that potential entrepreneurs should start their business planning processes with the financial plan. They argue that, until the entrepreneur determines what the proposed venture will cost and whether or not it is feasible, other planning is fruitless.

A Crucial Step. All experts agree that the financial plan must be developed very carefully. Poor financial planning at the start of a business venture almost inevitably leads to overall business failure. Therefore most bank loan officers carefully scrutinize all four categories in the financial plan.

Organization, Management, and Staffing Plan

Although opening day may be a long way off, the entrepreneur must determine how many employees the business will require and what their responsibilities will be. Such concerns are addressed in the organization, management, and staffing plan section of the business plan.

Organization Chart. The organization chart deals with the actual management of the business. The chart defines who will be responsible for tasks such as purchasing, advertising, accounting, and hiring personnel. The chart also shows who reports to whom in the organizational hierarchy.

Employee Requirements. Planning for an appropriate number of employees is essential. If too few employees are hired, there will not be enough people to meet customers' needs. On the other hand, if too many employees are hired, the excessive labor costs will unnecessarily decrease profits. During the business planning phase the entrepreneur should use information such as the organization chart and projected sales figures to estimate how many employees will be needed.

Resumés, Personal Financial Statements, and References. If opening a new business will require bank financing, each borrower must prepare a resumé, a personal financial statement, and a list of references. The resumé outlines the borrower's education and work experience. Banks use the resumé to help them determine whether the entrepreneur has the necessary background for the proposed business. The personal financial statement describes the borrower's financial condition. In particular, it shows what assets the borrower could use as collateral—something of value pledged as security—for the loan. Banks use the personal financial statement to evaluate the borrower's ability to repay the loan. The list of references contains the names and addresses of people who can supply information concerning the character and habits of the potential borrower.

Special Considerations

The last component of the business plan deals with any special considerations that apply to the entrepreneur's chosen business. Some small businesses will have many special considerations; some will have none.

If the business will be to manufacture a product, the list of special considerations may be quite lengthy. If the entrepreneur's business will consist exclusively of selling a service, however, the only special consideration may be a facility. Other special considerations may include training for the entrepreneur or employees, land and utility needs for the operation, and research and development of the proposed product or service. The entrepreneur's goal is to recognize and deal with all of these special considerations during the planning process.

DECIDING WHETHER OR NOT TO GO INTO BUSINESS

Once the business plan is complete, the entrepreneur can make the final decision as to whether or not to go into business. The three most useful pieces of information are the marketing plan, the financial plan, and the personal financial statement. If the entrepreneur has planned carefully, these items should reveal whether there is a market, how much money it will take to reach that market, and whether enough resources are available to pull it all together.

SOURCES FOR PLANNING ASSISTANCE

Many an entrepreneur has a great deal of enthusiasm plus a wealth of technical knowledge in a chosen field. What usually is lacking is management expertise and specific information about the nuts and bolts of starting a business. If that is the case, a variety of resources can offer assistance. Three of the most commonly available resources are described below.

Local Community Colleges

Many community colleges have small business development centers designed to assist local businesses.

Chamber of Commerce

In many communities, the chamber of commerce has a small business development committee that can offer guidance to entrepreneurs.

Small Business Administration

The Small Business Administration (SBA) is an independent federal government agency with offices in most metropolitan areas. The SBA offers a range of services including seminars, counseling, and loans.

Accountants and Attorneys

Though not one of the three commonly available resources, accountants and lawyers should not be overlooked as sources for planning assistance. During the planning process, the entrepreneur should establish a working relationship with an accountant and an attorney who have experience with small businesses. The accountant should review or, in some cases, help to develop the financial plan. The attorney should be consulted to determine the legal requirements of the proposed business.

These professionals are a necessary part of the planning process regardless of whether you are starting a new business, buying an existing business, or purchasing a franchise. Their fees, which usually run $100 an hour and up, must simply be viewed as part of the expense of doing business.

Illus. 2-5 In many communities, the chamber of commerce has a small business development committee that can offer guidance and assistance to entrepreneurs.

Photo by Alan Brown/Photonics

THE FASHION ATTIC

Laura took the advice of a friend and attended a seminar called "How To Write a Business Plan" at a local community college. Upon leaving she was feeling overwhelmed by the amount of work that the instructor advised in researching a business idea. She realized that there was much more to it than just coming up with an idea. Market research, financial planning, organization structuring—all were planning functions that would require a lot of time and hard work.

She had heard of consultants who would do the work for aspiring entrepreneurs. She wondered if it would be easier to hire a consultant, even though it might cost more. After class she asked the instructor if that would be a good idea.

"Laura, if you let someone else do it for you, you won't learn what must be learned," the instructor explained. "This is to be your business, not someone else's. An outsider will only give you general industry information. It's up to you to find out the information as it applies to your business, its location, and the community and market it will serve. Don't waste your money. If you're not ready to do the work necessary to plan a business, you're not ready to own one."

Laura went home and started to write out her goals. She realized that there were no shortcuts in developing a business plan.

SUMMARY

Planning is critical to the ultimate success of a small business. At the heart of the process is the business plan, which contains the following components:

1. Concept History and Background
2. Goals and Objectives
3. Marketing Plan
4. Legal Requirements
5. Form of Ownership
6. Financial Plan
7. Organization, Management, and Staffing Plan
8. Special Considerations

The completed business plan contains the information a potential entrepreneur needs to decide whether or not to start the business. Planning assistance is available from community college business development centers, the chamber of commerce, and the Small Business Administration. An entrepreneur should also engage the services of an accountant and an attorney during the planning process.

VOCABULARY BUILDER

On a separate sheet of paper, write a brief definition of each word or phrase based on your reading of the chapter.

1. Business plan
2. Marketing plan
3. Financial plan

REVIEW QUESTIONS

1. Why is careful planning crucial to developing a small business?
2. What are the eight components of a business plan?

3. How can a business plan help an aspiring entrepreneur decide whether or not to go into business?
4. What are three sources of assistance available to entrepreneurs?
5. What services can an accountant and an attorney provide during the business planning phase?

DISCUSSION QUESTIONS

1. What are the two key components of a business plan and why are they so important?
2. Why must entrepreneurs consider the competition when developing a business plan?
3. What is the importance of staffing to business success?
4. What is the importance of the form of ownership to the business operations of a small business?

CRITICAL THINKING

Sue Lee is a young woman who lives in your hometown. Recently she has been thinking about starting her own small business. After a lot of thought and discussion with friends and local store owners, she has decided to open an import shop dealing in original Japanese art and gift items.

Assuming that you are the banker who reviews her business plan, what are the good and bad points of the plan? This exercise should make you think about how the components of the business plan should be written.

1. Choose one of the eight components of the business plan (refer to the outline) and write it as if you were Sue Lee. Create explanations that sound convincing, well researched, and realistic.
2. Next, choose another component and write it so that it is lacking in good thought, development, and practicality. Then trade papers with a classmate and "correct" each other's weak components of the business plan by improving them with your own ideas and words. When you are finished, talk about how the changes you made improved Sue's business plan.

SHORT CASE: TO LOAN OR NOT TO LOAN

Michael Hardin lives in a small town 50 miles north of Atlanta. Recently he has been thinking about starting his own small business. After a lot of thought and discussion with friends, he has decided to open a video rental store.

Knowing that he needs a loan to get his business started, Michael went to his bank. He had been doing business at First State Bank since he was a teenager. Before going, he called ahead and made an appointment with Bob Swanson, the commercial loan officer. Bob is the banker who talks to all of the people who want business loans.

After Michael explained his idea, Bob's first question was, "How much money do you need?" Michael's answer was that he thought ten or fifteen thousand dollars should be enough.

"There's a lot of difference between ten thousand and fifteen thousand dollars, Michael," said Bob. "Let me see your business plan and I'll help you figure the exact amount you need."

Michael hesitated for a moment, then asked, "What's a business plan?"

Questions

1. Do you think Mr. Swanson will loan Michael the money he needs? Would you? Why or why not?
2. Which part of the business plan will Mr. Swanson probably want to see first? Why?
3. What is the first thing Michael needs to do after leaving the bank if he doesn't want his business dream to die?

PROJECT CHALLENGE

In the last chapter you decided what type of business you were interested in investigating. As the first step in the business planning process, start a business plan notebook. Briefly respond to each of the following:

a. Write a one or two paragraph description of the product or service that your business will market.
b. How did you get the idea for this business?
c. What experience do you have in the intended business?
d. Develop two goals you hope to attain during the first year in business. Develop two goals you hope to attain within five years.

Now, using your responses to the items above, write the first component of your business plan—the concept history and background. Remember that this should include a description of your product or service, an idea history, and a summary of your experience and qualifications. As you proceed through the chapters of this text, you will be adding other components of the business plan to your notebook.

3
Purchasing An Existing Business

After mastering the information in this chapter, you should be able to:

3-1 List sources of business for sale opportunities.

3-2 Describe the advantages and disadvantages of buying an existing business.

3-3 Describe how to identify a good business opportunity.

3-4 Explain how to evaluate a business for sale opportunity.

3-5 Know what information to acquire before deciding to buy a business.

market value, the value of similar goods, homes, properties, businesses, etc., in similar markets

PURCHASING AN EXISTING BUSINESS

For many aspiring business owners, the best way to enter the world of entrepreneurship is through the purchase of an existing business. Before deciding to open a new business, it is wise to investigate the business for sale market. Why? Talking to someone who has a business for sale is an excellent way to learn about the market conditions of the community in which you wish to operate. The potential buyer will be able to see the sales revenues of an industry member and a possible future competitor firsthand. In addition, it provides the opportunity to find out the potential **market value** of the particular type of business *after* it is established and any start-up problems have been worked out. Furthermore, it might lead to an opportunity to enter the market at a lower cost than originally anticipated. For these reasons it is wise for potential small business owners to inquire about businesses for sale, even if it was not the original intention.

How to Find Businesses for Sale

Business owners wishing to sell their businesses commonly advertise their intentions to sell by advertising in the classified section of newspapers, by listing their businesses with business brokers, or by getting the word out through industry and community sources.

Classified Advertising. Potential buyers should check first in the business opportunities pages of the classified section of local newspapers. There they will find numerous advertisements similar to the one shown in Figure 3-1.

Information provided in such advertisements is often very general. However, a telephone call or mail inquiry should provide enough basic information to determine whether it is worth investigating. If the idea

Figure 3-1   Business for sale advertisement

> **RESTAURANT**
> Good location. Seats 50.
> Established 3 Years.
> Profitable,
> family oriented. Must sell.
> $65,000.   Call 404-555-1060.

shows promise, you should arrange a time to meet with the seller to discuss the opportunity. Since buying a business requires very intensive research, the first meeting is normally a general discussion of why the business is for sale and how the seller foresees the future performance of the business. If you are still interested after this meeting, you and the seller should schedule meetings to discuss the opportunity further and for you to observe business operations during working hours.

Business Brokers. **Business brokers** act as selling agents for business sellers, just as real estate brokers do for people selling homes. Brokers represent sellers and assist them by bringing potential buyers and sellers together. As part of handling a business sale, brokers advise sellers to have specific information available that will be needed to answer potential buyers' questions. Brokers also handle advertising businesses for sale. Many sellers use brokers to keep their intention to sell confidential. Brokers advertise without giving the name of the business and provide their own business phone number and address for interested parties to contact. Only when they have screened the prospects and identified qualified buyers do they tell the prospects how to contact the seller. Business brokers may also assist in drawing up sales contracts and arranging financing. Brokers are paid for their services by receiving an agreed-upon percentage of the selling price. The percentage is normally 10 to 15 percent.

business broker, agent who brings business buyers and sellers together

Industry Sources. Many businesses are sold by announcing to industry members that a business is for sale. This works either through referral from salespeople or by advertising in industry publications. Since potential new business owners frequently ask industry suppliers

Illus. 3-1 Owners wishing to sell their businesses commonly make their intentions known by advertising in the classified section of newspapers.

about business opportunities, both are effective ways to learn about businesses that are for sale. Many companies have referral systems in place to put individuals making inquiries in touch with those who wish to sell. Industry sources will normally only get involved with the selling process as a referral.

Entrepreneurs may also find businesses for sale through other sources, such as the following:

- landlords/leasing agents
- attorneys
- bankers
- SBA
- Small Business Development Centers
- management consultants
- shopping center management offices
- venture capitalists
- chamber of commerce offices
- acquaintances
- bankruptcy announcements

Often the best business opportunities will come from businesses that are not for sale. If there is an existing business that meets all of the requirements a potential business buyer is looking for, the buyer can make the owner an offer. The owner may, of course, refuse. However, if the offer is attractive enough, he or she might consider the opportunity to sell.

Advantages of Purchasing an Existing Business

There are many advantages to buying an existing business, particularly for entrepreneurs with little experience. It is an ideal way to "learn the ropes" because, in many cases, the previous owner will stay on for a period of time to train the new owner and/or be available for consultation.

It is also a less risky way to become self-employed. The existing business has a track record—procedures are in place, suppliers are lined up, and a customer base is established. New owners will have an idea about what they can expect for revenues, expenses, and profits. These figures are easier to forecast for an established business than for a start-up business. If new business owners have some of the security anchor characteristics described in Chapter 1, buying a business will certainly alleviate some of the anxiety of getting started in owning and operating a business.

Purchasing an established business may also be financially advantageous. Sellers often assist with financing arrangements to sell their businesses. It is not uncommon for sellers to accept an initial partial payment with the agreement that the balance will be paid off in monthly installments in the form of a promissory note. This arrangement may reduce or eliminate the need for bank financing and is often negotiated at a lower interest rate. If the seller does not wish to help finance the purchase of the business, buyers are still (in most cases) more likely to receive financing from a bank or other financial institution for an *established* business than for a *start-up*. Why? It is less risky for the lender.

Entrepreneurs sometimes purchase businesses because it is the only way to successfully enter the market. If a particular business dominates the market because of its superior location and reputation, buying that business might be the best way to ensure success. Other advantages of buying an existing business may include the following:

- No business start-up is required.
- Suppliers have already been tried and tested.
- The company has survived the start-up phase (the first year or two) and has a better chance of succeeding.
- Experienced employees will already be functioning and probably will not require much, if any, training.

Disadvantages of Purchasing an Existing Business

Many businesses are for sale due to internal problems. It is not a good idea for aspiring business owners to assume someone else's problems. If a business has a poor reputation with customers, has trouble with suppliers, or is poorly located, it is unlikely that new ownership will automatically change customers' negative opinions about the business. Too many business buyers have learned the hard way that it takes a long time to restore customer confidence.

Another disadvantage is that buying a profitable business will initially cost more. The seller has built a business, poured time and energy into it, and will usually expect to be rewarded with a selling price that reflects his or her efforts. Capital limitations on the part of the buyer, however, might prevent the purchase of an existing business. It might be more economically feasible to take the risk of creating a new business with a smaller capital investment.

Some entrepreneurs might consider purchasing part of, or investing in, a business. The risk is that there might be a lack of compatibility between the parties that more or less have been forced together for economic reasons. A bad partnership arrangement prevents a business from building the comradery that is so essential for small business success.

Another drawback to purchasing an existing business is that the employees currently working in the business may have to be replaced. Poor training by the former owner or unacceptable work habits may not be tolerated by the new owner. It may also be necessary to invest money to modernize the operation.

Reasons Why Businesses Are Sold

In considering the purchase of a business, the potential buyer should determine why the business is for sale. This will help the buyer determine the price he or she feels is fair for the business. If sellers are under great pressure to sell, they may be more flexible about the selling price. The following is a list of some of the many reasons businesses are sold.

- Insufficient profits
- Owner's retirement
- Death or illness of a working partner
- Business heirs are uninterested
- Partner or shareholder dispute

Illus. 3-2   An owner's plan to retire is one of the many reasons a business is offered for sale.

- Management "burnout"
- Business is growing too fast or too slowly
- Forced liquidation or sale
- Fear of new competition
- Fear of current or predicted economic conditions
- Lack of desire or capital to do necessary remodeling
- Owner's desire for a change of career
- Owner's desire to take advantage of another opportunity requiring the liquidation of business assets

HOW TO PURCHASE A BUSINESS

Buying a business is an intricate process that requires the same thoroughness as creating a business plan for starting a business from scratch. As a potential business buyer, you should follow these steps.

1. Write clear, specific personal and financial objectives about what kind of business you want to buy. Whatever the type of business for sale, it must match these statements before you consider it for purchase.
2. Locate business opportunities that offer growth and provide an attractive return on investment. Read classified advertisements,

discuss opportunities with business brokers, and check industry sources as you formulate a list of potential opportunities.
3. Meet with business sellers or brokers for an introduction to specific business opportunities. The initial information provided by the seller should include a brief financial report, the history of the business, the selling price, and the reason for sale.
4. Request a second meeting to probe for more information if the seller's material fits the objectives you stated in Step 1.
5. Inspect the facility closely to determine how well it has been maintained.
6. Prepare a checklist of information needed. The checklist should include the following:

- A complete financial accounting of operations—the income statements and balance sheets—for at least the past three years, or from the beginning of operation if the business is less than three years old—federal income tax returns, and state sales tax forms should be included;
- A list of all assets to be transferred to the new owner—this should include an itemized list of all inventory as of the last accounting period;
- A statement about any past or pending legal action against the business;
- A copy of the business lease or mortgage;
- A list of all of the business's suppliers.

7. Once you examine all of the information you receive, you should then meet with several key individuals to receive their professional recommendations or approvals before going any further.

First, consult an accountant and a lawyer. They should be able to provide you with any further interpretation of the financial and legal information you received. Your accountant will review all of the financial information regarding the business. He or she may uncover flaws or inaccuracies that may provide a more accurate financial picture than what the seller presented. Your lawyer will need to check, among other things, to see if the lease or title may be transferred to you. You need to conduct an on-site meeting with the landlord or mortgage holder to ensure the facility is in satisfactory condition. In the case of a lease, you should discuss the expiration date and, if possible, negotiate the terms and price to fit your needs.

Potential buyers are wise to consult the chamber of commerce and other local assistance centers to discuss the future of the

market and the location. It would be in your best interest to contact industry representatives presently selling to the business to validate the sales reported and to obtain their assessment of the likelihood of the business's future growth.
8. It is essential that potential buyers arrange a convenient time with the seller to observe operations. Evaluate employee and customer satisfaction and/or dissatisfaction, as well as the pros and cons of the operation in general. All of these considerations enter into the final sales price.
9. Determine a fair purchase price to offer the business owner. In some cases, the owner will have already stated a price; you now must make a counteroffer based on your research. Determine what financing arrangements are available through a lending institution or with the seller. Present the offer in writing to the seller. You should present a letter of intent which, in essence, says, "I will purchase the business at the stated price and under the stated terms provided that an audit shows that the inventory, work in process, accounts payable, and accounts receivable are as shown to be."

    At this point, there will normally be some negotiation. You will have to use your best persuasion techniques to point out the fairness of the offer and the advantages to the seller for accepting it. Either party may bring his or her attorney, or another agent, to assist in negotiations.
10. If an agreement is reached, an attorney should draw up a suitable sales contract. Usually, there are many terms included in a business sale contract as details need to be clarified, and questions answered, such as whether the seller is permitted to open a competing business within the buyer's market area. Which party will be responsible for paying any unreported claims, liens, or unpaid taxes on the business following its sale? What should be done about customers' long-standing debts? What about union contracts for unionized employees? Employee benefits and pensions? How will costs for insurance coverage, taxes, and utilities be divided? As you can see, a lawyer can be very helpful at a business closing and can protect you from costly, unforeseen entanglements. The contract should be contingent upon examination of all assets to validate that what is represented is true.
11. Before signing a sales contract, the buyer should be present when the seller takes final inventory of assets.

EVALUATING BUSINESS FOR SALE OPPORTUNITIES

Normally an investigation of businesses for sale produces opportunities that range from bad to promising to good. Categorizing a business opportunity as bad, promising, or good helps prospective buyers determine the value of the business and, therefore, the price they are willing to offer.

Types of Opportunities

The first sign of a bad business opportunity is poor bookkeeping. If a business owner has been negligent in maintaining proper financial records, it is more than likely that the business has suffered because of it. Failure to present adequate verification of sales revenues and expenditures is often a sign that the seller is attempting to hide information. It is wise to avoid this type of situation.

Many business opportunities are not easy to classify or measure. For example, a business's recordkeeping may be adequate, but not entirely complete; a solid but unspectacular customer base may have been established; or relationships with suppliers may be satisfactory, but not as efficient as they could be. Many times these are the best business opportunities because their greatest need is better management. Proper management might generate greater sales, better customer reception, and create **goodwill.** Goodwill is the value of the effort of building a successful business which has a good reputation with customers and with the community. Since previous management has not been able to reach all of its objectives, the selling price of the business should not include goodwill. Therefore, it might be a bargain for the right buyer.

An example of a promising business opportunity is a store that has leveled off in sales at a certain point and cannot seem to increase them even though the market is good. Management is evidently not doing some things right or else does not have the capital available to aggressively pursue the market. If a new owner can make some changes, such as remodeling, adding new inventory, or increasing advertising expenditures, he or she could quite possibly increase profits and receive a healthy return on investment. Potential buyers should look for this type of opportunity.

Good businesses keep good records and maintain a good customer image. Buying a business that has been properly managed is

margin note: **goodwill,** the value of a business's image and community relations

Illus. 3-3 Remodeling an existing business is often enough to increase profits.

© 1988 Jon Feingersh/The Stock Market

an asset to the new owner. He or she will not have to spend time convincing customers that they will be given better service, quality, and/or prices under the new management. However, if a business has been profitable and managed well, it will be more costly to purchase. In cases of successful businesses for sale, it is customary for the seller to specify a dollar value for goodwill.

Evaluation Considerations

Unfortunately, there is no easy, standard formula to use to compute the value of a business. Many deals are based on how motivated both the seller and the buyer are to close the deal. Sometimes the terms are more important than the price. However, the following evaluation methods will help to generate a price at which you can begin negotiating.

Prospective buyers must evaluate opportunities for buying businesses in terms of profit earnings and return on investment. The most important factor to look for is the business's potential to make money. Unfortunately, this is not always easy to determine because the buyer is dealing with what he or she *thinks* might happen. To help, buyers use a method called the **earnings approach**. Using this

earnings approach, the method of determining the value of a business by calculating its potential profit and return on investment

Illus. 3-4 The prospective buyer should determine the immediate cash value of all assets in case the business must be sold.

© *David Hundley/The Stock Market*

approach, buyers determine whether the business will be able to pay them for their time. Potential buyers should identify their proposed changes and develop pro forma (projected) financial statements to examine the impact of the changes on the business. If this forecast looks positive, they then need to examine their return on investment.

Entrepreneurs should expect earnings to provide a return on investment over a period of time. Usually that period of time is five years, or 20 percent per year. Too often, businesses are bought with the assumption that as soon as the new management takes over, business will improve dramatically. However, it takes time to change operations procedures, employee performance, and customer buying habits. Therefore, opportunities must be evaluated by considering the long-term potential.

Potential buyers must also research the market value of the business for sale. This requires learning the selling prices of similar businesses and comparing them to the price of the business being considered. It is a good way to get a general idea of the market, but since no two businesses are exactly alike, this is not always accurate. Buyers would be wise to hire an appraiser to appraise the building and other assets.

Buyers must determine the **replacement value** of the assets they are considering for purchase. Since the value of assets such as equipment, furniture, fixtures, and inventory listed on a balance sheet is based on their previous purchase price, the buyer should determine the *current* replacement value of the assets listed. The replacement value is usually higher than the asset value.

A final measure should be the **liquidation value** of a business's assets. Using a worst-case scenario, the prospective buyer should determine the immediate cash value of all assets (including the present value of future income) in the event a problem arises that requires the immediate sale of the business.

It is a good idea for prospective buyers to review the current income statement of a business for sale and indicate any foreseeable adjustments to that financial statement due to the new ownership. Table 3-1 is an example of such a list of adjustments.

replacement value, the cost of purchasing new assets at current market value

liquidation value, the value of assets if liquidated or sold immediately

Table 3-1

INCOME STATEMENT
FOR YEAR ENDING DECEMBER 31, 19____

ACTUAL		COMMENTS FOR NEW OWNER FOR FIRST YEAR
Sales and revenues	$180,000	should increase 10 percent
Less cost of goods	93,000	add $25,000—new inventory
Gross profit	87,000	minus approximately $7,000
Operating expenses		
Payroll	26,000	– $5,000, cut one employee
Rent	19,500	no change
Utilities	2,200	no change
Maintenance	1,600	+ $500 for new lights
Insurance	2,400	+ $200, cover added inventory
Accounting	2,000	– $1,000, keep own books
Advertising	2,800	+ $550, announce new owners
Supplies	4,100	+ $600, new bags, boxes
Miscellaneous	4,000	+ $1,000, other changes
Total operating expense	$64,600	minus approximately $3,150
Net operating profit	$22,400	approximately $18,550

Inadequate review and investigation in buying a business can lead to problems like those experienced by Bailey Robinson, as recounted in the following paragraph.

Bailey Robinson bought a retail clothing business believing she could increase profits as soon as she took over. The business financial statement looked like this:

Sales	$ 250,000
Cost of goods	−130,000
Gross profit	120,000
Operating expenses	− 95,000
Net profit	25,000

To buy the business, Bailey borrowed from the bank with a promise to pay back $20,000 per year. She knew that this would only leave $5,000 per year for her salary, but she was sure that she could immediately increase sales by $50,000. This would allow her a salary of $25,000. One year later she was forced to sell the business. Although she had increased sales by $10,000, it was not enough and she ran out of time.

THE FASHION ATTIC

The seminar instructor had advised that before starting a business, prospective business owners should investigate businesses for sale and franchise opportunities. He had stressed that this should be done as a learning tool even if the entrepreneur wished to start a business of his or her own.

Laura decided to take this step and visited the owner of a fashion store located on the outskirts of Johnson City in a large discount shopping center. The owner said that he was selling the business in order to pursue an opportunity in another state.

He showed her financial statements that illustrated sales of $150,000, a profit of $15,000, and an inventory at a cost of $22,000. Fixtures, equipment and furnishings were valued at $18,000. The asking price was $75,000.

Laura reviewed the situation with an accountant. The final decision was not to buy the store. They had calculated that to make this enterprise successful, sales would have to increase by 50 percent. This would require investing more money into inventory and advertising, thereby making the total investment approximately $100,000. It also did not have the look Laura desired, nor did it serve the market she had envisioned.

However, Laura did learn a lot through the investigation. She learned much about the Johnson City market, including colors and styles that seemed to sell well. For future reference, she had an idea of the market value of an existing store. In addition, the experience gave her a firsthand look at a future competitor. She learned the store's sales history, the type and amount of inventory, from whom the store purchased merchandise, and the pricing strategy employed. From this she decided that she could do better than this competition. Why assume an operation with an image that wasn't her own?

SUMMARY

Many entrepreneurs choose to buy an existing business rather than create a business. To find business for sale opportunities, prospective buyers research the classified sections of the newspaper, make inquiries to business brokers, discuss their interest with industry representatives, and inquire throughout the community.

The advantages of buying a business, as opposed to starting one from scratch, include owning a business with a history, which reduces risk because buyers know what to expect. In addition, the new business owner will inherit an immediate customer and supplier base and often will receive preferable financial arrangements through seller financing. However, many businesses that are for sale have poor customer relations and/or negative images that take a long time for new ownership to improve.

Buying an existing business requires detailed research and planning, just as in starting a new business. Buyers must make sure that all documents presented are accurate and that the final price is fair. If the opportunity does not appear to be a good investment, it should be avoided. The buyer should realistically project what impact the change of ownership will have on the business. Business buyers should not expect an immediate turn-around of profits and growth.

VOCABULARY BUILDER

On a separate sheet of paper, write a brief description of each word or phrase based on your reading of the chapter.

1. Market value
2. Business broker
3. Goodwill
4. Earnings approach
5. Replacement value
6. Liquidation value

REVIEW QUESTIONS

1. Why is it a good idea to investigate business for sale opportunities before deciding to start a new business?
2. What are three sources of finding business for sale opportunities?
3. What are three advantages of buying an existing business?
4. What are three disadvantages of buying an existing business?
5. Why is it important to determine why a business is for sale?
6. What information should a prospective buyer collect to properly evaluate a business opportunity?
7. What is a sign of a bad business opportunity?
8. What does an earnings approach determine when used to evaluate a business for sale?
9. What is determined when calculating liquidation value?
10. Why is it wise to make a pro forma (projected) income statement before purchasing a business?

DISCUSSION QUESTIONS

1. What are some characteristics of a promising business opportunity?
2. What is the advantage of using seller financing as opposed to conventional financing?
3. What steps should an entrepreneur take to investigate a business for sale opportunity?
4. A business is advertised as for sale for $100,000. The stated profit is $25,000 after all salaries, including the owner's, are paid. Is this opportunity worth investigating? Why?
5. How does replacement value differ from the asset value listed on a balance sheet? Why should prospective buyers determine the replacement cost?

CRITICAL THINKING

Some business sellers are hesitant about disclosing all of their business's financial information to potential buyers. They believe they should only have to show sales results and asset totals, not tax returns or confidential payroll information. As a prospective buyer, how would you react to this attitude? How would this affect your purchase decisions? Explain your answers.

SHORT CASE: A BUSINESS FOR SALE OPPORTUNITY

Henry Murphy studied the two business propositions before him, trying to judge which was the better opportunity. Both restaurants were offered for sale for $50,000. The income statements reveal the following profits before the owner's salary is deducted.

	Restaurant 1	Restaurant 2
Sales	$135,000	$160,000
Food purchases	45,000	68,000
Gross profit	90,000	92,000
Operating expenses	65,000	73,000
Net profit	$25,000	$19,000

Restaurant #1 showed greater profits; however, Restaurant #2 had more assets—$35,000 compared to Restaurant #1's assets of $24,000. Restaurant #1 is 10 years old and has experienced a slight downturn of sales during the past year. Restaurant #2 is only three years old and has had a 22 percent sales increase during the past year. Restaurant #1 underwent a recent remodeling and appears to be operating under better management than Restaurant #2. Both are located on main thoroughfares in the same growing community. Henry is looking for a business that can afford to pay him a $14,000 salary with a good return on investment. He is confused about which restaurant offers the better opportunity.

Questions

1. Based on this initial information, what restaurant would you recommend that Henry purchase? What are your reasons for recommending that particular restaurant?
2. Describe a strategy to increase profits for the restaurant you chose.

PROJECT CHALLENGE

Review the classified section of the newspaper to find a business for sale opportunity for a business similar to the hypothetical one you are planning. Also, contact business brokers and inquire if they have any current listing of similar businesses. How do the newspaper or brokers' descriptions compare with what you have learned about your business project? Write a report that analyzes the existing business opportunities and compares them with your planned new business.

4

Purchasing a Franchise

After mastering the information contained in this chapter, you should be able to:

4-1 Define the terms associated with business franchises.

4-2 List some of the classifications of franchises that are available in the United States.

4-3 List some advantages and disadvantages of franchising.

4-4 Understand and explain some of the legal aspects and requirements of franchising.

4-5 List questions to ask before purchasing a franchise.

franchise, a right or privilege to conduct a particular business using a specified trade name

A person who has a burning desire to become an entrepreneur and own a small business may have no real idea what particular business to choose or how to run a business. This aspiring entrepreneur may want to consider a **franchise.** There are thousands of franchises in the United States from which entrepreneurs can choose. These businesses currently account for about one-third of the U.S. retail economy—more than $600 billion of business per year. Well-known franchises include Computerland®, McDonald's®, Kentucky Fried Chicken®, Coca-Cola®, Midas®, Wendy's®, Century 21®, Dunkin' Donuts®, Dairy Queen®, Video Connection®, and Ramada Inn®.

There are numerous benefits—as well as some drawbacks—to **franchising.** One of the benefits of franchising is business experience. When someone purchases a franchise, the past experiences of other entrepreneurs who have chosen that franchise are included in the purchase. In other words, practical business advice, based on the

Illus. 4-1a, 4-1b, 4-1c Well-known franchises.

experiences of all other owners of the same franchise, comes with the franchise. This advice is a valuable asset.

Purchasing a franchise is certainly a desirable option for some entrepreneurs. For others, it is not. Read the following information carefully and decide if a franchise may be the right decision for you.

DEFINITION

The U.S. Department of Commerce defines franchising as a method of doing business in which a **franchisee** is granted the right to engage in offering, selling, or distributing goods or services under a marketing format that is designed by the **franchisor.** The International Franchise Association defines a franchise as a continuing relationship between franchisor and franchisee in which the sum total of the franchisor's knowledge, image, success, manufacturing, and marketing techniques are supplied to the franchisee for a consideration.

Franchising is described in the following terms[1]:

1. Franchising is a business opportunity. An owner (producer or distributor) of a service or trademarked product grants rights to an individual for distribution and/or sale of goods or services and receives a payment or **royalty** in return.
2. Franchising is a pattern or method of doing business. A franchisee is granted a right to offer, sell, or distribute goods or services under the marketing format designated by the franchisor.
3. Franchising is a licensing relationship. A franchisor of a product, service, or business grants distribution rights to affiliated dealers (franchisees). These rights often include exclusive access to a defined geographic area.
4. A franchise is a continuing relationship. Franchisors provide a licensed privilege to do business. Many also provide management and technical assistance and training.

CLASSIFICATIONS

Franchising opportunities are available in many types of business in all areas of the United States. A publication that is offered by the U.S.

franchising, method of doing business by which a franchise is guaranteed the right to engage in offering, selling, or distributing products or services under a specified marketing format

franchisee, the person who buys a franchise from a franchisor

franchisor, the person or company that offers the franchise to others

royalty, an ongoing fee paid to a franchisor at specific intervals—usually a percent of gross revenue or net sales

---
[1]Robert T. Justis and Richard J. Judd, *Franchising* (Cincinnati: South-Western Publishing Co., 1989)

Department of Commerce, the *Franchise Opportunities Handbook,* lists by category the franchise opportunities that are available. Entrepreneurs have more than three dozen categories from which to choose. The publication includes information about costs, capital required, number of franchises already operating, etc. A current copy can be obtained by contacting the U.S. Government Printing Office in Washington, D.C.

Some of the categories in the *Franchise Opportunities Handbook* are the following:

- automotive products/services
- business aids/services
- campgrounds
- clothing/shoes
- cosmetics/toiletries
- dental centers
- educational products/services
- employment services
- foods
- motels/hotels
- printing
- real estate
- security systems
- vending

Other sources for finding franchise opportunities include the *Wall Street Journal, Forbes* magazine, *Barron's* magazine, the *Info Franchise Newsletter,* "The Franchise Annual" (published by Info Press, Lewiston, NY), "Franchise Yearbook" (published in Los Angeles, CA), "Franchising for Free" (published by John Wiley & Sons, New York, NY), *Venture* magazine, and *Entrepreneur* magazine.

ADVANTAGES

There are many advantages to purchasing a franchise. The entrepreneur should evaluate these (as well as the disadvantages) carefully before deciding to purchase.

A franchise provides an established product or service. One of the most challenging problems any entrepreneur faces when starting a new business is that of product/service acceptance by the consumer. The process of becoming established can take years. With a franchise, the process has already been underway for some time and is usually reinforced by large-scale advertising.

Many, but not all, franchisors offer management and/or technical assistance. Management assistance usually includes provision of the knowledge needed to start the new business and handle daily operations as well as crisis management. This assistance is available through on-site training or classes at the franchisor's base. Technical

Illus. 4-2 Franchisors provide management, technical assistance, and training.

© *Brian Seed/Tony Stone Images, Inc.*

assistance can include anything from site selection and building design to equipment purchase and food recipes.

For consumers, one of the main attractions of franchised businesses is consistency. A franchise contract mandates a certain level of quality. That level of quality is determined by past business experience. Most franchisees realize that they must match or exceed the quality available in related franchises if they are to be successful. The consumer knows that a franchised business in New Jersey will offer the same basic range of products or services as the same franchised business in California. It is unlikely that there will be any major surprises.

The operating capital required for a new business can be considerable. Association with a franchise may reduce some of these expenses. General supply purchases are a good example. Franchisors may be able to negotiate low prices because of the large volume they purchase. Independent entrepreneurs usually do not have that advantage. The same holds true for equipment, insurance, and other expenses.

A franchise contract may provide for the franchisee's professional growth. If the contract guarantees a certain geographic territory to the franchisee, future competition within that territory cannot come from within the same franchise. Any growth in the territory is limited to the purchase or sale of additional locations by the original franchisee. For example, if you purchased a franchise for a certain service station and, as part of the contract, were given an exclusive geographic territory, you may be able to purchase franchises for additional locations or sell franchises to others.

DISADVANTAGES

Entrepreneurs who purchase franchises may have certain expectations as to services that they are to receive from the franchisor. If these services are not clearly included in the contract, they may not be provided. The franchisor's only legal responsibilities are those included in the contract.

A franchisee is required to pay the franchisor on an ongoing basis. If the value of the services the franchisee receives does not at least offset the payment, the payment becomes a financial drain on the new business.

Franchisees may depend heavily on the advice of the franchisor at first, but should be careful not to become overdependent. Overdependence often clouds common sense and interferes with sound business practices. The level of dependence should decrease as time passes.

The franchise package will usually carry restrictions that involve products or services to be offered, types of customers to be served, geographic territory, and pricing. Many entrepreneurs object to this type of control because it inhibits the freedom they sought as business owners.

Franchise contracts usually control the terms of a sale or closure to a degree. This means that a franchisee may have little or no say about the terms of a termination of the franchise agreement.

For franchises that are part of a chain, the performance of existing locations may influence the success of new businesses. If service and quality slip at one location, customers may associate that slip with the other locations as well.

LEGAL ASPECTS OF FRANCHISING

An entrepreneur should not sign a franchise contract without the advice of a competent attorney. Only an attorney can properly analyze

Illus. 4-3 An entrepreneur should seek the advice of a competent attorney before signing a franchise contract.

the legal documents that are required for a franchise arrangement. Two of these documents are the disclosure document, or the Uniform Franchise Offering Circular (UFOC); and the Franchise Agreement.

The Disclosure Document

The Federal Trade Commission (FTC) requires that a franchisor disclose certain information to a prospective franchisee, in writing, at least ten business days prior to any legal commitment to purchase.

The franchisor can meet the disclosure requirements of the FTC by following the format of the UFOC, developed by the North American Securities Administrators' Association.[2] This format requires including information under the following headings:

1. The Franchisor and Any Predecessor—description and background of the company, owners' prior business experience, and details about any business that preceded the one being offered.
2. Prior Business Experience of Persons Affiliated with Franchisor: Franchise Brokers—identity and business experience of the franchisor's directors, executive officers, and **franchise brokers**.

franchise broker, a person who obtains the right from a franchisor to sell franchises within a certain territory—the franchise pays royalties to the franchise broker, who pays royalties to the franchisor

[2]Justis and Judd, *Franchising.*

3. Litigation—details of any involvement in criminal, civil, or administrative law complaints. If none, so stated.
4. Bankruptcy—details of any bankruptcies. If none, so stated.
5. Franchisee's Initial Franchise Fee or Other Payment—a detail of the franchisee's purchase cost and terms of payment.
6. Other Fees—a detail of fees that must be paid by the franchisee on an ongoing basis (such as royalties) and the terms of payment.
7. Franchisee's Initial Investment—a detail of the franchisee's estimated initial investment cost, how the funds are to be distributed, franchisor's policies regarding financing, and detail of any other costs to the franchisee, either direct or indirect. If none, so stated. NOTE: These costs are separate from the franchise fee.
8. Obligations of Franchisee to Purchase or Lease from Designated Suppliers—a detail of franchisee's obligations to purchase only from franchisor-designated suppliers. If none, so stated.
9. Obligations of Franchisee to Purchase or Lease in Accordance with Specifications or from Approved Suppliers—a detail of franchisee's obligations to purchase or lease certain items, such as equipment, advertising materials, and insurance; and details concerning restrictions in sources for purchases or leases. If none, so stated.
10. Financing Arrangements—information about what financing assistance (partial or full financing, assistance with application for third-party financing) is offered and the terms of such assistance. If none, so stated.
11. Obligations of Franchisor; Other Supervision, Assistance or Services—details of the provision, supervision, service, and assistance obligations of the franchisor and when those obligations must be met. If none, so stated.
12. Exclusive Area or Territory—information about territorial (geographical area) and sales restrictions, including details about any option for sub-franchise.
13. Trademarks, Service Marks, Trade Names, Logotypes, and Commercial Symbols—a detail of any particular formats that must be used in business operations. If none, so stated.
14. Patents and Copyrights—details of patents and copyrights that pertain to the offering and are owned by the company, and how they affect the franchisee. If none, so stated.
15. Obligation of the Franchisee to Participate in the Actual Operation of the Franchise Business—details about the personal participation obligations and staffing obligations of the franchisee.

16. Restrictions on Goods and Services Offered by Franchisee—details of limitations on the products or services the franchisee may offer, either within the offered franchise or in outside business transactions (e.g., a second business).
17. Renewal, Termination, Repurchase, Modification, and Assignment of the Franchise Agreement and Related Information—details about rights, obligations, or restrictions in renewal, termination, repurchase, modification, or assignment of the franchise agreement.
18. Arrangements with Public Figures—details about current involvement of any public figure in the franchise system—whether a famous person's name or image is used in conjunction with the franchise, what that person's true involvement is, what benefits that person receives, and what, if any, investment that person has made in the business; details of any restrictions on the franchisee's right to use a public figure. If none, so stated.
19. Actual, Average, Projected, or Forecasted Franchise Sales, Profits, or Earnings—details about the franchise's actual or projected revenues. If not available, so stated.
20. Information Regarding Franchises of the Franchisor—a detail of the operational franchises that the franchisor has sold, including franchisee names and franchise locations; history of cancellations, terminations, refused renewals, or reacquisitions; details about additional franchises to be offered, including location and number of offerings in each location. If none, so stated.
21. Franchisor's Financial Statements—audited financial statements, usually for the prior three fiscal years, should be attached. Statement of attachment is to be included in the UFOC.
22. Agreements—a detail of the documents that are included in the franchise, i.e., the franchise agreement and all related contracts and agreements.

The Franchise Agreement

The franchise agreement (contract), with all accompanying documents, must be delivered at least five business days before signature is required. It is the legal document that details the terms of the franchise purchase. This document, along with the accompanying documents, specifies the relationship between the franchisee and the franchisor. The entrepreneur should not sign such documents without

Illus. 4-4   A franchise agreement may include a list of tasks that must be completed prior to opening.

having an attorney review them. A typical franchise agreement may include the following[3]:

1. Grant of Franchise—general information about the nature of the franchise, a list of parties to the agreement, and details about any copyrights, patents, trademarks, etc., that are involved.
2. Exclusive Territory—statement regarding franchisor's right to operate or sell similar franchises within a specific territory. If none, so stated.
3. Term—specification of contract duration and renewal/termination requirements.
4. Development and Opening—list of tasks that must be completed prior to opening and time limits for completion; details regarding site selection and territory designation, site preparation, and, if the site is to be owned by the franchisor and leased to the franchisee, terms of the lease.
5. Payments—specific information about payments to be made to the franchisor, including franchise fees, continuing royalties, advertising fees, and interest penalties.

---

[3]Justis and Judd, *Franchising*.

6. Advertising—a detail of obligations, both franchisee's and franchisor's, related to advertising.
7. Trademarks—specifications regarding franchisee's use of symbols, logos, etc., and description of the process for franchisor's possible discontinuance of the use of any such marks.
8. Products, Supplies, and Equipment—specifications for franchisee's purchase and use of products, supplies, and equipment.
9. Standards and Procedures—detail of requirements that franchisee must meet in relation to management, personnel, personal participation, and insurance.
10. Training and Assistance—detail of obligations, both franchisee's and franchisor's, in relation to training required for successful operation of the business.
11. Business Conduct—detail of franchisee's responsibilities in business communications.
12. Reports and Inspections—a detail of the accounting documents and reports that the franchisee must provide to the franchisor, and at what intervals; details about the franchisee's and franchisor's rights concerning inspection.
13. Relationship of the Parties—specifics concerning the franchisee's relationship with the franchisor, limitations, and rights in transactions concerning the franchisor.
14. Assignment of Franchise—specifications for franchisee's right to transfer ownership of the franchise, and any obligations that must be met prior to such transfer.
15. Termination—detail of reasons for franchisor's termination of contract.
16. Rights and Obligations of the Parties Upon Termination or Expiration—detail of franchisee's responsibilities at termination of the contract.
17. Enforcement and Construction—specific information about enforcement and construction of the franchise agreement.

As you can see, the franchise agreement can be very long and complicated. All of the items must be included so that there is no misunderstanding between the franchisor and the franchisee.

QUESTIONS TO ASK

Entrepreneurs should ask several pertinent questions before they purchase a franchise. The final decision to purchase should not be made until these questions have been answered satisfactorily. These questions involve the franchise, the franchisor, the franchisee (entrepreneur), and the franchisee's market.

The Franchise

The following are questions that prospective franchisees should ask about the franchise in general.

1. Was the franchise agreement approved by a lawyer?
2. Are any of the requirements of the contract illegal in the area where business is to be conducted?
3. Will the franchisee receive an exclusive territory for the duration of the franchise term or can the franchisor sell additional franchises in the territory?
4. Is there a connection between the franchisor and any other franchise company dealing in similar merchandise or services?
5. If there is a connection between the franchisor and another franchise company, is the franchisee protected against competition from the second franchise company?
6. What is required if the franchisee wishes to cancel the contract?
7. Will the franchisee receive any payment for goodwill (customer loyalty) if the franchise is sold?[4]

The Franchisor

Prospective franchisees should ask these questions about the specific franchisor with which they are dealing.

1. How long has the company existed, and how long has the franchisor been in business?
2. Do other franchisees consider the franchisor honest and fair?
3. Has the franchisor shown the franchisee profit statements for several franchise locations? Have they been verified by the franchisee at each location?
4. Does the franchisor provide the following services?

- credit
- capital
- management training
- employee training
- marketing and/or marketing assistance
- merchandising assistance
- site selection assistance

---

[4]*Franchise Opportunities Handbook,* U.S. Department of Commerce, Washington, D.C., 1982.

5. Is the franchisor on firm financial ground?
6. Is there an experienced management team from which the franchisee can seek advice?
7. What services or opportunities can the franchisor provide that the franchisee cannot otherwise obtain?
8. In what kind of detail has the franchisor investigated the franchisee and the franchisee's ability to run a profitable business?
9. Has the franchisor followed all state, federal, and local laws that govern the sale of franchises?

The Franchisee

Each prospective franchisee must determine the answers to these questions before he or she can make a decision about investing in a franchise.

1. How much money is required to open and run the business until it becomes profitable?
2. Does the value (monetary and/or psychological) of the franchise outweigh the loss of the freedom of being an independent business owner?
3. Does the franchisee have what it takes to open the franchise and turn it into a profitable business?
4. What kind of commitment is the franchisee willing to make to the franchise? Is the franchisee willing to devote years to its success?

The Franchisee's Market

And, finally, prospective franchisees should consider these questions about the market and location of the franchise.

1. Has the franchisee conducted in-depth marketing research to determine that the franchise will be successful in the intended location?
2. What does marketing research indicate about potential future changes in the intended location?
3. What is the projected demand for the franchised product or service in the area surrounding the intended location?
4. What is the competitive environment for the franchised product or service?[5]

---

[5]*Franchise Opportunities Handbook,* U.S. Department of Commerce, Washington, D.C., 1982.

Illus. 4-5 The entrepreneur must analyze the competition for the franchised product or service.

THE FASHION ATTIC

Before starting to write her own business plan, Laura decided to investigate the possibilities offered by a franchise. She arranged an appointment with a sales agent for a national ladies apparel franchisor. The presentation by the sales agent seemed very appealing.

The franchisor would choose the location site, handle the merchandise selection, determine pricing, design the store, and take care of many other planning functions. It would greatly ease Laura's burden and workload. Additionally, the franchisor offered a well-known name and a history of being able to generate above-average sales.

However, after much discussion and consulting with her friend Paula, Laura decided a franchise wasn't for her. She determined this after asking herself the following questions:

1. What could the franchisor do that she couldn't do for herself? *Answer:* Nothing that she couldn't learn on her own. Sure, the franchisor could make the business process easier, but there wasn't anything that she couldn't learn with experience. Besides Laura had studied fashion design and could count on Paula for help in setting up a retail operation.

2. Was she willing to give up some of the freedom of being an independent business owner? *Answer:* No. Freedom and the right to make the decisions were two of the main reasons Laura decided to start a business. She did not want to give up these very important aspects of business ownership.
3. Was the name recognition of a franchise important? *Answer:* Possibly, but Laura and Paula felt that in a town the size of Johnson City (population 75,000) effective advertising and good customer service would in time be just as effective.

No, franchising was not for her. Laura decided the cost was too high for the benefits received. She liked the freedom of being independent and wanted to run the new business in the manner she chose.

Who knows? Someday the business might be so successful that Laura could start her own franchising operation. Wouldn't that be something?

SUMMARY

A person who wants to become an entrepreneur and own a small business may not know what particular business to choose or how to run a business. This person may want to consider a franchise. There are thousands of franchises from which entrepreneurs in the United States can choose. These businesses currently account for about one third of the U.S. retail economy.

The U.S. Department of Commerce defines franchising as a method of doing business in which a franchisee is granted the right to engage in offering, selling, or distributing goods or services under a marketing format that is designed by the franchisor. Franchising opportunities are available in many types of business.

Advantages and disadvantages of purchasing a franchise should be evaluated carefully before a decision to purchase is made. An entrepreneur should not sign a franchise agreement without the advice of a competent attorney. Only an attorney can properly analyze the legal documents that are required for a franchise arrangement, such as the disclosure document and the franchise agreement.

> The Federal Trade Commission requires that a franchisor discloses certain specified information to a prospective franchisee, in writing, at least ten business days prior to any legal commitment to purchase. The franchise agreement, with all accompanying documents, must be delivered at least five business days before signature is required. Several pertinent questions should be asked and answered before the entrepreneur purchases a franchise. These questions involve the franchise, the franchisor, the franchisee (entrepreneur), and the franchisee's market.

VOCABULARY BUILDER

Write a brief description of each word or phrase based on your reading of the chapter.

1. Franchise
2. Franchising
3. Franchisee
4. Franchisor
5. Royalty
6. Franchise broker

REVIEW QUESTIONS

1. What are two descriptive phrases for franchising? What information do they provide?
2. What U.S. Department of Commerce publication contains information about franchise opportunities, costs, capital requirements, and number of franchises already operating?
3. What are four advantages of franchising?
4. What are four disadvantages of franchising?

DISCUSSION QUESTIONS

1. What are royalties? What effect do they have on business profits?
2. What is the Uniform Franchise Offering Circular? Why is it important?
3. What is the purpose of the franchise agreement?
4. What are three of the questions entrepreneurs should ask about a franchisor before purchasing a franchise?
5. What are three of the questions you should ask yourself—a prospective franchisee—before purchasing a franchise?

CRITICAL THINKING

Chris, a 28-year-old, has worked as a clerical assistant at City Hall for the past nine years. She recently inherited a considerable amount of money from her grandmother and is thinking about using the money to start her own business. She is considering the purchase of a motel franchise.

1. Is a franchise purchase a reasonable consideration for Chris?
2. Are there any special attributes Chris needs to look for in selecting a franchise?

SHORT CASE: CAREER DECISION

Joe Ramos is a third-generation Mexican-American who lives in a suburb of Chicago. He has worked for his uncle Paco in the restaurant business for 20 years. Uncle Paco's restaurant, Casa del Mexico, is very successful.

When Joe began working for Uncle Paco, he bussed tables. Over the years he has successfully performed every job in the restaurant, including chef. Since Uncle Paco went into semi-retirement five years ago, Joe has managed the restaurant.

Joe has always been very happy working at Casa del Mexico. He figured that he would stay there until he retired. All that changed recently, however. Uncle Paco's oldest son, Luis, moved back from the West Coast and began working at the restaurant.

During the six months that Luis has been working with Joe in the restaurant, things have been changing. Joe is sure that it is just a matter of time before Uncle Paco makes his son manager of Casa del Mexico. Joe sees his career experiencing a serious setback when that happens.

Because of what is happening, Joe has decided that going into business for himself might be a good idea. Joe has always invested a portion of his earnings and he now has quite a nice nest egg. He plans to either purchase a franchise or open a small restaurant on his own.

Questions

1. Would you advise Joe to purchase a franchise or open a restaurant on his own? Why?
2. What should Joe consider as he decides which option is best for him? What questions should he ask?

PROJECT CHALLENGE

Choose a franchise, gather as much information as you can, and answer the questions that were presented in this chapter to decide if this franchise would be a viable option for you. Then answer the following questions.

1. What are the advantages and disadvantages of purchasing a franchise in your particular situation?
2. Is purchase of the franchise you chose a suitable option for you? Why or why not?
3. If purchase of this franchise is not a suitable option for you, might you consider the purchase of a different franchise? Why or why not?

THE WRONG BUSINESS PLAN

Unit 1 Case

Aaron was feeling uncomfortable as he waited for his appointment with Mrs. Kimura, a vice president with First National Bank. His wife, Carmen, had suggested going to the bank for advice on how to get his idea started. Mrs. Kimura was a family friend who he believed would be helpful. Entering her office, he suddenly felt very anxious about the meeting. What questions should he ask?

"Hi, Aaron, it's good to see you. Have a seat. How's Carmen and that future president you two are raising?"

"We're fine, Mrs. Kimura. Jason is keeping us busy, and so are our jobs. Sometimes it seems as if we're constantly on the run. That's the reason I'm here to see you. I have an idea for starting a business and I need some guidance. I want to open my own retail antiques shop. I gained sales and marketing experience while I was assistant manager of the big antiques mall downtown, and I've been buying and learning about antiques for myself for as long as I can remember."

"My goodness, Aaron, that's quite a step. Have you carefully considered all the risks involved in owning a business? What information have you collected to support your idea?" she asked.

"Actually, Mrs. Kimura, I have nothing except for a few notes I've made in an old notebook. How do I get it all together?" asked Aaron.

"It's a big job, Aaron. You'll need some assistance. You might want to visit with a business consultant for help, or better still, either go over to the Small Business Development Center at the college or go downtown to the Small Business Administration and ask for assistance. They can help you write a business plan. Then come back and see me and we'll see if the bank can help you get started financially."

Aaron went home and looked in the yellow pages of the telephone book. He jotted down the telephone numbers of several professional consulting firms, the Small Business Administration, and the Small Business Development Center at the local college. He thought he found exactly what he was looking for on his first call to B&B Consulting Services. They would create a complete business plan for an antiques store on their computer after meeting with him to get the essential information. "Wow, that's easy," thought Aaron, "I'll have to pay a fee, but I'll have a business plan in less than a week."

Sure enough, after Aaron told them about the type of store he envisioned on a quiet but accessible side street, they produced a 15 page report providing general market information, location considerations, money needed, and a personnel plan. Although the report cost $800, Aaron was pleased with its professional appearance and went to share it with Mrs. Kimura.

Her reaction shocked him. "Aaron, I can't use this. It's simply a compilation of statistics about antiques stores. It has very little to do with you or the local market. You must personalize a business plan to your own situation. I'm afraid you spent money for information you could have found at the library for free. Why not take this information, and your idea, to one of the federal assistance agencies and they can show you at no charge how to write a business plan."

The next day Aaron and Carmen visited Tom Porter at the nearby Small Business Development Center. Tom explained the ingredients for a business plan and directed Aaron and Carmen to the proper resources for information. He commented, "To start a project this big, simplify your approach as much as possible. I would suggest you go home tonight and sit down and write out a two-paragraph description of your objectives. The first paragraph should address your personal objectives, meaning the personal satisfaction you seek from this endeavor. The second paragraph should address your financial objectives. State these in terms of the minimum amount of money you must make in the first year to support your family, and then how much money you anticipate you will make after you run the business for three years. Once you have done this, you should list all the things that must be done to complete the business plan. Don't worry too much right now about the formal structure of the final plan—we can do that later. The main thing now is to start writing it out. Putting an idea down on paper begins to make it real and helps clarify your thoughts. By putting your objectives in writing you will have started down the path that leads to owning your own business."

That evening, with Carmen's help, Aaron wrote the following paragraphs.

◆

PERSONAL OBJECTIVE: For the purpose of achieving self-employment, I wish to open a retail antiques shop in Stillwater selling nineteenth and early twentieth century American furniture and small household items. As a business owner, I will be able to control my own destiny and be responsible for all decisions I make concerning the business. I will have the opportunity to use my interest in antiques, as well as my management experience and my creative instincts in retail merchandising. I can own a business I will be proud of, and receive recognition from the community for my efforts. It will be an enterprise that I can share with family members.

FINANCIAL OBJECTIVES: I am willing to invest the amount of money and time needed in an antiques shop if I feel confident that the business will make an initial profit the first year of $15,000. I anticipate profits will rise to more than $25,000 per year by the end of the third year. I am hopeful the store will be opened within a year.

◆

"Hey, Carmen, I'm excited," Aaron said with a smile. "We've taken the first step. Now let's list everything we have to do for the business plan."

Case Questions

1. Why is it not possible for a consulting firm to do a complete business plan?
2. Help Aaron and Carmen by listing the main components of a business plan.

UNIT 2
MARKETING THE SMALL BUSINESS

5 **Getting to Know Your Customers**

6 **Getting to Know Your Competition**

7 **Deciding on a Location and Facilities**

8 **Developing the Marketing Plan**

9 **Pricing and Sales Planning**

10 **Promotional Strategies**

5

Getting to Know Your Customers

After mastering the information contained in this chapter, you should be able to:

5-1 Describe a market.

5-2 Understand the importance of customers' needs.

5-3 Understand the steps of the research process used to learn about markets.

5-4 Explain how to conduct a demographic study.

5-5 Determine market potential.

customer, an individual who has the means to satisfy his or her needs

market, a group of consumers who have an unsatisfied need for a particular product or service

WHAT ARE CUSTOMERS?

Customers are the most important part of a business. Without customers, there can be no business. To be sure of having customers, entrepreneurs must make an effort to determine the needs of the **market** and identify groups of consumers that are likely to have an unsatisfied need for the product or service to be offered.

Potential customers' perceptions of need differ as a result of many environmental factors. When he formulated his theory on the hierarchy of human needs in 1920, Dr. Abraham Maslow cited five levels of need that we all share. Even though they are common needs, they vary in intensity depending on environmental background. Environmental background includes size of family, cultural orientation, upbringing, family values, and anything else that influences people during childhood and early adulthood.

All of us share physiological needs (basic survival needs such as food and water) in a similar degree of need satisfaction. We also share safety needs (protection needs such as shelter and clothing) in similar degrees of need satisfaction. It is at the love and belonging needs (social needs such as friends, family, and group identification) level of the hierarchy that most people begin to differ. The intensity of our need to be surrounded by people and our reliance on their support largely depends on the environment in which we were raised. Self-esteem needs (individual needs such as achieving status and recognition in the eyes of others and the need for self-respect) also vary widely depending on personality makeup. Many people reach as far as possible to meet their self-actualization needs (feeling accomplishment and achievement, and fulfilling personal capabilities), while others accept personal limitations at a fairly low level.

Illus. 5-1 The buyer of a luxury car is not shopping simply for transportation but may be seeking to fulfill self-esteem and self-actualization needs.

© SuperStock, Inc.

It is important to know that we all have these needs, and that the importance we place on them differs. It is sometimes difficult to recognize the need level. For example, the buyer of a basic, no-frills sedan is shopping for transportation. The need level being addressed is, in all probability, the love and belonging need. By having transportation, the buyer will be able to get to work, go shopping, and visit others. All of these activities relate to social need. The buyer of a luxury car, however, is not shopping for transportation. Purchasing a luxury car will fulfill self-esteem and self-actualization needs. The buyer hopes to receive recognition from others through the car's image. Also, being able to purchase such a car will enhance the buyer's sense of achievement, accomplishment, and fulfillment of personal capabilities.

WHERE ARE THE CUSTOMERS?

The starting place for approaching a market is determining what group of customers has the strongest need and motivation to buy

Unit 2 Marketing the Small Business

what is being sold. It is essential to learn how many customers there are and where they are located.

Entrepreneurs use **market research** to learn about the characteristics of their market. The more entrepreneurs know about the people or companies they will be serving, the more successful they will be at making wise, well-informed decisions. Since many business decisions will be based on the information found in the research of the market, the information must be accurate and timely. Collecting and properly analyzing information reduces the risk in making a decision.

Market Research

Properly conducting market research requires completing six steps (see Figure 5-1).

Define the Question. The first step in the market research process is to define the question. Often, entrepreneurs have concerns or are not sure about certain aspects of their businesses. By putting these concerns into words, they define the question. A typical question entrepreneurs ask themselves is, "Which people are most likely to buy from my business?"

Determine Needed Data. After the question has been identified, data must be collected to provide the solution. Entrepreneurs must determine what kind of data will help answer the question. Not all data will provide the needed information. For example, data about the number of customers who visit a certain mall each year does not indicate what those customers purchase.

Collect Data. Entrepreneurs determine if there is a market for a product or service by collecting and studying information about the consumers in the desired market. Collecting data begins with a **demographic study** of the market.

Entrepreneurs, in conducting demographic studies for consumer-oriented products or services, should collect data about age, employment status, education, **per capita income, ethnic ratio, gender ratio,** and **economic stability** of the target population. The **psychographics** of the market should also be researched. Are the people socially active or do they keep to themselves? Do they have a lot of leisure time? The answers to these questions will be important in determining if the intended product or service can be sold successfully.

If the product or service is industry oriented, such as selling surgical equipment to hospitals, the entrepreneur should conduct a study

---

market research, systematic gathering, recording, and analyzing of information concerning the market for goods and services

demographic study, a study of the statistics for the population in the proposed market

per capita income, average amount of money made or received, per person, on an annual basis

ethnic ratio, the proportion of a particular ethnic group to total population

gender ratio, the proportion of each gender to total population

economic stability, an economy's ability to withstand changes

psychographics, psychological variables (personality, attitude, beliefs, self-concept) and life-style values

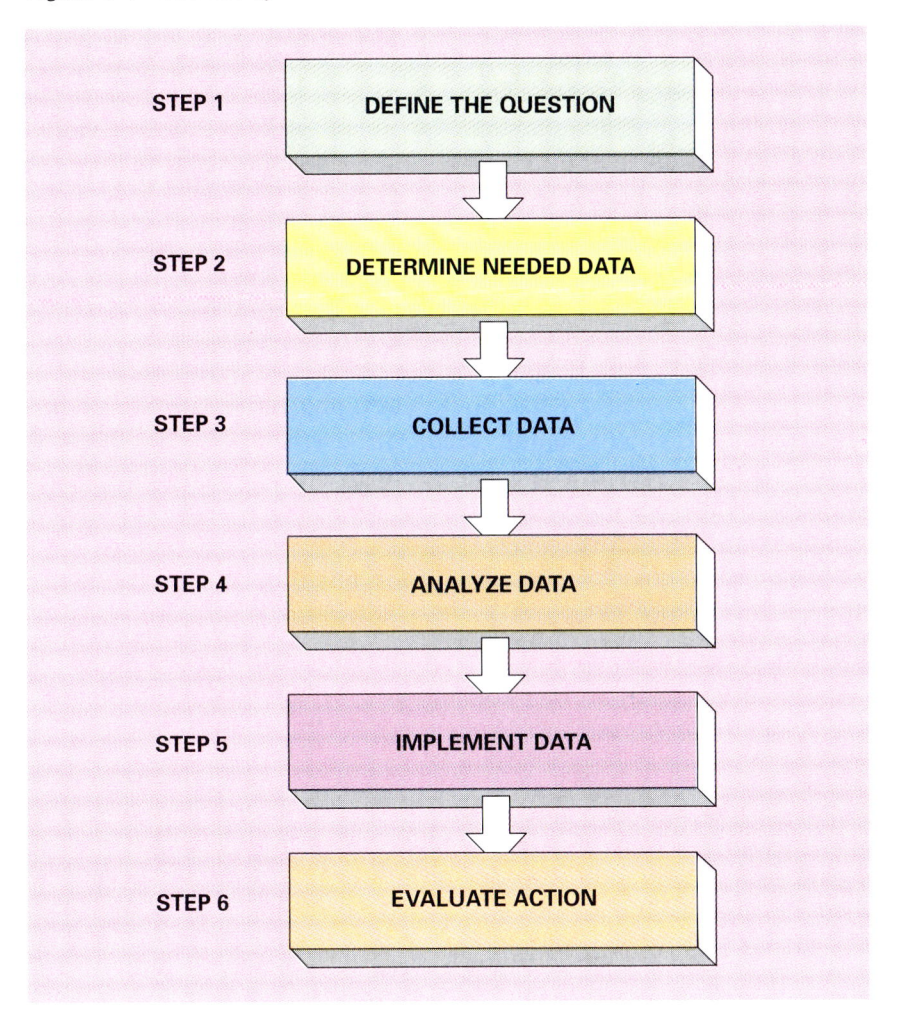

Figure 5-1 The Entrepreneur's Practical Guide to Market Research

STEP 1	DEFINE THE QUESTION
STEP 2	DETERMINE NEEDED DATA
STEP 3	COLLECT DATA
STEP 4	ANALYZE DATA
STEP 5	IMPLEMENT DATA
STEP 6	EVALUATE ACTION

of the targeted industry. Data for a study of an industry would include the number of potential customers in the industry, their locations, and the sizes of the companies or organizations in terms of sales revenues and number of employees. It is also necessary to learn the particulars of the industry, such as economic trends and which companies are leaders, to fully understand the needs of the market.

The information collected will include **secondary data** and **primary data.** Secondary data is available at a local chamber of commerce, library, or community college. These institutions provide published information about the number of people living in a

secondary data, information already published and available

primary data, information collected for the first time for a specific project

community, average education level, per capita income, and gender ratios. Such data were collected by Alison Nichols, an entrepreneur who wants to learn more about five potential new markets for her family's retail chain of shoe stores.

Table 5-1 is a population chart for the five communities Alison is considering, all located in Spring County. The table is an example of how secondary data acquired from a chamber of commerce can be assembled. It shows the 1980 population of each community, the 1990 population, and the projected population for the year 2000.

Additional research enables entrepreneurs to compile the types of information provided in Table 5-2.

In addition to collecting data about specific communities, entrepreneurs should collect data about geographic areas larger than the intended market so they understand the "big picture." In this case, Alison collected data about Spring County and other counties in the state. She then compiled the data (see Tables 5-3 and 5-4) so she could compare them easily.

Alison also collected data about the cities in the state with the highest rate of income growth. The results are shown in Table 5-5.

Analyze Data. After compiling secondary and primary data, entrepreneurs must analyze the information in a systematic manner. The analysis should include a written summary that includes results and

Table 5-1 Community Population Estimates

Community	1980	1990	2000 (projected)
Spruce City	52,000	75,000	99,000
Wallington	25,000	28,000	31,000
Henry	17,600	17,800	17,500
Riceville	24,300	26,300	28,500
Newton	33,600	39,500	47,400
TOTALS	152,500	186,600	223,400

Table 5-2 Age and Ethnic Structure

Community	Median Age	White, non-Hispanic (%)	African American (%)	Asian (%)	Hispanic (%)	Native American (%)
Spruce City	32.1	87.5	6.9	1.6	2.3	1.7
Wallington	34.5	91.6	4.4	0.0	1.8	2.2
Henry	37.0	83.2	10.5	3.3	0.7	2.3
Riceville	42.5	76.4	14.6	4.8	0.0	4.2
Newton	38.4	92.0	3.2	1.2	2.6	1.0

Table 5-3 Average Head-of-Household Income, by County

County	Average Income
A — Jackson	$20,427
B — Spring	19,978
C — Concord	19,865
D — Wilson	18,696
E — Newton	18,480
F — Walton	18,205
G — Cory	17,680
H — Denton	17,435

Table 5-4   Per Capita Income—Top 5 Counties in State

County	1980	1990	2000 (projected)
Atlas	$12,940	$15,540	$19,500
Spring	12,861	15,120	19,380
Desmond	12,140	14,800	18,700
Concord	11,985	13,980	17,310
Pacific	11,620	13,870	16,940

Table 5-5   Income Growth—Top Eight Cities in State

City	Income Growth (%)
Springfield	38.8
Smithville	37.8
Winston	37.0
Spruce City	35.4
Canton	34.7
Jonesborough	31.8
Green City	31.5
Howard	29.6

an interpretation of what they mean. Care should be taken to ensure that all useful data collected are included in the analysis. The analysis and interpretation can provide answers to many kinds of questions.

The information in Table 5-1 provides not only basic population figures, but also an idea of growth patterns. We can see which areas of the county are growing fastest and which are likely to continue growing. If a business is to grow, it is important for the entrepreneur to consider what may happen in five years, ten years, and even after that.

The information in Tables 5-1 and 5-2 tells us that Spruce City's population is young, densely situated, centrally located, and growing faster than the population of any other community in the county. The information in Tables 5-3 and 5-4 tells us that the county's head-of-household income and per capita income are higher than average, and are expected to continue to grow. These facts are positive indicators for the possibility of opening a new business in Spruce City in Spring County.

A county map might be helpful in determining the best location for a new business. Circle or pinpoint the communities' population centers and the traveling distance between each. This allows the entrepreneur to estimate the traveling time between population centers to determine the accessibility of the business to its potential consumers.

Another item of value to the entrepreneur is a breakdown of sales in the county by industry classification (see Table 5-6).

Table 5-6   County Annual Sales, by Industry Classification

Store Type	Total Sales	Per Capita Sales
Restaurants	$7,340,000	$389.71
Apparel	3,419,000	182.61
Furniture	1,760,000	89.89
Shoes	792,000	40.18
Records, Music	388,000	20.16
Gifts/Novelties	313,000	16.85

By comparing the information in Table 5-6 with the same information from other counties, an entrepreneur can tell how the sales of a particular category of products compare, on a per capita basis, with those of surrounding counties. Major producers of the intended product can provide information about the average per capita sales of the product or service in the national or regional market. This information will let the entrepreneur know if sales of the product in the intended market area are higher or lower than average. Product manufacturers may also be able to help entrepreneurs determine how many people it will take to support a new business.

After all information has been gathered, a rough scenario of the market can be drawn. Let's use the Nichols family's shoe store as an example. Alison has learned that it takes an average of 8,000 people to support a shoe store. There are presently 16 stores that sell shoes in Spring County. Dividing the population of approximately 200,000 by 16 stores means that there is only one shoe store for every 12,500 people in this county. The average per capita shoe sales in the local market total $40 (see Table 5-6). The neighboring county has average per capita sales of $44, and the national average is $42. The intended market is evidently not purchasing its expected share of shoes. The following are indicators of a community need for more family shoe stores:

- The research showed that the per capita income is higher than normal and the unemployment level is lower, indicating a healthy economy.
- Since the neighboring county sells more shoes, it might be that consumers are shopping for shoes in the neighboring town.
- Based on the total population, this county does not have as many shoe stores as it should.

market potential, total potential sales dollars for a particular market

If Alison's family opens an upscale shoe store and the average per capita shoe sales increase to $42 per year, the same as the national average, the **market potential** is $8,400,000.

$42 (average spent per capita) × 200,000 (population) = $8,400,000

The average sales per store would be $494,117.

$8,400,000 (total sales) ÷ 17 (number of stores [16 existing plus 1 new]) = $494,117

Using primary data about the other stores and the psychographics of the consumers, the entrepreneur may be able to determine what percentage of the market a new store will attract. This will depend on the location, how well the new store is managed, and how much money is available for inventory, fixtures, and equipment. A big store located in Spruce City (the largest and most central community) will do more business than a smaller store located in Riceville. However, the store in Spruce City will be more expensive to open and operate.

Implement Data. The next step in the market research process is to use the research data for decision making. A plan of action based on the information revealed in the research of the market is developed.

The shoe store is an example of how data can be used. The market research will help Alison and her family decide whether it would be better to open a big store and reach for a large, general market share, or to open a small store and sell to a smaller, more specialized share of the market.

Evaluate Action. The last step in the market research process is evaluation. Entrepreneurs should not be satisfied with just developing a plan of action—the actions taken as a result of the analysis should be evaluated regularly after implementation.

To be sure the market research will accomplish its purpose, the entrepreneur must consider the following: (1) Demographic information is only valuable if compared to the same information for other markets. (2) The process of market research should be ongoing because the marketplace is constantly changing. It is important to stay informed about current events and changes in the marketplace and continually try to project what may happen next. (3) To keep up with and take advantage of the changes requires knowledge. Knowledge is the result of research. (4) Determination and creativity are necessary for success.

Determining Community Need

Suppose an entrepreneur wants to know how much need there is for a particular product or service within a community. Determining community need identifies the product's potential profitability. For example, anyone can open an ice cream shop and sell some ice cream, since many people enjoy ice cream. But can enough ice cream be sold to make the business profitable? If the shop owner pays $2,000 rent per month in addition to paying employees, utilities, taxes, and other operating expenses, he or she might have to sell $250,000 of ice cream per year to make a profit—$250,000 is a lot of scoops of ice cream. The owner must be sure that the community need for ice cream is that great. Deciding to sell a good product is not enough; market research must be used to determine the size of the market or the business will probably fail.

Illus. 5-2 An enterprise as simple as an ice cream shop might have to sell $250,000 worth of ice cream per year to cover rent, pay other operating expenses, and realize a profit.

© *Steve Leonard/Tony Stone Images, Inc.*

Gathering and using information is something that can be done by entrepreneurs engaged in any type of business activity. For manufacturing or wholesale businesses, entrepreneurs would collect information about the size of the industry to which they plan to sell their product or service, how many potential customers there are, how much competition there is, and whether there are indications that the intended market is being inadequately served.

Entrepreneurs who wish to sell to industry rather than consumers can find information about the components, or members, of an industry in reference books such as the *Thomas Register of American Manufacturers* at the local library. The *Thomas Register of American Manufacturers* includes volumes that classify products and list the companies that make them. Other volumes in the set include company listings that provide addresses and phone numbers, and others contain reprinted product catalogs. Other good sources of industry information are industry directories and membership lists from trade association publications. Beginning with this type of basic secondary data, entrepreneurs can continue the research by talking with those already established in the industry.

Many corporate entrepreneurs are product-development managers. They develop new ideas for company products or services and then complete consumer research for the company. If research shows there is a need for the new product or service, the company executives may decide to produce and sell it.

If you were to undertake a small business venture at your school, your market research might take this form. Imagine that you want to sell T-shirts imprinted with your school's name. You would collect information about the students who go to your school to identify potential customers. You would need to ask these questions:

1. How many students are there in each class year?
2. How do students spend their extra money?
3. Is anyone else selling school T-shirts?
4. What colors are most popular with students?
5. What would be the best location for sales?

You could get this information by collecting secondary data from the school office. Reinforce this by collecting primary data—ask students questions and record the information—then compile tables and charts and study the information. If you find there is a need for T-shirts, you could go to a local T-shirt imprinter and purchase the shirts, then sell them at a higher price. How many shirts you sell will

Illus. 5-3 Collecting primary data—by asking questions and recording the information—can help determine the need for a new enterprise.

Photo by Jay Bachemin

determine how much money you make. Of course, if you don't sell enough shirts to cover your investment, you will lose money. That is the entrepreneurial risk.

THE FASHION ATTIC

Laura went to work on the first step of market research—identify the question. She knew that to be successful, she must be able to determine what her potential customers want and need and use this information to determine the proper product mix.

To answer this, she decided to collect data about the buying habits of potential customers. Laura used secondary data about the fashion industry to learn what well-dressed women were wearing nationally. She collected numerous magazine articles and researched the history of the fashion industry at the library. She also attended a fashion trade show and collected as much printed material as she could. In addition, she collected primary data from people within the industry through interviews and letters. When she returned home, she interviewed local women to reinforce the industry findings.

Laura analyzed the data by illustrating the information in a pie chart (see Figure 5-2). To implement her findings she drafted a rough plan for the initial inventory purchases in the following breakdown: dresses 20 percent, coordinates 35 percent, separates 10 percent, sweaters 10 percent, accessories 15 percent, evening wear 10 percent.

The next question for her was to determine if there really was a community need for a new fashion boutique in Johnson City. She collected the following demographic information about Johnson City.

- Population: 1980, 68,000; 1990, 75,000; 2000, 87,000 (projected)
- Per capita income: $15,500 (12% higher than the state average)
- Average age 27.1 (3 years younger than the national average)
- Average spent per capita on ladies specialty apparel: $42 ($3 less than national average)
- Average number of inhabitants served per ladies specialty apparel store: 7,500 (75,000 population ÷ 10 existing stores = 7,500), national average = 6,000.

Using this information, Laura made the following calculation. 75,000 (population) × $42 (average spent per capita) = $3,150,000 market potential ÷ 11 stores = $286,364 average store revenue potential.

It appeared that there may be a need for another ladies specialty apparel store in Johnson City.

Figure 5-2 Product Mix for the Fashion Attic

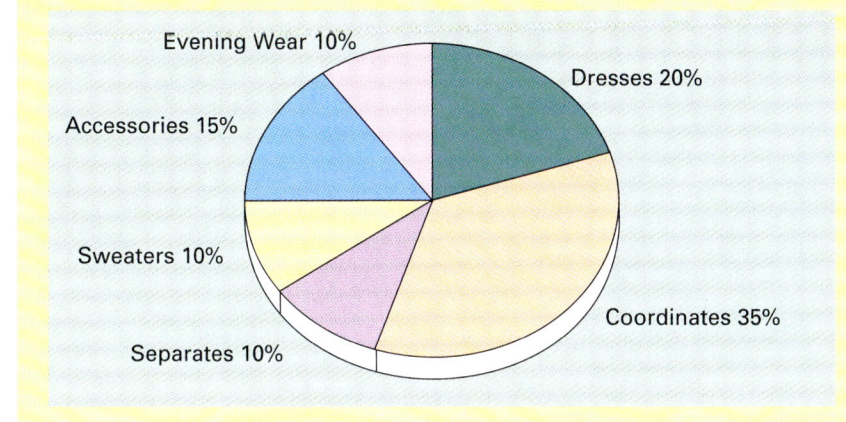

- Evening Wear 10%
- Dresses 20%
- Accessories 15%
- Coordinates 35%
- Sweaters 10%
- Separates 10%

SUMMARY

It is imperative that entrepreneurs do thorough studies on the size of potential markets and the makeup of potential customers before opening a business. The purpose is to determine if there are customers for the product or service and if there is a community need for the product or service.

The starting place for such a study is market research. To conduct market research, a six-step research process may be used: (1) define the question, (2) determine needed data, (3) collect data, (4) analyze data, (5) implement data, and (6) evaluate action.

Entrepreneurs must learn how to collect adequate information and put it to use effectively. Using the proper resources will significantly decrease the risk factor of the business venture. Data collected should include demographic information. The demographic study will provide information about the size of the market and the characteristics of its members. It should also indicate whether unsatisfied needs exist. Successful

> entrepreneurs know what needs the product or service to be offered will satisfy. By making comparisons with other markets for similar products and services, entrepreneurs will be able to project the potential for sales.

VOCABULARY BUILDER

On a separate sheet of paper, write a brief description of each word or phrase based on your reading of the chapter.

1. Customer
2. Market
3. Market research
4. Demographic study
5. Per capita income
6. Ethnic ratio
7. Gender ratio
8. Economic stability
9. Psychographics
10. Secondary data
11. Primary data
12. Market potential

REVIEW QUESTIONS

1. What is the starting point for approaching a market?
2. Why is it necessary to know the need levels of potential customers?
3. What are the six steps of the research process used to learn about markets?
4. Which of the six steps in market research involves gathering secondary and primary data?
5. What does *implement data* mean?
6. Why is it important to learn the psychographics of a market?
7. What information can an entrepreneur retrieve from a complete demographic study?
8. What is the difference between primary data and secondary data?
9. What is meant by the phrase *per capita income*?

DISCUSSION QUESTIONS

1. What factors in an individual's background would affect need levels?
2. What resources are available in your community that would help you do a demographic study?
3. What methods can be used to do a psychographic study?
4. Can the six steps of the research process apply when you are doing a school assignment?

CRITICAL THINKING

The town of Springfield has 100,000 residents. It has a healthy economy, with an above-average per capita income. It has three fine jewelry stores. The average per capita purchase of fine jewelry in Springfield is $49 annually. The national average is $52, and the per capita average for the neighboring community of Johnson City is $50. On average, a fine jewelry store serves 25,000 inhabitants. Do you think that there are enough customers in Springfield to support another jewelry store? Would you open one? Why or why not? If so, what is the potential for sales per store?

SHORT CASE: NOT ENOUGH INFORMATION

"Why not?" thought Carol. "A fine china department would add a great new look to the store and we could get out of our summer doldrums by selling to newlyweds." There were no china shops in this town of 40,000 people. The only china retailers in the area were a local jeweler, a local florist, and a department store 30 miles away. Carol was sure that a complete china department in her 4,500 square foot gift shop would outsell the competition. She set out to research the market.

First, she talked to Victor Blanco, a sales representative for the Cardinal China Company. Victor was very encouraging and showed Carol impressive sales figures from china shops in small towns. He suggested incorporating a 600 square foot department into her store that would sell Cardinal fine and everyday china, silverplate and sterling eating utensils, and accessories that would appeal to the newlywed market. Installing a plush white carpet, elegant wallpaper, and chandeliers would make it a very exciting department.

Carol then visited a friend who worked in the china department of a department store 200 miles away. She discussed her idea with the friend and the store manager. They both thought her idea was a good one.

Working with Victor she drew up a sales projection based on the sales history of her store. It looked great on paper, and she made plans to move ahead.

The department opened and drew many compliments from customers. "How beautiful." "Just what our town needs." "I'll be back." These were typical statements.

The china department was a failure. Sales were only 25 percent of projections. There were not very many weddings in the community. The department store, 30 miles away, still got a lot of the china business, as did the jeweler and the florist. A year later Carol liquidated the department.

Carol wondered what she had done wrong. Maybe she should have researched the idea with a demographic study similar to the one she did when she opened her store four years earlier.[1]

1. What information that would relate to a china shop would a demographic study have provided?
2. Is it necessary to do a demographic study for business expansions?
3. Why was research of a department store 200 miles away not useful?

PROJECT CHALLENGE

In your business plan notebook, do a demographic study for your hypothetical business. First, determine the size of the total market. Then compare the demographic statistics to those of a nearby community. Using the information you collect, estimate the total market potential and decide what share of the market you wish to gain.

---

[1] Case study entitled "Not Enough Information" reprinted, with permission, from book #3511 *Why Entrepreneurs Fail: Avoid the 20 Pitfalls of Running Your Own Business* by James W. Halloran. Copyright 1991 by Liberty Hall Press/TAB Books, a division of McGraw-Hill, Blue Ridge Summit, PA 17294 (1-800-233-1128 or 1-717-794-2191).

6
Getting to Know Your Competition

Once aspiring entrepreneurs get to know their potential customers, they need to get to know the businesses that will compete for those customers. The reason for this is simple: new businesses need new customers. Getting the store open is only a small part of future success. Real success will occur only if there are customers—many, many customers.

Where are these customers currently shopping? Entrepreneurs must answer that question, as well as many others. After all, they start out with no customers at all. Everyone who wants to buy products similar to theirs is buying from future **competitors.** The only way to get customers is to convince them to stop purchasing from other business. To do that, entrepreneurs must have as much information about their competition as possible.

Illus. 6-1   Customers are the key to success.

Photo by Alan Brown/Photonics

After mastering the information contained in this chapter, you should be able to:

6-1 Describe competitive impact.

6-2 Understand competition and its relationship to private enterprise.

6-3 Describe direct competition.

6-4 Describe indirect competition.

6-5 Explain the concept of geographic distribution of customers.

6-6 Explain the importance of analyzing competitive strengths and weaknesses.

competitor, an individual or business that sells the same products or services as another business and appeals to the same types of customers

THE IMPACT OF COMPETITION

competition, a rivalry between companies that sell similar products or services

competitive impact, competing effectively with other businesses

Competition, when used in a business sense, means a rivalry between companies that sell similar products or services. If you are to survive in the business world, you will have to get to know your competition. You must have **competitive impact,** which means effectively competing with other businesses.

Competition grows out of the fact that, in a country such as ours, consumers have freedom of choice. They can spend their money anywhere they please. Consumers make the decision to spend their money in your store or down the street at another store that is in competition with yours.

Because there is freedom of choice in spending, you as a business person must be as competitive as possible. Your store must be of the highest quality and your merchandise of the type demanded. These positive attributes must then be combined with prices that are less than or at least equal to those of your competitor's. Every day that the doors of your business are open to the public, you must strive to develop better products and better ways to serve your customers. If you do not, your competition will. At the same time, you have to keep an eye on your competition and what they are doing. They cannot be allowed to get a competitive edge on you. Once they do, then *your* customers will become *their* customers.

COMPETITION AND PRIVATE ENTERPRISE

Competition is a very necessary part of private enterprise. If a private enterprise system is to serve the people efficiently, there must be competition among those who produce the products and among those who sell them. That competition is created by the following factors.

Similar Products and Services

Competitors offer similar products or services for sale. In the case of a sporting goods store, all businesses that sell sporting goods of any type are potential competition for the store. The management must consider all sporting goods stores as competition for customers.

Multiple Buyers and Sellers

If there is to be competition within an economic system, there must be many buyers and many sellers. When these conditions exist in a market, no individual or business can exert undue pressure. For example, if there were only one sporting goods store in town, that store's owner could charge whatever price he or she wanted for the products. Local customers would have no choice but to pay the price or travel out of town to shop. Likewise, if there were only one buyer, the buyer could exert undue pressure on the sellers to give price concessions. Multiple buyers and multiple sellers ensure competition by offering choices. Choices, in turn, help keep prices at fair levels.

Freedom to Enter or Exit Business

Competition in private enterprise means that a new business can start at any time. It also means that a company or an individual can stop doing business whenever he or she wants. This freedom is what gives private enterprise its strength. Because new people are entering the marketplace on a regular basis and others are leaving, competition is assured.

The Guarantee of Fair Competition

Competition is a critical component of private enterprise, but private enterprise can be effective only if fair competition is guaranteed. The United States government, along with many state governments, has taken steps to ensure fairness in competition. Through the enactment of certain laws and the creation of the **Federal Trade Commission** (FTC), the U.S. Congress has attempted to create an environment in which entrepreneurs can receive fair treatment from competitors, no matter how small or large their companies are.

Three laws that protect competition are the **Sherman Antitrust Act,** the **Clayton Act,** and the **Robinson-Patman Act.** Collectively, these laws help prevent monopolies. When a business has a **monopoly** on a market, it sets prices, prevents other businesses from entering the market, and controls the available supply of the product or service. Because these practices are anti-competitive, the government does not approve of them. The only monopolies the government allows to exist are those in industries in which the product or service offered necessitates one supplier. This is often the case with local utilities. The following paragraphs describe the specific laws and the regulatory agency that help protect fair competition in the United States.

Sherman Antitrust Act. This act, passed in 1890, makes any business deal illegal that unreasonably restricts trade or commerce among states. It outlaws **price fixing,** an illegal practice that leaves

Federal Trade Commission, a regulatory agency that enforces and monitors fair competition and other business practices

Sherman Antitrust Act, makes any business deal illegal that unreasonably restricts trade or commerce among states, and outlaws price fixing

Clayton Act, a follow-up to the Sherman Antitrust Act that further prohibits monopolies from forming and makes tying agreements illegal

Robinson-Patman Act, adds to the Clayton Act by outlawing price discrimination

monopoly, a business agreement whereby a single company controls a specific supply of products or services

price fixing, the agreement between competitors to establish and maintain prices of their goods and services

customers with few price choices. The act also makes owners or directors of a violating business guilty of a crime.

Clayton Act. This 1914 legislation is a follow-up to the Sherman Antitrust Act that provides needed strength for dealing with companies involved in illegal deals. Specifically, it prohibits businesses from acquiring companies that would create a monopoly environment and reduce competition. It also makes **tying agreements** illegal.

Robinson-Patman Act. This act extended the Clayton Act in 1936 by outlawing **price discrimination.** It also outlaws mergers in which large companies acquire all the stock of competing companies.

Federal Trade Commission. The FTC is a regulatory agency that was established to enforce and monitor these laws. It ensures fair competition among businesses, encourages free trade, carefully reviews business mergers and acquisitions to prevent monopolies from forming, and regulates advertising so that it is not deceptive.

TYPES OF COMPETITION

As stated earlier, every business that sells sporting goods of any kind is a potential competitor for a new retail sporting goods store. Not all the businesses are the same, though. Some compete more directly than others. As entrepreneurs analyze their competition, they must first consider into which classification the competing firms fall—direct competition or indirect competition.

Direct Competition

Direct competition refers to businesses that derive the majority of their profits from the sale of products or services that are the same or similar to those sold by another business. A good way to start the analysis is by looking in the yellow pages of the telephone book for other stores that deal in the same product.

Another method of identifying direct competition is to contact the local chamber of commerce. A quick review of the list from the chamber should identify organizations that will be direct competition. Many communities have planning departments that compile annual data books. In these books, cities are divided into shopping zones, and the number and types of retailers in each zone are listed.

The last thing to do is a physical check of the geographic market. To do this, entrepreneurs should drive through all retail centers

---

tying agreements, the practice of a seller requiring a customer to buy one type of product in order to be permitted to buy another type

price discrimination, charging different prices to different customers for the same goods

direct competition, competition by businesses that derive the majority of their profits from the sale of products or services that are the same or similar to those sold by another business

Illus. 6-2 The yellow pages are an excellent resource for identifying direct competition.

within the competitive area and attempt to identify competitors not already known. The check should include a walk-through of any enclosed malls.

The number of direct competitors identified and their behavior in the marketplace will ultimately have a profound effect on the new business. It is important to evaluate these findings and try to determine the reputation of the competitors. For example, these questions should be addressed: "What are they doing that appeals to customers? What could I do better? What have I seen that I want to avoid?"

Indirect Competition

Indirect competition is competition by businesses that derive only a small percentage of their profits from the sale of products or services that are the same or similar to those sold by another business. If a business sells sweatshirts, for example, its competitors might be Wal-Mart, K-Mart, Target, and other large general merchandise retailers.

indirect competition, competition by businesses that derive only a small percentage of their profits from the sale of products or services that are the same or similar to those sold by another business

If the entrepreneur has lived in the area for quite a while, identifying indirect competition should not be much of a problem. Entrepreneurs should take time, however, to make sure all stores that fall into this category are included.

Indirect competition can often prove to be the most dangerous kind of competition. For a business like the sweatshirt store owner's, indirect competition will almost always come from a large national chain like one of those named previously. It usually has more capital than a small business and is capable of purchasing in much greater quantities. Because the large chain does not have to rely only on the one product line, it can choose to deal in only those items that produce the most profit. It can carry as little or as much of an item as is desired.

Small business owners do not have that option. Not only can they not be as selective, they cannot buy in as large a quantity either. To attract and keep customers, the sweatshirt store owner must try to satisfy all customer needs for athletic apparel and merchandise. In addition to high profit items, the entrepreneur must also carry items that are in demand even though they produce much lower profits.

Just as the number of direct competitors and their behavior in the marketplace will ultimately have a profound effect on the new business, so will that of the indirect competitors. Entrepreneurs should evaluate their findings about indirect competitors and try to determine the reputations and roles of those competitors in the marketplace.

GEOGRAPHIC DISTRIBUTION OF CUSTOMERS

As entrepreneurs begin the process of formally getting to know the competition for the planned business, they need to be concerned with geography—not geography in the sense of the *world* but instead in the sense of *customers*.

Getting to know customers is a critical ingredient in the success formula for a new company. Part of that knowledge concerns where the potential customers live. Entrepreneurs need to ask, "How far will customers travel to do business with me?"

To determine customer geographic distribution, acquire a map of the area in which the business will be located. On the map, mark in some fashion the probable location of the business. The exact location probably has not been chosen yet (see Chapter 7), but the entrepreneur should have an idea of the general business district where it will be.

Next, mark the areas on the map in all directions that represent the farthest distance customers would be willing to travel to do business. After this has been marked, a circle should be drawn on the map that includes all potential customers.

If the business is a small retail store, the circle drawn on the map may be relatively small and cover only a portion of the city. If, on the other hand, the intended business is a production facility with widely based appeal, the circle might include one or more states. It could even cover entire regions of the country.

The circle on the map represents the geographic distribution of potential customers. It also, to some extent, represents the geographic distribution of future competition. Have you ever noticed that fast-food restaurants tend to come in clusters? That's because they have all determined where their potential customers live and work and how far they are likely to drive for a hamburger and a soft drink. This is just one illustration of the fact that once you have located the customers, you have probably located the competition as well.

Illus. 6-3 The circle on the map represents the geographic distribution of potential customers as well as main access roadways.

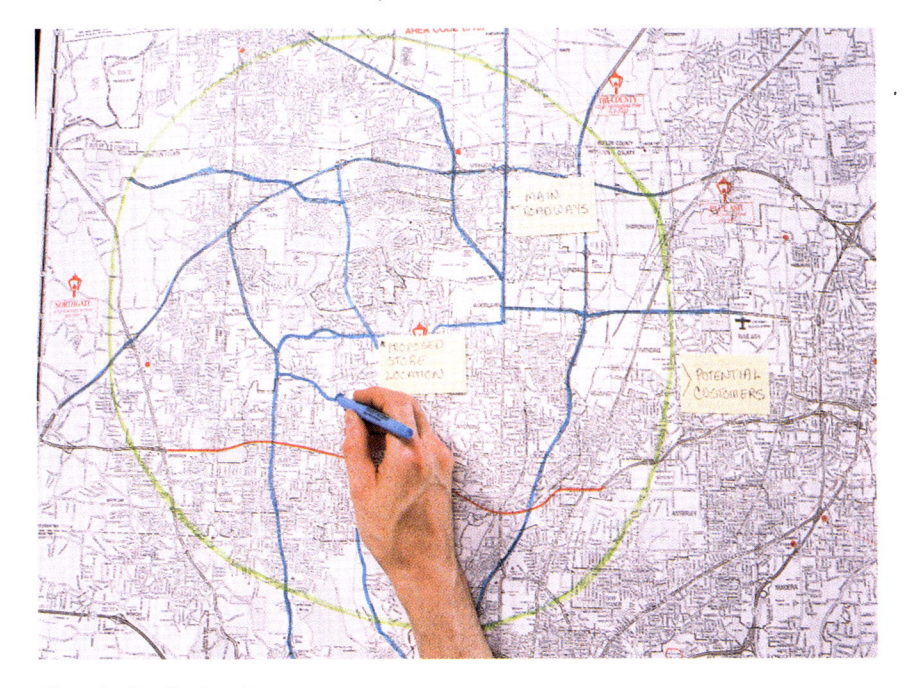

Photo by Jay Bachemin

ANALYZING COMPETITIVE STRENGTHS AND WEAKNESSES

Now that aspiring entrepreneurs have identified their competitors, it is time to do a more detailed analysis. Identification was just the first step. Now the real work begins.

Competitive analysis is important because understanding the competition is critical to a new business's success. From this analysis comes the information necessary to pinpoint strengths and weaknesses. Knowing strengths and weaknesses, both yours and the competition's, is a necessary ingredient for marketing success.

competitive analysis, identifying and examining the characteristics of a competing firm

Analyzing Competitors That Have Failed

Not only should all the identified direct and indirect competitors be analyzed; so should any that can be identified who have recently gone out of business. Most of these would probably have fallen into the category of direct competitors. It is important to analyze these so that you can benefit from their mistakes. To take advantage of this, though, the reasons for the mistakes must be determined. Analysis provides that information.

Table 6-1 is a form designed for analyzing competitors who have failed. To use the form, entrepreneurs should list as many competitors that have failed as possible. To identify these, they may use chamber of commerce records, community data books, personal knowledge, yellow pages from previous years, and any other source of local business data. After identifying failed competitors, the entrepreneurs should try to determine why they failed. Some of the reasons for failure are listed in the columns. They include poor management, under-capitalization, lack of knowledge about the business, and competition's influence. Also, any trends in the failures should be identified in the space given.

Analyzing Direct and Indirect Competition

The next step is to look at both direct and indirect competition from an analytical perspective. Table 6-2 is an expedient way of recording data from that analysis. As competition is examined, five factors must be analyzed: price, location, facility, competition type, and rank.

Price. In this sense, price refers to the price range into which each competitor's prices fall for products or services that are the same or

Table 6-1 Competitors That Have Failed

Names	Poor Management	Under-capitalization	Lack of Knowledge	Competition	Other
1.					
2.					
3.					
4.					
5.					
6.					
7.					

REASONS FOR FAILURE

Trends

1.
2.
3.
4.

very similar to what the new business will offer. Based on the competitive analysis, the entrepreneur should indicate if the competition is in the high (H), middle (M), or low (L) range.

Location. The location of competitive businesses must be examined in comparison to the new business's anticipated location. Is the competition located in a better (B), worse (W), or in about the same (S) quality location?

Facility. Facility refers to the actual buildings occupied by competitors. In comparison to the new business's anticipated facility, is the competitor's facility better (B), worse (W), or about the same (S)?

Type of Competition. Based on the previous information presented, determine if other businesses are direct (D) or indirect (I) competition.

Table 6-2 Direct and Indirect Competition

Names of Competitors	Price (H/M/L)	Location (B/W/S)	Facility (B/W/S)	Direct/Indirect (D/I)	Rank (1–10)
1.					
2.					
3.					
4.					
5.					
6.					
7.					
8.					
9.					
10.					

Table 6-3 New Business Strengths and Weaknesses

Strengths

1. _____

2. _____

Weaknesses

1. _____

How I will overcome this: _____

_____

_____

2. _____

How I will overcome this: _____

_____

_____

Rank. The competitors should be ranked from 1 to 10 in terms of the degree of competitiveness. Number 1 should be the strongest competitor; number 10 the weakest.

Table 6-3 on page 104 is a form that takes the competitive analysis one step further. By completing the form, entrepreneurs can use the information recorded in Table 6-2 to identify their own strengths and weaknesses. To begin, identify two strengths of the intended business. After that has been done, two weaknesses should be listed. As each weakness is identified, the entrepreneur should try to determine how it might be overcome.

By this point, an aspiring entrepreneur should have the knowledge necessary for getting to know the competition. If entrepreneurs do a good job, competitors should not be able to surprise them in the future.

THE FASHION ATTIC

As Laura started the process that would allow her to get to know the competition, she became very interested in the various names that were used. Her interest grew out of the fact that she had not yet named her business. Laura knew that the name for her business was very important. She wanted a name that would identify what she sold and also give the image desired—fashion apparel in a unique environment. The name had to be easy to remember.

After much thought, and after looking at the names of the competition, Laura decided on a name for her new business. She discussed it with Paula and some other friends and they all thought it was great. Laura would name her store "The Fashion Attic." It clearly demonstrated what was sold and at the same time the word "attic" brought to mind the nostalgic image that she was planning for her store's interior.

Having decided on the name, Laura proceeded to analyze her competition. In her community of 75,000 people, she realized that she had to consider both direct and indirect competitors. This included everything from department stores, discount merchandisers and specialty stores such as her own. She started by making a list of those who had failed and why (see Table 6-1a).

Laura found three direct competitors who had failed during the past two years. There were no real trends that she could discover. Laura figured they just didn't know what they were doing

Table 6-1a Competitors That Have Failed

REASONS FOR FAILURE

Names	Poor Management	Under-capitalization	Lack of Knowledge	Competition	Other
1. The Clothes Tree			X	X	
2. Bonnie's Boutique				X	
3. Fashions Galore	X	X			
4.					
5.					
6.					
7.					

Trends

1. No real trends are evident
2.
3.
4.

and that there was no reason to look any further. Do you think she was right in not looking harder for the true reasons these competiors failed?

Laura then proceeded to analyze her current direct and indirect competition. It took some time, but she eventually completed Table 6-2a.

She was able to identify seven competitors—two indirect and five direct. From the seven direct competitors, she was able to determine two that were likely to be serious threats to her store. Can you identify the two? What other information on Table 6-2a is relevant to Laura's future plans?

Table 6-2a   Direct and Indirect Competition

Names of Competitors	Price (H/M/L)	Location (B/W/S)	Facility (B/W/S)	Direct/Indirect (D/I)	Rank (1–10)
1. Around the Town	M	S	B	D	1
2. Norma's	H	W	W	D	6
3. The Fashion Barn	H	W	W	D	7
4. J.C. Penney's	M	W	W	I	2
5. Fashion Bug	M	W	S	D	4
6. Rose's Dept. Store	L	W	W	I	3
7. What's New	H	W	S	D	5
8.					
9.					
10.					

SUMMARY

A knowledge of competition is vital to all entrepreneurs if they are to survive in the business world. Competition and private enterprise are dependent upon each other. Competition in the United States is created by the following factors: similar products and services, multiple buyers and sellers, freedom to enter or exit business, and the guarantee of fair competition. Fair competition is ensured by three acts of Congress: the Sherman Antitrust Act, the Clayton Act, and the Robinson-Patman Act. In addition, the Federal Trade Commission regulates business activities to prevent unfair competition.

There are two types of competition, direct and indirect. All competitors, whether direct or indirect, must be identified and analyzed. The geographic distribution of competition is one of the first factors for an aspiring entrepreneur to consider. Businesses that have failed in the recent past must also be identified. Those establishments that have failed should be analyzed to determine why each failed and to see if there are any trends evident among the failures.

> Current competitors must be analyzed in five areas: price, location, facility, type of competition, and rank. After competitors are analyzed, the information should be used to identify strengths and weaknesses of the new business.

VOCABULARY BUILDER

On a separate sheet of paper, write a brief description of each word or phrase based on your reading of the chapter.

1. Competitor
2. Competition
3. Competitive impact
4. Federal Trade Commission
5. Sherman Antitrust Act
6. Clayton Act
7. Robinson-Patman Act
8. Monopoly
9. Price fixing
10. Tying agreements
11. Price discrimination
12. Direct competition
13. Indirect competition
14. Competitive analysis

REVIEW QUESTIONS

1. What is competitive impact?
2. How does competition relate to private enterprise?
3. What is the difference between direct and indirect competition?
4. What is meant by geographic distribution of customers?
5. Why is it important to analyze competitive strengths and weaknesses?

DISCUSSION QUESTIONS

1. What are the four factors that create competition in our country? Briefly explain each factor.
2. How does a monopoly eliminate competition?
3. What role do customers play in determining the geographic distribution of competition?
4. Why is it important to analyze competitors that have failed?
5. What are the five factors to consider when analyzing current competitors?

CRITICAL THINKING

Jan Cohen lives in a small town in Mississippi called Clarksdale. Jan has wanted to own and manage a model train store ever since she was a young child. After looking around town, she decided to lease a small shop located in a strip shopping center on the northwest side of town. However, before she signs the lease, she knows she should check out the competition.

1. If you were advising Jan, what is the first thing you would tell her to do?
2. Look in the yellow pages of the telephone book and prepare a list on a separate piece of paper of all businesses that sell model trains. If your city is large, concentrate only on your section of town. (For the purposes of this activity, limit your list to about ten businesses.)
3. After you have prepared the list, indicate whether each competitor is direct or indirect competition.
4. Based on your knowledge of the businesses listed as competitors for Jan's model train store, rank them in order. Number 1 should be the strongest competitor and the last number should be the weakest.

SHORT CASE: "A GOOD JOB" FOR THE COMPETITION

Benjamin Dinges opened his new business two weeks ago. His store is called "Sporting Life." It offers a full range of athletic equipment designed for weekend athletes.

Business has been very slow for Ben, and he is getting discouraged with his new business venture. It has not lived up to his expectations at all. In the beginning, he thought that once he got enough money together to open the store, customers would automatically start coming in. He managed to get the money after putting up the equity in his home as security. He did the necessary work to get the rented facility ready. He was sure that he had chosen the right kind of merchandise. He even had a few customers come in.

The problem was that most of the customers left without buying. He had been so frustrated that he even asked several of them why they didn't buy. They told him that they could get the same merchandise at a lower price from the competition. When he pressed them for names, they mentioned several. The problem was that he had only heard of one of the competing stores.

When he had been thinking about opening his new store, he knew there would be competition, but he didn't worry about it. "Just do a good job," he had told himself. "That's all it takes. Let the competition worry about me. I'm going to be the problem, not them."

Questions

1. If you were a friend of Ben's and he asked you for advice, what would you say to him at this point?

2. Do you think there is any chance of salvaging Ben's business? What is the biggest mistake he has made so far in his new business venture?
3. Do you think Ben gave himself good advice when he said, "Just do a good job?" Why?

PROJECT CHALLENGE

As you continue the planning process for your new business, it is now time to take the information presented in this chapter and use it to get to know your competition. To assist you in the process, complete the following steps in your business plan notebook.

1. Choose a name for your new business.
2. Take a map of your area and put a star in the general area of the site of your new business. Now take a marker and draw a circle around your anticipated geographic market area.
3. Using the yellow pages and other available resources, make a list of businesses that are potential competitors.
4. Try to discover if other businesses such as yours have failed in the past year. List those businesses on a separate sheet of paper.
5. Now make your own copies of Tables 6-1, 6-2, and 6-3. Complete the tables as fully as you are able.

7

Deciding on a Location and Facilities

You might have heard that the three most important ingredients in starting a successful business are location, location, and location. Although this is something of an exaggeration, for some businesses it is close to the truth. Choosing the proper location is one of the most important decisions entrepreneurs will ever make.

THE IMPORTANCE OF CONVENIENCE

Our society demands convenience. Driving along a busy commercial strip with all of its fast-food restaurants, or visiting a super-sized shopping center gives us an idea of the extremes that businesses go to in order to be accessible to their customers. The question is no longer whether to eat pizza; rather it is from what pizza restaurant to order and whether to go out to eat it, pick it up, or have the restaurant deliver it. The aspiring entrepreneur who knows that being in the right place at the right time is important is the one who is most likely to succeed.

Entrepreneurs must understand the relationship, or correlation, between time and place. Whether the prospective purchases are consumer goods or services or industrial products, customers' decisions are affected by what they perceive to be convenient. Making a business convenient to patronize intensifies the consumer's wants. In other words, if it is convenient to buy pizza, people buy more. If they have to drive 10 miles to buy pizza instead of 5 miles, they will buy fewer pizzas. Therefore, it is important that businesses create situations that their customers perceive as convenient.

Convenience saves time, and time is finite. By *finite* we mean that time cannot be created or extended. There are only 24 hours in a day. In Americans' increasingly busy lives, saving time has become very important. By offering convenience, the entrepreneur saves time for the consumer, thus persuading the consumer to buy more.

After mastering the information contained in this chapter, you should be able to:

7-1 Explain the importance of choosing a proper location for a business.

7-2 Describe the different types of goods.

7-3 Describe the different types of locations available for selling consumer goods or services.

7-4 Describe the location considerations of those who produce and sell industrial and technological goods.

7-5 Explain the importance of properly evaluating potential facilities and their surrounding environments.

Illus. 7-1 Choosing a convenient location is one of the most important decisions an entrepreneur will make.

The fact is, we Americans have grown accustomed to obtaining the goods we need with little effort. If we are pressed for time and cannot find what we want easily, we often buy substitute goods or services. Many businesses profit from consumers' time limitations. Fast-food restaurants are an example of businesses that have grown because of people's time limitations. By being convenient to their markets, they take advantage of time limitations and sell more food as a consequence. Time and convenience are responsible for growth in many other industries, such as mail order sales and machine vending, and for the successes of small manufacturers, which are often able to deliver goods faster than large companies. It is very important to have the right assortment of goods and the right image, but if the goods are not easy to acquire, the entrepreneur will not be successful.

CLASSIFYING CONSUMER GOODS

To determine the best location for selling consumer goods and services, entrepreneurs must first classify their products as one of three types of goods.

Convenience goods are products that people expect to find in many places. There is very little decision making involved in making these purchases. Soft drinks, tissues, toothpaste, and newspapers are examples of convenience goods. These products are readily available

convenience goods, products that people purchase regularly in a variety of stores, including convenience stores, drug stores, and grocery stores. It is imperative for businesses that sell convenience goods to be accessible to large markets.

Shopping goods are products that are easily found, although they are not as widely distributed as convenience goods. They are normally available in sufficient quantity in all communities to meet expected average consumer needs. Tires, jewelry, popular fashions, and compact discs are examples of shopping goods. Purchase of these products often requires going to a particular type of store and usually requires more planning and decision making than does the purchase of convenience goods. Consumers often comparison shop for these products, looking for the best values. To sell shopping goods successfully, businesses must be convenient to intended markets.

Specialty goods are products that people are willing to go out of their way to buy. The purchases are usually planned in advance. Wedding dresses, cars, and computers are examples of specialty goods. Since these are usually major purchases, the consumer does not mind taking extra time to get the best product. Success in specialty goods sales requires that the business be accessible, that its location be known to potential customers, and that it be located in an area that is compatible with the image of the product or service.

shopping goods, products that people purchase occasionally

specialty goods, products that people purchase infrequently

CHOOSING A LOCATION

The first decision to make is which community will be the best one for the business. As discussed in Chapter 5, completing a demographic study can determine this.

If demographics for his or her own community support the business idea, the entrepreneur would be wise to locate there for several reasons:

1. The business owner will be working in a familiar area.
2. There will already be a small nucleus of customers, through friends and acquaintances.
3. The entrepreneur may know bankers, attorneys, or accountants who would be part of an important support system for the new business.

The grass might look greener in another community, but the hometown is usually the best bet.

Once the community is chosen, location possibilities can be considered.

Shopping Areas

Downtown Shopping Districts. In the past, the downtown area of a town or city was where the commercial activity was centered—almost everyone worked and shopped downtown. After World War II, however, a move toward the suburban areas began. More and more people chose to reside outside of cities, so retail establishments started to move to these areas.

Suburban shopping areas began as small shopping centers and grew to be major shopping facilities. As a result, the downtown stores branched out to the suburbs, which caused downtown areas in many communities to become almost deserted. In recent years, however, many cities have recognized deterioration in their downtown areas and have made efforts to change this. It is often difficult to rebuild these areas because of parking problems and limited shopping hours, but many towns do have attractive downtown shopping districts. These shopping districts offer advantages to business owners.

The chief advantage to locating in a downtown area is a lower cost of doing business. Since the buildings are often older, the rental costs

Illus. 7-2

The chief advantage of locating in a downtown area is the lower cost of doing business.

can be considerably less. Also, the hours of operation are shorter, which reduces operating expenses. However, when considering a downtown location, the entrepreneur must identify any disadvantages, such as parking limitations, and any repairs the facility might need. Although many of today's shoppers prefer evening shopping, if the downtown area is active during the day and the surrounding businesses are well maintained, it is certainly a location worth considering.

Shopping Centers. Shopping centers have come a long way since they began to appear some 50 years ago. There are four classifications of shopping centers, and each is indicative of the market it serves.

Neighborhood shopping centers often have a supermarket and small service and convenience goods stores. The customers are nearby residents; they shop in these centers for convenience. The populations of the nearby residential areas determine the amount of activity. Rental expense is usually reasonable—businesses that sell mainly convenience goods or services can be profitable in these centers.

neighborhood shopping center, a small shopping center, usually with fewer than 20 stores, that serves its immediate neighborhood

Community shopping centers are designed to serve residents of many neighborhoods. Although rent costs are usually higher than those in neighborhood shopping centers, locating in community

community shopping center, a shopping center large enough to provide convenience goods and shopping goods to several neighborhoods

Illus. 7-3 Businesses that sell primarily convenience goods or services can be profitable in neighborhood shopping centers.

Illus. 7-4 Community shopping centers are designed to service residents of many neighborhoods.

anchor store, a store large and strong enough to attract customers by itself

regional shopping center, a shopping center that usually has 3 or 4 anchor stores and more than 40 other stores

mall, an enclosed shopping center with a controlled climate

profit margin (markup), the difference between what the seller and the consumer pay for a product

shopping centers can mean more profit for businesses that sell shopping goods, convenience goods, or both. Normally, these centers have at least one, and sometimes two, major tenants called **anchor stores**, and 20 or more small stores. Anchor stores, which are often department stores, discount stores, large supermarkets, or large drug stores, advertise actively and attract customers from an entire community. The smaller stores can then attempt to attract those customers into their stores.

Regional shopping centers are designed to attract customers from a region, or more than one community. These large shopping areas usually have three or four anchor stores and more than 40 other stores. Many times large shopping areas are **malls,** which are the trend in contemporary shopping. A regional shopping center or mall usually offers convenience, shopping, and specialty goods, but due to the expense of renting space in such a center, the products sold often have a higher **profit margin,** or **markup,** than most convenience goods can support.

The entrepreneur who sells shopping goods or specialty goods and needs a large amount of pedestrian traffic to be successful might want to do business in a regional shopping center, but the high cost of operation might make this risky.

Super regional shopping centers are found in major metropolitan areas and have hundreds of stores, including the most contemporary ones. For example, the West Edmonton Mall in Edmonton, Canada, and the Mall of America in Bloomington, Minnesota, each have approximately 800 stores. These giant shopping complexes often have entertainment facilities, such as skating rinks or miniature golf courses, hotels, or amusement parks attached. They are the wave of the future. Stores in these centers are very expensive to operate and are not usually recommended for new business owners. Most tenants are part of chain operations that can make large investments in their operations.

If the new business is to be located in a shopping center, the entrepreneur must research the advantages and disadvantages of each type of center. For example, the high cost of the large center is offset by its appeal to customers and, theoretically, more people shopping means more chances to sell. However, malls charge rent based on traffic flow. A location in a high-traffic mall will cost more than one in a low-traffic mall. Entrepreneurs need to determine whether the extra traffic will generate enough additional sales to offset the expense of the higher rent. Stores that depend on a large number of fairly low-cost transactions must locate where there is a large amount of pedestrian traffic. Also, larger shopping centers usually have larger advertising budgets.

super regional shopping center, a colossal shopping mall made up of many anchor stores and sometimes hundreds of smaller stores

Illus. 7-5   *Within 4.2 million feet of enclosed space, the Mall of America has hundreds of speciality shops along with a seven-acre amusement park.*

© *SuperStock, Inc.*

The super regional, regional, and some of the community shopping centers have **merchant associations.** The dues collected by these associations are used to advertise and to pay for entertainment events that are designed to attract customers. Special attractions at shopping centers, whether they be Christmas decorations, antique automobiles, or circus clowns, have usually been arranged by the merchant association.

merchant association, an organization of merchants who work together to promote shopping at their shopping area

Stand-Alone Stores. **Stand-alone stores** often depend on drive-by traffic. They must have ample parking, good signing, and effective lighting if they are to be successful. Stand-alone stores are often located away from shopping areas. They can also be located adjacent to large malls, or on streets leading to malls, to take advantage of the traffic flow. The buildings are often owned by the business owner. Even if the owner is leasing, however, rental costs are usually lower than those for shopping center spaces. Restaurants—both eat-in and carryout—and auto dealers are examples of businesses that often are successful in stand-alone locations.

stand-alone store, a store that is not located in a shopping area

Locations for Industrial Businesses

Manufacturers and wholesalers must also recognize the importance of location, but for different reasons. It is important that these businesses efficiently address transportation and communication needs.

Illus. 7-6   Certain types of businesses such as this muffler shop are often successful in a stand-alone location.

CarX Service Systems, Inc.

A sizable part of the operating expense of an industrial company is shipping cost, both for materials received and for products shipped. These businesses must deliver their products in a timely manner; therefore, the manufacturer or wholesaler will want to locate near transportation facilities and, if possible, close to customers. Also, locating close to customers allows the business to make personal sales calls with a minimum of expense.

Industrial Parks. **Industrial parks** usually provide space at a reasonable cost and often provide good access to transportation. The cost is often partially subsidized by the community to attract industrial businesses, creating jobs and thus increasing the community's tax base. The industrial entrepreneur should investigate this option if a large amount of space is needed.

industrial park, a section of land allocated for use by industrial businesses

Incubators. In recent years a need for small businesses, particularly new ones, to locate together and share some common operating expenses has been recognized. **Incubators** allow a small number of businesses to share certain operating expenses, such as rent, utilities, property taxes, office equipment, and support employee salaries. They are often found within industrial parks and are usually funded by state or local agencies using federal funds, rather than being managed by a leasing company. The entrepreneur who needs only a small amount of space, for technological development or small manufacturing, for example, should find out whether there is an incubator with available space within the community.

incubator, a facility that houses a number of small businesses, usually fewer than 10, which share certain operating expenses

Home-Based Businesses

There has been a tremendous growth in **home-based businesses** during the past 10 years, and for some very good reasons.

- Doing business from the home is an excellent way to run a business on a limited budget. Rent charges, utility costs, and maintenance fees are avoided, so there is more money to purchase income-producing inventory and for advertising expenditures.
- Home-based business owners are not subject to the restrictions and obligations imposed by lease agreements.
- The owner can be at the business site around the clock.

home-based business, a business conducted from the owner's residence

A home-based business is excellent for the part-time entrepreneur. Many businesses are operated from the owner's home, on a part-time basis, until a demand is established. Then the entrepreneur can better afford to move to a larger site.

You might recall the story of Mary Lawrence in Chapter 1. Mary successfully turned a part-time jewelry business into a full-time career. She started a home-based business selling hand-made jewelry to retailers. She worked in her basement to fill the orders, then took the finished products to a nearby shipping office. When a steady demand for her merchandise was established, she hired four people and moved to an industrial park to have more working space and better access to shippers.

Anyone can operate a home-based business. Many services, such as babysitting, house and office cleaning, and lawn maintenance, can be coordinated from a home. All that is needed is a telephone to contact customers and a word processor. It is also possible to sell goods, via mail order, from a home. The goods can be offered through advertisements or catalogs or by direct mail. Orders can be sent to the home or a local post office box, then filled and shipped from a local post office or shipping company.

Professional Office Space

Many entrepreneurs need a professional office to effectively sell to their clients. Doctors, lawyers, real estate agents, accountants, business consultants, and architects are examples of entrepreneurs who need office space for their businesses. It is important that the offices present a professional image and be conveniently located. Many types of offices are available, from small suites in stand-alone buildings to penthouse suites at the tops of skyscrapers. The spaces are leased, and expenses vary depending on location, size, and what services the landlord offers to the tenants. Some office complexes offer shared office expenses in an arrangement similar to that of an incubator.

LEASING

Unless they work from home-based businesses, business owners must make lease arrangements or buy a business property. Lease agreements for **commercial leases** are usually long and complex contracts that the **lessee** and possibly an attorney should review carefully. The lease should have complete details of all conditions and costs, including basic rent costs and other costs, such as maintenance fees, utility costs, insurance costs, and, in the case of larger shopping centers, merchant association dues. Since the **lessor** often requires at least three years of tenancy, the entrepreneur must feel confident that

---

commercial lease, a signed legal agreement that specifies the terms (length of time, cost, conditions to be met) for use of a business property by someone other than its owner

lessee, the person who promises to pay a specified sum of money for the use of space

lessor, the person who allows someone to use his or her property under certain terms

all conditions are satisfactory. Too often business owners must fulfill lease obligations for businesses that have failed and no longer exist.

EVALUATING A FACILITY

Choosing the facility for a new business is an important decision for business owners. Once the best location has been found, the owner must determine whether the facility is suitable for the intended business operation. It must be large enough, and it must be structurally sound. Many leases assign responsibility for all maintenance of property to the lessee; if there is a leak in the roof or if the plumbing or air conditioning fails, the tenant will have to pay all repair costs. Therefore, it is imperative that the prospective tenant carefully examine the property for structural soundness before signing the lease.

It is very important that the chosen site fit the image of the intended business. Selling expensive, fine jewelry requires a different image from that of selling tires. People shopping for a $5,000 diamond ring will not shop in a rundown area of town. However, for most people, the price of a tire is more important than where it is purchased. If you are selling to a specific market, the facility and its surroundings must appeal to that market.

Illus. 7-7 (a and b)   The site must fit the image of the intended business.

Different businesses have different environmental requirements. For example, the aspiring restaurateur should consider the following:

1. Restaurants should not be in areas that are noisy, have unpleasant odors, or are frequented by vagrants.
2. The type of neighborhood will influence whether customers come in family groups, couples, or singly.
3. Restaurants located in industrial areas will be dependent on surrounding businesses and their employees' lunch arrangements.
4. Restaurants in residential areas will be most dependent on evening trade.
5. Restaurants should not be located near funeral homes or cemeteries.
6. Schools or churches are not particularly desirable as neighbors to a restaurant; they may cause congestion, and they can affect the restaurant's right to sell alcoholic beverages.
7. There must be good lighting and ample parking to provide convenient access for customers.

The prospective business owner will need to research the location and facility requirements for his or her intended product or service.

THE FASHION ATTIC

After completing her demographic research and studying her competition, Laura began her search for the perfect location for her business. Having classified her fashion apparel as both shopping goods and specialty goods, Laura knew she needed a location with heavy pedestrian traffic. She ruled out Johnson City's deserted downtown area and concentrated on the shopping centers in the community. There were seven centers that had more than ten stores each: three were neighborhood shopping centers, two were community discount plazas, and two were community malls. There were two competitive stores in the neighborhood shopping center and one in each discount plaza. Both community malls had ladies' wear stores, but only one had a store with the high-fashion look of Laura's plan.

Laura visited the managers of the two community malls. They were both interested in adding a store such as hers, so she began a search to decide which would be the best location. After collecting and reviewing her information, she was confused.

Shopping mall A (see Figure 7-1), with 45 stores, had 2 anchor stores—a nationally known department store and a

Figure 7-1 Shopping Mall A

Figure 7-2 Shopping Mall B

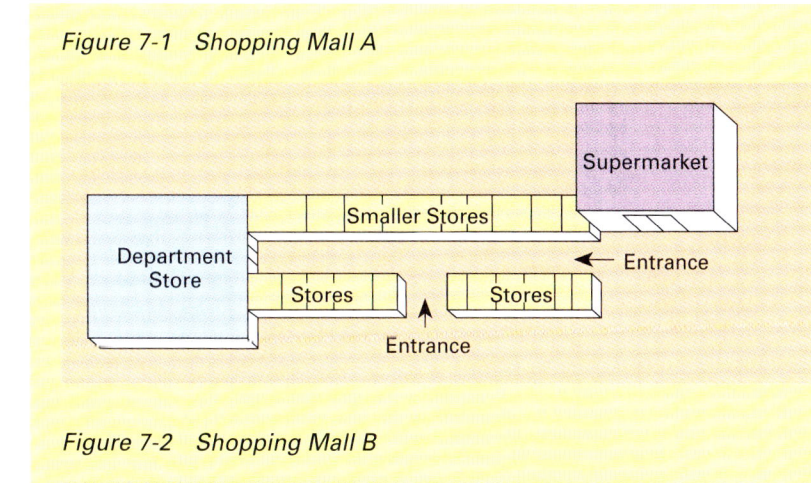

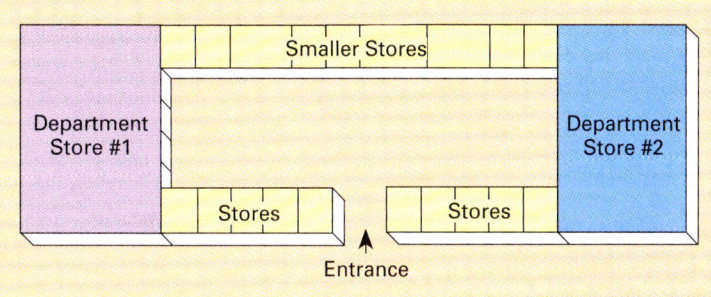

large supermarket. The anchor stores were located at opposite ends of the mall. Mixed in with the smaller stores were a well-known drug store, a large variety store, and a movie theater. The base rent for a 1,500-square-foot space, the size recommended by industry representatives, was $1,500 per month.

Shopping mall B (see Figure 7-2) was located two miles north of shopping mall A on the same main road through town. It was about the same size as shopping mall A and had the same tenant mix: 2 anchor stores, 40 small stores, a drug store, a variety store, and a movie theater. The biggest difference was that the anchor stores were both department stores. The rent for 1,500 square feet of space in this center was $2,000 per month.

The manager of shopping mall A pointed out that the department store in his center was well recognized throughout the country and that the supermarket was the largest in the community. The manager of shopping mall B pointed out that the two competing department stores stimulated a great flow of pedestrian traffic from one end of the mall to the other. He also pointed out that a supermarket anchor is of questionable value to a fashion apparel retailer; most people do not combine grocery shopping with shopping trips for clothes.

Laura decided to do a traffic count at each mall. She stood in front of the proposed location in each mall and counted the number of shoppers who passed during specific periods of time.

When she compared the results, Laura found that shopping mall B's traffic was almost 50 percent higher. She wondered if the extra traffic was worth the extra $500 per month in rent. If the 50 percent increase in traffic generated a 50 percent increase in sales, it could mean an additional $100,000, bringing her total projected annual sales to $300,000. She discussed the situation with Paula, since she was more familiar with the local retail market, and decided that an additional $6,000 of annual rent for a potential $100,000 increase in sales was a reasonable risk. The more expensive center also did not include Laura's most direct competitor, which she believed to be an advantage.

SUMMARY

Successful entrepreneurs know the importance of choosing the right location. Being in the right place at the right time is an important ingredient of success. Our society has become accustomed to accessibility and convenience, and we have come to expect it.

Entrepreneurs must classify the products to be sold in terms of the degree of convenience the consumer demands of the product. They can then determine what type of location should be chosen to successfully sell the products. This choice will depend on the product, the community, and the amount of money available to operate the business.

Entrepreneurs who sell or manufacture industrial goods might locate in an industrial park. Some small industrial and technological businesses locate in incubators.

Some entrepreneurs operate small businesses from their homes. Many successful businesses have been started in homes and then moved after a demand has been established. A home-based business is an excellent starting place for the part-time entrepreneur.

Unless entrepreneurs plan to buy a facility or work at home, they will need to make leasing arrangements. Commercial leases are legal contracts that should be signed only after a complete review of the document and a complete examination of the facility. The examination of the facility must include its surroundings. The location must be conducive to selling the intended product or service.

VOCABULARY BUILDER

On a separate sheet of paper, write a brief definition of each word or phrase based on your reading of the chapter.

1. Convenience goods
2. Shopping goods
3. Specialty goods
4. Neighborhood shopping center
5. Community shopping center
6. Anchor store
7. Regional shopping center
8. Mall
9. Profit margin (markup)
10. Super regional shopping center
11. Merchant association
12. Stand-alone store
13. Industrial park
14. Incubator
15. Home-based business
16. Commercial lease
17. Lessee
18. Lessor

REVIEW QUESTIONS

1. Why is choosing the proper business location important?
2. What are the differences among convenience goods, shopping goods, and specialty goods?
3. Why should entrepreneurs classify the products to be sold before choosing a location?
4. What are the differences among neighborhood shopping centers, community shopping center, regional shopping centers, and super regional shopping centers?
5. What is a merchant association?
6. What is an industrial park?
7. What is the purpose of an incubator?
8. What is the primary reason for starting a business in the home?
9. What is a commercial lease?
10. Why is the environment surrounding a business important to its success?

DISCUSSION QUESTIONS

1. Why have accessibility and convenience become so important to consumers?
2. What would happen if a convenience grocery store were located in a rather deserted downtown area? Why?
3. Where do people shop most often, and why?
4. What can happen to business owners who do not take the time to study and learn leasing considerations?
5. Why would opening an expensive jewelry store in a discount shopping center be risky?

CRITICAL THINKING

Make a list of businesses that you could operate from your home. What are the risks of each? What is the potential for each?

SHORT CASE: THE WRONG SIDE OF THE STREET

Sally Watkins had wanted to open a gift shop on posh St. George's Avenue since moving to the area seven years ago. The tree-lined shopping area comprised four blocks of unusual boutiques. There were gift shops, fashion boutiques, jewelry shops, craft stores, European-style restaurants—a dazzling collection to please the most discriminating shoppers. The area was so successful that openings for new stores were rare. When a vacancy did occur, the leasing agent would contact the next person on the long tenant waiting list.

When Sally learned that the old movie theater across the street was to be converted into a three-story shopping complex of small stores, she contacted the developer. The developer's plan provided for 18 store spaces of approximately 800 square feet each. The developer was hoping for a balanced tenant mix of specialty retail stores and food services. The idea was to have a restaurant, a gift shop, an apparel store, and three other stores on each level. This would ensure a good traffic flow throughout the complex. Sally leased the ground floor gift shop location, just inside the entrance—a sure winner. She had carefully scrutinized the gift shops across the street; they all seemed to be very successful.

During the nine months of remodeling, Sally planned an exciting presentation. She went to the leading merchandise marts to buy her inventory and consulted with top professionals on store layout. The finished store was truly a fine one. It had the latest in fixture design, elegant color-coordinated decor, and a sophisticated cash register.

The Theatre Shopping Galleria opened with great fanfare. Of the 18 spaces, 15 opened on time, and the initial reaction was quite enthusiastic. Sally was very pleased with the first 10 days' receipts, and the compliments seemed endless. After 30 days, however, she became concerned—the initial curious shopping crowd thinned, and it was not replaced by consistent, everyday traffic. Sales were inconsistent; some days were so hectic she could hardly keep up, and others were so slow it seemed that a barricade had been placed in front of the entrance. She was puzzled when she learned that business was still at a brisk, consistent level for the gift merchants across the street.

A year later Sally contemplated closing. Six of the original merchants had already moved out. Four had been replaced, but the new tenants did not have the quality or stature of the original stores. Meanwhile, businesses on the other side of St. George's Avenue continued to prosper.

1. Examine Figure 7-3. Can you see some of the reasons why the Theatre Shopping Galleria had difficulty attracting shoppers?
2. Based on your knowledge of the importance of convenience, what could be done to help the stores in the Galleria?
3. Do you think Sally should close her store?

Figure 7-3 St. George's Avenue

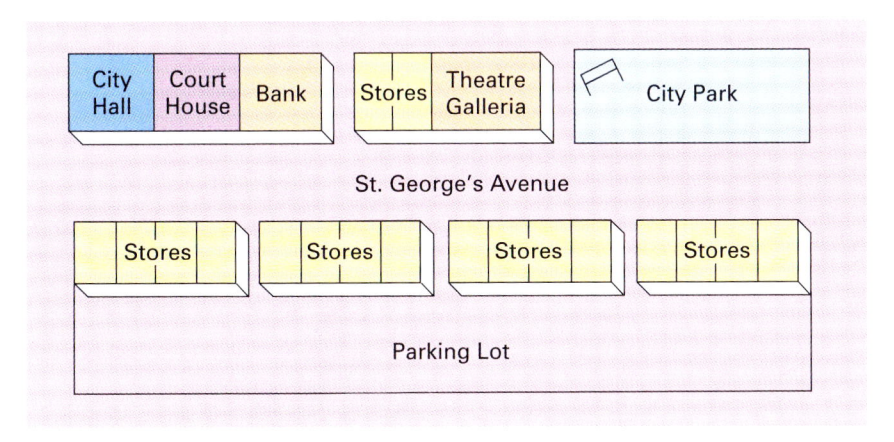

PROJECT CHALLENGE

Choose a potential location for your business, applying what you have learned in this chapter.

If your business is the sale of a consumer product or service you should consider the following:

1. Classify your product or service as a convenience, shopping, or specialty good.

2. Visit shopping areas in your community where you would expect to find similar products. Make notes about how successful these areas seem to be, based on the number of shoppers and how well the businesses appear to be doing.
3. Call leasing agents and inquire about costs and other leasing considerations.

If you are starting an industrial, wholesale, technological, or professional business, ask leasing agents for information about industrial parks, incubators, and professional office space, including terms and considerations.

If you want to start a home-based business, decide how you would use your home as a place of business.

Now make your location decision. Remember to consider the surrounding environment and the facility itself in making your decision. Explain why you chose the location.

8
Developing the Marketing Plan

THE MARKETING CONCEPT

Small business owners who want to become successful need to develop effective marketing plans. To develop effective marketing plans, entrepreneurs must utilize the **marketing concept.** The first step in utilizing the marketing concept is identifying the customer.

MARKET SEGMENTATION AND TARGET MARKETING

Identifying the customer begins with **market segmentation.** Since a small business cannot possibly serve an entire market, the entrepreneurs must determine which portion of the market is most likely to buy the product or service offered. An example of market segmentation would be to separate country music fans from those who like to listen to rock, then classifying listeners as different market segments. After completing the market segmentation process, entrepreneurs identify their customers through **target marketing.** For example, a radio station concentrating its efforts on rock listeners from the ages of fourteen to twenty-two would be target marketing. It is imperative that the small business target its marketing to a small, manageable segment of the market that can be effectively reached and influenced. Entrepreneurs need to make sure, however, that the targeted market is stable, permanent, and large enough to support the business. Focusing on a manageable segment will enable the business owner to design a marketing program that aims directly at the best market for the product or service. Target marketing begins with market research, as explained in Chapter 5.

Remember Tim Holton and his baseball plaques from Chapter 1? Tim did his market research before deciding to sell his baseball plaques. He wanted to find out if there was a large enough market for

---

After mastering the information contained in this chapter, you should be able to:

8-1 Explain the marketing concept.

8-2 Understand market segmentation and target marketing.

8-3 Explain marketing research and its importance.

8-4 Define the components of the marketing mix.

8-5 Explain advertising, sales promotion, personal selling, and visual merchandising.

8-6 Define the process involved in the development of marketing strategies.

---

marketing concept, the belief that consumer wants and needs are the driving force behind any product development or marketing effort

market segmentation, process of dividing the market into groups of similar consumers

target marketing, marketing to a selected group of consumers

his product before spending money to produce it. By researching publications, he found that there were more than 20 million collectors of baseball cards. He then continued his research to find out to what publications baseball card collectors subscribe. When he felt confident that he had found publications with good circulation to his market, he ran test advertisements in the publications to determine consumer interest. He analyzed the results by comparing the number of orders received with the circulation of each publication. With this information, he was able to determine where to place his advertisements to get enough orders to make a profit. He could then decide how many plaques to produce and how much to spend on advertisements. Tim followed the steps for market segmentation and target marketing.

As discussed in Chapter 5, to effectively sell a product or service, the entrepreneur must know as many market characteristics as possible, such as where the people who comprise the prime market live and how much money they have to spend. Identifying the ideal customer keeps the entrepreneur from spending money unwisely by trying to attract customers who are not interested in the product or service offered.

TARGET MARKETING QUESTIONS

Target marketing is achieved by answering the following questions:

1. Where do my customers live and work?
2. What level of income is needed to purchase my product or service?
3. What is the lifestyle of the people who are most likely to need my product or service?
4. Which of my potential customers will receive the greatest benefit from my product or service?
5. Which group of consumers will buy the most of my product or service?

customer profile, a recorded and complete description of the ideal customer for a business

The answers to these questions can help entrepreneurs achieve their goals, which are to create **customer profiles.** An example is shown in Figure 8-1.

Place a customer profile in the center of a target as the bull's-eye. The outer rings of the target will have descriptions of customers who have some of the characteristics of the ideal customer and *might* buy your product. However, the bull's-eye is where the entrepreneur's marketing arrow should be aimed. Figure 8-2 shows the target market for a retail store that sells expensive women's clothing.

Figure 8-1 Customer Profile

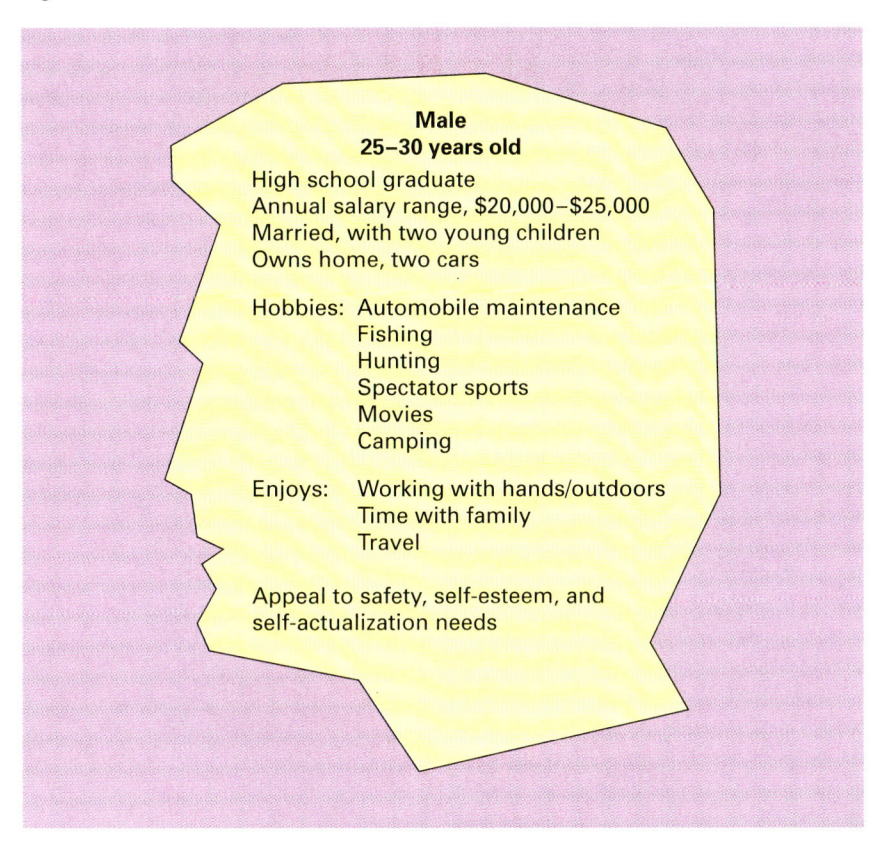

**Male
25–30 years old**
High school graduate
Annual salary range, $20,000–$25,000
Married, with two young children
Owns home, two cars

Hobbies: Automobile maintenance
Fishing
Hunting
Spectator sports
Movies
Camping

Enjoys: Working with hands/outdoors
Time with family
Travel

Appeal to safety, self-esteem, and self-actualization needs

Source: Reprinted, with permission, from book #3511 *Why Entrepreneurs Fail: Avoid the 20 Pitfalls of Running Your Own Business* by James W. Halloran. Copyright 1991 by Liberty Hall Press/TAB Books, a division of McGraw-Hill, Blue Ridge Summit, PA 17294 (1-800-233-1128 or 1-717-794-2191).

MARKETING RESEARCH

How do entrepreneurs determine what their potential customers want? A useful tool in this process is **marketing research.** As defined by the American Marketing Association, "marketing research refers to the systematic gathering, recording, and analyzing of data about problems relating to the marketing of goods or services."[1]

marketing research, the systematic gathering, recording, and analyzing of data relating to the marketing of goods or services

---

[1] From American Marketing Association, "Report of the Definitions Committee of the American Marketing Association," Chicago, 1961.

Unit 2   Marketing the Small Business

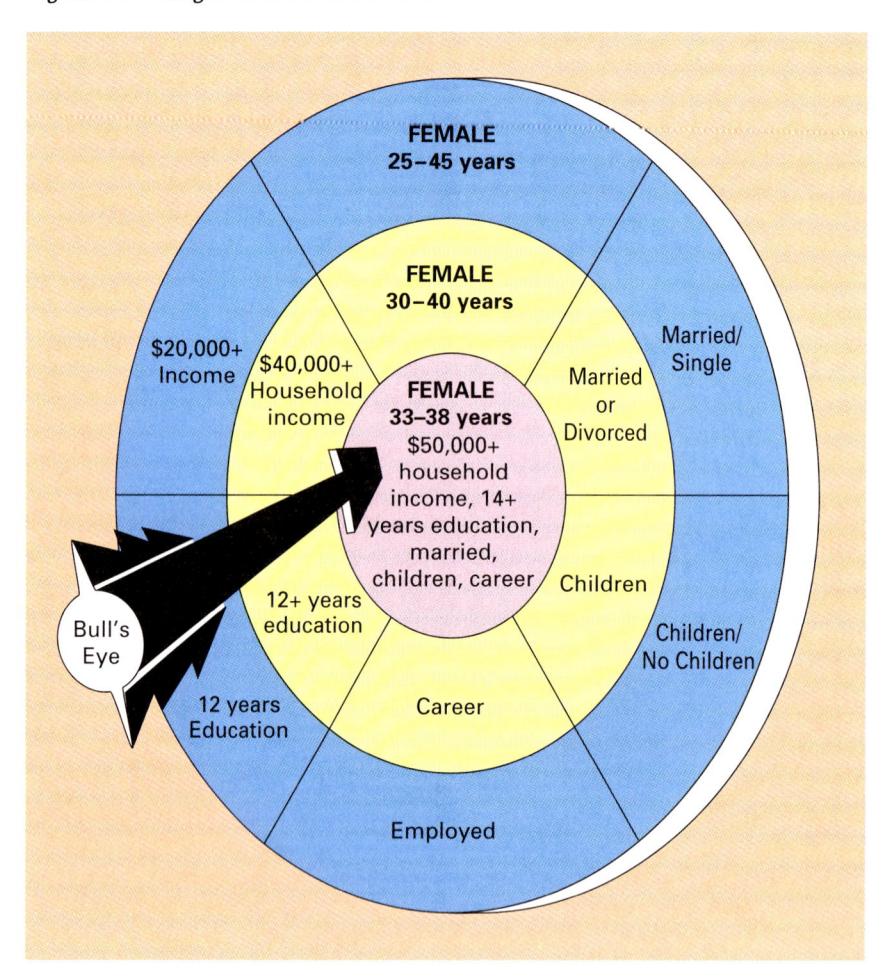

Figure 8-2   Target Market Illustration

Source: Reprinted, with permission, from book #3511 *Why Entrepreneurs Fail: Avoid the 20 Pitfalls of Running Your Own Business* by James W. Halloran. Copyright 1991 by Liberty Hall Press/TAB Books, a division of McGraw-Hill, Blue Ridge Summit, PA 17294 (1-800-233-1128 or 1-717-794-2191).

There are many times when the data obtained through marketing research can prove very useful. One of those times is during the start-up phase of the business. Another is when the business has unexplained difficulties, such as low sales, reduced store traffic, or frequent merchandise returns. Expansion of the business also requires research. Any time a business owner needs to make a decision, marketing research should be considered.

Marketing Research at Work

Entrepreneurs can use the six research steps discussed in Chapter 5 (see **Market Research**) to make effective management decisions concerning marketing. Following these steps can solve many kinds of problems for entrepreneurs, once they learn the process as demonstrated below.

Define the Question. Mei-ling Chan wants to open a bookstore, but she needs to decide what types of books and related merchandise to carry. She defines the problem by asking herself, "Exactly what types of merchandise and specific product lines should I offer for sale?"

Determine Needed Data. If Mei-ling makes a decision without adequate information, she is just guessing. Guessing about the solution to a problem is not a good way to run a business.

For Mei-ling, the problem is what to sell. She needs to know what kind of books and related merchandise customers want to purchase. Therefore, she has to collect data concerning the buying habits of her targeted customers.

Illus. 8-1 Entrepreneurs, like Mei-ling Chan, can use local libraries to begin their market research.

Collect Data. Now that Mei-ling has identified the data she needs to collect, she has to figure out how to collect it. Since she is basically a lone operator on a tight budget, that may be a difficult task.

Mei-ling worked in the consumer book publishing business several years ago, so she has access to some secondary data, including several lists of bestselling books. These lists were compiled and published by national newspapers, consumer book clubs, and the local newspaper. She also has access to new book reviews through the periodical index in her local library, which allows her to locate magazine reviews. These data will tell her which books will be in high demand. She also has information concerning how much money was spent the previous year on hardcover and paperback books. Finally, she has a breakdown according to the type of book purchased; for example, the number of mysteries, romances, science fiction novels, and biographies that were sold in hardcover and paperback. If she adds this to her demographic research (see **Collect Data** in Chapter 5), her volume of data should be significant.

Secondary data can provide much useful information. The smart entrepreneur will seek out all available sources of secondary data before proceeding to more direct collection of data. If Mei-ling does not have enough secondary information to make her decision, she must collect primary data. In Mei-ling's case, the primary data will be consumer data. As an entrepreneur operating on a small budget, Mei-ling's task may be accomplished in one of two ways. She may either observe consumers or survey consumers using a questionnaire. Whichever approach is used, Mei-ling should observe or question as many consumers as possible.

Analyze Data. After Mei-ling has analyzed her data, she will know what her customers are most likely to buy. If an entrepreneur has a problem with frequent merchandise returns, the analysis may indicate that customers find that products made by a certain manufacturer don't operate as they should or that the workmanship is of poor quality.

Implement Data. Mei-ling Chan can now use her analysis to make good buying decisions. She decides to carry a full range of fiction and nonfiction in her bookstore, with an emphasis on self-help books. In addition, a large selection of periodicals will be prominently displayed to entice customers to come in to browse. Finally, a selection of specialty stationery items will round out her new store's offerings.

Evaluate Action. After Mei-ling has made her buying decisions, she will closely monitor sales to determine if changes in product selection will be needed. If she does need to alter her stock, Mei-ling can use these same six research steps to help her decide what changes to make and when to make them.

MARKETING MIX

After the marketing research is completed, entrepreneurs can make informed decisions about the **marketing mix.** Often referred to as the four *P*'s of marketing, the marketing mix variables form the heart of the marketing plan (see Figure 8-3).

marketing mix, four variables—product, place, price, and promotion—that must be manipulated to ensure success in marketing

Figure 8-3 The Marketing Mix

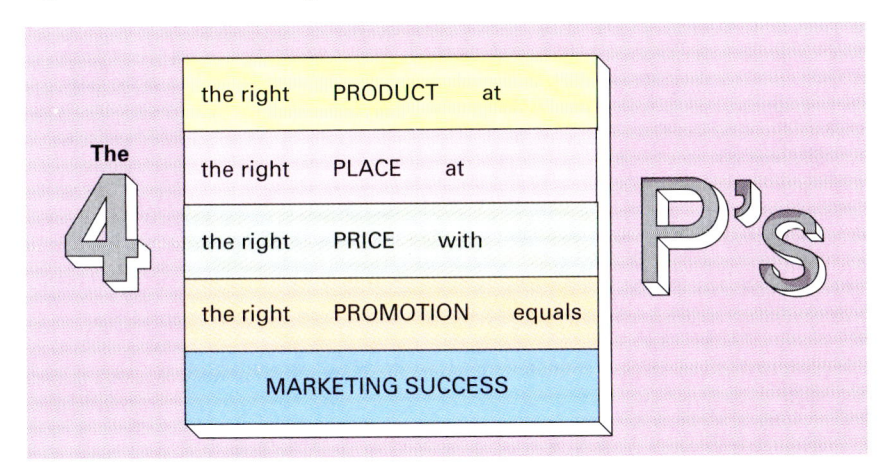

The 4 P's

the right   PRODUCT   at
the right   PLACE   at
the right   PRICE   with
the right   PROMOTION   equals
MARKETING SUCCESS

Product

Most entrepreneurs think that the product or service part of the marketing mix is the easiest with which to deal. After all, they chose that product or service when they first decided on their business venture.

It is not always that easy. Mei-ling, for example, knew she wanted to open a book store. But what kind of books would sell best? She still had to make a product decision. What would happen if she made the wrong product choice? Choosing the right product may be difficult. Entrepreneurs often have a little doubt about whether or not the product they offer will sell.

Place

The place, or distribution, decision means the entrepreneur has to make sure that the right product is in the right place at the right time. The product must be on the shelves ready to be sold when the consumer walks into the store. If it isn't, then all the marketing planning in the world will not make the business a success.

Price

The price decision is critical to marketing success. The price charged for the product must be low enough that consumers will want to buy. At the same time, it must be high enough for the entrepreneur to make a reasonable profit.

Another consideration is whether or not the price is competitive with those of other businesses offering the same product or service. If it is not, there must be a reason for the difference. The reason must be readily apparent to the customers. Pricing is such a critical *P* in the marketing mix that Chapter 9 is devoted to pricing strategies.

Promotion

Promotion, like the other *P*'s, is very important to marketing success. It is through promotion that the entrepreneur informs the potential customer about the product or service. Promotion includes advertising, sales promotion, personal selling, and visual merchandising.

advertising, paid nonpersonal public notice

Advertising. Although **advertising** can be an expensive aspect of starting a business, it is a factor that cannot be ignored by entrepreneurs offering products or services directly to consumers.

Advertising is important to entrepreneurs starting new businesses and to owners of established businesses. There are several reasons for this importance. Advertising accomplishes the following:

- Lets customers know that the new business exists
- Informs customers about the products or services that the business offers
- Provides communication with customers
- Keeps the business's name in front of the buying public

As an entrepreneur, you must select the form of advertising that best suits your business. Newspaper advertisements are probably the most common form of advertisement for entrepreneurs. The other common types of advertising are radio and television (TV). Radio and TV can reach many, many people; but TV advertising, in particular, is quite expensive. Other types of advertising that might be considered are telephone directory ads, direct mail, billboards, and specialty

Illus. 8-2 Direct mail is just one of the many effective methods of advertising.

advertising. Examples of specialty advertising are calendars or key rings with the business's name imprinted on them.

Sales Promotion. To ensure effective **sales promotion,** entrepreneurs must understand the communication channel (see Figure 8-4 on the next page). The communication channel consists of the five steps in sending a message—message sender, encoding, message vehicle, decoding, and message receiver. The message sender decides what message is to be relayed, creates the message (encoding), and determines the best method for relaying the message (written, verbal, or by means of a second person). Once sent, the message is interpreted (decoded) and absorbed by the message receiver. The sender waits for feedback, or a response, from the receiver. The feedback might be a returned message or an action taken as a result of the message.

In sales promotion, the entrepreneur is a message sender hoping for a positive response from the message receiver, such as confirmation of a sale. To maintain an effective communication channel, the entrepreneur must recognize that distortions and interruptions will disrupt

sales promotion, things other than advertising and personal selling that will have a positive impact on the purchasing decision

Figure 8-4 The Communication Channel

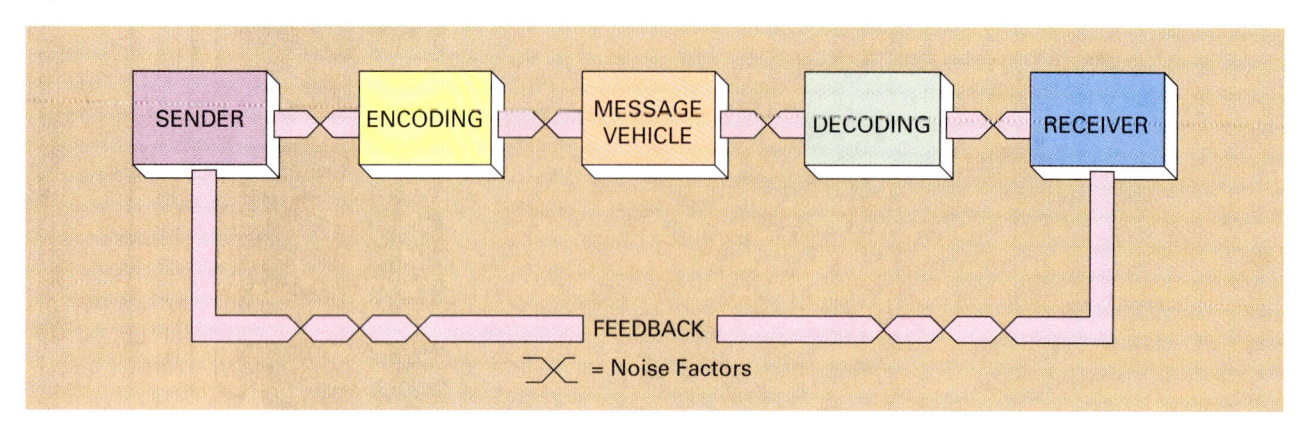

Source: Reprinted, with permission, from book #30049 *The Entrepreneur's Guide to Starting a Successful Business* by James W. Halloran. Copyright 1987 by Liberty Hall Press/TAB Books, a division of McGraw-Hill, Blue Ridge Summit, PA 17294 (1-800-233-1128 or 1-717-794-2191).

the messages. The distortions, called "noise" factors, will impose severe limitations on how intended messages are received and interpreted. A simple example is the game of sending a message around a group—each person whispers the message to the next person, passing the message to each person in the group. The message received by the last person often has little resemblance to the original message. Try this in your class or with a group of friends and see what happens.

In sales promotion, the best way to get a message across is through repetition. The more times a message is sent, the better the chances that it will be received in its intended form. This is why advertisements are repeated many times. The advertiser believes that with continual exposure, the intended message will eventually be received, resulting in more sales.

One of the most common tools for sales promotion currently used by businesses is coupons. Businesses provide coupons to their targeted customers through newspapers, magazines, and direct mail materials. Other examples are free samples and free gifts. The smart entrepreneur chooses sales promotion tools carefully. Because they can be very expensive, sales promotions should be well planned and implemented for specific reasons.

Personal Selling. The importance of **personal selling** to the success of a business cannot be overstated. Customers are more likely to purchase a product or service if they like the person selling it. Entrepreneurs may hire salespeople or have family members help out, but they often do the majority of the personal selling themselves. This is because of the small number of employees in most new businesses and because the entrepreneur often knows the product or service being sold better than anyone else in the company. Because of their confidence, determination, and need to achieve, entrepreneurs are often natural salespeople. Nevertheless, since personal selling is critical to the success of the business, the entrepreneur should take the time to satisfy the needs and wants of customers by making use of personal selling skills. Personal selling skills—involving a sales approach, presentation, and a close—can be developed by study and observation. Time spent in this fashion will almost certainly pay off in increased sales and customer satisfaction.

personal selling, face-to-face communication between the buyer and the seller

Visual Merchandising. Window displays are a very common form of **visual merchandising.** Visual merchandising also includes any

visual merchandising, creative display of merchandise for attracting customers' attention and creating a desire to purchase

Illus. 8-3 Visual merchandising includes any interior display of merchandise to attract customers' attention.

interior use of merchandise to attract customers' attention. Examples are the use of shadow boxes, display cases, and mannequins.

MARKETING STRATEGIES

marketing strategy, planned activity designed to increase sales of a business's products or services

To develop **marketing strategies,** entrepreneurs must analyze previously gathered data about customers, community, facilities, and competition. Once the analysis is complete, decisions about the marketing mix can be made.

Consider the 4 *P*'s

Entrepreneurs who are planning to sell products must make final decisions about the source for the products and how they will get to the place of business. From whom will the products be purchased? When? How will they be transported? Can sources ensure timely delivery? What type of inventory system will be used? Remember, if the product is not there when the customer is ready to buy, the sale may be lost forever. Final pricing decisions also need to be made. What will the price range(s) be for the products or services?

When entrepreneurs get to the promotion phase of the marketing mix, they are at the point where most marketing strategies are decided. The majority of the strategies will be promotional in nature.

Implement Marketing Strategies

Now is when entrepreneurs can put their months of research to work. They can use their accurate information to develop effective marketing strategies. Six steps must be carried out to arrive at a complete marketing strategy.

Establish an Advertising Budget. A certain amount of advertising has to be done to launch a new business toward success. Entrepreneurs need to decide what kind of advertising will best serve their type of business. To get assistance, the entrepreneur should contact the newspaper, radio station, or whichever medium is to be used. Professionals will be available to discuss schedules, costs, and other necessary information. A little extra time should be devoted to comparing the costs for different types of advertising as well as the costs between competitive advertising media, such as two radio stations or two newspapers. The information gathered from this investigation should be used in developing an advertising budget. Although the entrepreneur may feel the expense is excessive, it is necessary.

If the entrepreneur feels that no money is available for advertising, there may not be enough money to start the business. Perhaps a delay in the business start-up should be considered.

Whatever the type of business, some form of advertising is usually necessary to say, "Hey, we're open for business!" The advertising budget may be devoted to direct mail or other means of informing potential customers about the opening. Direct mail might be in the form of a sales letter or a catalog, or it might be a circular informing potential customers of the opening of the business and of special sale items.

Plan and Schedule Advertising. Once the advertising budget has been determined, a plan should be developed. Working with the media specialists discussed above, the entrepreneur should plan and schedule actual advertising.

Make Decisions about Sales Promotion. Entrepreneurs should make decisions about sales promotion well in advance of the planned opening of the business. For example, entrepreneurs who plan to use coupons as promotional tools must design the coupons (or have them designed), contact printers to obtain quotes for the work, select a printer, order the coupons, and distribute them in time for the opening. This process could take weeks or months.

Decide How Personal Selling Will Be Handled. Many decisions have to be made concerning personal selling, such as whether to hire salespeople, how many to hire, when to hire them, how to compensate them, and how to train them. These decisions and others will have to be made and acted upon long before the business is open and ready for customers.

Make Decisions about Visual Merchandising. If the new business is retail, visual merchandising is an important concern. The entrepreneur cannot wait until the merchandise arrives. Decisions have to be made much earlier so that visual merchandising supplies and props can be ordered and/or constructed.

Develop a Strategies Calendar. After strategies have been developed, they should be scheduled. Using a scheduling device (see Figure 8-5) allows the entrepreneur to plan strategy implementation. It also provides a method for keeping track of the implementation.

Figure 8-5   Strategies Calendar

Strategy	Begin Planning	Complete Planning	Implement Plan	Strategy Complete
1.				
2.				
3.				
4.				
5.				
6.				
7.				
8.				
9.				
10.				

If a calendar is used, start by listing the strategies, then set a date to begin planning, write down the date by which planning must be completed, and set the date to implement (start) the strategy. When the strategy is completed, put a check mark in the last column.

THE FASHION ATTIC

Let's see how Laura is doing. She has decided what types of fashions to carry and has information concerning her competition. Laura now needs to find out who her best customers will be. She segmented the market as follows:

1. Women in the age group of 25 to 40 years, the greatest spenders per capita for the type of fashions that Laura will be selling.
2. Career oriented women, who are socially and professionally active have the greatest need for an up-to-date wardrobe.
3. Ladies who prefer to shop in a specialty store environment because of individual service and attention.
4. Women who have a higher than average income and education level.
5. Women who read contemporary fashion magazines.
6. Women with a high level of confidence and self esteem.

Having made these determinations, Laura drew up a customer profile and a target of her market (see Figures 8-6 and 8-7).

Figure 8-6 Customer Profile—Ladies Fashion Buyer

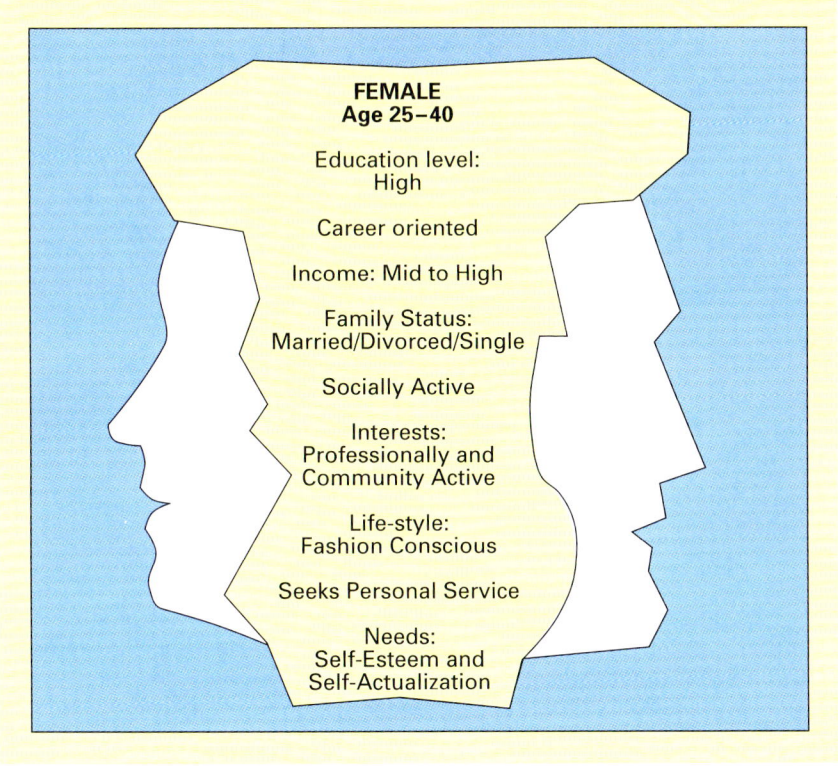

**FEMALE
Age 25–40**

Education level:
High

Career oriented

Income: Mid to High

Family Status:
Married/Divorced/Single

Socially Active

Interests:
Professionally and
Community Active

Life-style:
Fashion Conscious

Seeks Personal Service

Needs:
Self-Esteem and
Self-Actualization

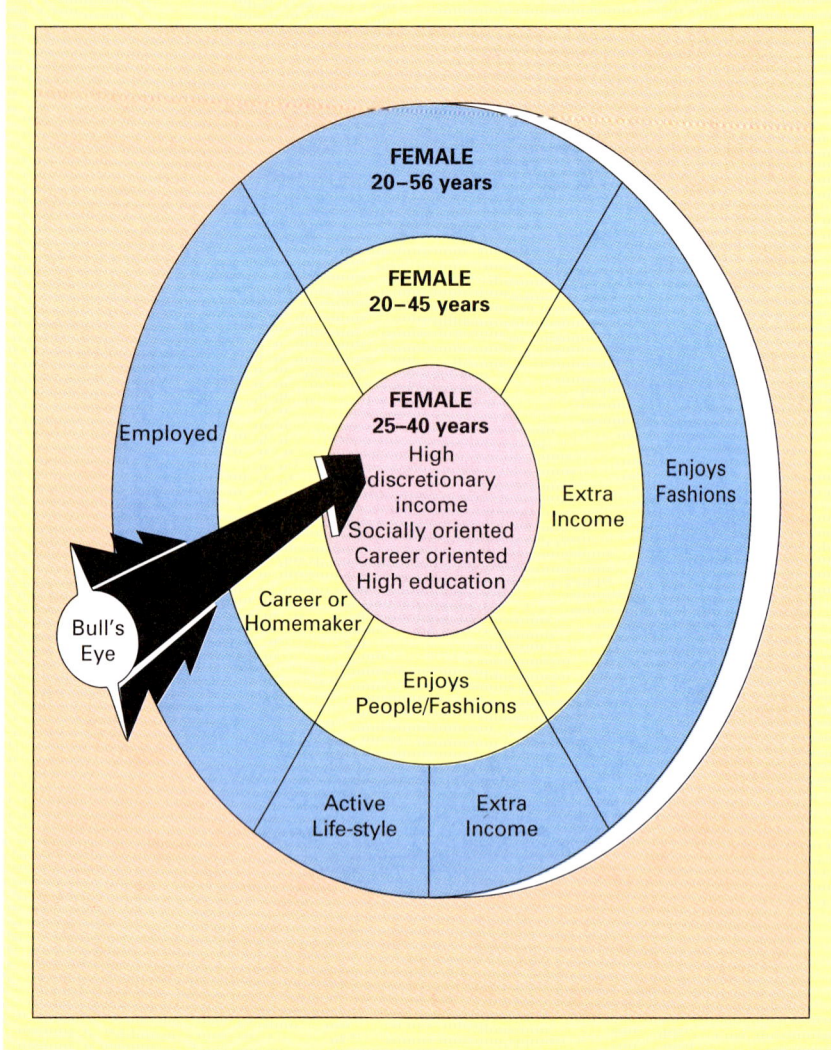

Figure 8-7   Target for Ladies Fashion Customer

FEMALE 20–56 years
FEMALE 20–45 years
FEMALE 25–40 years
High discretionary income
Socially oriented
Career oriented
High education

Employed
Extra Income
Enjoys Fashions
Career or Homemaker
Enjoys People/Fashions
Active Life-style
Extra Income

Bull's Eye

   Based on what she learned through her research, Laura is making progress on determining her marketing mix. She feels the most important part of the mix is the product selection. She also feels very satisfied with her choice of location—the mall.
   Now it is time for Laura to start to develop her marketing plan. She must first address her pricing strategy and then her promotion plan. When this is done, she will have completed her research of the 4 *P*'s of the marketing mix.

SUMMARY

As entrepreneurs begin the marketing plan process, they must understand the marketing concept. They must then use the data collected in their market research to segment the market, breaking it down into manageable groups of potential consumers with similar characteristics. Additional information allows entrepreneurs to target the market to a very specialized group of customers with similar characteristics and needs. The final step is creating a customer profile that describes the ideal customer for the planned business.

To effectively plan, decisions need to be made regarding the marketing mix, or the 4 *P*'s: product, place, price, and promotion. The promotion part of the mix includes advertising, sales promotion, personal selling, and visual merchandising.

Once the marketing plan is developed, the entrepreneur will have a list of marketing strategies to implement:

- Establish an advertising budget;
- Plan and schedule advertising;
- Make decisions about sales promotion;
- Decide how personal selling will be handled;
- Make decisions about visual merchandising;
- Develop a strategies calendar.

The ultimate goal of the business is to offer the product or service to potential customers at a convenient location at an affordable price, so the business will make a profit. If this happens, both the consumer and the business owner will be satisfied.

As each strategy is completed, the dream of being a successful business owner will be one step closer to becoming a reality.

VOCABULARY BUILDER

On a separate sheet of paper, write a brief description of each word or phrase based on your reading of the chapter.

1. Marketing concept
2. Market segmentation
3. Target marketing
4. Customer profile
5. Marketing research
6. Marketing mix
7. Advertising
8. Sales promotion
9. Personal selling
10. Visual merchandising
11. Marketing strategy

REVIEW QUESTIONS

1. Why is it important that entrepreneurs study and learn the segment of the market to be served?
2. Why must entrepreneurs concentrate on a target market?
3. What is the value of drawing a customer profile?
4. What are the six steps of marketing research?
5. List the four variables of the marketing mix.
6. What are the five steps of the communication channel? Briefly describe each step.
7. What are marketing strategies?
8. What are the steps involved in the development of marketing strategies?

DISCUSSION QUESTIONS

1. What is the marketing concept?
2. What would be included if you were writing a customer profile about one of your classmates?
3. What is marketing research and why is it important?
4. From what sources might you obtain secondary and primary data for your own use?
5. What is advertising and why is it important?
6. What are some examples of "noise" factors that distort messages?
7. How can various forms of sales promotion help a business?
8. What is personal selling?
9. Why is a strategies calendar necessary?

CRITICAL THINKING

Gene Chin is planning to open a men's clothing store in the local mall. The majority of his products will be for professional men 30 years of age and older. At this point in his marketing planning, he is working on advertising.

1. If Gene lived in your town, what would his advertising options be?
2. To give Gene some ideas, collect ads from three similar businesses. Try to get examples from at least two media. Explain how each of the ads succeeds or fails in letting customers know the business exists, informing customers about the business's products or services, communicating with customers, and keeping the business's name in front of the buying public.
3. Based on Gene's target market and your knowledge of local radio stations, recommend the local station that you think he should use. Give reasons for your recommendation.

SHORT CASE: SELECTING A PERSONAL SHOPPER

Kathy O'Neill plans to open a business in three months. Her business will offer what she considers a needed service in her community. Kathy plans to offer customized shopping for senior citizens who wish to avoid the hassle of going to the grocery store or are simply unable to go themselves.

By researching her community, Kathy has collected the following data:

- Twenty percent of her city's population are senior citizens. Current city population is 115,000.
- The average annual income for each senior citizen household is $25,000.
- Most senior citizens (80 percent) live in the same section of town, the south side, because of a concentration of retirement housing.

Although Kathy knows that she wants to sell her services as a personal shopper, she hasn't decided exactly what specific services senior citizens would be willing to buy.

Questions

1. Do you think Kathy has an idea that will work? Why?
2. What would you suggest Kathy do to determine the specific services to offer?
3. What other information (if any) do you think Kathy needs to complete her marketing plan?

PROJECT CHALLENGE

At this point in your overall business planning, it is time to concentrate on the marketing plan. In your business plan notebook, complete the following as they relate to your hypothetical business:

1. Decide if you believe in the marketing concept;
2. Determine what information you will need when developing your marketing mix;
3. Design a marketing research process for gathering the information you need; Gather the data;
4. Develop your marketing mix.

9
Pricing and Sales Planning

After mastering the information contained in this chapter, you should be able to:

9-1 Understand the importance of price.

9-2 Define and calculate a markup.

9-3 Describe different pricing strategies and understand why each is used.

9-4 Describe the steps of the selling process.

economics, the study of how the resources of a society are allocated

To be successful, entrepreneurs must offer products that fulfill unsatisfied needs and that are conveniently available to the intended market at an acceptable cost. They must also educate the market about the products' features, advantages, and benefits. This is how the four *P*'s discussed in Chapter 8—product, place, price, and promotion—are interrelated. We have discussed having the right product at the right place; now we will discuss the importance of offering the product at the right price with the right sales plan.

A product or service that is not properly priced cannot be sold successfully. Determining proper price begins with understanding supply and demand.

UNDERSTANDING SUPPLY AND DEMAND

If you take a course in **economics,** you will learn the relationship between supply and demand. Proper allocation of goods and services to the market at an affordable cost helps maintain a healthy economy. We can buy only what we can afford, so the higher the price of the product or service, the smaller the market will be. If the price of a product is perceived as being too high by the market, then the demand for the product will be low. This will cause a surplus of the product in the marketplace and production will have to be slowed or stopped. Conversely, if a product is priced below the perceived value, the demand for the product will be great. This will cause a shortage in the marketplace, and production will need to be increased to bring supply in line with demand.

The entrepreneur's goal is to find the price point that allows a balance of demand and supply. When a price is set high enough to ensure a profit for the seller, certain portions of the market will switch their demand to other products. This guarantees that the supply of the

Chapter 9   Pricing and Sales Planning

higher-priced product will be adequate for demand. On a supply and demand graph (see Figure 9-1), the balance, or equilibrium, point is reached when the demand line intersects with the supply line. To read the graph, use the vertical (price) scale in conjunction with the supply line. Use the horizontal (quantity) scale in conjunction with the demand line. For example, if an item costs $2, read across the graph until you reach the point where the demand line intersects the horizontal "2" line. The demand for a $2 item would be eight units.

The prices that entrepreneurs set need to be low enough to encourage a high demand for their products or services, but they must also be high enough to ensure a profit. Low prices will certainly increase demand, but they may mean little or no profit. High prices could mean more profit, but only if demand does not drop. Therefore, it is important to find a price point that is acceptable to the buyer and yields a satisfactory profit to the seller. In our relatively free marketplace, the determination of the acceptable price point ultimately comes from the buyers; they will not buy what they cannot afford. The entrepreneur attempts to determine what that price is, using various strategies employed in a marketing plan.

The consumer's decision about how to spend money is based on **utility satisfaction.** For example, the consumer has $15. That $15

utility satisfaction, using one's money (utility) for the product or service that will bring the greatest need satisfaction

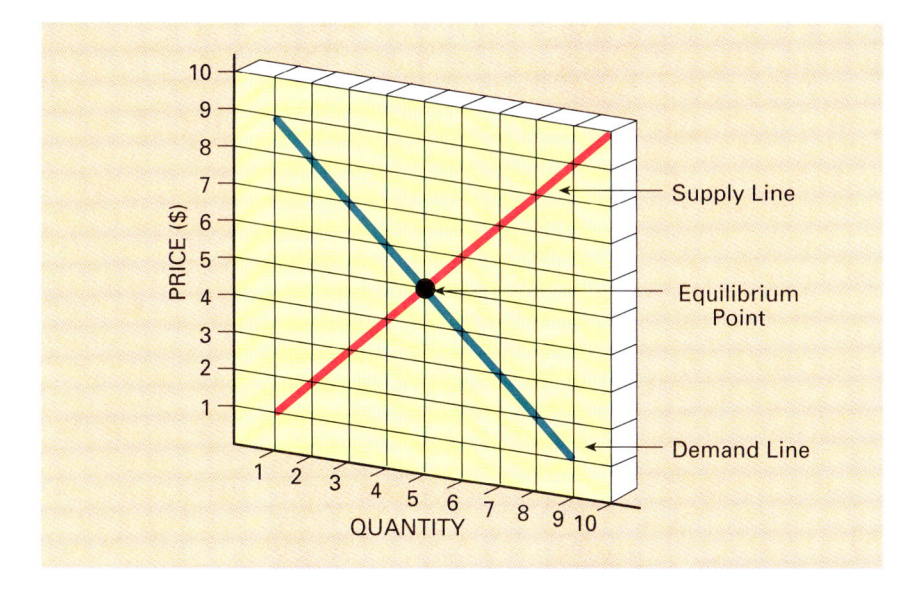

Figure 9-1   Supply and Demand Graph

can be used to buy a new CD or to take a friend to a movie. The decision will probably be based on what is perceived to give the greatest need satisfaction. The consumer must weigh considerations such as who the recording artist is and how popular the CD is. On the other hand, the consumer must consider the popularity of the movie and the desire to spend time with a friend. In this instance, the CD industry is competing against the movie industry. A change in price, such as a sale—two CDs for $15—or a discount for matinees might affect the decision. Ultimately, the consumer determines where the money is spent, but businesses *can* influence those decisions.

DETERMINING PRICE

Proper pricing of a product or service addresses two objectives. The first objective is for the price to serve as a customer relations tool. A fair price tells the customer that the business offers good value, encouraging a demand for the product or service. The second objective is for the price to ensure profit to the seller, thereby allowing the business to continue serving the market.

Illus. 9-1 Fixed and variable costs must be determined before pricing each unit.

Price setting begins with determining a **break-even point.** The entrepreneur determines the break-even point by properly analyzing **fixed costs,** such as rent, utilities, and insurance, and **variable costs,** such as the cost of goods or materials, salaries, and advertising, to determine the cost of each unit sold.

Once the break-even point is reached, additional sales will mean profit for the entrepreneur. The more units sold, the more profit that will be made. Total profit can be projected by multiplying the amount of money that will be made per unit by the number of units that will be sold, then subtracting the total cost (fixed plus variable) of selling. Figure 9-2 is a graphic illustration of the break-even point for a small manufacturer of a product—let's call it a Gizmo. The price, $10, will cover all fixed and variable costs of making the Gizmos when 1,000 units have been sold. If fewer than 1,000 units are sold at this price there will be a loss; each sale in excess of 1,000 will mean profit.

The price of a product or service must accomplish the following:

1. The total cost of the item to be sold must be covered, including the direct expenses of manufacturing or buying the product and the operating and overhead expenses incurred in operating the business.

break-even point, the price at which the costs of producing and/or selling a product or service are covered

fixed cost, a cost that does not vary even though there are changes in production and/or sales volume

variable cost, a cost that fluctuates with changes in production and/or sales volume

Figure 9-2 This break-even point graph illustrates that selling 1,000 Gizmos at $10 each would equal $10,000 in total revenues.

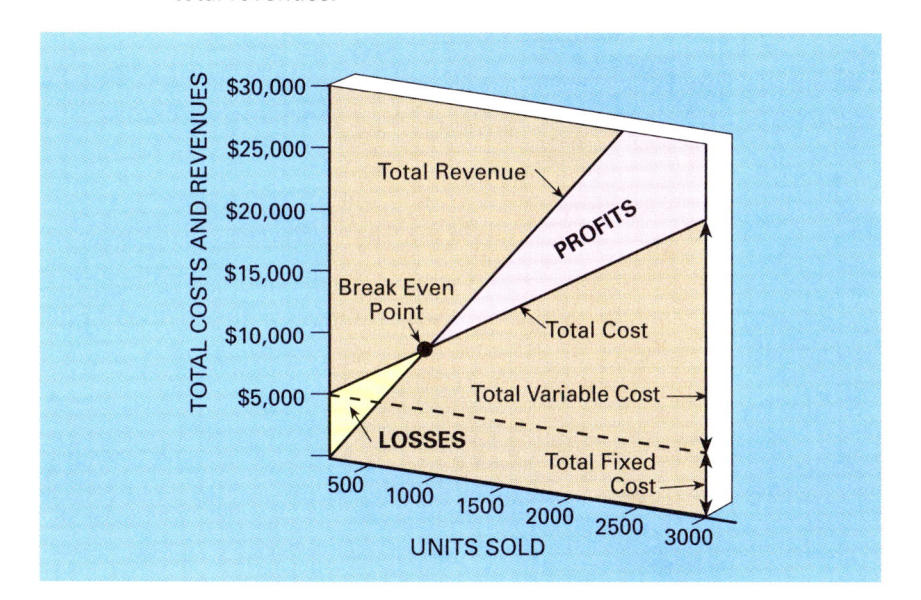

total pricing concept, prices are set to compete successfully, build good customer relations, and ensure the long-term success of a business

2. A contribution to the long-term stability of the business must be made—enough profit must be made to generate retained earnings.
3. The entrepreneur must be rewarded for the effort expended and risk assumed in owning and running the business.
4. Customers must perceive the price as giving fair value.

By satisfying these requirements, the entrepreneur is operating under the **total pricing concept.**

Once they know the break-even point, entrepreneurs can take the next step. With the total pricing concept in mind, as well as profit goals and the condition of the market, entrepreneurs must determine the selling prices of their products.

Markups[1]

markup, the amount added to the cost of an item to arrive at a selling price

Markups can be stated in dollars or by percentage. They vary widely depending on the industry and market conditions. If an item costs $5 and sells for $10, the markup is $5, or 50 percent, of the selling price.

To calculate a selling price at a 50-percent markup when the cost is known, divide the cost by the reciprocal of the markup percent. To get the reciprocal, subtract the markup percent from 100. The reciprocal of a 40-percent markup is 60 percent; the reciprocal of a 45-percent markup is 55 percent. A cost of $5 divided by 50 percent, or 0.5, equals a $10 selling price. For a cost of $6 and a desired markup of 40 percent, divide $6 by the reciprocal of 40 percent, or 60 percent.

$$\$6 \text{ (cost)} \div 60 \text{ percent} = \$10$$

To calculate the cost when the selling price and the markup percent are known, multiply the selling price by the markup and subtract the answer from the selling price.

$$\$10 \text{ (selling price)} \times 40 \text{ percent} = \$4 \text{ markup}$$
$$\$10 \text{ (selling price)} - \$4 \text{ markup} = \$6 \text{ cost}$$

To determine the markup percent when the cost and the selling price are known, subtract the cost from the selling price and divide the difference by the selling price.

$$\$10 \text{ (selling price)} - \$6 \text{ (cost)} = \$4$$
$$\$4 \div \$10 \text{ (selling price)} = 0.4, \text{ or } 40 \text{ percent}$$

---

[1] These examples reprinted, with permission, from book #30049 *The Entrepreneur's Guide to Starting a Successful Business* by James W. Halloran. Copyright 1987 by Liberty Hall Press/TAB Books, a division of McGraw-Hill, Blue Ridge Summit, PA 17294 (1-800-1128 or 1-717-794-2191).

These examples apply to markups for a retail business. Manufacturers, wholesalers, and service businesses use similar formulas. Determining a markup percent is a complex process that is affected by the many variables of the industry, the market, and the operating expenses of the business. Once determined, a markup percent must be closely monitored.

Many small businesses do not adequately protect their profit objectives—their markups are too low. For example, a retail store sells its products at a 50-percent markup: a $1 product has been purchased by the entrepreneur for $.50. The profit on each dollar of sales is calculated as follows:

Sale	$1.00
Cost of product	− .50
Gross profit	$ .50
Operating expenses	− .34
Net profit before taxes	$ .16

At a 50-percent markup, the owner receives $.16 in profit per item sold—this must cover the owner's salary, taxes, loan payments, and retained earnings. If the markup were only 40 percent, the product cost would be $.60, and if all expenses remained the same, the profit would be $.06. The owner would need to sell more products to make the same amount of money. Too often entrepreneurs discount their markups and severely decrease potential profits.

Markdowns

If a product cannot be sold at the selected price, a **markdown** must be taken. When a product is "on sale," the original selling price of the item has been reduced. To calculate a markdown, decide on the percent of the markdown. Multiply the original selling price by the percent of the markdown. Then subtract the result from the original selling price to get the sale price. There are a number of reasons for taking markdowns:

1. Damaged merchandise—A defective item usually cannot be sold at its original selling price.
2. Old merchandise—Some merchandise that remains in the store too long becomes out of style or obsolete.
3. Broken assortments—Merchandise intended to be sold in sets loses its appeal when part of the set is damaged or missing.

markdown, the difference between the original selling price and the price at which an item is actually sold

4. Special promotions—Low prices are offered to increase customer traffic and, therefore, demand.
5. Competitors' prices—If the competition is offering the same merchandise at a lower price, the entrepreneur must either lower the price or increase services to effectively compete.
6. Space considerations—Sales must be increased to make room for new merchandise.

Business owners must consider the possibility of future markdowns when setting prices for new merchandise. The initial markup must be high enough to accommodate periodic markdowns.

Pricing Strategies

As previously mentioned, the customers ultimately determine price; they will not buy if they do not perceive the price as being fair. However, in the initial stages, entrepreneurs must set prices for products or services to determine what is acceptable to customers. This is done by following the rules of the total pricing concept and then determining the marketing objective of the business to determine a pricing strategy. Following are some common strategies that business owners use.

Illus. 9-2 Business owners must consider possible markdowns when setting prices for new merchandise.

Short-Term Profit Strategy. A short-term profit strategy is used for products that are not expected to remain on the market. These products are fads that take advantage of current, but temporary, demands in the marketplace. The products are sometimes tied into a current market happening, such as a popular movie, record, or fashion trend. These products are produced with the expectation of selling a lot quickly, then getting out of the market. Prices are set very high, anticipating that the short selling period will encourage customers to pay a high price for the "in" product. These products have a high risk: sales are dependent on whether or not the fad or craze catches on. The idea is to make as much profit as possible in a short period of time.

One example of a fad product is the Pet Rock—a novelty product that appeared in the late 1970s. It was an ordinary rock packaged in a small carton that looked like a doghouse. The marketing strategy suggested that customers train their rocks to do tricks; training instructions were even included. It caught the public's imagination—millions were sold during a six-week period, then it quickly disappeared from the marketplace. The price for a common rock, a humorous box, and a sheet of instructions was $5.95—truly a price set with a short-term profit strategy.

Market Penetration Strategy. Sometimes entrepreneurs use a strategy opposite to the short-term strategy. Using a market penetration strategy means selling at the lowest possible price. Entrepreneurs often use this strategy when introducing a new product. The idea is to get people to try the product, then raise the price to a profitable level. This is a method of gaining **market share.** By gaining market share, the entrepreneur increases demand for the product.

Loss Leader Pricing Strategy. Using the loss leader pricing strategy, retailers purposely price some of their products at a level that will produce little profit or incur a loss. This is done to increase customer traffic, thereby increasing the likelihood that other products will be sold at a normal or high profit. This strategy is frequently used in grocery stores, drug stores, and toy stores. By enticing customers to come in and buy certain products at bargain prices, business owners hope that those customers will also buy other products at full price to offset the loss on the bargain products.

Status Quo Pricing Strategy. Most businesses will settle into a status quo pricing strategy in which price levels are firmly established and remain relatively fixed until something happens in the market that makes a change necessary. A price change may become

market share, the portion of a particular market that uses a particular product or service

Illus. 9-3 Loss leaders are products that retailers sell at or below cost to increase customer traffic.

necessary with new competition, changes in established competition's pricing strategies, changes in demand due to market shortages, or overflows or changes in the economy.

The profit goals of the business can be reached only if entrepreneurs use the right pricing strategy. Entrepreneurs must be realistic in their expectations and knowledgeable about the supply and demand conditions of the market to be served to determine the best pricing strategy. This requires constant evaluation of pricing policies and market conditions.

THE SALES PLAN

sales plan, any planned attempt to stimulate a potential customer's attention, interest, and desire

A **sales plan** emphasizes a product, service, or business through advertising, personal selling, customer referrals, publicity, or promotional events. The major objective of a sales plan is to educate potential customers by informing them of the features, advantages, and benefits—FAB—of a product or business.

The ability to sell a product or service is essential to every business. Selling keeps the activity going. Without sales there could be no production; therefore there would be no business, and unemployment would increase. All businesses sell in some manner.

Entrepreneurs must design sales plans that address the needs of the markets their businesses serve. Since different products satisfy different needs, a sales strategy must be tailored to the particular needs of the target market. Selling automobiles requires a different selling strategy from selling life insurance because the two products satisfy different needs. A good sales plan is one that is designed to identify the needs of the customers and motivate the customers to satisfy those needs for themselves. Successful salespeople believe in their products and are convinced that they are helping their customers by persuading them to buy. Entrepreneurs and their employees must know their products thoroughly if they are to successfully persuade customers to purchase the products or services.

Salesmanship

There are many different ways to sell, and many different techniques are used. Whatever method of selling is employed, the entrepreneur must learn the parts of an effective sale.

Sales Approach. In a personal selling situation, the **sales approach** might be an opening statement about the benefit of the product or service. In a retailing situation, it might be a display that draws attention to how a product looks or how it makes a buyer feel.

> **sales approach,** the part of the selling process that is intended to attract the potential buyer's attention and stimulate interest

Sales Presentation. The **sales presentation** should create a desire, develop a positive attitude in the buyer, and instill confidence that the product will satisfy a need. A good presentation will persuade, build trust, ask for participation, and prove the seller's statements. It will SELL: S—show features, E—explain advantages, L—lead into benefits, L—let the customer talk.

> **sales presentation,** the part of the selling process that emphasizes the features, advantages, and benefits of a product or service

Sales Close. The **sales close** is the final step of selling. It involves helping customers make decisions, encouraging them to purchase the product or service offered. It should be thought of as helping customers make decisions that will benefit them. Closing a sale requires asking for the order. Often, salespeople will inject trial close questions during the presentation to determine where the customer stands in regard to the decision-making process.

> **sales close,** the part of the selling process that requests an action, such as an order or purchase

When making a sale, the salesperson will often encounter objections. A good sales plan provides methods for handling objections. One method is to use the objections to emphasize the benefits of the product. Many times an objection can be turned into a question that will lead into a benefit. For example, a common objection is price. A good salesperson can easily defend the price by knowing and presenting the advantages of the product and using a question as an illustration, i.e., "If I can show you how this product can actually save you money over the lifetime of its use due to its quality, would you reconsider?"

Entrepreneurs must also understand the importance of instilling a good feeling about the product or service in the customer, even if a sale is not made. Goodwill leads to repeat business, which is important to all businesses.

In order to create a successful sales plan, the entrepreneur must have a thorough knowledge of both the product and customer. A customer typically collects and evaluates information to determine if the product will, in fact, satisfy a need. The entrepreneur is, therefore, challenged with identifying the customer's needs and using the product's FAB (features, advantages, and benefits) to demonstrate how it will fulfill those needs.

Sales Strategies

A complete sales plan is supported by the tools discussed in Chapter 8. One of those tools, advertising, is used to draw attention to a product, service, or business. Advertising can be considered a sales approach. Its importance varies with the type of business or industry. Some businesses, such as automobile dealerships, invest a greater portion of revenues in advertising than others. Small manufacturers often limit their advertising expenditures to reaching a small group of potential clients within their industry. Since the purpose of advertising is attracting the attention of the business's target market, the amount of advertising needed depends on how large the potential market is. Although there is much disagreement about the value of advertising in relation to its costs, there is no disagreement about its importance in the sales plan.

Although it is the slowest method of selling, getting the message about the business to potential customers through satisfied customers is the most effective selling strategy. Referral advertising refers to a satisfied customer telling a potential customer about the benefits of a product, service, or business. This reference is considered the most creditable of all promotion: it can be a very effective selling tool. However, if it is a bad reference, it can be very damaging. Entrepreneurs must maintain a positive image with customers to ensure that references are positive. This is done through an effective program of building sound customer relations.

Illus. 9-4   A good display will draw attention to the look or feel of a product.

When a business exhibits interesting aspects that are noteworthy and newsworthy, it gets **publicity.** A positive newspaper article about a business is more valuable than a paid advertisement. Entrepreneurs should try to have news about their activities publicized through media releases. For example, if an entrepreneur is selling an unusual product or service, it is newsworthy. Publicity can also be generated from seasonal products and events. Community newspapers, television and radio stations, and industry publications are media vehicles that bring attention to a product, service, or business.

Businesses often use planned events or activities, such as contests, entertainment, or giveaways, to attract attention. Promotional events are effective elements of a sales plan; they are image-builders, designed to create goodwill and increase sales activity and profits. Creative entrepreneurs recognize the value of promotional events in relation to both customer and employee involvement: they are fun for everyone and encourage good referrals.

publicity, advertising that does not incur cost to a seller

THE FASHION ATTIC

Laura was moving quickly toward her goal. Having found a location for The Fashion Attic, she set a timetable to open for business: 16 weeks. She turned her attention to selecting her products and developing a pricing strategy.

After completing her research on the products she would sell, Laura knew the following:

1. Merchandise normally could be purchased at a cost of approximately 50 percent of the retail selling price.
2. Manufacturers often offered discounts on invoice totals, when they were paid early. These discounts varied by manufacturer; however, they could be as high as 8 percent, which would have a significant impact on the gross profit received for the product.
3. Suppliers offered specials on older merchandise and broken assortments of merchandise. Buying these specials would allow Laura to make significantly higher markups, which would help offset markdowns that she would have to periodically take on some of her products.
4. In the fashion industry, manufacturers cut and assemble designs by order; therefore, they do not take returns and orders must be placed well in advance of the season needed.

Laura realized that to be successful as the leading fashion store in Johnson City, she would have to get new fashions first. She knew that this meant early ordering, early delivery dates, and, to receive the benefit of the highest markup, early payment. She also learned that to maintain a profitable storewide mark up percentage, specials should make up approximately 10 percent of her purchases to offset the 10 percent anticipated markdowns she would probably be taking in the future.

Laura's research of the industry showed that successful retail fashion stores maintain an average gross margin between the sale and the cost of goods of 46 percent. On average, a $100 retail sale should leave the owner $46 after paying the supplier for the product and the cost of shipping and handling. The $46 should be enough to pay all overhead and operating expenses, make a contribution to building the business for the future, and give Laura enough profit to reward her for her efforts. Laura calculated her markup as follows:

90 percent of all purchases would be made on a 50-percent-of-retail-price basis. In other words, for every $100,000 purchased at cost from suppliers, $90,000 would be priced at retail for $180,000.

10 percent of purchases should be purchased at discounts to assure selling, on average, at three times the cost of the product. For every $100,000 purchased at cost from suppliers, $10,000 would be retail-priced at $30,000.

Using this formula, Laura calculated the result of each $100,000 purchased as:

```
   $180,000 retail sales – 50 percent markup
+    30,000 retail sales – 67 percent markup
    210,000 total retail sales
–   100,000 total cost from suppliers
    110,000 gross margin before store markdowns ($10,000)
            and freight and handling costs ($4,000)
–    14,000
  $  96,000 total gross profit on $210,000 in sales (46%), or
            $.46 on each dollar sold
```

If all worked as planned, this should give Laura enough gross profit to be successful. She could also improve her margin by taking advantage of early-pay discounts.

Her objective was to make a minimum of $.15 net profit on each dollar sold in her business. Following her plan, she would have $.31 from each dollar sold to use to pay operating expenses.

Revenue	$1.00
Less cost of goods	– .54
Gross profit before expenses	$ .46
Less operating expenses	– .31
Net profit before taxes	$ .15

SUMMARY

If products or services are not properly priced, customers will not buy. The entrepreneur's goal is to set prices low enough to ensure a demand for the product and high enough to ensure enough profit to successfully operate the business. Consumers will buy what they perceive will bring them the greatest need satisfaction for their money.

Successful entrepreneurs follow the total pricing concept by pricing their products to ensure good customer relations and long-term profits. To accomplish these objectives, entrepreneurs must find the break-even point for a product, service, or business, then learn markup formulas and decide on the best pricing strategy for the business.

After determining the proper price, entrepreneurs can design sales plans that fit the target market. Since sales are essential to all business enterprises, it is important to understand the steps of making a sale: approach, presentation, and close. The total sales plan includes provision for promotional tools such as paid advertising, customer referrals, publicity, and planned promotional events.

VOCABULARY BUILDER

On a separate sheet of paper, write a brief description of each word or phrase based on your reading of the chapter.

1. Economics
2. Utility satisfaction
3. Break-even point
4. Fixed cost
5. Variable cost
6. Total pricing concept
7. Markup
8. Markdown
9. Market share
10. Sales plan
11. Sales approach
12. Sales presentation
13. Sales close
14. FAB
15. Publicity

REVIEW QUESTIONS

1. What is the relationship between price and demand?
2. To what does the term *utility satisfaction* refer?
3. What two objectives are to be accomplished when determining price?
4. What is the difference between markup and markdown?

5. If the cost of an item is $50 and it is sold for $100, what is the markup percent? If an item retails for $50 and has a 40 percent markup, what was its cost to the seller?
6. What are five possible reasons for making a markdown?
7. When is a seller most likely to use a short-term profit strategy? A market penetration strategy? A loss leader pricing strategy? A status quo pricing strategy?
8. What are the three steps of making a sale?
9. What marketing tools are used to support a sales plan?

DISCUSSION QUESTIONS

1. How might you spend $100 in terms of utility satisfaction?
2. How do discount stores sell at low prices and operate profitably?
3. Bring an advertisement that appears to utilize a loss leader pricing strategy to class. What items might this business be selling at a full markup?
4. Sell a common item, such as a pencil, to the person next to you. Use a sales approach, a sales presentation, and a sales close. Be prepared to handle objections.

CRITICAL THINKING

One option for retail pricing is selling at a price that is below the suggested retail value, or discounting. To do this and be successful, the business owner must increase the number of units sold to make up for the loss of profits that results from reducing the price. If the price on a unit with a suggested retail price of $1 is reduced by 20 percent, to $.80, unit sales increase by 20 percent, and all other costs remain constant, profits will be reduced. The following example illustrates the profit difference for 100 units sold at $1 and 120 units (20 percent increase) sold at $.80.

	Before Discount	After Discount
Sales revenues	$100	$96 (120 @ $.80)
Cost of goods	− 50	− 60 (120 @ $.50)
Gross profit	$ 50	$36
Operating expense	− 34	− 34
Net profit	$ 16	$ 2

How many units would have to be sold at $.80 to make more than a $16 profit? What are the risks involved in using the discounting strategy? Discuss aspects of this strategy that would increase operating expenses, such as the need for more inventory and, therefore, a larger investment; additional space needed to house the larger inventory; the need for more insurance coverage; and the additional personnel needed to handle the increased sales.

SHORT CASE: THE SALES "DEAL"

George was disappointed by the sales reports lying on his desk. All three of his salespeople were performing below expectations. Although the number of sales calls had increased, sales revenues were below the previous year's total for the same month. He wondered whether the new sales strategy he had introduced four months ago was doing any good.

The new sales plan had been implemented after George had heard a lecture at a convention. The speaker had discussed "selling to the max" in a very motivating presentation, and George was impressed. The theme was to refuse to relent when selling—the more you ask for, the more you will sell. Do not give up and do not take no for an answer. Persistence pays off.

The timing of the speech had been appropriate—the packaging industry was in a slump. Five years' worth of healthy sales increases had come to a halt for George and for most of the industry. It seemed everyone was searching for ways to reverse the slowdown. George had been pondering ways to get more from his sales force. They too had been disappointed, since their sales commissions had fallen. Maybe, thought George, we need to push harder.

When he had presented the new sales philosophy to the sales force, George had received a lukewarm response. His plan was to increase the number of calls per client, offer price discounts for immediate delivery of large orders, and remind clients of the expense of handling small orders. Judging from the reports, however, the new plan was not working. He asked Carla Wilson, his top salesperson, for some feedback about why she thought sales were down.

"George, I feel like a used car salesman half the time and a hatchet man the other half. I am not used to selling 'deals.' I'm used to selling pride in our product. I am also hesitant to imply that we might not be able to accept small orders. Some of our small accounts will gladly tell you how much they have ordered over the years. Add to that the extra sales calls and it is obvious that we are gaining resentment rather than sales."

George had a sinking feeling. He knew Carla was right.[2]

---

[2] Case study entitled "The Sales Deal" reprinted with permission from book #3511 *Why Entrepreneurs Fail: Avoid the 20 Pitfalls of Running Your Own Business* by James W. Halloran. Copyright 1991 by Liberty Hall Press/ TAB Books, a division of McGraw-Hill, Blue Ridge Summit, PA 17294 (1-800-233-1128 or 1-717-794-2191).

1. What is George forgetting about designing a sales plan that fits the needs of his clientele?
2. What support tools might George provide to his salespeople?
3. Would George be better off to review effective sales approach, presentation, and close techniques with his salespeople instead of radically changing the business's sales philosophy?

PROJECT CHALLENGE

Research the price range for the product or service that you wish to sell. Make a list of competitors' prices. Determine what pricing strategies they are using, and explain why you think they are using those strategies.

What pricing strategy will you use? Answer the following questions about your pricing strategy:

1. Is it competitive with those for similar market offerings?
2. What markup percent is desirable? (Check with industry sources for opinions.)
3. Does your price meet the qualifications of the total pricing concept? (Is it a customer relations tool that will cover all costs, ensure a fair profit for you, and contribute to the long-term stability of your business?)

10
Promotional Strategies

After mastering the information contained in this chapter, you should be able to:

10-1 Understand the importance of promotional planning.

10-2 Describe the guidelines and considerations used in selecting the proper advertising resources.

10-3 Understand the principles of creating effective advertising copy.

10-4 Understand the necessary considerations of staging a successful promotional event.

10-5 Define the different selling methods and understand how each is used.

The final step of the 4 *P*'s in the marketing mix, promotional planning, is to implement communication strategies to entice customer acceptance of the product or service. Once the product has been determined, the place selected, and a price set that insures a comfortable profit margin, the entrepreneur turns his or her attention to the most effective method to entice the potential customer to buy.

Our free enterprise system offers a myriad of choices to communicate with a business's intended target market; however, many are not within the budget constraints of the small enterprise. It is important that the entrepreneur learns to out-think the competition because, in many instances, he or she will not be able to outspend them. There will be hard choices to make in regard to spending money on advertising,

Illus. 10-1

The opening of a business should be a promotional event.

© *David Harry Stewart/Tony Stone Images, Inc.*

promotional events, and developing sales programs. To be successful in developing an effective marketing strategy, it is imperative that entrepreneurs have a thorough understanding of their customers' needs as well as the methods that are available to satisfy those needs.

ADVERTISING

Advertising is the function of drawing attention to the benefits and advantages of a product or service through an impersonal presentation of a sales-creating message. However, since the heart of the small business entrepreneur's existence is the personal, customer-oriented approach, he or she should adopt a more personal presentation than the larger businesses.

A business can advertise in different formats and use many vehicles to draw attention. Some of these vehicles, such as prime-time major network television advertisements or multiple page advertisements in major newspapers, are too impractical and impersonal for small business owners. Entrepreneurs must concentrate on the most

Advertising, drawing attention to the benefits of a product or service through an impersonal sales-creating message.

Illus. 10-2 Effective advertising can be simple and inexpensive.

effective method(s) of reaching their particular target market. It is not necessary to spend lavishly to achieve the desired results from an advertising program.

Guidelines

It is not possible to evaluate the results of an advertisement in strictly quantitative terms, therefore, there are no definite rules to follow. However, experience does generate some guidelines for effective advertising for small businesses.

1. A business that engages in advertising must design a consistent approach. Too many businesses jump in and out of the marketplace depending on impulse and cash flow fluctuations.
2. Entrepreneurs must be careful not to overreach their intended market. Too often small businesses assume that they are more powerful in attracting customers than they really are. Small businesses tend to overreach their target market by paying for advertising circulation that extends beyond their market. For instance, a single retail unit should not spend advertising dollars in a metropolitan newspaper that is distributed to areas that are not part of the business's marketplace. This situation costs the business as much to reach readers twenty miles away as it does to reach those in the immediate marketplace.
3. Small businesses must keep their advertising message and approach on a personal basis. They should utilize advertising vehicles that allow a one-on-one presentation.
4. Business owners must understand the stage of development their business is in to determine effective copy.

Stages

New businesses are in the *pioneering stage* of development and therefore should concentrate their strategies on introducing themselves to the marketplace. Key words such as "introducing," "welcome," "brand new," and "announcing" are often used in this stage.

Once the business has settled into the marketplace, it enters the *competitive stage* of advertising. In this stage distinctive or exceptional features of the product, supposedly not shared by others, are emphasized. Here themes such as "better than," "compare," and "less expensive than" are used in an effort to increase market share. Often this stage is entered when the competition reacts to the new business by increasing its advertising.

Once firmly established, the *retentive stage* is entered with the intention of maintaining market share. Often themes such as "established since," "reliable," and "serving your needs since" are used to remind customers of loyalty and dependability. This is considered the least effective form of advertising and is used only for businesses and products that are well known in the marketplace.

Advertising in the first two stages is normally **product advertising,** since it focuses on the benefits and advantages of buying the products or services of a business. **Institutional advertising** is used in the retentive stage as it emphasizes the benefits and advantages of doing business with the institution itself.

Businesses in the retentive stage should look for ways to reenter the pioneering stage by adding a new dimension to their products or services. It is important to offer a new look or feature at this stage, or the business may slide into obsolescence. Often a new look can be achieved by expanding selection, remodeling, or showing new uses for the same product. You may recall Arm and Hammer Baking Soda placing its product back into the pioneering stage by emphasizing its value as a freezer deodorant. Johnson Baby Shampoo did the same thing when it advertised a football player using the shampoo and thereby entered the adult shampoo market. We often see advertisements announcing "the new and improved" or "bigger and better" product in a business's attempt to reenter the pioneering stage of advertising. Small businesses often announce "come see our new look," or "we now carry the new" in order to accomplish the same thing.

product advertising, advertising that draws attention to the features, advantages and benefits of a particular product or service.

institutional advertising, advertising that promotes the advantages of doing business with a particular business or organization.

ADVERTISING VEHICLES THAT WORK FOR SMALL BUSINESSES

Advertising rates are based on exposure, whether it is to readers, listeners, or viewers. Small business owners are constantly on the watch for the media that most directly reaches their specific market, without needless exposure to markets that will not react to their message.

Local Newspapers

Small enterprises should use newspapers only if they are circulated to their specific target market and do not reach into areas outside their domain. Often these newspapers are community dailies or weeklies that serve the market where the enterprise derives the greatest percentage of its business. In some larger markets the

zoned editions, sections of newspapers or magazines that are printed for and circulated only to specific areas of the total circulation.

column inch, formula for calculating the cost for newspaper advertising

metropolitan newspaper will run **zoned editions** or sections that are only distributed in the marketer's area of business. By limiting the circulation to the immediate market, the entrepreneur has saved money that would have been spent on needless exposure.

Rates for newspaper advertising are declared on a cost per **column inch.** Newspapers are laid out in a six- or eight-column format. The total number of column inches per advertisement are calculated by multiplying the width of the newspaper measured in terms of columns, by the depth, measured by lines, of which there are fourteen to an inch. Therefore, if an ad is a 4×4 column inch ad, it would be four columns wide by four inches (56 lines) deep. If the rate charged was $18 per column inch, the cost of the ad would be 16 (4×4) times $18, or $288. The charge per column inch is derived from the stated circulation number of the newspaper. A metropolitan newspaper with a circulation of 100,000 copies might be $25 per column inch as opposed to a zoned edition, or local community newspaper, charge of $12 with a circulation of 30,000. Newspapers generally allow discounts on their published rates if the advertiser signs a contract guaranteeing to buy a stipulated number of column inches over a specific period of time.

Due to the competitiveness and size of the larger business advertisements, it is very difficult for the smaller businesses to compete in size of advertisement. The size of an ad is the single most important ingredient for an ad to be noticed, as evidenced by the survey results shown in Figure 10-1.

It is clear that if the entrepreneur cannot afford to run an impact size ad in a major circulated newspaper, he or she should concentrate on the less costly, but more target marketed newsprint media. For example, a 6×8 column inch advertisement (approximately $\frac{1}{2}$ page) in the 100,000 circulation newspaper would cost $1200 ($48 \times 25), as opposed to $576 ($48 \times 12) in the local 30,000 circulation newspaper, which is better targeted.

Radio

Many small businesses use radio advertising effectively, citing its affordability. Radio advertising is charged on a cost per spot fee. The rates are based on listenership, which is derived from independent survey companies. The largest is the Arbitron Company. These surveys are published throughout the industry and denote the listenership of particular stations at specific hours of the day, including the age group

Figure 10-1 Survey of 32 newspapers and 6,400 personal interviews conducted by the Starch Marketing Reporting Service

Size of Ad	Women Noted	Women Read Most	Men Noted	Men Read Most
1 page or more	48%	19%	34%	11%
3/4 to 1 page	43%	13%	30%	8%
1/2 to 3/4	36%	10%	31%	9%
1/4 to 1/2	29%	10%	22%	7%
1/8 to 1/4	28%	10%	20%	7%
under 1/8	15%	5%	13%	5%
All ads	31%	11%	24%	7%

of the listening audience. The more listeners a radio station has, the higher its rates. Charges are usually quoted on 30- or 60-second basis. They are also quoted based on the time of the day the spot is run, with prime time (often called drive time in the radio industry) being the highest charge period. Rates will vary significantly between stations as well as within the time periods the advertiser wishes to run his or her advertisement. A 30-second drive time spot might be $12 for one station and $50 for another, depending on the surveyed listenership. Radio stations, like newspapers, offer discounts to frequent users.

The small business owner should be more concerned with the makeup of the listenership than the number of listeners. It does not matter how many listeners there are, if the listeners are not the target market of a business. Entrepreneurs must choose the station that their customers tune to in order to receive results. For example, if a business sells western wear, it might consider using country western stations, but if the business sells to teenagers, hard rock stations might be targeted.

Television

The expanding number of stations due to cable television has opened opportunities for smaller businesses to use television advertising. When the three major networks dominated all markets, it was too competitive and costly for small enterprises to engage in TV advertising. However, with the growth of local programming through cable television, advertising on TV is now a viable option for smaller businesses. With such a large assortment of stations and programming, businesses may choose television stations on the same premise as radio—by the target market served. The objective is for the advertiser to chose a program of interest for its specific target market; i.e., a local sporting goods store may wish to sponsor the televising of a local high school football game.

Rates are based on viewership, which is surveyed by independent companies such as the Nielsen Company. The rates quoted may be comparable with local radio rates; however, there is a onetime charge for taping the advertisement and, depending on the degree of complexity, this can prove quite costly.

Billboard Advertising

Many businesses find billboard advertising invaluable. Restaurants, motels, and tourist attractions are examples of businesses that typically consider this media. Its appeal is to businesses that target car travelers, particularly those travelers who are visiting an area or who are passing through it.

Rates for billboard advertising are based on the number of exposures of a location, determined from drive-by surveys. This information is available through a state's department of transportation. Rates will fluctuate as to the amount of traffic, whether the sign is lighted or unlighted, and its size. Usually advertisers are billed on a monthly basis stipulated by a signed contract covering a specific period of time. The design, artwork, and setup charges are billed separately.

Yellow Pages

Small businesses selling consumer products or services should consider Yellow Page advertisements since the telephone is such an important convenience tool for any consumer. Yellow Page rates are determined by telephone books in circulation and the size of the advertisement. Charges are billed monthly as part of the telephone

Illus. 10-3   Billboard advertising can be very creative.

bill. The challenge here is to place ads where the target market of a business will look. Many areas overlap, and there is a temptation to advertise under multiple headings that overreach the market. Overreaching can become very expensive. Once again, the better the entrepreneur understands the target market, the more effectively he or she will control advertising expenditures.

Direct Mail

For many small businesses the most cost efficient and effective advertising vehicle is *direct mail*. If designed properly, it is a media that allows the desired one-to-one situation. A direct mail piece directly places a message in front of the potential customer, often with a minimum amount of the noise factors that cause distortion. The challenge is utilizing a format that will be read.

Strategies.   Since the small business is personal, the direct mail piece should be as personal as possible. The advertiser must be sure to address the mail piece to an individual, i.e., "Mrs. Mary Jones," rather than to "Resident." The address should appear typewritten, or in some cases handwritten, in order that it not appear to be part of a mass mailing. In a crowded mailbox of advertisements, the reader will open mail pieces that have the appearance of being personally addressed.

The same holds true of the salutation and the message itself. "Dear Mrs. Jones," or in the case of a regular customer whom the entrepreneur knows personally, "Dear Mary," will be much better received than "Dear Customer." Whenever possible, the message should begin with a personal approach such as "Thank you for . . . ," or some reference to an acknowledgement of appreciation or past relationship.

Besides being personal, a direct mail message must also be professional. The use of photographs, graphs, or illustrations shows professionalism and breaks the monotony of the written message. The entrepreneur should select a quality paper to insure that the desired image is created for the enterprise.

Mailing Lists. Direct mail can be used for sending information letters, brochures, or catalogs. The cost is controlled by the numbers of names, or addresses, needed. Mailing lists are available through mailing houses and can be tailored for the intended market. The best mailing list is comprised of customers who have used or visited the business in the past. Most businesses should design an effective system for collecting and maintaining a database of past and current customers.

CREATING COPY

The best source of information needed for creating advertising copy is the entrepreneur. It is important to recognize that any promotional piece will carry the image of the enterprise. The entrepreneur is responsible for maintaining that desired image; therefore, it is his or her responsibility to screen all representations of the business. Certainly the art departments of print medias and the production design skills of radio and television personnel should be utilized, but control should remain in the hands of the entrepreneur. He or she knows the product and the target customer the best.

The writers of ads often use two acronyms to guide them in creating copy—AIDA (attention, interest, desire, action) and KISS (keep it simple, stupid).

An effective advertisement must of course attract the *attention* of the target market. Usually this is accomplished through a headline, photograph, or illustration that demonstrates the benefit of the product or service. *Interest* is created by effectively explaining the

Illus. 10-4   It is the entrepreneur's responsibility to screen all advertising.

© *Chuck Keeler/Tony Stone Images, Inc.*

features of the product with clear, concise language or illustrations. *Desire* will be gained by showing the advantages that the customer will receive upon purchase. The *action* part of the advertisement asks the customer to do something to gain the intended satisfaction. "Buy now," "come on down," and "save today" are illustrations of action statements. All advertisements, whether print media, radio, television, billboards, yellow pages, or direct mail should contain the four AIDA ingredients. See Figure 10-2.

The other component of effective advertising is simplicity. The entrepreneur must keep in mind that the customer is busy and will not take the time to decipher long, complicated messages. The ad must be clear, concise, and understandable to all—KISS.

EVALUATING ADVERTISING RESULTS

Rarely can an entrepreneur effectively measure the results of an individual advertisement. An entrepreneur who spends $400 on a onetime advertisement with the objective of selling enough of the

Figure 10-2 Diagram of an ad

AIDA

Attention, Interest, and Desire:

Wilson's Record Shop
announces a **member's only** club!
❖ ❖ ❖
Receive a **free record** with every purchase!
❖ ❖ ❖
FREE RECORDS

Action:
Come in and register today.
Wilson's Records
Springfield Mall
Highway 405
843-1121

product to pay for the ad plus make a profit will, in most cases, be disappointed in the results. The entrepreneur must take into account the long-term benefits of image enhancement and customer exposure. An entrepreneur must look at the long-term effectiveness of the total advertising program. To evaluate properly advertising expenditures, a long-term approach and consistency are important to planning an advertising program. Consistency will assure the regular exposure that will keep the business in front of the customer. Large businesses know the importance of consistency and that is the reason they run advertisements repeatedly through television, radio, and print media. The more times people are exposed to an advertisement, the more likely those in the target market are to remember it.

The small business should work from an annual calendar. An annual calendar helps an entrepreneur to budget effectively and highlight certain sales periods. Leading merchandisers use a calendar that features at least one such event per month. For example, January's sales event may be a white sale, while February may feature a President's Day or Valentine's Day sale, and August might feature a Back-To-School sale. If the entrepreneur markets on an irregular basis, the competition may take away customers and change their buying habits.

STAGING A PROMOTIONAL EVENT

A **promotional event** is a planned program created to build goodwill for a business by offering an added value to customers. An event can be as simple as distributing pens or calendars to customers, or staging elaborate contests and gimmicks to gain attention. Planning a promotion for a small business can be a very rewarding and surprisingly affordable method of increasing sales and exposure.

> **promotional event,** a planned activity that is designed to promote goodwill for the business that is conducting the event.

Promotions should be fun for the customer and the business. The primary objective is to create goodwill. A simple contest of counting jelly beans for a prize creates excitement for the customer and leaves the participants with a good feeling for the business. The cost is nominal and might include a fish bowl, jelly beans, copies of entry forms, and a prize that is normally a product or gift certificate from the business. In exchange, customers enjoy participating and often discuss the contest with friends and family members, giving the business a broader exposure. Once the word is out, potential customers will stop in to enter the contest and, of course, be exposed to the offerings.

Many businesses, particularly retailers, are very socially oriented. People enjoy visiting the store to see what is new and also to interact with other friends, customers, and staff in a social environment. In staging promotions, the business is entertaining them in a manner that promotes good feelings and, in the long run, increases sales.

Many businesses also benefit greatly from staging a grand opening promotion. A grand opening serves multiple purposes and is an exciting method of announcing that the retailer is open for business. By incorporating entertaining promotions, it also announces that the business is fun, cares for its customers, and is socially oriented. Customers enjoy new things, and they will respond to the invitation. By serving refreshments, having a ribbon cutting ceremony, and providing entertainment, the new business has created goodwill, received excellent exposure, and will be assured that new customers will return.

As in advertising, a promotion judged strictly in terms of dollars returned for a particular event might be disappointing. Promotions must be evaluated as part of the overall marketing package that allows a business to reach its sales goals.

THE DYNAMICS OF SELLING

A sales plan may consist of several methods of selling. The entrepreneur must decide the best means for educating the potential customer as to the features, advantages, and benefits of his or her product or service.

Retailing

Retail selling is the easiest sales method because the customer comes to the seller. The seller must make sure that he or she creates an environment that encourages buying and that salespeople are knowledgeable in their presentations. The mere fact that the customer has chosen that particular store in which to shop or browse announces to the seller a need for her or his product.

Door-to-Door "Cold" Calling

The most difficult sales method is cold calling on a door-to-door approach. In this situation, the salesperson must be armed with techniques designed to determine needs quickly. Door-to-door selling is often not a time-effective selling method, particularly in regard to business-to-business selling. This approach requires spending time waiting for the availability of the intended customer.

Telemarketing

Telemarketing has become an effective sales method for many small businesses, but only when done properly. **Telemarketing** is selling that involves interacting with customers by telephone. A special feature of telemarketing is being one-on-one with the potential customer but it often has been abused to the point of creating a negative image. Small service companies can utilize this method as their products do not have to be seen or touched. Telemarketing can reach large numbers of prospects in a relatively inexpensive manner. However, the rules of etiquette require the use of sales personnel who have good articulation, are naturally enthusiastic, and are knowledgeable about the product or service.

A good telemarketing script proceeds through the following steps:

1. Address the customer by name, and identify yourself, your company and the reason you are calling.
2. Pause. Ask if the time is convenient; if not, arrange a better time.

telemarketing, using the telephone as a vehicle to sell or introduce a product or service to potential customers.

3. Make an opening interest statement. Tell the benefits.
4. Determine if the prospect qualifies by asking fact-finding questions.
5. Overcome any objections.
6. Sell the benefits.
7. Use a trial close.
8. Close.
9. Summarize and confirm.
10. Express your appreciation for the time or order.
11. Determine a follow-up method and date.

The most effective way of using telemarketing is as a follow-up to a direct mail piece, particularly if the direct mail piece closes with the announcement that a service representative will be in touch at a later date. When used in this manner, the telephone is viewed less as an intrusion and more as a tool that offers additional information. The bottom line of telephone etiquette is not to use any method that the caller himself or herself would find objectionable, and not to violate times normally reserved for family matters or privacy, such as dinner hours.

Trade Shows

Trade shows bring industry buyers and sellers together. A **trade show** is a gathering of many producers in the same industry to display products to customers. This promotional tool is normally used to communicate with businesses who purchase a product for the purpose of using it within their own production process or reselling it to another organization. Since the potential client is part of the seller's industry, product knowledge is extremely important. Smiles and personalities alone will not sell to the informed buyer who is looking out for what is best for his or her business.

trade show, a gathering of many producers in the same industry to display products to customers

Product Demonstrations

Often part of the cold caller's repertoire, demonstrations show how a product is used to bring the desired benefits. Also used in on-site industry presentations, or in staged promotional events, demonstrations present an excellent format for effectively handling objections.

This sales method will only be successful if the full support of the company is behind the sales representative and the product. Sales personnel must be equipped with knowledge, support tools (warranties, dependable shipping schedules, etc.), merchandising aids, and the confidence that the company supports them.

Illus. 10-5 A cold caller often demonstrates the product in the customer's home or business.

Photo by Alan Brown/Photonics

Sales Training

sales training, planned education techniques which demonstrate selling techniques and motivate sales personnel.

A good **sales training** course or manual will help motivate and bring out selling skills of individuals. It will not transform the highly technical introvert into a dynamic salesperson; however, it will provide proven sales techniques. A training program must be chosen that matches the sales philosophy and approach of the business. The primary requirement for successful sales training is having motivated individuals who want to become professional salespeople. Since sales training programs act as motivators, it is important that these programs be used on a regular basis. In order to keep motivation high and skills sharp, salespeople should undergo further training at planned intervals.

THE FASHION ATTIC

Laura is enjoying deciding how to implement strategies for communicating with her customers. It allows her to use her creativity. She realizes that the Fashion Attic is in the pioneering stage of the advertising cycle and that her advertisements must tell her customers in an exciting manner what she sells. She has decided to use a number of different media. Since the community is neither large nor geographically spread out, the local newspaper, *The Johnson City Ledger,* should not overreach her potential market. Laura can back this up with advertising on the local soft rock or easy listening radio station that her target market listens to at work, in the car, and at home. In order to use a direct mail strategy in the future, she will begin to create a database of customers immediately upon opening. She also has some exciting promotional events in mind that should be fun and at the same time create goodwill with her customers.

The first promotion will be her grand opening. This is the time to pull out all the stops. Laura realizes that customers can't buy from her if they don't know she is there. She has decided she will open on a Thursday evening at seven o'clock, after dinner and work. That evening there will be a ribbon cutting by the mayor, a fashion show, refreshments, and door prizes. The fun will continue throughout the weekend with special prices, more giveaways, and more fashion shows. Laura will advertise in the newspaper on Wednesday, Thursday, and Saturday mornings and on the radio station throughout the weekend.

Having an annual advertising budget of only $2000, Laura will have to be very careful on what and how she spends her resources. She has allocated a special budget of $1500 for the grand opening that is separate from her regular advertising budget. This budget includes a grand opening announcement in the local newspaper (see Figure 10-3). She knows that it is important to be consistent, particularly when she can't afford to be extravagant. After researching the advertising rates, Laura was able to develop an advertising calendar to follow for the first twelve months (see Figure 10-4).

Everyday things are getting more exciting for Laura—the grand opening is just eight weeks away.

Figure 10-3   Grand Opening Announcement

GRAND OPENING!
Thursday 7:00 P.M.
The Fashion Attic
Offer good 'til Nov. 18th
Holiday Merchandise **25% off**

Fashion Shows   Door Prizes
8:00 and 9:00 P.M.   Refreshments

Don't miss it!   Thursday, Nov. 11

Special Hours 7:00 A.M. – 10:00 P.M.
Mon-Fri, 10:00 A.M.-7:00 P.M.   Sat 9:00 A.M.-10:00 P.M.
555-9508   Lakeside Mall

Figure 10-4 Advertising Calendar

December 1994	
December 1	Holiday Fashion Show Ad—Newspaper
December 2	Radio Spots on Fashion Show
December 3	Repeat Thurs. Fashion Show Ad—Fashion Show
December 5	Copy for Thurs. Due to Newspaper
December 7-10	Radio Spots to Run
December 8	Under the Tree Ad—Newspaper
December 12	Copy due for Weekend
December 14-17	Radio Spots to Run
December 15	Last Minute Shop Ad—Newspaper
December 19-24	Radio Spots for Stocking Stuffers
December 19	Copy Due for Weekend
December 21	Copy Due for After Xmas Sale
December 22	Stocking Idea Ad—Newspaper
December 25	After Xmas Sale Ad—Newspaper

SUMMARY

Due to limited capital resources, entrepreneurs must be very careful in developing promotional strategies that communicate directly with their intended target market. A common mistake is to overreach a business's market, causing additional expenditures. Small businesses should use strategies as much as possible that allow a one-to-one presentation. Direct mail, telemarketing, and media with specific target markets are viable communication vehicles to use.

Planned promotional events often are effective tools for the entrepreneur in building goodwill and bringing attention to particular features of the product and business.

Small enterprises must select selling methods that reflect the image and philosophy of the business. The business owner must insure that all sales personnel are properly trained in regard to product knowledge and presentation skills.

VOCABULARY BUILDER

On a separate sheet of paper, write a brief description of each word or phrase based on your reading of the chapter.

1. Advertising
2. Product advertising
3. Institutional advertising
4. Zoned editions
5. Column inch
6. Direct mail
7. AIDA
8. KISS
9. Promotional event
10. Telemarketing
11. Sales training
12. Trade show

REVIEW QUESTIONS

1. What is the function of advertising?
2. Why should small businesses try to be as personal as possible in their choice of advertising media and messages?
3. What are the three stages of advertising?
4. What is the difference between product and institutional advertising?
5. How are advertising rates determined?
6. What types of businesses use billboard advertising?
7. What is the greatest hazard to using direct mail?
8. What is an advertising calendar?
9. How does a promotional event build goodwill?
10. Name five different methods of selling.

DISCUSSION QUESTIONS

1. Discuss the techniques employed in the various advertising stages.
2. Give an example of an advertiser overreaching the intended market.
3. What suggestions would you have for someone who is planning to employ a direct mail advertising program?
4. Keeping the acronyms AIDA and KISS in mind, draw a grand opening announcement for a new shoe store.
5. Describe the effectiveness of a recent promotional event that you attended in regards to creating goodwill and encouraging product acceptance.
6. How are sales training programs considered motivational as well as educational?

CRITICAL THINKING

Ken Clark is preparing to open a new family style restaurant. Unfortunately, he has not planned a budget to announce the grand opening. With only $300 available and the opening just two days away, he feels there is nothing he can do to generate excitement for the event. Can you help him? What options from the list below might work? What other creative ideas can you offer?

1. newspaper advertisement
2. radio spots
3. direct mail
4. television
5. advertising flyers passed out in parking lots
6. telemarketing

SHORT CASE: CREATING AN ADVERTISEMENT

Bill Myers was disappointed with the results he was receiving from the television commercials for his car dealership. They seemed to be like all the rest, and very few customers were being enticed by the commercials. He had always left the advertising copy decisions up to Wayne Fontane, the sales representative at WATZ television, since he felt that Wayne had experience in this area. Now he was wondering if Wayne was missing the mark.

At his next meeting with Wayne, Bill addressed the issue. "Wayne, if you can't create some excitement in those commercials, I am going to drop my ads and do something else. Why can't my ads feature some fun instead of just that boring spokesman talking about great deals? Spark it up! I want my customers to be happy when they think about my car dealership."

"Bill, why don't you design your own ads?" replied Wayne. "I'll help with the production techniques and make sure they look good. You know your business the best, and I think you need to get involved."

Bill swallowed hard. It was either put up or shut up time. Maybe he should get involved, but he knew nothing about creating ad copy.

1. Give Bill some suggestions about creating ad copy.
2. Do you agree with Wayne that Bill should design his own commercials?
3. Can you give Bill some ideas that would make a fun and exciting commercial?

PROJECT CHALLENGE

Take a blank sheet of legal size paper and write the acronyms AIDA and KISS in pencil lightly across the top. Design a newspaper ad that announces the opening of your business.

Also using the same acronyms, write the copy for a 30-second radio spot telling customers why they should use your business. Read it aloud and make sure that it fills exactly 30 seconds. Remember, you can use music or any other background noise to help get your message across.

MARKETING FROM SCRATCH

Unit 2 Case

Ray Heath had lived in California all of his life. For 25 years he worked in the aerospace industry in Long Beach. Then, after a successful corporate career, Ray retired with a handsome retirement income.

His company had made it a policy to give employees one share of stock for every two they purchased. Beginning with his second year of employment, Ray invested ten percent of his annual income in company stock. At his retirement, Ray's company stock was worth more than $300,000.

◆

Though Ray enjoyed his many years with the company, yet he resented the times he was affected by a decision in which he had had no input. Ray knew that someday he wanted to be in a decision-making position. He repeatedly shared with his wife, Jill, his desire to start his own business someday.

◆

Ray's retirement meant that "someday" had arrived. Now he could start his own business and run it the way he thought best. There would be no more corporate boardroom politics to affect decisions. He would make decisions based on what he thought was most appropriate for his business.

◆

When Ray and Jill had dreamed about and planned for their retirement, they talked about buying a small motel. So for the past year, as the retirement date approached, they had focused their attention on motels. They read everything that was available about motel management. They tried to determine which parts of the country were experiencing growth— or had growth potential—in the travel and tourism industry. They concentrated their research on coastal areas, since they both enjoyed the ocean very much.

◆

Both Ray and Jill knew that they needed to identify an area that had growth potential and was not fully developed. Property there should still be reasonably priced. That way, they could afford to buy a small motel and turn it into a profitable retirement venture.

◆

After much research, they found the perfect spot—a section of the Texas Gulf Coast adjacent to a high-growth zone. Within the next ten years, Ray and Jill thought, the area would grow to match or even surpass its high-growth neighbor. They pinpointed the small town of Port Aransas, as the most desirable location.

◆

After Ray retired, he and Jill sold their home and moved to Port Aransas. They spent the next month talking to real estate agents trying to locate the type of property they wanted. Of the 13 motels in the immediate area, only two of the owners were interested in selling. After visiting both properties and talking to the owners, the Heaths decided on a motel overlooking Aransas Pass, a major shipping lane leading into Corpus Christi Bay.

◆

The motel had 35 rooms, an outdoor swimming pool, and a spacious lobby with a view of the shipping activity. The stucco building was about 40 years old. The only apparent problem was that the rooms were decorated in an outdated olive green, orange, and gold color scheme. The swimming pool was in good shape, though some of the tiles on the deck of the pool were loose and crumbling a little bit. In general, the Heaths fell in love with the grounds and the view. They planned to make some changes, and Jill's brother, an engineer, said he would inspect the place when he came to visit in a month or so.

◆

After offers and counteroffers, the owners of the motel accepted Ray and Jill's contract. A month later the Heaths moved into the motel, which was open for business for the quiet off season. Now all they had to do was make it a profitable venture. The start of the tourist season was about six months away. By the time a steady flow of tourists began, Ray and Jill wanted to have everything in top condition.

◆

Ray and Jill knew they could not just keep the motel going without making changes and assume that it would make money. They needed business and marketing plans to guide them through the experience of motel ownership.
To get the business planning process underway, Ray and Jill developed the following list of questions that they felt they needed to answer.

1. Who are our competitors and how much will they affect our motel business?
2. Who are the potential customers for our motel?
3. Is the motel facility adequate or does it need remodeling?
4. How much should we charge for the rooms?
5. How should we market our motel?

◆

Ray and Jill needed to begin working on the answers to their questions right away. The accuracy of their answers could mean the difference between business success and business failure. Case questions occur on the following page.

Case Questions

1. How can Ray and Jill determine who their competitors are and how much those competitors will affect their business?
2. How can the Heaths determine who their potential customers are?
3. What criteria should the Heaths use to determine whether their facility is adequate in terms of structure, decor, etc.?
4. How should the Heaths decide what to charge for their rooms and any other services they offer?
5. How do you think the Heaths should market their motel?

UNIT 3
FINANCING THE SMALL BUSINESS

11 Personal Finances

12 Analysis of Financial Sources

13 Initial Capitalization and Financial Planning

11
Personal Finances

After mastering the information contained in this chapter, you should be able to:

11-1 Demonstrate the appropriate method of writing a personal resumé.

11-2 Explain how to select proper references.

11-3 Describe how entrepreneurs use their personal assets to start a business.

11-4 Identify what lending institutions consider to be good collateral.

11-5 Explain the different ways to put together initial capitalization for a new business.

When stepping out on their own, entrepreneurs must realize that the personal and financial contributions they must make will come primarily from their own pockets. This stage in the start-up process requires a thorough examination of personal and financial capabilities. Some entrepreneurial pursuits will rely heavily on the individual's talents and knowledge, while others will require a sizable financial investment. All require entrepreneurs to look first at what monetary contributions they can make before looking to others for financial help.

PERSONAL RESUMÉ

A business will be successful only if the entrepreneur has the personal skills to assume the responsibility of owning and managing it. To determine whether the individual has the necessary qualifications to make the business succeed, a personal resumé should be included in the business plan. Lenders and investors use personal resumés to determine whether an entrepreneur's background is suitable for the business he or she wishes to start.

If it is well written, a resumé can show that the leadership of the potential business is in good hands. A personal resumé, such as the one in Figure 11-1, includes the following information:

1. name, address, and telephone number;
2. a statement declaring the individual's objective and why he or she is qualified to achieve the objective;
3. a chronological list of work experiences; each position listed should include a brief description of responsibilities and accomplishments;
4. a description of all formal education and training programs undertaken by the individual;

Figure 11-1   Personal Resumé

PERSONAL RESUMÉ

James L. Sullivan
111 Meredith Circle
Fort Walton Beach, Florida 32548

Objective	To own and operate Precision Electronics Service Company to make use of management and vocational abilities
Employment and Business Experience	Executive Airlines 1520 Locust Drive Atlanta, Georgia 33604 Responsibilities: Supervised ten-person maintenance crew for charter aircraft carriers. Named 1990 Employee of the Year. 1983 to present Bureau of Land Management 907 Buena Vista Road Boise, Idaho 68745 Responsibilities: Repaired and installed radios. Supervised two employees. 1981 to 1983
Education	Marietta College Marietta, Ohio BA degree in Business Administration GPA 3.2/4.0 1981 Vocational Technical Institute Twin Falls, Idaho Television Radio Repair Course 1976
Community Activities	Fulton County Chamber of Commerce, Membership Committee South Metro YMCA Board of Directors Kiwanis Club, Treasurer
Hobbies	Ham radio operator, golf, model train collector
References	Mr. Milton Causey, Vice President Executive Airlines 1520 Locust Drive Atlanta, Georgia 33604 (404) 555-3440 Ms. Phyllis Charles, Personnel Manager Dr. William H. Hershey, Dean Executive Airlines School of Business Administration 1520 Locust Drive Marietta College Atlanta, Georgia 33604 Marietta, Ohio 38973 (404) 555-3440 (213) 555-6756

5. a list of personal activities that indicate character and ambition, including community work, significant hobbies, and awards and distinctions;
6. two or three references who have witnessed the achievements of the individual.

When individuals other than the owner, such as partners, active investors, or family members, will play significant roles in the start-up, entrepreneurs need to prepare a personal resumé for each person and include it in the business plan. The goal is to present a clear and complete picture of the skills and expertise that the new business will have available to ensure its success. If a resumé does not show the experience and expertise needed to operate a particular business, it is necessary for the entrepreneur to gain the appropriate qualifications. This might mean taking some related courses or going to work in the industry to gain knowledge and experience.

Resumé *Do's* and *Don't*s

A proper resumé will demonstrate the following:

1. how well a person communicates,
2. how positively a person thinks of himself or herself,

Illus. 11-1 A resumé should reflect the qualifications necessary to make a business succeed.

Courtesy, International Business Machines Corporation

3. ability to achieve results,
4. direction and focus toward goals,
5. personal character, as evidenced by community activities, personal interests, and hobbies.

The following characteristics are things to avoid when preparing a personal resumé:

- excessive length (one page is sufficient in many cases);
- poor organization;
- irrelevancies (a resumé should include only significant information that gives evidence of abilities);
- poor grammar, misspellings, or typographical errors;
- photos, fancy paper stock, or borders.

References

A proper resumé will offer as references people who can verify that what is represented is accurate. This can be done by listing two or three names with addresses and phone numbers or stating at the end of the resumé that references are available upon request. It is customary to ask permission from people you would like to use as references.

Illus. 11-2 Persons listed as references on a resumé should be people who have witnessed your accomplishments.

It is important that the references are people who have witnessed the accomplishments listed on the resumé. A reference list should not be a list of friends or relatives. The reader expects to be able to discuss the entrepreneur's career achievements with the reference, not whether the person is pleasant to be around. The higher the authority, the more credible the reference. Previous supervisors or colleagues who have worked with the individual on career or community efforts make good references. Former instructors also make good references since they have witnessed achievements in education.

FINANCIAL CONTRIBUTION

The primary financial contribution for a new business comes from the entrepreneur's personal savings and investments. Entrepreneurs must take a careful look at what financial resources they have and how much of those resources they can contribute to the business venture. Although it is important to show confidence in an idea by investing personal resources, it is foolish for entrepreneurs to risk *all* of their financial assets.

Calculating Net Worth

To determine their financial capabilities, entrepreneurs should use the method of calculation shown in Table 11-1.

The format used to determine a person's financial worth is the same as that of the business balance sheet to be discussed in Chapter 13. It lists the entrepreneur's assets (owned property) on one side and the liabilities (debts owed) on the other. The difference between the assets and the liabilities is the net worth.

Determining Available Cash

Entrepreneurs must identify which assets can be turned into cash for financing the business and which assets can be used as collateral for borrowing purposes. Let's look at each item listed in the assets column in Table 11-1 to identify which assets can be used to start a new business.

Cash on Hand. Cash on hand refers to all money held in checking and savings accounts that is readily available upon request. Frequently, entrepreneurs seek financial assistance from family members. If a family member offers money to help the entrepreneur, a personal note should be drawn up promising repayment after the

Table 11-1

NET WORTH CALCULATION TABLE				
ASSETS			**LIABILITIES**	
Cash on hand and in bank	$_____		Notes payable to bank	$_____
Government securities	$_____		Notes payable to others	$_____
Stocks and/or bonds	$_____		Accounts and bills due	$_____
Accounts and notes receivable	$_____		Real estate mortgage	
			Home	$_____
Real estate owned			Other	$_____
Home	$_____		Other debts	$_____
Other	$_____			$_____
Automobile	$_____			$_____
Cash surrender value— life insurance	$_____		Total liabilities	$_____
Other assets	$_____			
Total assets	$_____			
Net worth calculation				
Total assets	$_____			
Total liabilities	$_____			
Net worth (total assets less liabilities)	$_____			

business is firmly on its feet. This should be done only after the relative or friend reviews the business plan thoroughly to make certain that the risk is fully understood. Entrepreneurs must be aware that they are required by the federal government to pay interest on such loans if they are to be considered legally enforceable.

Government Securities. **Government securities** include savings bonds and treasury notes. Individuals may invest in the U.S. government by allowing the government to use their money in exchange for repayment, including interest, at a later date. Interest is the payment

government security, a certificate that bears evidence of money on deposit with a government agency

stock, a certificate representing ownership in a corporation

bond, a certificate that verifies a debt owed to an individual by a corporation or government agency

maturity date, the predetermined time that a bond becomes payable to the bondholder

made to lenders for the use of their money. Government securities can be redeemed for cash at federally insured financial institutions.

Stocks. Stocks are certificates representing ownership in corporations. Public stocks are normally bought and sold through stockbrokers. Stockbrokers are licensed agents who are able to buy and sell stocks in stock exchanges such as the New York Stock Exchange and the American Stock Exchange. If a person wishes to buy stock in a corporation, he or she could learn the price per share by asking a stockbroker or by checking the listings in the daily newspaper's business section. The stockbroker would then place a buy order through the exchange to find a seller. Buyers of stock are always available, although the selling price is never guaranteed until the transaction is actually made. To sell stock, thereby converting it to cash, individuals place a sell order with their stockbrokers. The completion of the sale normally takes only a few days, and the seller of the stock will receive his or her cash at that time.

Bonds. **Bonds,** similar to government securities, are contracts of indebtedness issued by corporations or governmental units that promise payment of a principal amount plus interest on a specified date. The date of promised payment is called the **maturity date.** An individual holding a bond can redeem the bond at any time for cash, although it will lose some of its original value if it is exchanged before the maturity date.

Illus. 11-3 (a and b)   Stock certificates (left), which represent ownership in corporations, are bought and sold by stockbrokers.

© Ralph Mercer/Tony Stone Images, Inc.   © Robert Mort/Tony Stone Images, Inc.

Profit Sharing and Pension Plans. Many individuals have accumulated investments in profit sharing and pension plans with current or former employers. Often, these investment plans are held by the company until the time that the individual leaves the company. Entrepreneurs who have worked for such companies and plan to resign and pursue self-employment can look to these investment plans as money available to start a business. They need to be aware, however, that money withdrawn before a specified date or age may be subject to taxes and/or penalties.

Insurance Policies. Another area that is often used for available money is the cash value of a life insurance policy. **Whole life insurance** policies are insurance policies that serve as investments to their owners. Over a period of time, insurance premium payments accumulate and the policy acquires a cash value because the insurance company uses a certain portion of the premium payments to make investments. As these investments grow, the cash value of the insured's policy will grow as well. Such policies allow the owner either to redeem the cash value at any time, or to borrow against the policy at a very attractive interest rate. The policyholder must be aware, however, that any money taken out or borrowed against the policy will decrease the amount of money distributed at the time of death.

whole life insurance, an investment that yields cash value from premium payments that are invested

To determine the amount of cash immediately available, entrepreneurs should add the cash on hand, easily converted investments, and any life insurance values. Automobiles are not usually considered sources of available cash since they are needed for transportation. Other assets may include personal belongings, such as furniture and jewelry, but these are also not usually counted as available assets. Entrepreneurs' homes are not considered to be readily available cash assets because they are used as residences and cannot be sold on short notice.

Borrowing against Collateral

Some assets that are not easily converted into cash can be used as **collateral** against which to borrow. This is true if the lender thinks that the assets can be converted to cash at a future date in the event that the borrower defaults on the loan.

collateral, assets used as security for the payment of a debt

Home Equity. The equity in one's home or other real estate is an excellent source of collateral because the real estate market is considered reasonably stable. **Home equity** is the difference between

home equity, the difference between the appraised value of a house and the amount owed on it

Illus. 11-4 The equity in one's home or other real estate is an excellent source of collateral.

the money owed (mortgage) on a home and its appraised value. For instance, the equity of a home that has a $75,000 appraised value with an outstanding mortgage loan of $25,000 is $50,000. A lending institution might lend money against a certain portion of this equity by holding the house as collateral. In the event the borrower cannot pay back the loan, the lender would have the right to force the sale of the house to recapture the money owed. To make sure the loan is well secured, or collateralized, the lender will usually loan only up to 80 percent of the equity in a home to protect itself in case the real estate market experiences a slump. In the previous example, the borrower could borrow up to $40,000—or 80 percent of the home equity of $50,000—if he or she is willing to place the home as collateral against a loan that would finance a new business.

Investments. Instead of selling their investments and using the cash to finance the start-up, many entrepreneurs decide to use their investments as collateral. This can be a good idea particularly if the investments are expected to grow at a rate equal to, or higher than, the interest cost of borrowing against them. Just as in the case of home equity, the lender will loan only a certain portion of the market value of the investment to protect against a downward turn of the market.

For example, stock owned by an entrepreneur might have a collateral value of 70 percent of its current value. The borrower could place $10,000 in stock with the lender and receive a $7,000 loan. The stock stays in the name of the borrower, but remains in the possession of the lender until the loan is paid.

Cash can be used for collateral when it is placed in a certificate of deposit with a bank. A **certificate of deposit** (commonly known as a CD) is money that is deposited for a specified period of time (six months, one year, or longer) and cannot be withdrawn without penalty. The interest rate is higher than that of a standard savings account, and, usually, the longer the duration of the CD, the higher the interest rate. When a CD is used as collateral, the bank keeps control over the certificate until the debt is paid. It is important to note that during the time stocks and/or CDs are held by a lender, the interest payments from CDs and dividends from stocks continue to be paid to the borrower.

certificate of deposit (CD), a certificate that shows evidence of money being held by a financial institution for a specified period of time bearing a specified interest rate

To determine their complete financial capabilities, entrepreneurs can add the total value of the readily available cash to the value of money available through collateral borrowing. Once this is calculated, entrepreneurs should carefully review the liabilities they must pay before determining the total amount that they can contribute to the business venture.

It is imperative that entrepreneurs set aside enough money to provide for personal emergencies. They should also keep enough for several months' living expenses in reserve in case the business venture does not work out as planned.

Putting It All Together

In most cases, aspiring entrepreneurs use a combination of the resources discussed in this chapter as well as many financial sources that are covered in Chapter 12. Lenders do not make a habit of lending the total amount needed for initial capitalization—and often there is not enough cash available from the individual's savings and investments—so the total capitalization plan can be pieced together by gathering a little here and a little there.

Precautions

Since many new businesses go through an adjustment period, new business owners should take certain precautions. As mentioned, an ample operating reserve should be available, at least until the business is stable. There are usually unaccountable surprises in the cash flow projections—sometimes good, sometimes bad. During the developing period the owner might have to make sacrifices. One very common sacrifice is the forfeit of a planned payday. Since entrepreneurs are the last to get paid if money is short in a particular week, they may have to delay receiving their paycheck. Whenever possible, it is wise for new business owners to have alternate sources of regular income. Holding a second job on a temporary basis or having a spouse hold a steady job can be a good idea.

THE FASHION ATTIC

Laura was now prepared to address the always difficult question of where the money would come from. She knew from the seminar and from her research that the bulk of it would have to come from her. She gathered the necessary information and completed a personal financial statement shown in Table 11-2.

Next, Laura reviewed the statement to decide how much of her assets she was willing to invest. She knew that it would not be wise to put everything she owned into the business; however, she was also confident that her business would succeed. Laura listed the assets that she would be willing to use, sell, or borrow against (see Figure 11-2 on page 204). If she invested $46,000, Laura would still have some cash and investments left, plus her automobile and personal belongings. Laura felt comfortable with her calculations, but she still wondered whether she would need more than $46,000, and if so, where would it come from?

Table 11-2

NET WORTH CALCULATION TABLE: LAURA WATSON

ASSETS		LIABILITIES	
Cash on hand and in bank	$18,000	Notes payable to bank (auto)	$ 2,000
Government securities	6,000	Notes payable to others	0
Stocks and/or bonds	14,000	Accounts and bills due	
Accounts and notes		Credit cards	2,000
receivable	0	Real estate mortgage (lot)	3,000
Real estate owned		Other debts	
Lot	10,000	College loan	3,000
Automobile	8,000	Total Liabilities	$10,000
Cash surrender value—			
life insurance	5,000		
Other assets			
Personal belongings	16,000		
Certificates of deposit	6,000		
Total assets	$83,000		

Net worth calculation

Total assets	$83,000
Total liabilities	10,000
Net worth (total assets less liabilities)	$73,000

Figure 11-2 Laura's Assets

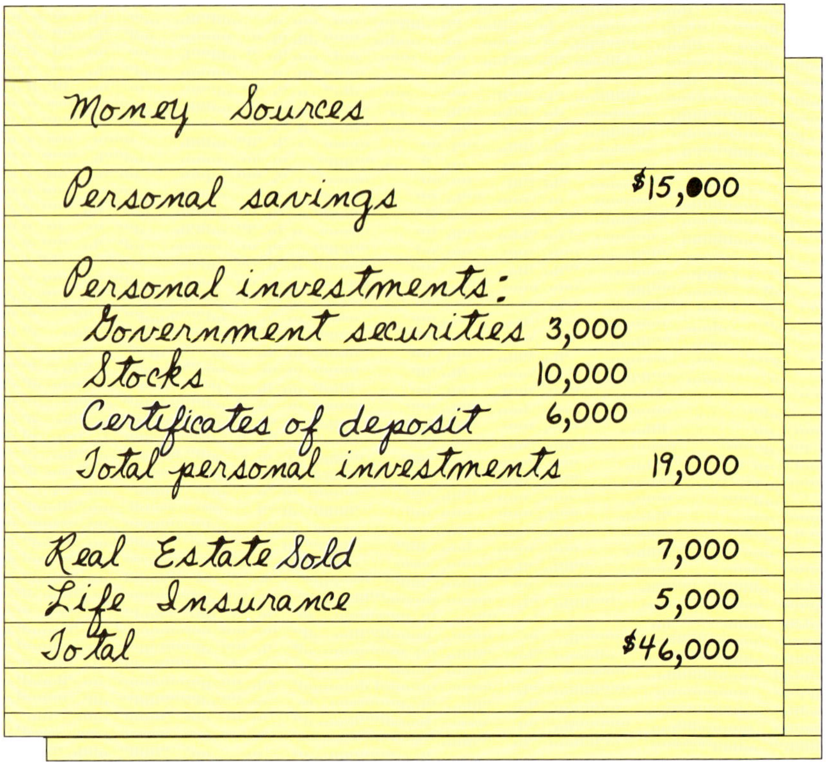

Money Sources		
Personal savings		$15,000
Personal investments:		
Government securities	3,000	
Stocks	10,000	
Certificates of deposit	6,000	
Total personal investments		19,000
Real Estate Sold		7,000
Life Insurance		5,000
Total		$46,000

SUMMARY

In putting together a business plan, entrepreneurs must look first at what they are able to personally contribute to the endeavor. When it is time to look for other financial sources, a personal resumé should be included with the business plan. A personal resumé gives an overview of the abilities and leadership capabilities of the person who will manage and operate the business. It must be a clearly written document that demonstrates the person's qualifications. A personal resumé should be prepared for each person actively involved in the proposed new business.

Entrepreneurs must also provide evidence of financial capability. A personal net worth calculation shows what financial resources can be used for the business. It indicates the amount of readily available cash entrepreneurs have and also what assets they own that can be used as loan collateral.

VOCABULARY BUILDER

On a separate sheet of paper, write a brief definition of each word or phrase based on your reading of the chapter.

1. Personal resumé
2. Reference
3. Government securities
4. Stocks
5. Bonds
6. Maturity date
7. Whole life insurance
8. Collateral
9. Home equity
10. Certificate of deposit

REVIEW QUESTIONS

1. Why is a personal resumé important to a business plan?
2. What information should a personal resumé include?
3. Why are references included in a resumé?
4. What types of people make good references?
5. How is a person's net worth determined?
6. What personal assets are considered good collateral against which to borrow?
7. What is the difference between stocks and bonds?
8. Before going to the bank for a loan, where do many new entrepreneurs find money to borrow?
9. What is a good precautionary step to take before opening a business?

DISCUSSION QUESTIONS

1. What should you avoid when preparing a resumé?
2. Approximately how much money would a bank be willing to lend as a home equity loan on an appraised $100,000 house that has a $40,000 first mortgage?
3. Why would an individual use stocks as collateral to borrow against, rather than selling them?
4. What is the net worth of an individual with the following assets and liabilities?

ASSETS		LIABILITIES	
Cash, savings	$ 3,500	Accounts payable	$ 2,400
Stocks, bonds	8,400	Automobile loan	4,200
Automobile	9,500	Home mortgage	32,000
House	65,000		
Other, personal	17,000		

How much money do you believe this person could raise for business purposes?

CRITICAL THINKING

Many businesses encounter problems shortly after opening due to lack of capital. They turn to the bank for help and often are rejected because they lack adequate collateral to secure a loan. What do you believe is the cause of this problem? How can it be prevented? Should banks be more helpful to these new businesses?

SHORT CASE: TOO SOON TO EXPAND

Mimi Shannon was so delighted with the results of her store after one year that she began looking for a second location. It was not hard to find there was a need in the neighboring community.

She thought it would be much easier to open and operate the second store than the first. She had learned a great deal, and she had established good credit with all of her suppliers. She did not see any reason to go through all the financial planning she had done for the first store. She could order all the inventory on credit and would not have to pay for it for 30 to 60 days. By then she would have sold enough to pay for the first orders. She also knew that the fixture and equipment manufacturers would give her a note for the total amount purchased since she had been paying on time for the first store's fixture-and-equipment note. Therefore, she opened without a cash reserve for operating expenses.

It didn't work. Business started at a very slow rate. After the first month, Mimi had barely sold enough to cover the operating expenses, let alone the initial inventory and monthly fixture note. At the end of 60 days, she was in serious trouble. She was forced to stock the new store with inventory from her other store because she could not order from her suppliers until she paid for the initial inventory shipments. This, of course, hurt business at the original store. Mimi had overestimated the success of the second store. She wondered what she should do.

Questions

1. What did Mimi fail to do?
2. What can she do now?
3. What will happen if Mimi fails to correct the situation immediately?

PROJECT CHALLENGE

Develop a personal resumé that you believe would be satisfactory for the type of business you wish to open. (Remember that it is hypothetical, so design a background that supports your idea.)

In your business plan notebook, calculate a net worth statement showing that you have the cash and investments to cover one half of the money you need to start your business.

12
Analysis of Financial Sources

FINANCING A NEW BUSINESS

Having access to enough capital, or money, is critical to the success of a business, especially in the start-up phase. What happens if you do not have enough capital to start your business? Should you give up your dream? Absolutely not! There are many sources of funds for entrepreneurs.

When trying to obtain additional funds, entrepreneurs must have well-developed, written business plans. Potential lenders and investors will want to see a well-prepared and reasonably accurate accounting of the business's projected development. By preparing this information carefully, entrepreneurs will be better able to determine how much money they need, when they will need it, and how decisions about sources of funds will affect cash flow and profits. Figure 12-1 shows the many sources from which entrepreneurs may obtain financing.

> After mastering the information contained in this chapter, you should be able to:
>
> **12-1** List potential sources of funds for a business.
>
> **12-2** List and explain types of financing.
>
> **12-3** Describe how to match financial sources to business needs.
>
> **12-4** Explain how the lending/investing decision is made.

DEBT CAPITAL

Debt capital, also called creditor capital, is borrowed money. Sources for debt capital might include friends and relatives, supply vendors, equipment vendors, state and/or local business development funds, and, under certain circumstances, the Small Business Administration. In most cases, collateral is required to obtain debt capital.

debt capital, money loaned to a business with the stipulation that the original amount borrowed, plus interest, will be paid to the lender within a certain time period

Friends and Relatives

Establishing trust is usually a requirement for borrowing money. Who trusts the entrepreneur more than friends and relatives? In many cases, it was encouragement from these people that prompted the idea to start the business in the first place.

Figure 12-1   Financial Sources

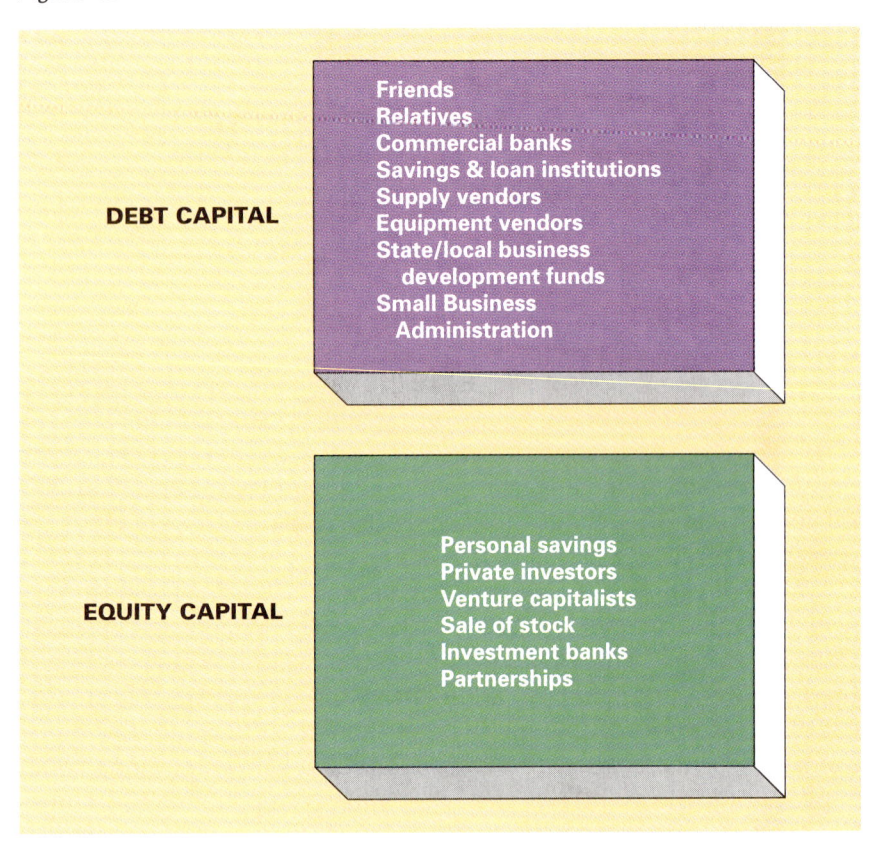

DEBT CAPITAL
- Friends
- Relatives
- Commercial banks
- Savings & loan institutions
- Supply vendors
- Equipment vendors
- State/local business development funds
- Small Business Administration

EQUITY CAPITAL
- Personal savings
- Private investors
- Venture capitalists
- Sale of stock
- Investment banks
- Partnerships

Most people use family money, if it is available, during start-up. Friends and relatives may be willing to lend more money than other sources would, and they will probably allow more time for repayment. In addition, they probably will not scrutinize the business plan as closely as another lender would, and they are usually more understanding than other lenders during times of hardship. However, borrowing money from friends and relatives may also encourage interference. They may feel that since you used their money, you should also take their advice.

Commercial Banks

Most entrepreneurs think of commercial banks when it comes to borrowing funds. Most of us have a bank we deal with on a regular basis, and we are inclined to begin our quest for funds there.

• Have a local banker visit your class to explain how banks evaluate potential business loans.

Illus. 12-1 An entrepreneur's personal bank is a good starting point in the quest for funding.

However, you may find that your bank is not able or willing to meet your business needs. If this happens, check with other sources. The results may not be the same.

Before approaching a bank for funds, entrepreneurs should understand the various types of financing available. Seven different types are briefly described in the following paragraphs.

Traditional Loans. Often referred to as commercial loans, traditional loans are short-term loans. This type of loan is often unsecured, which means that no collateral is required. Traditional loans may not be available to new business owners.

Line of Credit. There are two types of line of credit financing—the regular line of credit and the revolving line of credit. The regular line of credit allows business owners access to a preapproved, prearranged amount of money for a specific period of time—usually one year. The revolving line of credit also allows business owners access to a certain amount of money, but it provides an option for renewal at the end of the original term.

The interest rate for a line of credit is usually 1.5 to 3 percent above the **prime rate of interest.** In most cases, interest is charged only on the amount drawn, but the bank usually charges a fee (1.5 to 2 percent of the total credit line) for reserving the funds.

prime rate of interest, the publicly stated rate that major commercial banks charge their most creditworthy business customers for short-term loans

A business owner who needs extra cash several times during the year may be able to save time and money by obtaining a line of credit. Once a line of credit is approved, loans of this amount are automatic. No additional paperwork or approval are required up to the pre-approved amount. A line of credit helps business owners through the highs and lows that can occur during the course of a year. If a retail business has a dip in sales in October, it may not have the money to stock up on inventory for the busier Christmas season. A line of credit can provide the funds to increase inventory when sales are slow.

Installment Loans. Entrepreneurs often use installment loans to finance equipment. The term of the loan is based on the expected life of the asset purchased. If an entrepreneur purchases an expensive piece of equipment, such as a computer system, it is likely that the business will not generate enough profit to pay for it in one year. If the loan is spread out over several years, however, the computer will add enough value to the business to justify its expense.

The interest rate on installment loans is based on the bank's cost of funds and is usually 2 to 4 percent higher than the prime rate of interest. Installment loans for business equipment are handled in the same manner as installment loans for personal assets. They are often obtained through the private lending division of the bank rather than the commercial lending division.

Mortgage Loans. Mortgage loans are given to businesses that have property to use as collateral for the loan. Two types of mortgage loans are usually available to entrepreneurs. The first is a loan on new property, such as a building to house the business. For this type of loan, the building becomes the collateral. The maximum amount of the loan is determined by the value of the property. Many commercial banks will approve a loan of up to 90 percent of the appraised value of a building.

The second type of mortgage uses property that is already owned, such as the owner's residence, as collateral. This is known as an equity loan. The maximum amount for this type of loan is determined by the amount of equity the owner has in the secured property. Equity is the appraised value of the property, less the existing debt. Many banks will approve a loan of up to 80 percent of the equity amount.

Acquiring a mortgage loan may require payment of closing costs, including loan origination, appraisal, and other fees. Interest rates for these loans vary. Some are based on the prime lending rate, and some are based on the treasury bond interest rate.

Accounts Receivable Financing. This type of loan is available to businesses that have accounts receivable. Accounts receivable businesses permit their customers to charge merchandise or services. If an entrepreneur has accounts receivable worth $10,000—in other words, the customers owe $10,000—then the bank will offer a loan based on that amount. Banks will loan a business up to 85 percent of the face value of the total accounts receivable. As the receivables come in, payments are forwarded to the bank. The interest rate for this type of financing is often higher than that for other types of loans, but interest is charged only on the unpaid portion of the loan.

Inventory Financing. If entrepreneurs choose this type of financing, the inventory that is held by their businesses is used as collateral for the loan. Banks will probably require that the value of the inventory be at least double the amount of the loan. This type of loan is available only when entrepreneurs have paid for the inventory.

Sales Contracts. Some entrepreneurs own businesses that sell products or services on a contract basis. For example, Michael Jacob owns a small furniture manufacturing plant in North Carolina. He recently obtained a contract with a large chain of retail furniture stores. He will supply them with 8,000 entertainment centers over a period of three years.

Illus. 12-2   Inventory is sometimes used as loan collateral.

Photo by Alan Brown/Photonics

Michael's company has never had such a large order, and he does not have enough equipment or employees to produce the merchandise. To meet his contractual obligation, he must buy four new machines and add six employees. He does not have enough money to cover these costs. The contract is with a well-known business, so Michael can take the contract to the bank and request a loan based on the value of the contracted sales. Most banks are receptive to this type of request and will try to meet the entrepreneur's needs.

Savings and Loan Institutions

Many of the loans that are available at commercial banks are also available at savings and loan institutions, and often at a lower cost. These institutions also provide some types of financing that commercial banks generally do not, such as factoring.

Factoring is another method of using accounts receivable to obtain funds. In this case, the lender actually purchases receivables from the entrepreneur for an amount that is less than their total value. Customers are notified that their debt has been transferred, unless the entrepreneur makes other arrangements with the bank.

Supply Vendors

A company that supplies merchandise to a business can provide a source of working capital known as **trade credit** to that business. Typically, trade credit gives the business 30 to 90 days to pay for merchandise.

As discussed in Chapter 8, one of the four *P*'s of the marketing mix is place, which means having the right product at the right place at the right time. Place takes on great importance in the area of trade credit. If entrepreneurs plan carefully, their products will arrive at the time they are needed, and at least part of the order will be sold before payment is due. Receipts from the sales can be used to pay vendors. By using trade credit, entrepreneurs need less working capital to maintain inventory.

Equipment Vendors

Equipment vendors often allow entrepreneurs to lease equipment or buy it on credit. The vendor will usually require a down payment of 25 to 35 percent of the cost of the equipment. The balance of the cost is paid in installments over a specified period. By allowing entrepreneurs

margin note: **trade credit,** a type of financing that allows delayed payment for merchandise

Illus. 12-3   Equipment vendors often allow entrepreneurs to lease or buy equipment on credit.

Photo by Alan Brown/Photonics

to pay for equipment in installments, equipment vendors allow businesses to use profits from the use of the equipment to cover their costs.

A large part of the cost of starting a new business is often the purchase of equipment. When vendors allow entrepreneurs to lease or buy on credit, they provide a reduction in current expenditure and, therefore, an increase in working capital.

State and Local Business Development Funds

Most states and many communities have funds available for business start-ups. An example of this type of funding at the state level is the Colorado First Customized Training Program. This program, which began with the passage of a law in 1984, provides money to new businesses for employee training.

An example of financial assistance for new business start-up at the local level is Economic Opportunity Planning Associates, Inc., in Toledo, Ohio. This fund provides loans to qualified small businesses in northern Ohio.

Small Business Administration

The Small Business Administration (SBA) was established in 1953 to aid the development of small businesses. One of its primary purposes is to provide financial assistance to small business owners, either directly or indirectly.

The SBA's loan guarantee program is for small business owners who are unable to obtain financing through a bank or other private source. The SBA guarantees the lender that in the event the borrower is not able to repay the obligation, the SBA will use funds appropriated by Congress to pay the guaranteed portion of the loan. The maximum amount of the loan guarantee is 85 to 95 percent, depending on the amount of the loan. SBA "contact banks" include most commercial banks, some savings and loan institutions, and some finance companies.

Direct loans from the SBA are available to only a few specific groups, such as Vietnam-era veterans and people with certain disabilities. Also eligible are small firms engaged in manufacturing, selling, installing, servicing, or developing specific energy conservation methods; development companies that aid small businesses in urban and rural communities; and small companies involved with export activities. Only businesses not qualified for a guaranteed loan are eligible for a direct loan.

Illus. 12-4

Direct loans from the SBA are available only to a few specific groups.

© *Peter Menzel/Stock Boston*

EQUITY CAPITAL

Equity capital, also referred to as owner capital, is the money invested in a business by the owner or owners. This might include the owner's personal savings; or investment by others, such as private investors, venture capitalists, stockholders, investment bankers, or partners.

equity capital, money invested in a business in return for a share in ownership and, therefore, in the profits of the business

Personal Savings

The best source of equity capital is personal savings. One of the advantages of using personal savings to start the business is that the entrepreneur keeps more of the business's profits.

Entrepreneurs who need additional funds and wish to finance their businesses entirely through equity capital will need to locate **investors.** Entrepreneurs who want people to invest in a business may be required to provide a substantial portion of the needed capital themselves. Many potential investors consider the amount of money the entrepreneur is willing to invest an indicator of the degree of dedication to the new venture. However, if the business is one that involves a truly innovative idea, someone may be willing to invest the entire amount needed.

investor, a financial source that provides capital in return for partial ownership of the business

Private Investors

Entrepreneurs may be able to obtain financial assistance from people who have excess income available for investment purposes. A personal banker, lawyer, or accountant may be able to provide a referral for such a source. These investors usually have a conservative investment philosophy. They may not be willing to finance businesses that involve high risk.

Venture Capitalists

Financial assistance from **venture capitalists** should usually be considered only as a last resort. Venture capitalists do not often invest in start-ups. They prefer to invest in established businesses and businesses that have potential for an extremely high return on investment.

Venture capitalists often insist on being involved in the management of the business. They usually require that agreements be executed that will allow them to take full control of the business if it is not meeting their expectations. Profit becomes the highest priority, often overriding the entrepreneur's ideas about product quality or how the business should be run.

venture capitalist, an investor who specializes in funding high-risk business proposals that are not acceptable to banks

Sale of Stock

Established businesses can raise capital by selling stock, or small pieces of the business. This process will be discussed in detail in Chapter 14.

Investment Banks

Investment banks specialize in bringing together entrepreneurs who need funds and individuals or groups that have money to invest. These individuals or groups include, for example, insurance companies and pension fund administrators. Most major metropolitan areas have investment banks. Entrepreneurs in other areas may not have access to this funding source.

Partnerships

partnership, a voluntary association of two or more persons to carry on as co-owners of a business for profit

Entrepreneurs who establish **partnerships** may seek a partner or partners for two reasons. They may want to increase the business's capital or acquire expertise in areas that are unfamiliar to them. Percentages of ownership will usually be based on the portion of the capital each partner invests.

Illus. 12-5   Establishment of a partnership may increase the business's capital and/or provide greater expertise.

© Ken Fisher/Tony Stone Images, Inc.

OTHER SOURCES OF FUNDS

Small Business Investment Company

Some small businesses are eligible for Small Business Investment Company (SBIC) loans. An SBIC is usually one that is established by a small group of local investors. These companies can provide debt capital, equity capital, or both, to small businesses.

Debt capital is provided in the form of long-term loans to provide small businesses with funds needed for sound financing, growth, or expansion. Equity capital is usually provided as a loan and requires the business owner to issue a security to give the SBIC the right to purchase a portion of the business.

An SBIC is not permitted to control a small business on a permanent basis. The SBA may, however, allow the SBIC to assume temporary control to protect its investment in a high-risk business. All SBIC loans to small businesses have a minimum term of five years. Early repayment may be subject to penalty.

Small Business Innovation Research

The Small Business Innovation Research (SBIR) program provides grants to small businesses for innovative research and development. These grants can be obtained only by applying to the SBA in Washington, D.C. Applications and information about the program are available at local SBA offices.

MATCHING FINANCIAL SOURCES TO BUSINESS NEEDS

When considering sources of additional funds, entrepreneurs should remember that the best source is the one that fulfills the business's particular needs at the lowest cost. Cost can refer to either a monetary loss or ownership reduction, which forces entrepreneurs to give up a portion of their interest in the business.

Entrepreneurs must be knowledgeable about financial sources available and how each could apply to the business. It is important that entrepreneurs take time to determine the true cost—both monetary and ownership—of capital obtained from each financial source. Alternatives should be chosen since the first choice may not be available. For example, an entrepreneur who doesn't have enough capital to purchase inventory should probably try to make use of trade credit or seek a short-term loan from a bank. If equipment is needed, entrepreneurs might consider equipment vendors or banks.

HOW THE LENDING/INVESTING DECISION IS MADE

In Chapter 11, you learned about personal financial statements, resumés and references, and types of personal collateral. Lending institutions will usually require this information, as well as information on cash flow projections and an operating statement. These documents are very important to the lender or investor.

When combined with the other elements of the business plan, this information lets the financial source know that the business venture is well planned. The thoroughness and knowledge demonstrated by the entrepreneur in putting this information together will have a direct bearing on whether or not the necessary capital is obtained.

THE FASHION ATTIC

The Fashion Attic is well on its way to becoming a reality. Laura has done quite a bit of research to get to know her customers and competition, and to establish her pricing strategy and sales plan. She has also given her location and facilities, as well as her marketing plan, a lot of attention.

In Chapter 11, Laura analyzed her personal financial position. Based on how much funding she can provide through her own savings and investments, Laura knows that the Fashion Attic may never get past the dream stage unless she obtains some kind of financial assistance.

Laura has compiled a list of potential sources of financial assistance for the Fashion Attic (see Figure 12-2).

Laura wants to have complete control of her business, so she has eliminated the idea of acquiring a partner. She also knows that the business will not be large enough—or profitable enough—to attract venture capitalists. Laura also considered the SBA as a source for a loan, but she discovered that it prefers to make larger loans than what she will need.

Then, an offer of assistance came from Laura's family. Although she did not directly ask for help, her parents sensed

Figure 12-2   Financial Sources for the Fashion Attic

> Friends
> Relatives
> Commercial banks
> Savings and loan institutions
> Supply vendors
> Equipment vendors
> State/local business development funds
> Small Business Administration
> Personal savings
> Private investors
> Venture capitalists
> Sale of stock
> Investment bankers
> Partners

her enthusiasm and offered to lend her $8,000 for five years at an interest rate two percent lower than what the banks were charging. Laura readily accepted the offer.

She was surprised and delighted when her friend Paula also volunteered to help. Paula was so convinced that Laura's idea would work she pledged to loan $5,000 for three years at an interest rate slightly above the banks'. Paula was happy to be receiving better interest than what she could get from the bank, and she was glad to be helping her friend. Added to Laura's money, these loans brought the total amount available to invest to $59,000. It sounded like a lot; however, Laura was beginning to think that it would still not be enough.

Laura decided to turn to her industry for additional assistance. She discovered that she could purchase fixtures and equipment on an installment note from the manufacturers. They asked for 50 percent down and financed the remainder over a five-year period, with the fixtures and equipment serving as collateral in the event that something goes wrong. She also learned that after paying for the initial inventory shipment in advance, she would be granted trade credit for the replacement merchandise. Although this credit was granted for only 30 days after delivery, it would give Laura time to sell some merchandise before paying for it.

"Well," Laura thought to herself, "I'm getting closer to my goal, but I'd better keep looking." She decided to visit Mrs. Hickham, a loan officer at the bank. Laura presented all of the information she had compiled to Mrs. Hickham and asked for her recommendations.

After reviewing all of Laura's data, including her resumé, Mrs. Hickham responded. "Laura, you've been doing a good job on your plan up to this point. It appears to be a very worthwhile endeavor, and one in which you're putting a great deal of energy. Although we normally do not loan start-up capital to new enterprises without sufficient collateral, I will carefully review your plan after you have finished your total capitalization package."

Immediately upon returning home, Laura called Frank Duffy, a friend who is an accountant, to arrange an appointment to put together a capitalization plan for the bank to review.

SUMMARY

The entrepreneur has many financial sources to choose from, including debt capital (friends and relatives, commercial banks, savings and loan institutions, supply vendors, equipment vendors, state and/or local business development funds, and the SBA); equity capital (personal savings, private investors, venture capitalists, sale of stock, investment bankers, and partners); the Small Business Investment Company program, and the Small Business Innovation Research program.

Matching financial sources to business needs is very important. The entrepreneur should remember that the best source of financing is the one that fulfills the business's needs at the lowest cost.

The lending/investing decision is based on several factors, including, but not limited to, personal financial statements, resumés and references, collateral, cash flow projections, and operating statements. The degree of skill shown by the entrepreneur in putting together the required documentation will have a direct bearing on whether or not financing is secured.

VOCABULARY BUILDER

Write a brief description of each word or phrase based on your reading of the chapter.

1. Debt capital
2. Commercial bank
3. Savings and loan institution
4. Prime rate of interest
5. Trade credit
6. Supply vendor
7. Equipment vendor
8. Equity capital
9. Personal savings
10. Private investor
11. Venture capitalist
12. Sale of stock
13. Investment banks
14. Partnership

REVIEW QUESTIONS

1. What are the sources of equity capital?
2. What are the sources of debt capital? Name some of the advantages and disadvantages of each.
3. What are seven types of financing available from commercial banks?

DISCUSSION QUESTIONS

1. Why is it important to prepare well before seeking financing?
2. Describe the advantages and disadvantages of using venture capitalists.
3. How can entrepreneurs use a line of credit effectively?
4. What two costs must entrepreneurs consider before accepting financing from a source? Why?

CRITICAL THINKING

Mary Slovic is planning to open a small engine repair shop in your community. She has asked you for advice. What would you tell her if she asked these questions?

1. Should I use friends and relatives as a source of capital?
2. What are the advantages or disadvantages of using a commercial bank instead of a savings and loan institution?
3. How can I purchase the equipment and supplies I need without working capital?

SHORT CASE: TO BUY OR NOT TO BUY

Mike Joyner is planning to open a karate studio in a large city in your state. Mike is a fifth-degree black belt who has won the state title in his weight class for the last four years. He has received a great deal of publicity concerning his karate skills. As a result, he is very well known in the city and has become something of a hero to the young people in town.

Mike has been doing a lot of work on his business plan during the past few months. He is now ready to start thinking about financing his new studio. Although Mike will not need very much equipment for his studio, he does feel that he needs a certain type of building in the right part of town.

Mike does not like the idea of renting. He thinks that renting a building is a poor investment of his money. He would much prefer to buy a building.

A friend of Mike's, who happens to be a realtor, recently found a building that he thought was perfect for the new karate studio. It is in the right part of town and is definitely large enough for the business. After seeing the building, Mike agreed enthusiastically.

In addition to planning for the building, Mike has also started to sign up students for the new studio. Because of his reputation and popularity in town, he has already signed up 100 students. Each student signed a one-year contract agreeing to pay $30 per month for karate instruction.

Since Mike really likes the building his friend found for him, he has decided to buy it. His only problem now is to find a source of financing.

Mike already has a little experience in financing real estate. He feels fairly comfortable in this area because he bought a home five years ago. He has equity of $20,000 in his home.

Questions

1. Where is the first place Mike should go to get financing to buy his building?
2. What type(s) of financing do you think will be available to Mike?
3. Do you think Mike will be successful in obtaining financing? Why or why not?
4. Should Mike consider venture capitalists as a possible source of financing? Why or why not?

PROJECT CHALLENGE

Your hypothetical business planning has now progressed to the point where you need to start thinking about acquiring capital. Begin this process by doing the following:

1. Develop a list of all possible funding sources in your community. (Not all of the sources discussed in this chapter are available in all communities.)
2. Include all information pertaining to the type and amount of funding available from each source and what the cost will be.
3. Rank the sources based on the type of business you are planning. The first source on the list should be the source you consider to be your best alternative for financing.

13
Initial Capitalization and Financial Planning

After mastering the information contained in this chapter, you should be able to:

13-1 Describe the ingredients for a new business's financial plan.

13-2 Explain the procedure for determining the capital needs of a new business.

13-3 Understand the importance of proper financial planning.

13-4 Describe the financial statements used in making a financial plan.

13-5 Describe the parts of a basic bookkeeping system.

capitalization, obtaining the necessary capital assets needed to operate a business

The obstacle that prevents many entrepreneurs from fulfilling their dreams of starting a business is initial capitalization. **Capitalization** is the activity of obtaining all capital assets necessary to operate a business. A business's capital assets include all the equipment, inventory, and operating resources (including cash) that the business owns and uses in the operation of its activities. The challenge of capitalization for the entrepreneur is determining where to obtain the money necessary to purchase and/or lease the items needed to successfully start a business.

PUTTING TOGETHER A FINANCIAL PLAN

Before a business plan is completed, entrepreneurs need to ask themselves how much money they need for the type of business they are considering. The path to the answer starts with the personal financial objective of the entrepreneur. How much income is needed for personal living expenses? What amount of profit does the entrepreneur consider necessary to make the venture a worthwhile and realistic endeavor? An entrepreneur should write an objective statement declaring how much profit needs to be gained from the business. Whether the objective is $1,000 per year for a part-time business, or $100,000 for a heavily invested enterprise, the financial objective statement will direct the business plan.

Stating the amount of profit needed will dictate the amount of capital necessary to achieve the objective. For example, if the entrepreneur's objective is to make $25,000 per year, the financing or capitalization plan must be designed to ensure that there are enough capital assets purchased or leased to achieve the sales volume that will ensure a $25,000 net profit. Net profit is the income left over after all expenses, including taxes, are paid. If a business must sell $150,000 to net $25,000, the business owner must purchase or lease whatever inventory, equipment, and other capital assets are necessary to ensure that he or she achieves sales revenues of $150,000. A problem many entrepreneurs encounter is that they do not develop a realistic plan of investment to earn the needed profits. When entrepreneurs are not able to obtain the resources needed to successfully complete the business's objective, the enterprise is considered **undercapitalized.** Planning the amount of capital needed starts with making the sales projection, as discussed in Chapter 5.

undercapitalized, the failure of a business owner to obtain the needed resources to meet operating expenses in the early stages of business

COMPUTING INITIAL CAPITAL NEEDS

As an example of computing initial capital needs, let's discuss two entrepreneurs, David and Sara, and their new store, "Novelties." David and Sara have set an objective of making a $25,000 profit selling a retail product with an average markup of 50 percent. The $25,000 objective is the minimum amount of money needed for David and Sara to maintain a desired standard of living. They hope to make more than that eventually; however, $25,000 is the amount they need to meet all of their personal obligations during the first year of operation. They need a plan to help them achieve their objectives.

In researching the industry, David and Sara learned that successful stores selling that particular product can expect to make a profit of 16 percent of gross, or total, sales. This means that their store's sales must be at least $150,000 per year, since 16 percent of $150,000 would equal a profit of $24,000. They must therefore purchase whatever inventory, fixtures, and equipment is necessary to ensure sales of $150,000.

Entrepreneurs need to estimate the number of times the inventory will turn over. If the average **inventory turnover** rate for a product is five, the owner can divide the projected sales by 5 to determine the minimum amount of inventory available at all times. To make $150,000 in sales, David and Sara's store should sell $30,000 worth of retail inventory five times each year. Since the markup is 50 percent, they must have a minimum of $15,000 ($30,000 × .50) of initial inventory to open the business.

inventory turnover, the number of times a business sells the amount of its base inventory in a year

One-Time-Only Costs

Many starting costs are incurred only once by the business—during this start-up phase. Once the minimum amount of inventory is calculated, entrepreneurs should determine how many and what kind of fixtures (shelving units, gondolas, tables, etc.) they require to house

Illus. 13-1 Start-up costs are incurred only once by a business.

leasehold improvement, the remodeling performed on a store or business to appeal to its customers

and display the initial inventory. Next they should find out how much money they need for **leasehold improvements.**

In addition to inventory, fixture, and leasehold improvement costs will be the one-time-only costs of an appropriate sign, cash register(s), stockroom shelves, advertising for a "grand opening," utility deposits, change for the cash register, and all other miscellaneous expenditures incurred in opening the business. Building and equipment costs can be reduced considerably by leasing, rather than purchasing. Table 13-1 shows the one-time-only capital-needed statement for such a retail business.

This amount of money will get the door open. However, money will also be needed to sustain operating expenses while the business gets started.

Monthly Operating Expenses

Entrepreneurs must also estimate the average monthly operating cost to keep the business running smoothly. It will take time to generate sufficient sales to cover all expenses, so the business owner must set aside money to pay the initial expenses without depending on sales revenues at all. Entrepreneurs should have three months of operating expense capital available in an operating reserve account so they can concentrate on increasing sales without the worry of how they're going to pay

Table 13-1 One-Time-Only Capital Needs

Fixtures and equipment	
Decorating and remodeling	
Installation cost	
Starting inventory	
Utility deposits	
Legal and other fees	
Grand opening promotion	
Cash on hand	
Other	
Total one-time-only expenses	

the bills. To estimate operating expenses, calculate the monthly rent and employees' salaries, and determine the average cost of utility services, insurance premiums, and other charges, as shown in Table 13-2. Multiply the total projected monthly operating expenses by three (representing three months) to arrive at the amount of money that should be available in the initial capitalization plan for operating expenses.

By adding the total amount of one-time-only capital needs to the amount of initial operating expenses, entrepreneurs will know the total amount of money needed for the business idea. Once this is determined, a plan must be devised to make sure this money is available to the business owner.

FINANCIAL STATEMENTS

Pro Forma Statements

Pro forma financial statements are projected statistical reports used to illustrate the expected financial status of a business at a future date. To demonstrate the validity of a business idea, entrepreneurs

pro forma financial statement, a projected statistical report used to illustrate the expected financial status of a business at a future date

Table 13-2 Initial Operating Expenses

Item	Expenses (One Month)	Multiply by 3	Expenses (Three Months)
Owner's salary	$2,000	3	$6,000
Other salary	900	3	2,700
Rent	1,600	3	4,800
Advertising	250	3	750
Supplies	270	3	810
Utilities	300	3	900
Accounting	165	3	495
Insurance	200	3	600
Loan principal and interest	225	3	675
Taxes, licenses	125	3	375
Miscellaneous	150	3	450
Total monthly expenses	6,185		18,555

must project success in the form of pro forma income statements and balance sheets. These projected financial statements are an important part of the business plan.

Income Statements

income statement, a financial report that shows a business's revenues collected and expenses paid out over a specified period of time

An **income statement** shows the revenues, or monies collected, and the expenses, or monies paid out, of a business over a specified period of time. It also reveals the business's profit. New business owners must make pro forma income statements for the first year of operation and also for future years. If properly done and if a realistic profit is shown, it will serve to support the reasons for starting a business. A simplified pro forma statement for the first year of operation for David and Sara's $150,000 business might look as shown in Table 13-3.

This statement makes use of the itemized expenses from the initial operating expenses statement (see Table 13-2). It shows the sales expected for a year and the accumulation of a projected year's operating expenses. In this case, it is evident that if this business is properly managed, and the location is suitable, David and Sara can expect to realize the goal of a $25,000 profit the first year.

Table 13-3 Simplified Pro Forma Income Statement

NOVELTIES
Income Statement
For Year Ending December 31, 19—

Sales	$150,000	
Cost of goods sold	78,000	
Gross profit		$72,000
Operating expenses		
Payroll	11,000	
Rent	19,000	
Maintenance and repairs	1,000	
Operating supplies	2,700	
Taxes and licenses	1,500	
Utilities	3,300	
Advertising	3,000	
Insurance	2,200	
Accounting and legal	2,000	
Miscellaneous	1,800	
Total operating expenses		$47,500
Net profit		$24,500

Future projections indicate the planned growth of the business. The growth projections can be made based on factors such as market population growth, business growth from becoming better known, and industry growth. David and Sara have determined that their business can expect growth in revenues of 15 percent in the second year ($150,000 ÷ $172,500 = 15 percent increase), and 10 percent in the third year ($172,500 ÷ $189,250 = 10 percent increase). The pro forma income statements for the second and the third years of the business are shown in Table 13-4.

Table 13-4 Simplified Pro Forma Income Statement—Second and Third Years

NOVELTIES
Income Statement

	Second Year	Third Year
Sales	$172,500	$189,250
Cost of goods sold	88,000	90,200
Gross profit	84,500	99,050
Operating expenses		
Payroll	12,000	13,000
Rent	19,000	19,000
Maintenance and repairs	1,100	1,200
Operating supplies	3,300	3,400
Taxes and licenses	1,600	1,700
Utilities	3,600	3,600
Advertising	3,400	3,800
Insurance	2,500	2,600
Accounting and legal	2,100	2,200
Miscellaneous	2,000	2,200
Total operating expenses	$50,600	$52,700
Net profit	$33,900	$46,350

Balance Sheets

A **balance sheet** is a financial statement that shows the worth, or value, of a business. A pro forma balance sheet projects the growth of a business with respect to how much capital value the business will have at a particular date in its existence. In the business plan, entrepreneurs should include a pro forma balance sheet for its opening date as well as one indicating what the business should be worth one year later. Table 13-5 shows a simplified pro forma balance sheet for David and Sara's store.

The balance sheet has two sides—assets and liabilities. The asset side shows all property and capital to which the business claims ownership. The liability side shows all the debts of the business. The net worth, or owner's equity, of a business is determined by adding all the values of what is owned (the assets) and subtracting from this the total debt of the business (the liabilities). The result is the net worth, value, or owner's equity. This table is called a balance sheet because the net worth is added to the liabilities to achieve the "balanced" totals on each side of the ledger, as shown.

Assets are listed as current and fixed. **Current assets** include cash and assets that are easily converted into cash, such as inventory

balance sheet, a financial statement that shows the worth or value of a business

current asset, property that is easily converted into cash

Table 13-5 Simplified Pro Forma Balance Sheet

NOVELTIES
Balance Sheet
July 1, 19—

ASSETS		LIABILITIES AND OWNER'S EQUITY	
Current assets		Current liabilities	
Cash	$ 6,400	Accounts payable	$5,200
Inventory	15,000	Current portion of long-term debt	3,300
Total current assets	21,400	Long-term liabilities	6,700
Fixed assets	17,900	Total liabilities	15,200
Total assets	$39,300	Owner's equity	24,100
		Total liabilities and owner's equity	$39,300

Illus. 13-2   Fixed assets take longer to convert into cash.

© Bob Krist/Tony Stone Images, Inc.

fixed asset, property that normally takes a longer time to convert into cash

current liability, debt that is to be paid within 12 months

long-term liability, debt that becomes due after 12 months, usually associated with the purchase of fixed assets

and accounts receivable. **Fixed assets** are those that would take a longer time to convert or liquidate into cash, such as property, equipment, and fixtures that require a special buyer.

Liabilities are listed as current and long term. **Current liabilities** are liabilities that are to be paid within 12 months of the date of the balance sheet. **Long-term liabilities** are often debts that will come due more than 12 months after the date of the balance sheet. Long-term liabilities are usually associated with the purchase of fixed assets such as mortgage notes on property and equipment. By understanding short- and long-term classifications, it is easy to see how much money the business could raise on short notice to use for emergency purchases or expansions. The goal of business owners is to always keep current assets greater than current liabilities, or the business will be considered "technically bankrupt."

Planning Cash Flow

To gain a close look at the business operation for the first year, entrepreneurs must break the year into a month-by-month projection, or a cash flow statement. This analysis allows business owners to gain insight into cash flow problems, which are caused by changing sales and payment patterns due to seasonal and industry fluctuations. Cash flow statements are also needed because goods are sometimes purchased and paid for by the business despite the fact that the goods are still in inventory. Cash flow statements tell entrepreneurs what their business's cash position *really* is. For example, since goods are frequently sold to customers on credit, the business may not receive payment (cash) for those credit purchases for a month or two. Although on paper it may appear that the business did receive payment at the time of sale, it was not a cash payment and the business may appear more cash-rich than it really is.

It is necessary for David and Sarah to understand how their $150,000 in sales will occur. Particularly in a retail business in which a great portion of sales are made during the end-of-the-year holiday season, owners must be aware of the impact that seasons have on the cash flow cycle of a business. Entrepreneurs should learn from industry sources the percent of total sales normally received each month of the year. This allows entrepreneurs to budget expenses to accommodate these fluctuations. Table 13-6 is an example of a form that is available from the SBA for calculating and recording cash flow.

Although the final outcome of the year should support the income statement, some months have excess cash coming in, and some months have too little cash coming in to meet obligations. Entrepreneurs must be aware of these circumstances to properly plan the best allocation of money in different cycles. It is not difficult for entrepreneurs to go bankrupt if cash is flowing out of the business much faster than it is flowing in. They may be making a profit on each item sold, but if the cash flows into the business too slowly, the business may have to close.

Once entrepreneurs put together the capital needs statements, pro forma income statements, balance sheets, and monthly cash flow projection, they will have a financial plan in place. The information gathered will indicate how much money they need to open and operate the business for the first three months; the income that the business should generate in its first, second, and third years of operation; and what the expected value of the business will be upon opening and at the end of its first year. These are essential ingredients of the business plan. Their results will determine whether the owner needs to borrow money for the idea or attract investors to share the risks and profits.

cash flow, how money comes in and goes out of a business operation during a specific period of time

Unit 3 Financing the Small Business

Table 13-6 Twelve-Month Cash Flow Cycle

	Pre-start-up position	Month 1	Month 2	Month 3		TOTAL Columns 1–12	
YEAR MONTH	Estimate / Actual	Estimate / Actual	Estimate / Actual	Estimate / Actual		Estimate / Actual	
1. CASH ON HAND (Beginning of month)							1.
2. CASH RECEIPTS							2.
(a) Cash Sales							(a)
(b) Collections from Credit Accounts							(b)
(c) Loan or Other Cash injection (Specify)							(c)
3. TOTAL CASH RECEIPTS (2a + 2b + 2c = 3)							3.
4. TOTAL CASH AVAILABLE (Before cash out) (1 + 3)							4.
5. CASH PAID OUT							5.
(a) Purchases (Merchandise)							(a)
(b) Gross Wages (Excludes withdrawals)							(b)
(c) Payroll Expenses (Taxes, etc.)							(c)
(d) Outside Services							(d)
(e) Supplies (Office and operating)							(e)
(f) Repairs and Maintenance							(f)
(g) Advertising							(g)
(h) Car, Delivery, and Travel							(h)
(i) Accounting and Legal							(i)
(j) Rent							(j)
(k) Telephone							(k)
(l) Utilities							(l)
(m) Insurance							(m)
(n) Taxes (Real estate, etc.)							(n)
(o) Interest							(o)
(p) Other Expenses (Specify each)							(p)
(q) Miscellaneous (Unspecified)							(q)
(r) Subtotal							(r)
(s) Loan Principal Payment							(s)
(t) Capital Purchases (Specify)							(t)
(u) Other Start-up Costs							(u)
(v) Reserve and/or Escrow (Specify)							(v)
(w) Owner's Withdrawal							(w)
6. TOTAL CASH PAID OUT (Total 5a thru 5w)							6.
7. CASH POSITION (End of month) (4 minus 6)							7.
ESSENTIAL OPERATING DATA (Non-cash flow information)							
A. Sales Volume (Dollars)							A.
B. Accounts Receivable (End of month)							B.
C. Bad Debt (End of month)							C.
D. Inventory on Hand (End of Month)							D.
E. Accounts Payable (End of Month)							E.
F. Depreciation							F.

MAINTAINING FINANCIAL RECORDS

Using an Accountant

Most small businesses hire accountants. **Accountants** are trained in the methods and procedures used in assimilating and maintaining financial records. They are often hired by businesses to assist in making sure that all financial activity is properly documented for the purposes of reporting taxes to the government and informing banks, investors, and owners of the progress of a business.

accountant, an individual trained in the methods and procedures used in assimilating and maintaining financial records

Basic Parts of A Bookkeeping System

Too many small business owners become too dependent on accountants for assistance in keeping business records. Basic bookkeeping for a business is a relatively simple, though sometimes tedious, process that entrepreneurs should learn and maintain. By doing their own bookkeeping, business owners will be better informed about the financial condition of their businesses. The basic parts of a bookkeeping system are outlined in the following paragraphs.

Sales Journal. This is a listing of revenues received each day from the business activity. It is also called a *receipts journal.* It should show the amount of cash received, any sales taxes collected, and charge account purchases. Table 13-7 is an example of a sales journal ledger sheet.

Disbursement Journal. This is similar to a personal checking account record. Its purpose is to show all payments made by check on a particular day, to whom the check was written, and the type of expense incurred. Table 13-8 shows a ledger sheet from a disbursement journal.

Accounts Payable Ledger. This is a listing, by account name, of all bills the business needs to pay. The amount owed, the due date, and the date actually paid are also recorded. Many times companies will offer a discount on a bill if it is paid promptly. If so, the amount of the discount should also be shown on the ledger. Table 13-9 is an example of an accounts payable ledger sheet.

Accounts Receivable Ledger. This record lists customers by name and the amount they owe the business for goods and services bought on credit. Table 13-10 shows a standard accounts receivable ledger sheet.

Furniture, Fixture, and Equipment Ledger. All purchases of current or long-term assets should be recorded on this ledger. It will help maintain a record of business assets and the date they were purchased.

Unit 3 Financing the Small Business

Table 13-7 Sales Journal Sheet

Table 13-8   Disbursement Journal Sheet

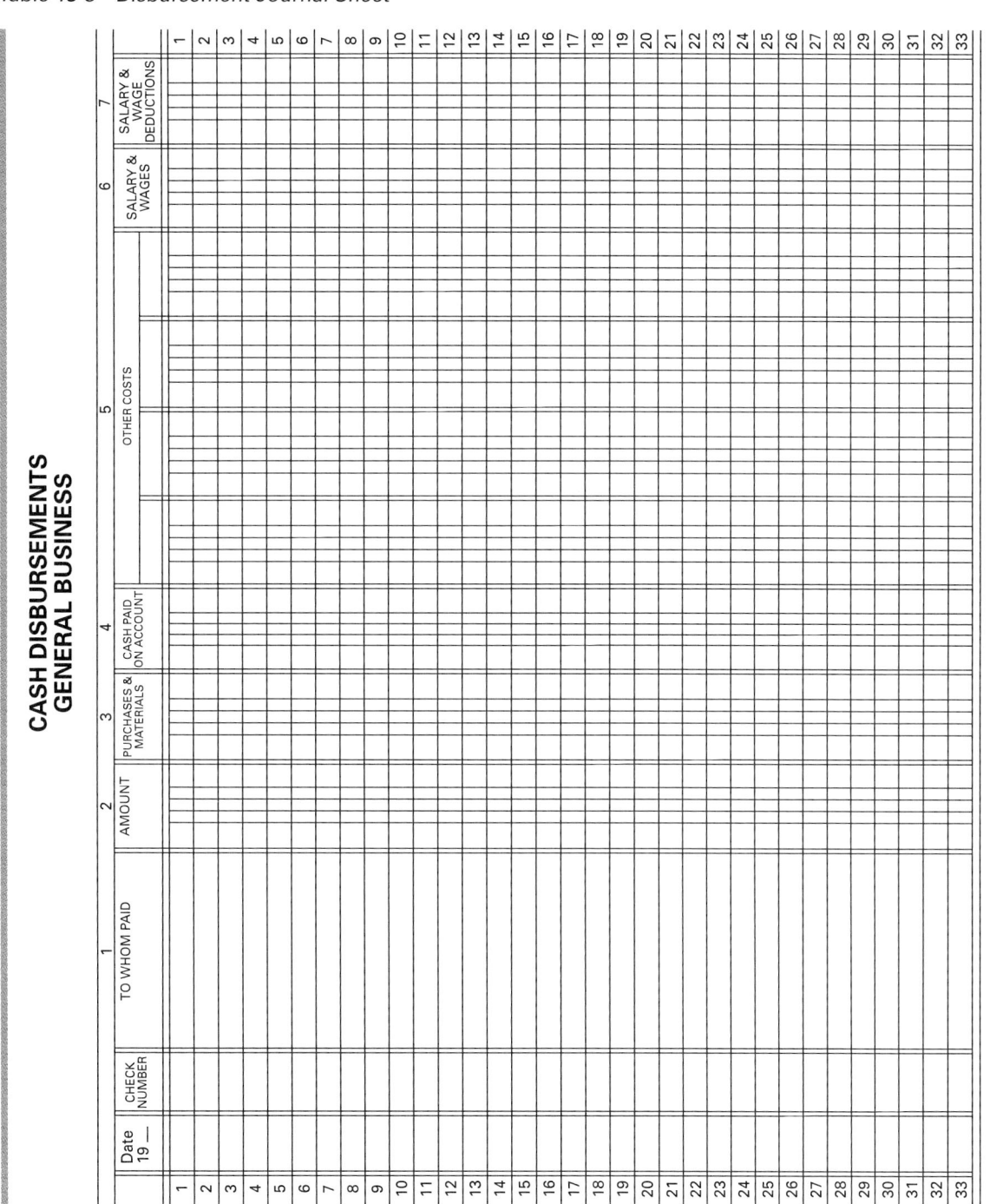

**CASH DISBURSEMENTS
GENERAL BUSINESS**

Date 19—	CHECK NUMBER	TO WHOM PAID	AMOUNT	PURCHASES & MATERIALS	CASH PAID ON ACCOUNT	OTHER COSTS	SALARY & WAGES	SALARY & WAGE DEDUCTIONS
		1	2	3	4	5	6	7

Unit 3 Financing the Small Business

Table 13-8 (continued)

Chapter 13 Initial Capitalization and Financial Planning

Table 13-9 Accounts Payable Ledger

Unit 3 Financing the Small Business

Table 13-10 Accounts Receivable Ledger

Notes Payable Ledger. Any money borrowed for business activity should be recorded, showing from whom it was borrowed, the date the note becomes due, the interest rate to be paid, and any special payment arrangements.

Using A Bookkeeping System

Entrepreneurs who use these six basic recordkeeping devices have a basic bookkeeping system. Using this information, they will be able to produce approximate income statements and balance sheets. A monthly totaling of the sales receipts journal and the columns of the disbursement journal will allow business owners to calculate net profit. The following calculation is used:

$$\text{Sales} - \text{Purchases} - \text{Expenses} = \text{Net operating profits}$$

By keeping tabs on the accounts payable, accounts receivable, assets purchased, and notes payable, a rough balance sheet can be kept if the owner keeps track of inventory on hand and cash in the bank.

Another part of a bookkeeping system is a payroll summary sheet for each employee. These show up-to-date totals of how much each employee has been paid during a given calendar year. There should also be separate records kept for posting sales and other taxes paid, and other miscellaneous accounts that pertain to a particular business.

Successful entrepreneurs do the basic recordkeeping and bookkeeping themselves, or hire a company bookkeeper. Accountants are used to formalize, summarize, and review financial records for tax reporting purposes. Learning basic bookkeeping is essential for those who wish to open a business. Bookstores offer many resources for non-financial business people who desire easy-to-understand books on accounting and bookkeeping.

THE FASHION ATTIC

Laura sat down at her desk with a large folder of information that she had put together and went to work on her capitalization plan. Her research had shown that a $200,000 initial sales volume for a ladies' fashion boutique was certainly attainable. Although she felt confident that her sales would be higher, since she would be located in the Lakeside Mall, she wanted to be conservative in her projection to make sure there would be no problems. From her discussions with industry suppliers and other sources, she conservatively estimated that she would have four inventory turnovers annually. This meant that she would have to have a minimum opening inventory of $50,000 in merchandise, plus at least a month's worth of replacement inventory en route. Laura decided that she would place initial orders of $50,000 for immediate delivery, as well as $20,000 of merchandise to be delivered at a later date, for a total inventory investment of $70,000. Based on the average markup percentage of 50 percent, Laura would need to have $35,000 ($70,000 × .50, the reciprocal of the markup percentage) available to purchase the initial inventory. Displaying and storing that much inventory in a 2,000-square-foot shop would require almost 50 fixtures, plus mannequins and counters, at a total cost of $20,000. In addition, Laura decided that she needed two cash registers, stockroom shelves, carpeting, paint, a sign, and what seemed to be a million other odds and ends. Laura determined that her one-time-only capital needs were as follows:

Table 13-11 One-Time-Only Capital Needs

Fixtures and equipment	$20,000
Decorating and remodeling	12,000
Installation cost	1,500
Starting inventory	35,000
Utility deposits	900
Legal and other fees	500
Grand opening promotion	2,500
Cash on hand	200
Other	1,200
Total one-time-only expenses	$73,800

Laura also knew that she must arrange financing for initial operating expenses since it would take some time for sales to reach the expected level. She listed the following estimated monthly operating expenses:

Table 13-12 Initial Operating Expenses

Item	Expenses (One Month)	Multiply by 3	Expenses (Three Months)
Owner's salary	$2,000	3	$6,000
Other salary	1,200	3	3,600
Rent	2,000	3	6,000
Advertising	500	3	1,500
Supplies	200	3	600
Utilities	550	3	1,650
Accounting	50	3	150
Insurance	100	3	300
Taxes, licenses	300	3	900
Miscellaneous	400	3	1,200
Total monthly expenses	$7,300	3	$21,900

Laura had been advised to have three months of operating expense money available, so she multiplied $7,300 by 3 to come up with $21,900. Her total capitalization plan to open the Fashion Attic would be $73,800 plus $21,900, for a total of $95,700. "That's a lot of money," Laura said to her friend Paula. "I'll certainly have to borrow some money from the bank, so I'll have to make sure the shop's going to be profitable enough to pay back loans."

Laura presented her research to her accountant, Frank Duffy, who helped put together a pro forma income statement.

Table 13-13 Pro Forma Income Statement

THE FASHION ATTIC
Pro Forma Income Statement
For Year Ending December 31, 19—

Sales		$200,000
Cost of goods sold including freight		110,000
Gross profit		$90,000
Operating expenses		
Payroll		
Owner's salary	24,000	
Employee's salary	14,400	
Rent	24,000	
Operating supplies	2,400	
Taxes and licenses	3,600	
Utilities	6,600	
Advertising	6,000	
Insurance	1,200	
Accounting and legal	600	
Miscellaneous	1,860	
Total operating expenses		$84,660
Net profit		$5,340

Using this statement as an operation guideline, Frank cautioned Laura that she should not enter into any loan arrangement that required a payback of more than $5,000 for interest and principal the first year. Using the sales growth projections of 15 percent the second year and 10 percent the third, and allowing a 5 percent increase in operating expenses for each year, Frank roughed in the projections of Laura's income statement.

Table 13-14 Simplified Pro Forma Income Statement—
Second and Third Years

THE FASHION ATTIC
Income Statement

	Second Year	Third Year
Sales	$230,000	$253,000
Cost of goods sold	126,000	139,150
Gross profit	104,000	113,850
Total operating expenses	88,893	93,338
Net profit	$ 15,107	$ 20,512

When the net profits from the first three years of operation are added together, profit estimates indicate that Laura's business should conservatively generate surplus cash of $40,959. This amount of money could be available for debt reduction and retained earnings for future growth.

Frank concluded that the business could comfortably pay back a loan of $15,000 plus interest over this period of time. The terms of the loan should allow a maximum principal reduction of 10 percent, or $1,500, the first year; 40 percent, or $6,000, the second year; and 50 percent, or $7,500, the third year.

Laura wondered whether $25,000 would be enough of a loan to capitalize this new business. Working with Frank they put together a rough calculation based on her previous research:

Total capital needed for opening and reserve	$ 95,700
Cash available from Laura, family, friends	−59,000
Fixture, equipment loan (50% x $20,000)	−10,000
Trade credit for replacement inventory	−10,000
Total capital deficit	$ 16,700

"Close enough," Frank announced. "Laura, assuming that you can get a $15,000 loan, the pro forma balance sheet for the business, on opening, would look similar to this." Frank placed an impressive balance sheet in front of Laura.

Much of what Frank told Laura sounded encouraging. However, it was dependent on getting a loan for $15,000. Laura scheduled another visit with Mrs. Hickham at the bank.

"Laura, as much as I like your business plan, I'm afraid your business does not have enough collateral for the bank to loan you that much money," Mrs. Hickham said. "Can you contribute personal collateral?"

"Well, I still have some stock and some savings left. How much more do I need as collateral?" asked Laura.

Mrs. Hickham made some calculations as she looked at Laura's personal financial statement. "If you would be willing to pledge $10,000 in stock, CDs, and securities as collateral, I will recommend that the loan committee grant you a $10,000 3-year note and a $5,000 line of credit to be renewed annually as long as it is properly handled. Since part of your request includes an operating reserve of $21,900, I don't really expect that you will need to use the line of credit, but it will be available just in case of emergencies."

Laura had hoped to keep some of her stock and assets out of the business, but she realized now that this was part of the risk of being an entrepreneur. Her business plan was good and her confidence level was high. She reached out to shake Mrs. Hickham's hand. "You've got a deal," she said.

Table 13-15   Pro Forma Balance Sheet

THE FASHION ATTIC
Pro Forma Balance Sheet
August 2, 19—

ASSETS		LIABILITIES AND OWNER'S EQUITY	
Current assets		Current liabilities	
Cash	$21,900	Accounts payable	$10,000
Inventory	35,000	Notes payable	2,500
Total current assets	56,900	Long-term liabilities	
Fixed assets			
Fixtures and equipment	20,000	Equipment loan	10,000
Utility deposits	900	Notes Payable	7,500
Leasehold improvements	12,000	Total liabilities	30,000
		Owner's equity	$59,800
Total assets	$89,800	Total liabilities and owner's equity	$89,800

SUMMARY

In starting any business operation, there must be a financial plan to arrange for the purchase of all necessary components. The plan starts with determining a realistic objective of desired profits and calculating what must be purchased to achieve that objective. Determining the amount of inventory needed, the equipment required, and how much money will be necessary to sustain initial operating expenses is done by researching industry sources and talking to suppliers.

Once a total figure is determined, pro forma income statements and balance sheets are used to validate whether or not the business is a good investment and whether it is potentially profitable. These financial statements also show whether or not it is necessary to borrow money or raise money from investors to open the business.

Many business owners will use an accountant to assist in this important decision. Accountants are important to the business owner because they instruct and assist in recording and maintaining proper financial records. However, successful entrepreneurs maintain basic bookkeeping systems themselves and use accountants for advisory consultation, special reports, and tax matters.

VOCABULARY BUILDER

Write a brief description of each word or phrase based on your reading of the chapter.

1. Capitalization
2. Undercapitalized
3. Inventory turnover
4. Leasehold improvements
5. Pro forma financial statements
6. Income statement
7. Balance sheet
8. Fixed asset
9. Current liability
10. Long-term liability
11. Cash flow
12. Accountant

REVIEW QUESTIONS

1. What are the capital assets of a business?
2. What is normally the starting point in determining the financial needs of a business?
3. What causes a business to be undercapitalized?

4. What is the recommended amount of money needed for operating expenses to start a business?
5. What is the difference between an income statement and a balance sheet?
6. Why should a business conduct a cash flow analysis?
7. What is the difference between current and fixed assets? Between current and long-term liabilities?
8. Why should a business use an accountant?
9. Why should a business maintain its own bookkeeping system?
10. What are the six parts of a bookkeeping system?

DISCUSSION QUESTIONS

1. Why is the financial plan such an important part of the overall business plan?
2. How does knowing the inventory turnover of a business help determine its capital needs?
3. What problems might entrepreneurs encounter if they do not conduct a cash flow analysis for their new businesses?
4. If the asset value of a business increases by $2,000 and the amount of liabilities decreases by $1,000, what would be the change in the amount of owner's equity?
5. What would be the net profit of a business that has total sales of $350,000, with a 50 percent markup and operating expenses of 35 percent of total sales?

CRITICAL THINKING

Entrepreneurs often undercapitalize new businesses, believing that they will be able to make quick profits to cover the difference. Suppose an entrepreneur has calculated one-time-only capital needs at $10,000 and estimated monthly operating expense at $3,000. The entrepreneur decides to open the business with only $12,000. The first year's profits are expected to be $30,000. What would you tell this person about the problems he or she may encounter as a result of undercapitalization?

SHORT CASE: CAPITALIZATION— A CAPITAL IDEA

Paula Zelski was excited about the prospect of mass-producing her own line of designer T-shirts. She had produced a limited number, 200, for distribution through three local boutiques that sold them immediately. Now, her phone was ringing with requests for more stock and more designs.

Paula expanded her line from three designs to six and entered into an agreement with Walt Crosby, a manufacturer's representative, to sell her shirts at a 15 percent commission. Her initial plan was to produce and sell 10,000 units, making a net profit of $1.12 per unit. If she could increase her production run to 20,000, the per-unit profit would increase to more than $3 per T-shirt.

She calculated her one-time-only capital needs at $14,500 and projected her average monthly operating expense at $3,200. She had $3,000 in the bank and borrowed $15,000 on a home equity loan. Once all the equipment was installed in her 1,000-square-foot production facility and the initial inventory was purchased, Paula had only one month's operating expenses available in the bank. But outside of that everything looked great. Walt had easily sold the 10,000 units to retailers at the regional fashion show in Chicago.

Paula worked like crazy during the next three months getting the orders out. However, she ran into some difficult cash flow problems because she did a poor job of planning for accounts receivable. Although most of her shipments were made on a cash-on-delivery basis, it still took turnaround time to actually receive payment from the shipping company. She sold to several customers on terms that requested payment within 30 days of receipt of merchandise. The average collection period on these became 60 days.

Paula ran out of money to meet payroll and rent expenses. She also had trouble purchasing extra materials needed to produce the T-shirts consistently. She was forced to borrow additional monies on a short-term basis at a higher rate of interest than her home equity loan.

Eventually Paula collected all that was due and paid all her debts, including the short-term note. The additional interest charges, however, reduced her net profit. Although the profit was slim, the product's reception was excellent. Walt came back from the next show with orders for 18,000 more shirts.

Paula's elation quickly turned to panic as she realized that she did not have enough money to pay for all the materials needed to produce that many units.[1]

Questions

1. What did Paula neglect to do in her initial capitalization plan?
2. What can Paula do now to keep the business going?

---

[1] Case study entitled "A Manufacturer Obtains a Shortsighted Loan" reprinted with permission from book #3511 *Why Enterprises Fail: Avoid the 20 Pitfalls of Running Your Own Business* by James W. Halloran. Copyright 1991 by Liberty Hall Press/TAB Books, a division of McGraw-Hill, Blue Ridge Summit, PA 17294 (1-800-233-1128 or 1-717-794-2191.)

PROJECT CHALLENGE

In your business plan notebook, make a one-time-only capital needs statement for your business idea. You may need to visit someone with experience in the industry that you are pursuing to receive the needed information.

Based on your sales projection, make a pro forma income statement to determine the feasibility of the idea. In addition, see if you can learn the revenue fluctuations of the business to make a monthly cash flow projection. A local Small Business Administration office or a Small Business Development Center will be glad to assist you.

THE BANKER

Unit 3 Case

Rebecca Thomas was reviewing Bill Moye's loan application for his proposed candy-making and distribution company. Rebecca had been a commercial loan officer at First National Bank for a little more than two years. Her primary responsibility was to review business loan applications and make a recommendation to the bank loan committee for approval or disapproval. Her recommendations were based on both careful scrutiny of the business plan and an interview with the applicant.

Rebecca had studied Bill's business plan last evening. Then she had spent the morning interviewing him. She was trying to discover whether Bill had the necessary expertise in candy making as well as the knowledge to run a business. She was pleased to find that Bill had an extensive background in candy making. He had worked for a large confectionery for quite a few years, and he seemed quite confident of his abilities.

Now it was time to see whether Bill's financial proposition was a good risk. New business loans were the toughest part of Rebecca's job. The bank directors were always cautious about new business loans, because so many new businesses often fail. While the bank usually required that a new business loan be 100 percent collateralized by easily liquidated personal assets, there were occasional exceptions when the loan officer was able to convince the committee that the applicant had a very strong business plan. Rebecca knew that Bill's loan would have to be one of those exceptions. Bill did not have enough collateral to fully support his $50,000 loan request.

Rebecca reviewed Bill's personal financial statement shown in Figure C3-1.

Figure C3-1   Personal Financial Statement

ASSETS		LIABILITIES	
Cash on hand	$ 2,500	Notes payable to bank	$ 3,500
Stocks and/or bonds	25,500	Accounts and bills payable	1,200
Real estate—home	70,000	Real estate mortgage	30,000
Automobile	8,500		
Personal assets	20,000		
Total assets	$126,500	Total liabilities	$34,700

Net worth calculation

Total assets	$126,500
Total liabilities	$ 34,700
Net worth (total assets less liabilities)	$ 91,800

The financial plan to start the business called for a total of $75,000. Bill, willing to contribute $25,000 from the sale of his stocks and bonds, was still $50,000 short of his goal.

Rebecca reread the statement to find more possible sources of collateral. She passed over the values listed for Bill's car and personal belongings because they could not be easily converted into cash if the bank had to request that the loan be paid. She did, however, circle the home equity shown on the statement. Bill had listed his home as having a $70,000 value with a $30,000 mortgage loan against it. The $40,000 difference represented equity which, once the house value was appraised, could be used to help secure the loan. The bank could loan up to 80 percent of the equity—$32,000 in this case. Rebecca felt confident that the committee would agree to use the house as collateral, and Bill had indicated that he would agree to that. There was still, however, an $18,000 deficit. Rebecca turned her attention to Bill's pro forma balance sheet shown in Figure C3-2.

Figure C3-2 Pro Forma Balance Sheet

```
                    HOUSE OF SWEETS
                      Balance Sheet
                       July 1, 19—

                                    LIABILITIES AND
         ASSETS                     OWNER'S EQUITY
Current assets                     Current liabilities

Cash                    $15,500    Accounts payable        $   300

Inventory                19,300    Current portion of
                                    long-term debt          16,700
Total current assets      2,200
                                   Total current liabilities 17,000
Fixed assets             37,500
                                   Long-term liabilities    33,300
Total assets             74,500
                                   Total liabilities        50,300

                                   Owner's equity           24,200

                                   Total liabilities and   $74,500
                                    owner's equity
```

Although Bill had planned on $50,000 in equipment and inventory, Rebecca knew that it would not make a good source of collateral since it would be difficult to sell if the need arose. In cases in which the bank had used such goods as collateral it had received only a small percentage of the collateral's listed value in the desperation sale. To find out how much he usually paid for such equipment that had to be sold on quick notice, Rebecca contacted a seller of used candy-making equipment. He told her that about ten percent of the original purchase price was common. Rebecca penciled in a collateral value of $5,000 for inventory and equipment and hoped that the loan committee would agree. She still needed to find $13,000 in collateral for a $50,000 loan.

◆

Next Rebecca reviewed the pro forma income and cash flow statements Bill had prepared. He had been quite thorough, including statements that showed the expected outcome of the business under both best- and worst-case scenarios. Rebecca studied the worst-case scenario to determine the level of risk involved (see Figure C3-3).

Figure C3-3 Pro Forma Income Statement

Pro Forma Income Statement
For Year Ending December 31, 19—

Sales		$250,000
Cost of goods sold		97,000
Gross profit		$153,000
Operating expenses	59,000	
Payroll (including owner)	18,700	
Rent	18,700	
Operating supplies	9,800	
Maintenance	6,700	
Utilities	9,600	
Interest	5,400	
Other	27,500	
Total operating expenses		$136,000
Pre-tax profit		$ 16,300

Based on Bill's most conservative projections, the business would be able to afford a $1,000 per month installment payment, the approximate payment required for a five-year payout of $50,000 at 12.5 percent interest. This would pinch Bill's cash flow a little during the first year; the second and third year projections indicated that by then the payments could easily be met.

◆

Rebecca again reviewed the capital needs statement. She noted approvingly that Bill had put in a reserve fund of $10,000 for unexpected expenses. Looking back at the cash flow statement, she saw no indications that there would be any months of great deficit.

◆

Rebecca assessed the information she had gathered and decided to propose to the loan committee that the bank loan

Bill $40,000 on a five-year note, collateralized by his home equity of $32,000 and business assets of $5,000. She would further recommend that the committee consider extending Bill a $10,000 line of credit to be used on a short-term basis in the event of a cash-flow shortage.

◆

She realized that the committee would have misgivings about issuing a loan to a new business that was less than 80 percent collateralized. She also knew that the bank would benefit from having the use of Bill's deposits of $250,000. Rebecca recognized the risks involved but using her best business judgment, she decided to offer this recommendation. If the business failed, the committee would hold her responsible for suggesting the loan. If the businesses succeeded, they would treat her opinion with even greater respect. Rebecca picked up her pen and wrote "Recommend Approval" on the top page of the application.

(See the following page for case questions.)

Case Questions

1. Do you think the loan committee should accept Rebecca's recommendation? Why or why not?
2. Do you think Bill should accept the loan as recommended, or should he hold out for his original request of a $50,000 long-term note?
3. Do you believe conventional lending institutions are too cautious about making new business loans? Can you think of anything that lending institutions could do to lessen the risks associated with new business loans?

UNIT 4
MANAGING THE SMALL BUSINESS

14 **Forms of Ownership**

15 **Human Resources Management**

16 **Management Control Tools**

17 **Computer Applications**

18 **Small Business Assistance**

14

Forms of Ownership

After mastering the information contained in this chapter, you should be able to:

14-1 Explain the nature of sole proprietorship.

14-2 Discuss the creation of a partnership.

14-3 List the types of partnerships.

14-4 Explain the importance of a partnership agreement.

14-5 Explain how a corporation is created.

14-6 Name and define the five classifications of corporations.

14-7 List the advantages and disadvantages of a sole proprietorship, partnership, and corporation.

sole proprietorship, a business established, owned, and controlled by a single person

QUESTIONS OF OWNERSHIP

A key decision for any entrepreneur is one of ownership of the new business. Will you choose to make a go of it by yourself? Will you establish a business with one or more other people? Or will you decide that you want a business in which many people share ownership?

All of these questions have to do with forms of business ownership. The form of ownership the entrepreneur chooses will have important legal, financial, and personal implications throughout the life of the business. Each form has its own set of advantages and disadvantages. As you read through this chapter, keep in mind the type of business you would like to start some day. Try to determine which form of ownership is right for you.

The three basic forms of business ownership are a sole proprietorship, partnership, and corporation. Which of these is best for the entrepreneur thinking of starting a new business? To answer that question, let's look at the various ownership options in detail. Carefully considering each will help you make the best ownership decision for you and your business.

SOLE PROPRIETORSHIP

Do you want to make a go of it by yourself? If you are willing to be solely responsible for all aspects of a new business, a **sole proprietorship** may be the best form of ownership for you.

Sole proprietorships come in all shapes and sizes. They may be very small businesses with only one employee, the owner. Or an entrepreneur may own a sole proprietorship, but he or she may hire a manager to run the business on a daily basis. Or a sole proprietorship can be a very large business with hundreds of employees. The owner realizes all the profits from the business and assumes responsibility for any losses. In this sense, the owner of a sole proprietorship is truly an entrepreneur.

The sole proprietorship is the most prominent of the three forms of ownership. In fact, more than 95 percent of all businesses in the United States are sole proprietorships. Because of the ease of formation and the almost unlimited control of the business, this form far outnumbers the other two forms of ownership. The very same characteristics that prompt individuals to be entrepreneurs—the desire to control one's own destiny, to achieve freedom from direct supervision, and the potential to achieve profits greater than a salary from someone else—prompt them to choose the sole proprietorship form of ownership.

Formation of a Sole Proprietorship

Of the three forms of ownership, the sole proprietorship is by far the easiest to form. The government exercises very little control over the establishment of new sole proprietorships. Start-up can be immediate and simple, providing you have all the necessary resources—capital, knowledge, and merchandise or a service to sell. You may need to obtain licenses or permits for your particular type of business, such as the license needed to operate a hair salon.

Illus. 14-1

In a sole proprietorship, the owner realizes the profits but also assumes responsibility for the losses.

© *Don Smetzer/Tony Stone Images, Inc.*

One important thing entrepreneurs do need to consider is the selection and registration of the business name. This should be done whether the entrepreneur is forming a sole proprietorship, a partnership, or a corporation. Most states require any business name that doesn't fully include the personal name of the business owner to be registered with a local government agency. For example, take Dana Simpson. Dana has decided to open a video rental store in a small town. She has narrowed the choice of names for the new business down to two possibilities: "Dana's Video" and "Dana Simpson's Videos to Go." If Dana chooses "Dana's Video," the name will have to be registered. On the other hand, if Dana chooses "Dana Simpson's Videos to Go," she can start the new store without registering its name. The difference is that most states require any business name that does not include the full name of the business owner to be registered with a local government agency.

Depending upon the state, entrepreneurs register the name with a county government office or with the Secretary of State's office. It is a very simple process to fill out the necessary form. The advantage of registering a business name is protection. Once the name is registered, it goes into state records and may not be used by anyone else in the state. This protects your future profits by ensuring that you are the sole user of the business name.

Operation of a Sole Proprietorship

Owners of sole proprietorships make all of the decisions regarding the operation of the business. Even though they have the luxury of being the boss, sole proprietors are not exempt from financial risk. They must still obtain the necessary funds to open and run the business, and they must pay taxes.

The assets of entrepreneurs who own sole proprietorships are not considered legally separate from the assets of the business. This means that if the business does not succeed and if any debts remain, the entrepreneur's assets may be taken to pay those debts. Despite this drawback, reporting taxes is fairly simple. Owners of sole proprietorships report the business income and expenses on their personal income tax returns.

Advantages of a Sole Proprietorship

To summarize, some of the advantages of a sole proprietorship are as follows:

- Sole proprietorships are simple to start.
- No formal action is required to establish a sole proprietorship.
- They may be started immediately.
- The owner has total control of all aspects of the business.
- The owner receives all the profit.
- The business itself pays no income tax; the owner pays income tax as an individual.

Disadvantages of a Sole Proprietorship

Listed below are some of the disadvantages of a sole proprietorship.

- The owner has unlimited responsibility for losses, debts, and other liabilities the business might develop.
- The owner must make all the decisions.
- The owner is the only person who can arrange financing or capitalization.
- The existence of the business ends upon the owner's death.

PARTNERSHIP

A partnership, according to the Uniform Partnership Act, is an association of two or more persons to carry on as co-owners of a business for profit. **Partners** with complementary skills or knowledge often team up to form a partnership. For example, a person experienced in manufacturing may form a partnership with an individual with marketing expertise. Entrepreneurs who may have originally wanted to form a sole proprietorship may choose to form a partnership because of the benefits of combined talents and finances.

The Uniform Partnership Act (UPA) has been adopted by almost every state in the nation to provide a degree of uniformity among states concerning partnership laws. Entrepreneurs should check to see if the UPA has been adopted by the state in which their new business is to be located. If it has not, then entrepreneurs should approach the formation of a partnership all the more cautiously. Without the UPA, there are no guidelines to protect entrepreneurs who are seeking to form partnerships.

partners, individuals who voluntarily agree to conduct a partnership

Partnership Agreement

One of the first things that must be done when two or more entrepreneurs are considering a partnership arrangement is to write a

partnership agreement, the official document forming the contract between partners

partnership agreement. Written partnership agreements are not required by law in all partnerships; oral agreements are perfectly legal for some types of partnerships. However, a written agreement is strongly recommended. Many future conflicts can be avoided by defining in writing all important aspects of the partnership. At a minimum, partnership agreements should contain, in detail, the following points:

- name of the business or partnership
- names of the partners
- type of investment of each partner (such as cash, equipment, real estate) and its value
- managerial responsibilities of each partner
- accounting methods to be used
- rights of partners to review and/or audit accounting documents
- information about how profits will be divided and how losses will be shared
- salaries/money to be withdrawn by partners
- duration of the partnership
- information concerning dissolution of the partnership
- how assets will be distributed upon dissolution
- procedure relating to the death of a partner

Figure 14-1 is an example of a partnership agreement.

Illus. 14-2   A partnership is an association of two or more persons working as co-owners of a business.

Figure 14-1   Sample Partnership Agreement

PARTNERSHIP AGREEMENT

We, L. J. Doray, Jake Meyer, and Janet Feldman, do mutually agree to conduct a business as general partners under the fictitious trade name of STYLE 'N SPEED, on the following terms and conditions:

PURPOSE, LOCATION

I The purpose of the business shall be the operation of an automobile body customizing shop to be located in rented quarters at 5500 Auto Row, Atlanta, Georgia.

DURATION, DISSOLUTION

II The partnership shall continue for a period of five (5) years, with the expectation that it will be renewed thereafter for additional five-year periods by unanimous mutual consent. However, any partner may withdraw without liability with ninety (90) days' notice in writing, sent by registered mail to the other partners, with time to commence five (5) days from date of posting. In such event, either or both of the other partners may decide to terminate the business. In the alternative, either or both may elect to continue the business, buying the interest(s) of the withdrawing partner(s) at book value with no allowance for goodwill. Book value shall be determined as of the date of withdrawal, by the firm's certified public accountant. Payment shall then be made in equal monthly installments over a three (3) year period, unless otherwise agreed, with interest at ten (10) percent a year on the unpaid balance. The continuing partner(s) may accelerate the payments at will. In the event of death of any partner, the same terms shall apply.

CAPITAL

III The initial capital shall be the sum of thirty thousand dollars ($30,000) to be contributed in equal amounts by the partners within ten (10) days of this agreement. Additional contributions of no more than ten thousand dollars ($10,000) from each partner may be required by majority vote at any time within one year from this date. Any further contributions of capital shall require unanimous agreement.

DUTIES AUDIT, BANK

IV Doray and Meyer shall work in the shop; Feldman shall run the office, promote sales, make all necessary purchases and disbursements, and keep or supervise . . .

. . . fiscal year by allocating the year's total profit to all working days equally. Any sum thus deducted shall be added to the share of profits of the partner(s) who remained at work on the day(s) in question.

COMMENCEMENT, WORK DAYS

VII Business shall commence on the day this agreement is signed. The work of this partnership shall constitute the full-time, gainful occupation of each of the partners. Unless and until otherwise agreed, the business shall be open from 8:00 a.m. until 6:00 p.m. every weekday. It shall be closed on Saturdays, Sundays, and officially designated federal holidays.

IN WITNESS WHEREOF WE HAVE SET OUR HANDS THIS _____ day of September, 19–.

L. J. Doray   *Jake Meyer*   *Janet Feldman*
L. J. Doray   Jake Meyer   Janet Feldman

Source: Reprinted from Mietus, Adamson, and Fisk, *Applied Business Law,* 12th edition, p. 645. © 1984 by South-Western Publishing Co.

Types of Partnerships

Partnerships may take many forms, but the general partnership and the limited partnership are the most common. Entrepreneurs should be familiar with the characteristics of each.

General Partnership. A general partnership is made up of two or more general partners. A **general partner** is a partner who actively engages in the day-to-day management of the business and is fully liable for any actions for, by, and against the business. General partners are sometimes referred to as "ordinary" or "regular" partners. Partnership agreements are not always required by law for this type of partnership. They are, however, advisable.

Limited Partnership. A limited partnership is made up of one or more general partners and one or more limited partners. A **limited partner** is a partner who does not actively engage in the day-to-day management of the business and has liability limited to the extent of his or her investment in the business. Limited partners are investors in the business. For example, if Marty Junkin wants to be a limited partner in Dana Simpson's business, she is limited in two ways. First of all, Marty could not participate in the day-to-day management of the video store. Secondly, Marty's liability would be limited to the amount invested in the business. If, for example, Marty invested $3,000 in the business, then $3,000 is the maximum amount that she could lose.

In a limited partnership, there must be at least one general partner. This means that there is at least one partner in the business who is both fully liable for losses *and* involved in the daily management of the business.

Unlike the minimal start-up requirements for a general partnership, there must be a partnership agreement in a limited partnership. States generally require that the limited partnership agreement be filed with the state in which the limited partnership is located. Entrepreneurs considering forming a limited partnership should seek the assistance of a competent attorney when writing and filing the limited partnership agreement.

Termination of a Partnership

A partnership may be terminated for any number of reasons. Any time a partner leaves or is added to the partnership, the partnership (as well as any partnership agreement) is terminated. Such circumstances include the following situations.

---

general partner, a partner who actively engages in the day-to-day management of the business and is fully liable for any actions for, by, and against the business

limited partner, a partner who does not actively engage in the day-to-day management of the business and has liability limited to the extent of his or her investment in the business

- Expelling a partner—the partnership agreement may provide for the expulsion of partners under certain circumstances, such as the unauthorized use of funds.
- Adding a partner—if a partner is added, the old partnership is terminated and a new one must be initiated.
- Partners agree to terminate the partnership.

The law also dictates the termination of partnerships under certain circumstances. These include the death, bankruptcy, or insanity of a partner. In addition, a partnership may be terminated if the purpose of the business is determined to be illegal.

Advantages and Disadvantages of Partnerships

Numerous advantages exist for the partnership as a form of ownership. They include the following:

- Start-up can be simple because the law does not always require a partnership agreement.
- The partnership, as an entity, pays no income tax.
- Partners share responsibilities of decision making, management, and capitalizing the business.
- Partners share any and all liabilities.
- Liability is limited in the limited partnership.

Just as there are advantages to the partnership form of ownership, there are also disadvantages. They include the following:

- There is a high percentage of partnership break-ups.
- General partners carry unlimited financial liability (in the general partnership).
- Each general partner carries liability for the errors of his or her partners.
- Partners, potentially, have less control due to shared decision making and shared management.
- Partners must share profits.
- Partnership termination may disrupt business.

CORPORATIONS

A **corporation** is a legal entity created by law. Characteristics of a corporation make it sound like an artificial person. For example, a corporation pays taxes, accrues debt, enters into contracts, can be held liable for negligence, and can make a profit.

corporation, a legal entity created by law

Illus. 14-3 (a and b)   Both large and small corporations are legal entities created by law.

Starting a Corporation

A corporation has to be created by one or more people. The individuals who start the process of incorporation—creating the corporation—are called **promoters.** The promoters file **Articles of Incorporation** with a state agency, usually the Secretary of State. Typically, Articles of Incorporation must contain the following information.

- the name of the proposed corporation
- the promoters' names and addresses
- the address of the corporate office
- an explanation of why the corporation is being formed
- the number of years desired for operation of the corporation (most states allow an indefinite number)
- the names and addresses of people who will direct the corporation

Once the Articles of Incorporation are in order, the promoters pay state taxes required for incorporation. When all requirements have been met, a state official—again, usually the Secretary of State—issues the **charter.** Entrepreneurs should have an attorney file the papers. The cost of incorporation varies from state to state.

Ownership and Management of a Corporation

Ownership of corporations is handled through the possession of stock. Stock represents a share of ownership in a corporation. The

---

promoter, a person who starts the process to create a corporation

Articles of Incorporation, an application asking the state for permission to form a corporation

charter, a document that allows a new corporation to do business in that state

promoters and/or executives of a corporation divide a specified amount of stock into a certain number of shares. People who buy these shares are called shareholders, or stockholders. All shareholders hold partial ownership in the corporation, according to the amount of stock they own.

The amount of ownership represented by one share of stock is determined by the amount of stock issued upon incorporation. If 1,000 shares of stock are initially issued, each share represents 1/1,000 ownership of the corporation. If the initial issue is 50,000 shares of stock, each share represents 1/50,000 ownership. The greater the number of shares of stock issued, the lower the value of each share.

After the charter has been issued for a new corporation, a shareholders' meeting is held. Any person owning stock in a company has the right to attend and vote on issues during this and all future meetings. During the first shareholders' meeting, a board of directors is elected. The board of directors is responsible for electing the senior officers of the corporation, setting their salaries, and deciding the corporation's rules for conducting business.

Classifications of Corporations

Corporations are usually classified in five categories. The categories are domestic, foreign, public, private, and closely held.

Domestic or Foreign. A corporation doing business within the state of incorporation is referred to as a domestic corporation. When employees of the corporation go out of the home state to do business, the corporation is considered a foreign corporation in the other states in which it does business. As an example, consider Leonard, Inc., a business that sells musical greeting cards. It is incorporated in the state of North Carolina. When it does business in North Carolina, it is a domestic corporation. When it does business in Texas, or any state outside of its chartered state, it is a foreign corporation. Foreign corporations sometimes need to obtain permission to do business in other states.

Public or Private. Corporations can be either public or private. Public corporations are incorporated government entities. For example, public utility companies fall into this category.

A private corporation is one owned by one or more individuals. It is, as a rule, more free to operate than public corporations because there are fewer regulations. Entrepreneurs who choose to incorporate form private corporations.

Closely Held. Closely held corporations are similar to private corporations. Closely held corporations are private; the difference is that stock is sold to people other than the promoters, but only on a small scale. Even though the corporate structure is used and shares of stock are issued, there is nothing in corporate law that requires large-scale or public sale of the stock. The promoters may choose to retain all or most of the stock themselves. Some notable examples of closely held corporations are Mary Kay Cosmetics and the Amway Company.

Advantages of the Corporation

Because of the legal structure of corporations, there are numerous advantages to this form of ownership. They are discussed in the following paragraphs.

Limited Liability. This is probably the primary reason many entrepreneurs choose the corporate form of ownership. In many ways it is less risky than other forms of ownership. In the corporation, the shareholders' liability—for debts, taxes, and lawsuits—is limited to the amount of money actually invested in the purchase of stock.

Illus. 14-4   Ben & Jerry's Ice Cream is an example of a closely held corporation (Ben Cohen, Chairperson of the Board, passes his hat to new president and CEO, Robert Holland Jr.).

© Bettmann/Reuters

However, you should be aware that most lenders require a top executive, such as the chief executive officer (CEO), of an incorporated small business to sign both personally *and* as the business owner, so liability may *not* be limited for that individual in some cases.

Ability to Raise Capital. The ability of a corporation to raise additional capital through the sale of stock is a very important advantage of this form of ownership. Lenders are generally more willing to loan money to corporations than to sole proprietorships or partnerships.

Continuity of Business. Unlike the sole proprietorship and partnership, in which business is directly affected by things such as the death or bankruptcy of an owner, the corporation is not directly affected by such occurrences. The business continues to operate and exist regardless of what happens to individual shareholders.

Transferable Ownership. Since shareholders (owners) do not manage the business, ownership can change through the buying and selling of stock without disrupting the day-to-day business of the corporation.

Disadvantages of the Corporation

The legal structure of the corporation can also lead to certain disadvantages. Such drawbacks are discussed in the following paragraphs.

Double Taxation. There are several instances in which individuals are taxed more than once on income generated from a corporation. Functioning as a legal entity, the corporation pays income tax on profits earned. Furthermore, shareholders pay additional income tax on any dividends they receive from the corporation. Employees who are shareholders must, of course, pay income tax on their salaries, so they are taxed one more time. This is a disadvantage especially for a closely held corporation.

Charter Costs. The cost to incorporate a business can be high. There are fees associated with attorneys and state requirements.

Regulation. A corporation is subject to a considerable amount of regulation that does not apply to the sole proprietorship or partnership. Examples include keeping records of board meetings, holding required board meetings, and completing public disclosure reports. A corporation's business activities are also regulated; they may pursue only the business activities stated in the charter. If the owners wish to expand those activities or, in some cases, do business in other states, they must complete the necessary paperwork.

Lack of Control. Ownership in a corporation does not guarantee any control or say in the day-to-day operation of the business. Remember, ownership of stock allows only the ability to vote for the board of directors. The president or CEO actually decides how the business is run. Even if you are a major stockholder, you may not be the president or CEO and, therefore, you may not have much control over the management of the company.

COMPARING FORMS OF OWNERSHIP

Table 14-1 summarizes selected advantages and disadvantages of the three forms of ownership.

Table 14-1 Forms of Ownership—Pros and Cons

Factors of Ownership	Sole Proprietorship	Partnership	Corporation
Simple to start	A	A (except for limited)	D
Liability	D	D (except for limited)	A
Regulation	A	A (except for limited)	D
Ownership control	A	A (except for limited)	D
Initial costs	A	A	D
Ability to raise capital	D	A	A
Taxes	A	A	D

A—This factor is an advantage of this particular form of ownership.
D—This factor is a disadvantage of this particular form of ownership.

THE FASHION ATTIC

When Laura was considering the form of ownership that she wanted for The Fashion Attic, she reflected on one of her original goals in becoming an entrepreneur: independence. She definitely did not want to feel that anyone had control over her. It was one of the things she had disliked about working for a large organization. She began to closely examine the options of sole proprietorship, partnership, and corporation.

The sole proprietorship was the one that would give Laura total control of her business. At the same time, Laura realized that the sole proprietorship had some drawbacks. She would be totally dependent on herself both financially and in all management decisions. She would be the only one responsible if she failed and she would be personally liable for all debts or losses incurred. On the other hand, Laura liked the idea that all potential profits would belong to her and that it would be easy to start a proprietorship with no costs except for the business license.

Laura considered asking her friend Paula if she wanted to become her partner. She could certainly use the money, and Paula also had some valuable experience that would come in handy. They could draw up a partnership agreement, which, if properly done, would prevent legal disputes over any major disagreements. However, Laura had heard numerous stories about how friendships could be ruined over business disagreements, and she was reluctant to do anything that might threaten their relationship. Laura's accountant suggested that she consider having Paula as a limited partner, whereby Laura would have total management control and Paula would have only a financial share. Laura thought the idea was worth considering; however, their friendship might still be in jeopardy if the business failed. Also, Laura didn't think that Paula would agree to making an investment and having to remain a quiet spectator.

Incorporating the business had some advantages—particularly the limited liability feature of a corporation. Laura certainly liked the idea that in the event of a lawsuit or major financial catastrophe, the corporation rather than her personally would be held financially liable. Her accountant recommended that if Laura chose to incorporate, she should form a Sub Chapter S corporation because hers would be a small, closely held corporation with less than 35 stockholders. This would give her some tax advantages as well.

Laura finally decided on a sole proprietorship. It was the choice that gave her the greatest control. It was also the easiest and least expensive option. She could still count on Paula for advice, and, although there was the risk of being personally liable in the event of problems, Laura believed that catastrophic lawsuits related to the operation of a fashion store were rare. Also, her accountant advised her that she could incorporate later, if her business needs changed. In deciding on a sole proprietorship, Laura would be totally responsible for mistakes and successes—just the way she wanted it!

SUMMARY

There are three basic forms of business ownership: the sole proprietorship, the partnership, and the corporation. A sole proprietorship is a business established, owned, controlled, and operated by a single person. The advantages of the sole proprietorship are that it is simple to start, may require no formal action to start, may be started immediately, owners have total control, owners receive all profits, and the business as an entity pays no income tax. Some disadvantages of the sole proprietorship are unlimited responsibility for any losses or debts, owners must make all the decisions, and owners have sole responsibility for capitalizing the business.

A partnership is an association of two or more persons to carry on as co-owners of a business for profit. The two major types of partnerships are general and limited. Some advantages of the partnership form of ownership include the following: It is simple to start; it pays no income tax as a business; partners assist in decision making, management, and capitalizing the business; liability is shared; and liability is limited in a limited partnership. Some disadvantages of the partnership are liability for errors of partners; entrepreneurs must share decision making and management, which may result in less control; partners must share profits; and partnership termination may disrupt the business.

A corporation is a legal entity created by law. Corporations may be domestic or foreign, public or private, or closely held. Some advantages of the corporation include limited liability, little difficulty in raising capital, continuity of business is not tied to individuals, and sale of ownership does not disrupt the business. Some disadvantages of the corporation include double taxation, charter costs, regulation, and lack of control.

VOCABULARY BUILDER

On a separate sheet of paper, write a brief description of each word or phrase based on your reading of the chapter.

1. Sole proprietorship
2. Partnership
3. Partner
4. Partnership agreement
5. General partner
6. Limited partner
7. Corporation
8. Promoters
9. Articles of Incorporation
10. Charter
11. Stock
12. Shares of stock
13. Shareholder

REVIEW QUESTIONS

1. What are the three basic forms of business ownership?
2. What are the two major types of partnerships?
3. What is the difference between a general partnership and a limited partnership?
4. What are the five categories into which corporations may be classified?
5. What advantages are there to forming a corporation?

DISCUSSION QUESTIONS

1. What are the characteristics of a sole proprietorship, including the advantages and disadvantages?
2. What are the characteristics of partnerships, including the advantages and disadvantages?
3. Why is having a written partnership agreement important to the individual partners?
4. What are the characteristics of the corporation, including its advantages and disadvantages?

CRITICAL THINKING

Allen Huang is planning to start a business that manufactures horse trailers. He has two friends who have expressed an interest in the business. One friend knows quite a lot about horse trailers, but the second knows very little.

1. Of the three forms of ownership, which one would you recommend to Allen? Why?
2. Is there a way the second friend could be involved in the business, but with limited liability? How?

3. If Allen decides to go into business with one or both of his friends, what is the first agreement they should negotiate? Do you think it is really necessary, since they are friends?

SHORT CASE: OWNERSHIP— SAFETY IN NUMBERS

Stan Beasley has been working for the past two months on a business plan involving a health club. For most of his life, Stan has been a very successful athlete. In high school he excelled in football and went on to earn a scholarship to a major university. After college he joined a professional team and, for ten years, he was the best defensive safety in the National Football League.

Because the only thing Stan really has any experience in is athletics, he decided that was the best area to pursue for starting a new business. With his tremendous success in the NFL, Stan is independently wealthy.

He doesn't really have to work again, but he thinks he needs to stay busy at something to be happy. Opening a health club seems to be the perfect business since he has been involved in athletic training for many years; after all, he has spent most of his adult life in training. He feels he possesses the level of technical knowledge necessary to start such a business and keep it running.

Stan is at the point in his business planning where he needs to give serious thought to the form of ownership he will use for his new business. As part of his deliberation, he has listed the following points as factors to consider before making the final decision about the form of ownership his business will assume.

1. Capitalization is no problem.
2. I possess technical expertise.
3. Health clubs have experienced great financial difficulty in recent years.
4. Lawsuits against health clubs have been increasing.
5. Several friends (ex-football players) have indicated an interest in participating in some way in the venture.

Stan has a very difficult decision to make. Give him some help by answering the following questions.

1. Should Stan give serious consideration to a sole proprietorship? Explain your answer.
2. There are at least two ways that Stan could involve his friends as owners of the new business. What are they?

3. If you were Stan, what would be your primary area of concern in relation to form of ownership?
4. What form of ownership would you recommend to Stan? Why?

PROJECT CHALLENGE

Now it is time for you to decide what form of ownership will be the best for your hypothetical business. Make this decision only after careful deliberation.

1. List at least five aspects of your hypothetical business that would be considerations in your decision about the form of business ownership.
2. Take the list from question #1 and rank the items in order of importance.
3. Choose two forms of ownership that are possibilities for your business. List the advantages and disadvantages of each form, being specific about your hypothetical business.
4. Choose your form of ownership and list the two most important reasons why you chose it.

15

Human Resources Management

After mastering the information contained in this chapter, you should be able to:

15-1 Explain the importance of an organization chart.

15-2 Explain how small businesses recruit efficient personnel.

15-3 Describe how small business owners direct and motivate employees.

15-4 Understand the importance of listening.

15-5 List and explain some of the laws that govern employment.

The successful entrepreneur knows the importance of having the right personnel. Capital, equipment, and inventory are resources that are essential to success, and so are people—they are the human resources. Without the right personnel, a business will flounder. Finding and keeping good employees requires competent performance of three management functions—staffing, directing, and controlling.

STAFFING

Staffing begins with determining how much money is available for personnel. Entrepreneurs use sales projections as guides for purchasing initial inventory and equipment. They also use sales projections to determine how to staff the business. Entrepreneurs should first determine how much money is available to pay employees, perhaps by checking with industry sources to find the percent of sales revenues normally available for payroll expenses and multiplying their own projected revenues by that percentage. This process will establish an approximate amount to use as a guide. The next step is to find out how much other businesses are paying for similar help. This information will help determine how much employees should be paid. Then the approximate payroll cost, including employer-paid taxes, should be calculated for each potential employee. This amount is subtracted from the amount available.

After entrepreneurs have determined how much money is available for personnel, they must decide how many employees are needed. The type of business will determine what skills are needed to effectively serve customers. Before staffing a business, the owner must carefully analyze the business's needs by means of an organization chart.

The Organization Chart

An **organization chart** is a picture of a business's distribution of its human resources. It identifies the positions in the organization and the general work responsibilities of each. The names of the individuals who hold the positions are added to the chart as they join the business. The organization chart should show primary job responsibilities. Organization charts are both planning tools and management tools (see Figure 15-1).

organization chart, an illustration of an organization's distribution of its human resources

Figure 15-1   Organization Chart for a Small Retail Store

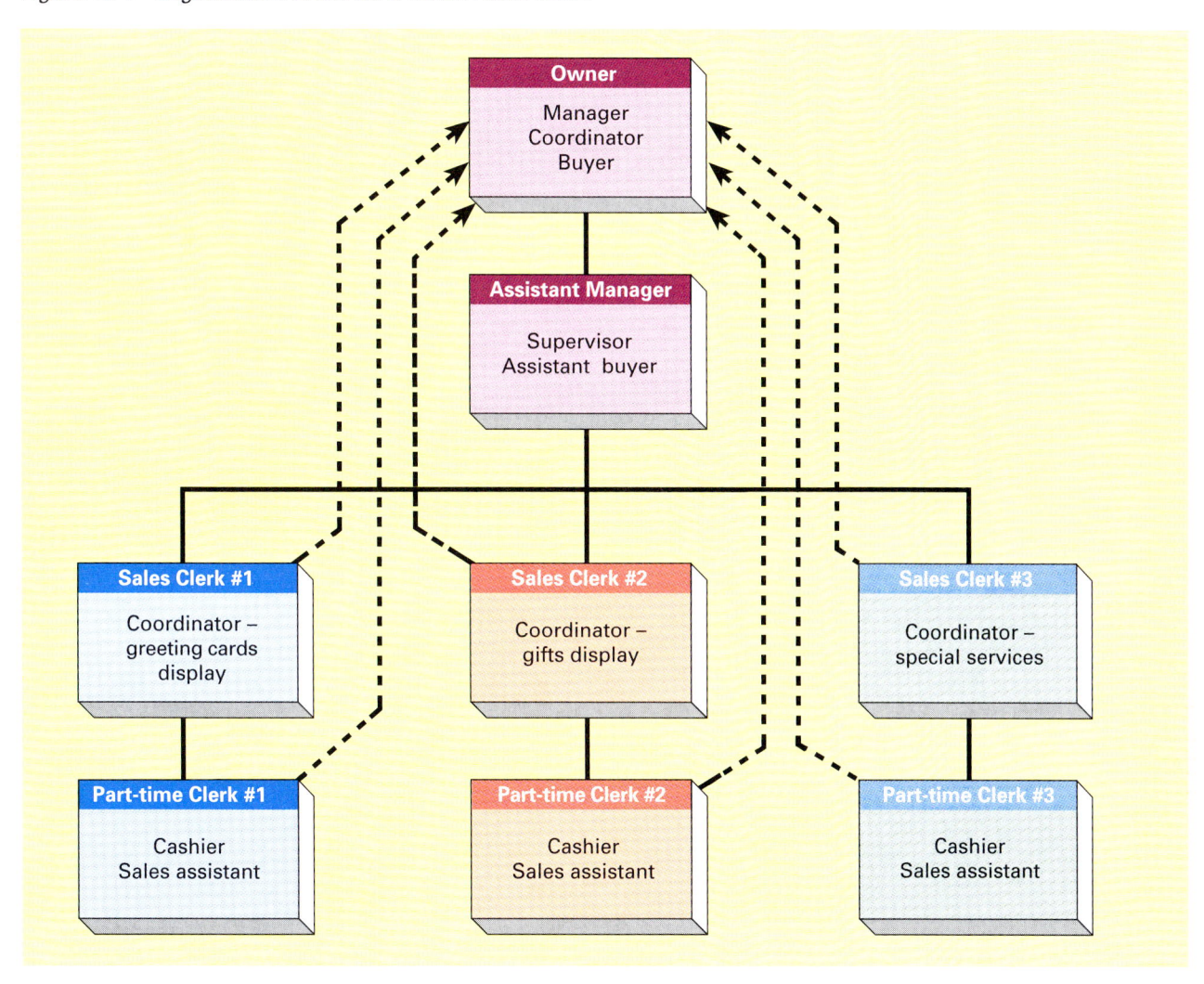

Owner
Manager
Coordinator
Buyer

Assistant Manager
Supervisor
Assistant buyer

Sales Clerk #1
Coordinator –
greeting cards
display

Sales Clerk #2
Coordinator –
gifts display

Sales Clerk #3
Coordinator –
special services

Part-time Clerk #1
Cashier
Sales assistant

Part-time Clerk #2
Cashier
Sales assistant

Part-time Clerk #3
Cashier
Sales assistant

chain of command, the reporting relationship of positions depicted on the organization chart

line organization, an organization in which all members are involved in performing duties directly related to creating and/or selling products or services

line and staff organization, an organization that has staff positions to assist the line functions

The lines on the chart indicate reporting relationships. It is important to include specific instructions about who oversees whom, or the **chain of command.** As Figure 15-1 shows, the solid lines indicate formal reporting relationships. The broken lines indicate that in small businesses all employees have direct access to the manager. Illustrating supervisory relationships in graph form eliminates confusion.

Management uses the organization chart to identify the positions that must be filled and the skills needed for each. It is an important part of the business planning process because it gives business owners a clear picture of their personnel needs. To identify the positions to be filled, entrepreneurs need to determine what type of organization the business is.

Small businesses are normally characterized as **line organizations.** A line organization's mission is to create and sell the products or services. Larger organizations, characterized as **line and staff organizations,** may have, for example, a personnel manager, safety officer, and company accountant to assist the line employees who perform the work involved with creating and selling the products or services. One staff position that is often found in a small business is that of bookkeeper.

Illus. 15-1 A common staff position often found in a small business is that of bookkeeper.

Photo by Alan Brown/Photonics

The organization chart is also a very important tool for employees. All employees have the right to know what their areas of responsibility are, to whom they must report, and what other positions they may pursue within the organization. If this information is not readily available, employees may not be motivated to do their best work, and morale—as well as productivity—may suffer. No matter how large or small the organization, an organization chart should be established as a reference tool for management and employees.

Too many small businesses overlook this tool, believing that because their organizations are small their employees automatically know what is expected of them. It is usually not that clear, however, particularly in a small business in which responsibilities may overlap. As is the case in most areas of small business management, personnel management must ensure a great deal of flexibility. A flexible staff is essential if all employees are to carry out their business activities efficiently.

Recruiting

Finding and recruiting the right employees for a new business is a difficult task. Entrepreneurs usually have capital limitations that can make the task even more difficult. Because they have limited capital, small business owners—and especially *new* small business owners—cannot always offer the same wages or salaries to prospective employees as large businesses can. The benefit packages they can offer may not be as lucrative as those offered by large businesses, which often offer incentives such as well-funded profit sharing plans, comprehensive insurance packages, and paid vacations. For these reasons, small business owners are often forced to hire less-experienced individuals. This obstacle can, however, be overcome and in some cases, works to the business owner's benefit. With efficient training, these employees can attain desired skill levels and perform the same functions as employees who join a company with prior training.

How do small business owners find and recruit quality personnel? The first step is to decide how to "shop" for applicants.

Classified Advertisements. Placing ads in the help wanted sections of local newspapers is usually an effective method of attracting large numbers of applicants. A descriptive ad should list job requirements, such as education or previous experience, as well as the responsibilities of the open position. Resumés should be requested from applicants in addition to cover letters. It is sometimes helpful to ask that specific information be included in the cover letter, such as salary requirements, date of availability, or other pertinent information. For those who do not wish to disclose the business's name, many newspapers offer mailbox facilities for use in conjunction with their classified ads. The business owner can then screen the resumés to determine which applicants are worth interviewing.

Employment Agencies. Employment agencies keep records of people who are looking for work and their qualifications. Seeking applicants through an employment agency saves some of the time involved in screening applicants, but the cost is much higher than that of classified advertising. Employment agencies charge a fee from either applicants or employers, or sometimes both.

College Placement Services. Many colleges offer a no-charge placement service. Placement departments keep records of students and alumni who are looking for work and their qualifications.

In-Store Advertising. Posting a sign in the business's window might attract pedestrians or motorists. When using this method, business owners have two options. They may either have applicants complete applications and inform them that they *may* be called for an interview, or have them complete applications and interview the applicants

Illus. 15-2 College career fairs offer entrepreneurs one means of finding employees.

Courtesy, University of Cincinnati

immediately. The first option allows the business owner to do some initial screening of the applicants. The second option requires the business owner to interview all applicants. This often means dedicating several days to interviewing alone, knowing that not much other work will get done during those days.

Referrals. An entrepreneur's friends or employees are often good sources of referrals. If the entrepreneur considers the person who is making the recommendation reliable, a referral may require very little screening. However, many business owners are reluctant to hire people related to, or too closely affiliated with, other employees. This practice is risky—there is a possibility of alienating one at the expense of the other, creating conflicts within the organization, or losing two employees if one decides to leave or must be let go.

Regardless of the methods used, it is to the business owner's advantage to attract a large number of applicants. Having more people to choose from allows more opportunity to be selective and find the *right* person.

Applications

Tailoring an employment application to a specific business is a good idea. By using a tailored application, business owners gather specific information that might not be included on a resumé, and they can use that information to decide what to ask during the interview.

Interviewing

Once job descriptions are written and candidates have been selected, the interview process can begin. As with any interview, the interviewer should plan carefully and have a written list of questions. A lot of information must be gathered in a relatively short period of time, and it is easy to get caught up in conversation and forget to ask important questions.

Interviews should be held in a quiet, relaxing environment. When conducting the interview, the business owner should focus on the applicant's personal characteristics with regard to teamwork and cooperation. Two characteristics to look for in applicants are a positive attitude and reliability. Skills are important, but, if they are inadequate, they can normally be taught; personal characteristics cannot. The discussion should enable the interviewer to determine whether the applicant will do well in the team environment of a small business.

In many cases, more than one interview will be needed before the final decision can be made. If the interview indicates that the applicant is right for the position, the business owner should take time to fully explain the job, show the applicant the operation, and give the applicant good reasons for joining the team. Following is a list of ways that a small business owner might appeal to a prospective employee.

- Appeal to the excitement of participating in a new venture. Many people prefer to work in an environment where they are able to see the outcome of their work. Employees of small businesses know their contributions are important to the operation of the business. They have strong self-actualization needs. For these people, working for a small business is worth a possible sacrifice of financial benefits.
- Tell potential employees how much the company needs them. By being direct about this, the business owner helps them visualize the roles they will play. They will understand that they will be direct participants in the business's activities.
- Share your values with the applicant. If it is clear that the goal is to create an ethical and responsible business, the employee will feel proud to be a part of the organization.
- Create an environment of flexibility and caring, and be sure to describe that environment to potential employees. Small businesses should not need to enforce the rules that are necessary in businesses that have many employees. Explain that the management understands that additional time off is sometimes required for family responsibilities. The owner should give the applicant the impression that there are many benefits to working in a friendly, informal environment.
- Establish a bonus system whereby employees benefit from the success of the company. Emphasize that if the business does well, the employees will benefit financially. When extra profits are generated, employees should receive bonuses in recognition of their contributions.

New employees should be hired on a probationary basis for a certain period of time—four to six weeks is common. Both parties must clearly understand that if either party is dissatisfied at the end of this period, the relationship will be terminated. Specific reasons for termination should be reviewed by emphasizing the importance of teamwork. Tardiness, dishonesty, unreliability, and poor attitude disrupt the activities of all and cannot be accommodated in a small business.

Thorough interviewing is important, because training new employees is expensive. An employee in training is not usually able to produce at full speed, and neither is the trainer. Therefore, two employees are performing at below-normal levels for a certain period of time, which ultimately results in added payroll expenses. If the interview and selection process is inadequate, the payroll expense will be high. There will be excessive turnover of employees and, therefore, a continual need for training.

DIRECTING

Once the business is staffed, efficient management is necessary to keep valuable employees. The business owner's success in keeping an efficient team together will depend on leadership abilities and management skills. Successful small business owners understand that they lead by example. A small business does not have an "ivory tower" where the boss sits and looks down on the employees. The boss is right in the middle of things, participating with the workers. If the boss is not willing to pick up the trash, employees won't be either.

Illus. 15-3

Employee teamwork is critical to the success of the business.

© *Daniel Bosler/Tony Stone Images, Inc.*

Motivating

The owner, as instructor and organizer, decides what must be done—a planning function—and how it will be done, a directing function. Enthusiasm for the work—and efficiency in completing that work—are dependent on employers' abilities to motivate employees. Good instructors are patient when giving instructions. They do not expect students to do the impossible, but they do expect students to do their best. By allowing plenty of time and creating a proper learning environment, the business owner can supply the employee with the tools needed for good performance. This requires coordination and attention to detail. The ability to give directions and assign tasks is one ingredient of success. Just as important is the owner's ability to continually motivate employees to do their best.

Management Styles

Douglas MacGregor, a professor of industrial administration at the Massachusetts Institute of Technology, observed two distinct management styles that he termed Theory X and Theory Y. He defines **Theory X managers** as those who direct with little consideration for human relations. They are very task oriented and are most concerned with being sure assigned jobs are completed in the most expedient manner. They operate under the assumption that workers prefer to be directed and do not wish to take on responsibility. They also believe that workers do not like work, and that getting paid is the prime motivation for their presence in the workplace.

Theory Y managers are very concerned about human relations. They direct under the presumption that workers like their work and enjoy responsibility. They believe that if given the opportunity, people will use their creativity and intellectual capabilities.

Effective managers operate under a Theory Y philosophy. They realize that, to build an effective team and accomplish all the work on hand, workers must receive satisfaction from the job itself and not just from the pay received.

This theory is reinforced by a study of job satisfaction factors made by Frederick Herzberg in 1959. The results of his study showed that worker enthusiasm is created by the following job satisfaction factors, ranked in order.

1. Sense of achievement
2. Recognition for achievement
3. Interest in the work itself
4. Opportunity for growth

> **Theory X manager,** a manager who directs with little consideration for human relations
>
> **Theory Y manager,** a manager who is very concerned with human relations

5. Opportunity for advancement
6. Responsibility
7. Peer and group relationship
8. Compensation
9. Supervisor fairness
10. Reasonable company policies and rules
11. Status
12. Job security
13. Supervisor friendliness
14. Good working conditions

This study clearly showed that employees are most concerned with job contentment. They prefer an environment that allows a sense of achievement and personal growth. They desire recognition for accomplishments and enjoy working with others who have similar goals.

Herzberg went on to separate job-related factors into two categories—**motivators** and **hygiene factors.** Motivators in the work environment include the following:

- The work itself
- Achievement
- Recognition
- Responsibility
- Growth and advancement

motivator, a work environment factor that provides workers with satisfaction and motivation

hygiene factor, a work environment characteristic needed to ensure job satisfaction

Illus. 15-4 *Supervisor friendliness helps create worker enthusiasm.*

Herzberg identified the following as hygiene factors:

- Salary
- Supervision
- Company policies
- Interpersonal relationships
- Working conditions

Workers will perform their assigned duties in a satisfactory manner when the hygiene factors are present, but if management expects peak performance, the workplace must also offer the motivators.

Many small businesses can offer a combination of Theory Y management and Herzberg's motivators better than large organizations can. Because of their size, large organizations must generally rely on rigid company policies and structured supervision to control operations. small business managers can work with all employees and instill a sense of involvement, achievement, and challenge.

CONTROLLING

The controlling function is often the most difficult function of human resources management to master. To excel in this function, business owners must constantly consider employees' roles in the business.

Listening

Employees who are in line positions work directly with the customers, and often with suppliers. A good manager listens to employees because employees know what customers want and expect. Entrepreneurs will better serve their markets if they are open to suggestions from employees.

Small business owners should seek input from the people they work with and include them when setting goals. Large businesses, of necessity, tend to set objectives from the top down; upper management sets sales goals and company policies often without direct employee input. Decisions made without collecting information from the people most affected—the employees—forces new policies on the employees, which hurts organization morale. The small business owner, who works closely with employees, should always get direct input from them before making important decisions. For example, a retail store owner who is considering adding a new product line should ask sales personnel for suggestions since they work with the customers daily. The same is true for a business owner who wants to make an accurate sales forecast. Asking sales personnel what they think is happening in the market and listening to their responses enables business owners to make better predictions about future growth.

If decisions are made at the top of the organization without valuable employee input, problems arise for employees at the lower levels of the structure. For example, when ABC company, a large organization, sets its sales goals for the upcoming year, they are typically set from the top down. The president of the company reports the results of the past year to the Board of Directors and awaits a response. If the company achieved a five-percent increase the previous year, the response might be to try for a six-percent increase in the coming year. The president, not wanting to disappoint the board, agrees to accept the challenge. He meets with the vice president of sales and sets a goal for a seven-percent increase—he wants to be sure that he will look good to the Board of Directors even if the sales team misses the mark. The vice president meets with the regional sales managers and sets their objective as an eight percent increase, using the same protective strategy the president did. The regional sales managers relay a nine percent sales increase objective to the district managers, who, using the same safety valve strategy, relay a ten percent sales increase objective to the sales personnel. In this case, the original goal has almost doubled by the time it reaches the unfortunate sales representatives. During the coming year, pressure to reach the objective will build, particularly for the sales representatives, who have received the most difficult assignment. This is top-down management; managers neither listen nor request information from the bottom-up as shown in Figure 15-2.

Business owners should obtain information from the customer contact level before making decisions. Most small business owners find that they are most successful when they are willing to listen.

Performance Evaluations

Large businesses usually have an elaborate system for appraising employees' work. This system often requires rating employee performance in selected areas of responsibility such as dependability, punctuality, attitude toward job and coworkers, and, sometimes, an analysis of success in achieving predetermined objectives. The ratings are used to let the employees know how their supervisors perceive their performance. They also serve as useful management control tools because they provide a means of determining whether

Unit 4 Managing the Small Business

Figure 15-2 Top-Down Goal Setting

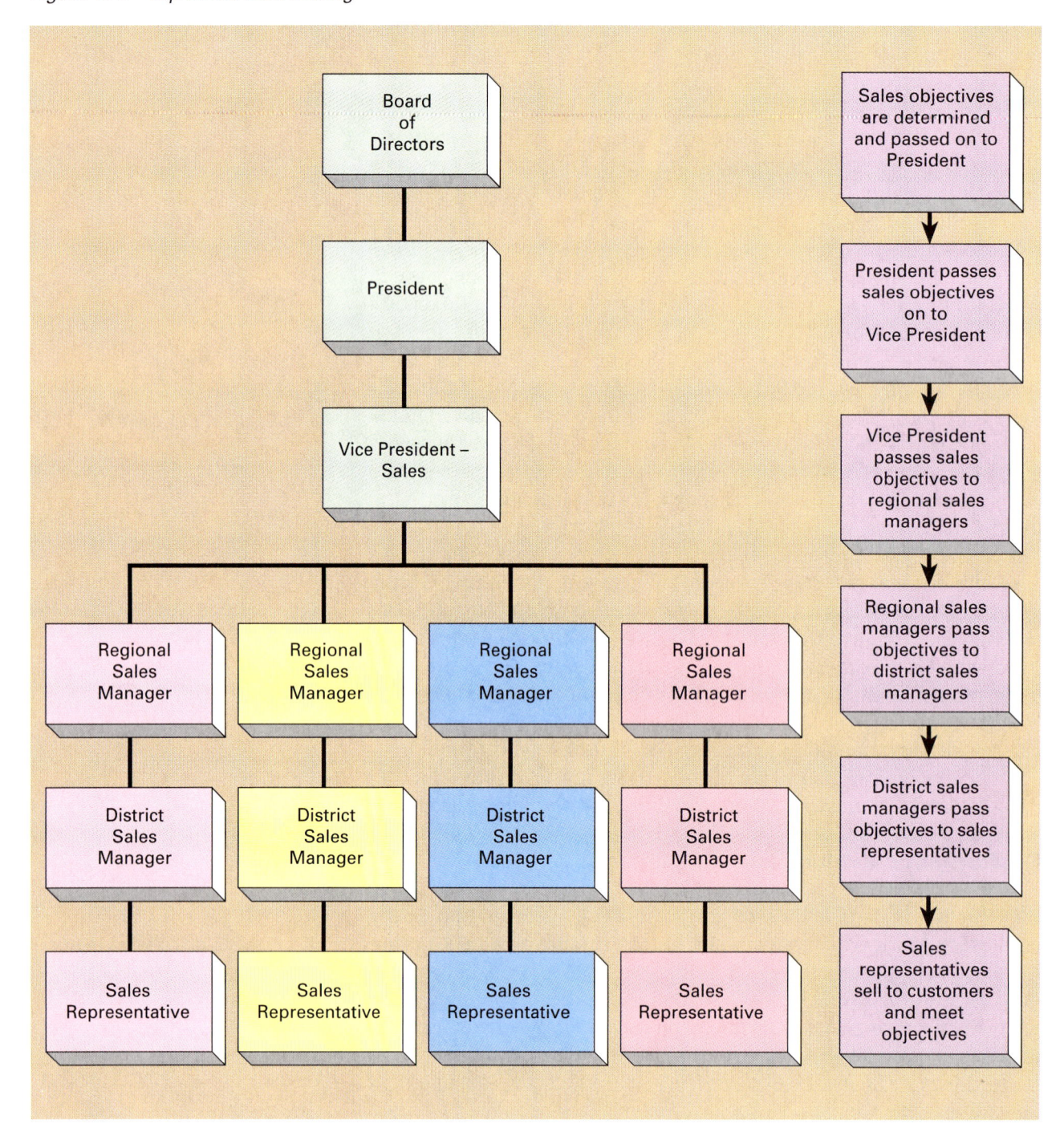

the objectives for a particular job are being met. Performance evaluations are conducted at regular intervals, usually every 6 or 12 months. They are an important management tool and should be utilized in every business.

Small business owners must realize the value of listening to employees during their evaluations. Evaluations are most productive when conducted away from the business, allowing employer and employee an uninterrupted amount of time to share thoughts about the direction of the business. Results can be reviewed and new objectives set in a nonthreatening way that proves helpful to all. Employees need to know how their employers feel about their performance.

Employee evaluations provide an excellent opportunity for praise and, when necessary, suggestions for improvement. Small business owners must devise employee evaluation plans. These plans may differ considerably from those of a large business. The best system does not use rankings or ratings—it uses comments. A list of the areas to be discussed should be prepared ahead of time, with space to record comments made during the discussion. It is important that employer and employee ultimately agree about the comments and the objectives set for future work performance. Clearly stating work objectives makes it easy to determine what has or has not been achieved. A good employee evaluation session focuses on positives rather than negatives. Figure 15-3 is an illustration of an effective evaluation form for a small business employee.

LABOR LAWS

Entrepreneurs who plan to hire other people must learn the regulations that protect them and their employees from unfair labor practices. There are many laws, and new ones are constantly being added, so the business owner must keep up with legislative activities that concern employment.

Small businesses can be susceptible to personnel trouble because often the person doing the hiring is *not* a trained personnel specialist. That is why familiarity with these laws and their provisions is important. Without the necessary knowledge, small business owners may infringe upon applicants' or employees' rights without knowing it. The five laws listed below are the ones with which every business owner *must* be familiar.

Figure 15-3   Employee Evaluation Form

Jan's Shoe Emporium
Employee Evaluation

Employee Name _____ Date _____

1. Employee's personal evaluation of his or her work accomplishments:

   Employer's comments:

2. Employee's personal evaluation of the company's overall performance, including areas that could be improved upon:

3. Employee's specific comments regarding: (a) employee morale, (b) customer relations, (c) policies and procedures:

4. Manager comments as to employee's contribution toward goals:

   Employee's comments, including points on which he or she agrees or disagrees:

5. Goals agreed upon for future development of the company:

- The Fair Labor Standards Act of 1938 established a minimum wage and required overtime pay for employees working in excess of 40 hours per week.
- The Civil Rights Act of 1964 prohibited discrimination based on sex, race, color, religion, or national origin.
- The Age Discrimination in Employment Act of 1967 prohibited personnel practices that discriminate against people aged 40 to 60. An amendment outlaws company policies that require employees to retire before age 70.
- The Occupational Safety and Health Act (OSHA) of 1970 ensures workers in the United States a healthy and safe working environment by regulating exposure to hazardous substances and setting requirements for safety equipment.
- The Immigration Reform and Control Act of 1986 requires employers to check identification for employees hired after 1986 to ensure that they are legal citizens of the United States.

Illus. 15-5 Owners of small businesses must be aware of the legal rights of applicants and employees.

Courtesy, International Business Machines Corporation

These laws and others are regulated by the Equal Employment Opportunity Commission (EEOC) a government agency established by Congress in 1972.

THE FASHION ATTIC

Laura turned her attention to how many employees she would need to help operate her shop. She began by projecting a payroll budget. Advice from industry representatives and her secondary research told her that no more than 10 percent of projected income should be used for payroll. Since Laura's most conservative projection was $200,000 in sales, she decided to allocate $20,000 (10 percent) for payroll expenses. She had also learned that the average hourly starting wage for the industry was the required minimum wage of $4.25 per hour. Laura decided that she would start her employees at the minimum wage and give them a $.25 raise after successful completion of a 30-days probationary period. By dividing the amount she could spend—$20,000—by the wage she planned to offer—$4.50 per hour—she determined that she could pay for 4,444 hours per year. She divided the 4,444 hours by 52 weeks to determine that she could pay for 85 hours per week. Allowing for employer-paid payroll tax expenses, Laura decided to hire one full-time employee (40 hours) and two part-time employees at 20 hours each, for a total of 80 hours. She then drew up her organization chart (see Figure 15-4).

Laura decided to advertise the positions in the Help Wanted section of the local newspaper, and she also called the placement office of the local community college. She was delighted to receive more than 20 responses to her classified advertisement and the placement office recommended five candidates. All of the candidates from the placement office seemed qualified. She screened the advertisement responses, found that she had five more candidates, and scheduled ten interviews for a two-day period. She planned to allow one hour for each interview.

Laura decided to ask the applicants to come to the shop, where she would be setting up fixtures and displays. She would show them the shop, then invite them to join her for coffee or a soft drink at the restaurant across the mall.

Six of the applicants Laura interviewed were very appealing. They each had the necessary qualifications plus a neat appearance and good attitude. As it turned out two of the six were eliminated due to scheduling conflicts, and one was not satisfied with the starting pay. In the end, Laura's new team would consist of Valerie, who had three years of retail experience, as the full-time employee; Cathy, a college student majoring in fashion merchandising; and Gina, a high school senior. Laura was pleased with the team. Its members represented three different backgrounds that would appeal to three different kinds of customers. Training sessions would begin three days before the grand opening.

Figure 15-4   Fashion Attic Organization Chart

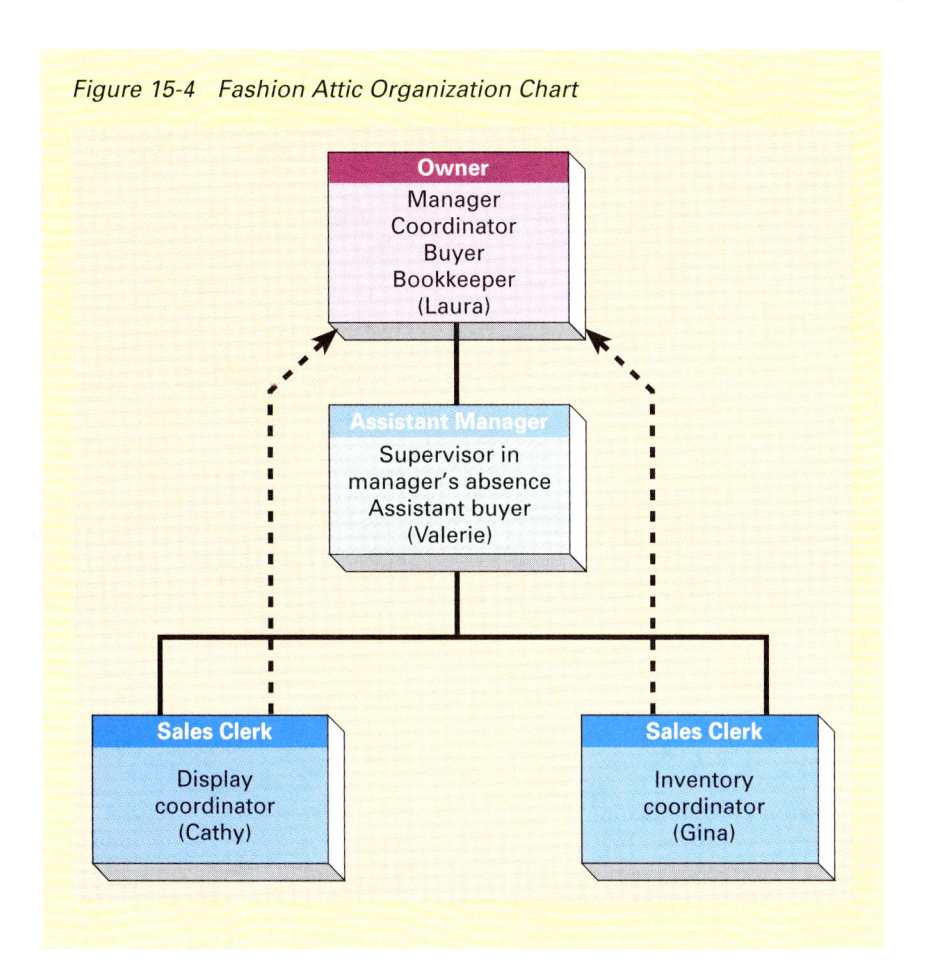

```
                    ┌─────────────────────┐
                    │       Owner         │
                    │      Manager        │
                    │    Coordinator      │
                    │       Buyer         │
                    │     Bookkeeper      │
                    │      (Laura)        │
                    └─────────────────────┘
                              │
                    ┌─────────────────────┐
                    │  Assistant Manager  │
                    │    Supervisor in    │
                    │  manager's absence  │
                    │   Assistant buyer   │
                    │      (Valerie)      │
                    └─────────────────────┘
                              │
                 ┌────────────┴────────────┐
        ┌────────────────┐         ┌────────────────┐
        │   Sales Clerk  │         │   Sales Clerk  │
        │     Display    │         │    Inventory   │
        │   coordinator  │         │   coordinator  │
        │     (Cathy)    │         │     (Gina)     │
        └────────────────┘         └────────────────┘
```

SUMMARY

Entrepreneurs must realize the importance of creating a well-coordinated team of employees that are well schooled in creating and/or selling the product or service. Creating a good team is achieved through effective leadership in a challenging and responsive environment. Entrepreneurs who are good managers participate with employees as coworkers, not exclusively as supervisors.

Developing an effective team requires creating an organization chart that clearly defines all positions, responsibilities, and reporting relationships. Small business owners must interview candidates carefully and train employees well. They must stay within budget guidelines when deciding how many people to employ.

Once the team is in place, the owner must be a skillful manager. Use of proper employee evaluation procedures and the ability to listen are essential. Employers can motivate employees by letting them know they are integral parts of the business and allowing them to assume challenging responsibilities. Finally, entrepreneurs must be familiar with the laws that govern employment.

VOCABULARY BUILDER

On a separate sheet of paper, write a brief definition of each word or phrase based on your reading of the chapter.

1. Staffing
2. Organization chart
3. Chain of command
4. Line organization
5. Line and staff organization
6. Directing
7. Theory X manager
8. Theory Y manager
9. Motivator
10. Hygiene factor
11. Controlling

REVIEW QUESTIONS

1. How do entrepreneurs determine how much money to allocate to payroll expenses for new businesses?
2. What is the purpose of an organization chart?
3. What do the connecting lines on an organization chart represent?
4. What effect might capital limitations have on the recruiting process?
5. What are five methods of finding potential employees?
6. In what ways can a small business owner interest potential employees?
7. Why are inadequate interviewing and employee selection methods expensive for small business owners?
8. What is the difference between a Theory X manager and a Theory Y manager?

9. What are the two kinds of job satisfaction factors and what effects do they have?
10. With what five labor laws should small business owners be familiar?

DISCUSSION QUESTIONS

1. What can happen in a business that does not have an organization chart?
2. What are some of the advantages of working for a small business? What are some disadvantages?
3. Have you ever worked for a Theory X manager? A Theory Y manager? Relate your experiences to the class.
4. What aspects of a job do you consider motivators? Hygiene factors? Does your list differ from Herzberg's?
5. Do you think minimum wage laws can cause increases in the cost of living? Why or why not? Could minimum wage laws affect job availability for certain groups of people (e.g., teenagers)?

CRITICAL THINKING

Grades are a form of performance evaluation. Are you glad you receive grades? What changes do you think could be made to improve your school's grade reporting system? Write a description of a better reporting method or form and explain the changes that you are suggesting.

SHORT CASE: INCONSISTENT MANAGEMENT

"I think you will find this store an enjoyable place to work, Susan. What we can't provide in wages we more than make up by providing a comfortable environment. I try to be as flexible as possible. Come with me, and I'll introduce you to Sharon and Jim. They'll be showing you the ropes."

Roger felt good about his new employee. It seemed likely that she would stay for a while, not the usual two or three months. He was anxious to get her trained.

Susan was happy to have found a nice store to work in that was not far from her home. Roger seemed sincere and she thought it was going to work out well.

Sharon and Jim were cordial, but somewhat reserved. They taught her the cash register procedures and explained the inventory control system. After two weeks, Susan felt comfortable with her assignments, but she still felt like an outsider with Sharon and Jim. She learned that although they liked the store and the customers, they were fearful of Roger's moods. Some days he was easygoing, but other days he was very temperamental and impulsive.

Susan's first encounter with one of Roger's mood swings occurred when she was at the cash register writing a ticket for a customer refund. "Who told you to write the ticket that way?" Roger demanded.

"Jim did," Susan answered.

"Well it's all wrong. Doesn't he know anything? I'll go talk to him. Meanwhile, please pick up that paper on the floor. This place looks like a pig sty." Roger abruptly took the refund ticket, went directly to Jim, and reprimanded him in front of a customer.

After this incident, Jim and Sharon accepted Susan. They often complained to each other about their boss's erratic behavior. Jim often vented his frustrations. "I will *not* be treated that way. When he is in one of those moods, I'm staying out of his way. I'll spend time in the stockroom, or say that I'm sick and leave early."

It wasn't long before Roger lost his temper and fired Jim. His replacement lasted less than two weeks; he was also fired on one of Roger's bad days. Sharon and Susan started looking for new jobs because they never knew when their turn might come. Susan didn't want to leave, but living with such inconsistency was causing anxiety—both on the job and off.[1]

Questions

1. What management style is Roger exhibiting in his bad moods?
2. What effect is Roger's inconsistency having on the production and payroll of his business?
3. What can Susan do about her situation?

PROJECT CHALLENGE

Develop a human resources plan for your hypothetical business. In your business plan notebook, write the decisions you make about the following issues.

1. Determine how many employees you will hire.
2. Create an organization chart.
3. Write a job description for each position. Include areas of responsibility. Determine whether all positions are line positions.
4. Decide how much you will pay your employees.
5. Decide how you will find and recruit your employees.
6. Describe your intended management style.

---

[1]From James Halloran, *Why Entrepreneurs Fail: Avoid the 20 Pitfalls of Running Your Own Business* (Blue Ridge Summit, PA: Liberty Hall Press/TAB Books, a division of McGraw-Hill, 1991).

16
Management Control Tools

In Chapter 15 we discussed how employee performance evaluations act as management tools to monitor progress toward stated objectives. There are many tools managers can use in all aspects of operating small businesses to ensure that employees meet objectives in a timely and efficient manner. Entrepreneurs must make sure that their businesses are operating as planned in terms of sales, inventory control, financial responsibilities, and operating procedures.

MANAGEMENT BY OBJECTIVES

By clearly stating the goals of the business and meshing them with the goals of the employees, entrepreneurs make use of a management technique called **management by objectives** (**MBO**). MBO serves as a planning tool when the objectives are being set, and as a control tool when the results are monitored and measured. Objectives should be set in all areas of business operations to ensure that resources are used efficiently. The planning function—setting objectives—should follow the steps shown in Figure 16-1.

The control function—monitoring results—can only be effective if the standards to measure against are fairly and uniformly established. Properly set measuring standards will allow an effective feedback system that will be consistent and clearly understood by all concerned. Figure 16-2 illustrates the steps involved in the controlling function of an MBO technique.

Both large and small businesses benefit from the MBO technique. Entrepreneurs must tailor a system to their particular businesses that fairly establishes and monitors their objectives. It is not enough just to announce what you expect to be achieved in a particular area of the business operation. Detailed objectives must be defined, discussed, and agreed upon by any and all employees and

After mastering the information contained in this chapter, you should be able to:

16-1 Describe the management technique of management by objectives.

16-2 Explain why it is important to closely monitor the results of business activities.

16-3 Demonstrate how to prepare a purchase plan.

16-4 Explain how inventory and sales fluctuations affect business operations.

16-5 Describe the use of computers in small businesses.

management by objectives (MBO), a management technique that clearly states the goals of the business and meshes them with the goals of the employees

Figure 16-1   MBO Planning Steps

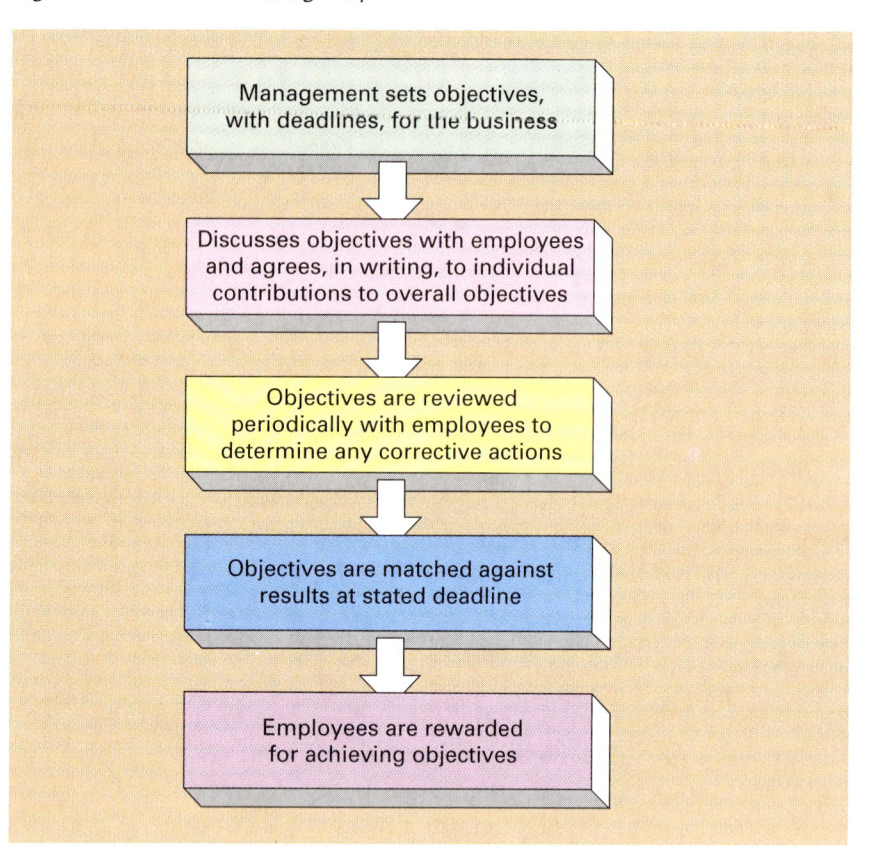

- Management sets objectives, with deadlines, for the business
- Discusses objectives with employees and agrees, in writing, to individual contributions to overall objectives
- Objectives are reviewed periodically with employees to determine any corrective actions
- Objectives are matched against results at stated deadline
- Employees are rewarded for achieving objectives

Figure 16-2   MBO Control Cycle

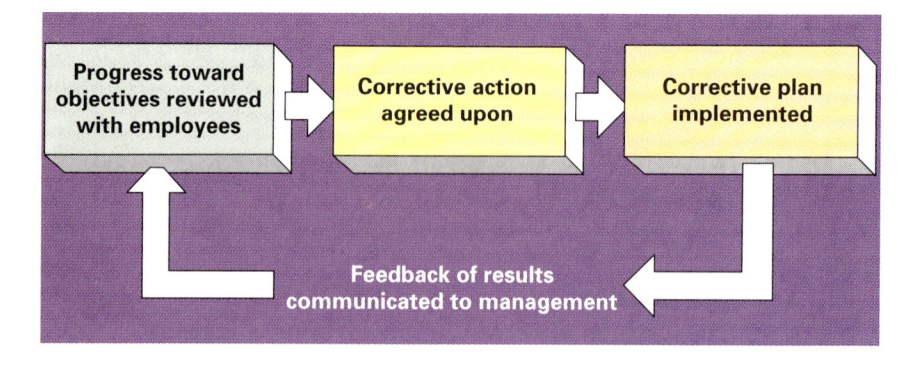

Progress toward objectives reviewed with employees → Corrective action agreed upon → Corrective plan implemented

Feedback of results communicated to management

managers concerned, and the results should be closely monitored. Small-business owners use a variety of reports that serve as checklists for achieving objectives. Sales objectives are the first objectives that should be set. Nearly every aspect of the business is dependent upon sales dollars. Therefore, business owners must effectively estimate what sales totals will be for different time periods. Sales affect inventory levels, cash flow, personnel scheduling, and all other operating conditions.

CONTROLLING REVENUES

If an entrepreneur set the business's sales objective at the beginning of the year at $200,000, the business would be in sad shape if the owner waited until November to find out that sales were running 40 percent behind the objective. It would be too late at that point to take corrective action. By monitoring the sales income daily, weekly, and monthly, the entrepreneur will discover any problems early on and can design and implement a plan to correct the deficiency. The sales plan that calls for sales to total $200,000 per year might require that seven percent of sales should be received in January. Therefore, the January sales objectives would be $14,000—approximately $3,500 per week or $500 per day. The comparison of actual sales results with sales objectives can be shown on a daily and weekly sales report or a monthly report. Examples of these reports are shown in Figures 16-3 and 16-4 on pages 300 and 301.

If the results of a daily or weekly report are higher or lower than the objective, the owner might need to make changes in the weekly and monthly sales objectives. For example, if the sales income for Monday and Tuesday was $1,400, and not $1,000 as projected, the business owner might wish to reset the weekly sales objective at $3,900 instead of the $3,500 originally set. If this objective is achieved, the monthly objective might be reset for an additional $400. The same logic would apply if sales were *not* meeting the daily or weekly objectives.

CONTROLLING INVENTORY

There is a direct correlation between sales and inventory. **Inventory** is the number of units, and the value of the units, that are available for sale or manufacture. Theoretically, the more units a business had

inventory, the number of units and the value of the units a business has available for sale or manufacture

Figure 16-3   Daily and Weekly Sales Report

DAILY AND WEEKLY SALES REPORT		
Week of _____		
Daily Sales	**Objective**	**+/(−)**
Monday _____	_____	_____
Tuesday _____	_____	_____
Wednesday _____	_____	_____
Thursday _____	_____	_____
Friday _____	_____	_____
Saturday _____	_____	_____
Sunday _____	_____	_____
Weekly total _____	_____	_____
Comments:		

on hand to sell or manufacture, the more it could sell. In this way, inventory affects sales, and inventory levels are controlled by sales levels. If the inventory is not sufficient, there will be a drop in expected sales revenues. If a business sells more units than expected, its inventory level will fall below the desired level. If a business does not sell the number of units the owner expects, the inventory will be higher than the desired level. Closely monitoring sales revenues allows the business owner to adjust inventory levels to the demands of the market.

Figure 16-4

MONTHLY SALES TO OBJECTIVES REPORT 19—				
Month	Sales	Objective	+/(−)	Comments
January	$21,200	$20,500	+700	Increase open to buy $500
February	18,400	18,550	(−150)	No action necessary
March	23,000	24,500	(1,500)	Decrease open to buy $1,000
April	26,700	24,300	+2,400	Increase open to buy $2,000
May	23,100	22,900	+200	No action necessary
June	19,650	19,900	(−250)	No action necessary

Business owners attempt to have the amount of goods available that will give the greatest amount of sales without over-investing in inventory. It is impossible to always have the exact amount of inventory that will yield the greatest profit. However, with proper controls in place, the business owner can maintain a level that will produce a healthy sales income and provide a profitable return on investment. For example, if an entrepreneur invests $10,000 in inventory and the profit received from the sale of that inventory is $5,000, the entrepreneur has received a return on investment of 50 percent. Business owners want and need to make a profit from the purchase of inventory. If they have leftover or unwanted inventory, they must sell it at a price that yields less profit. Therefore, it is important to avoid having too much inventory because if it doesn't sell, it will most likely decrease the return on investment. Having too little inventory is just as dangerous. This will cause lost sales, lost profit, and dissatisfied customers. Manufacturers who run out of parts are forced to shut down production until the replacement parts arrive. Retailers who run out of merchandise before a major holiday lose business at the time when they should be making great profits.

Illus. 16-1 Business owners strive to maintain an inventory of goods that will provide the greatest number of sales.

Photo by Alan Brown/Photonics

As you can see, it would be hazardous to guess at inventory levels. Inventory objectives must be planned carefully and monitored closely or the business could get into serious trouble.

Inventory Purchase Plan

The amount of inventory to purchase for a business can be derived from the sales forecast. Entrepreneurs need to ask the question, "How many units must I add to what is presently available to reach my sales objective for a particular period of time?" They also need to know the amount of inventory they want to have at the conclusion of that time period. For instance, if a business owner wishes to increase the amount of inventory on hand at the end of the period, he or she must add the amount of increase to the purchase plan. If less inventory is desired, the amount is subtracted. The formula used to plan inventory purchases is as follows:

$$\text{beginning inventory} + \text{purchase} - \text{sales} - \text{markdowns} = \text{ending inventory}$$

Suppose that a merchant has a $45,000 inventory and projected sales of $100,000 for a period of six months. He or she wishes to increase the inventory on hand to $50,000 at the end of six months and plans that $10,000 of the inventory will be marked down and sold at cost. Since markdowns represent inventory that is sold without profit, that amount should be subtracted from the plan. To find the planned purchase, the merchant inserts these figures into the formula, as shown:

(beginning inventory) + (purchase) − (sales) − (markdowns) − (ending inventory)
$45,000 + ?? − $100,000 − $10,000 − $50,000

In this case, the amount of inventory to purchase would be $115,000.

Once the inventory purchase amount is determined, the entrepreneur must make sure that the inventory arrives at the proper time. If all inventory arrived at the same time, such as at the beginning of the period, it would all have to be paid for at one time. This could cause serious cash flow problems. If this were to happen, there would be no controls available to raise or lower the inventory level in the event that sales were higher or lower than planned. The entrepreneur must break the plan into smaller periods of time and stagger inventory purchases. When a purchase plan is detailed, it is easier to maintain the desired inventory levels. A six-month purchase plan for the previous example could be broken into a month-by-month plan, which would resemble Figure 16-5.

Note that the example in Figure 16-5 applies to a retail store. A manufacturing company would have a new materials inventory, a

Figure 16-5 Six-Month Sales and Inventory Purchase Plan

Inventory Fluctuations (in dollars)	July	August	September	October	November	December	Total
Beginning Inventory	45,000	45,800	47,600	48,200	50,600	55,600	
+ Purchases	14,000	15,000	16,000	20,000	27,000	23,000	115,000
(−) Sales	12,000	12,000	14,000	16,000	20,000	26,000	100,000
(−) Markdowns	1,200	1,200	1,400	1,600	2,000	2,600	10,000
= Ending Inventory	45,800	47,600	48,200	50,600	55,600	50,000	

work-in-process inventory, and a finished-goods inventory. However, we will address the purchase plan in terms of a retail operation. Also note that in Figure 16-5, the merchant plans to gradually increase the inventory level as the Christmas selling season approaches. It is imperative that the inventory level at the beginning of each month be sufficient to produce the projected sales of that particular month. The key to proper inventory levels is being flexible and changing course midstream, when necessary, to adjust to sales that are higher or lower than projected.

In other words, if September's sales are $5,000 lower than the objective, there will be a $5,000 inventory surplus (in terms of sales dollars) on hand at the beginning of October. As soon as the entrepreneur sees sales slipping, such as on September 10, he or she should swiftly alter the purchase plan to reflect this situation. Otherwise there is a risk of ending up with the $5,000 inventory surplus at the end of the month. Conversely, if sales are higher than projected, the entrepreneur may have to order additional inventory.

Small business owners should keep a running written record, called a **perpetual inventory,** at all times. By recording the amount of inventory a business receives and how much it sells on a daily, weekly, or monthly basis, entrepreneurs will have a record available that shows the approximate inventory level at all times. This record will not be exact because it does not accurately take into account defective or stolen inventory or, often, the amount of markdowns taken. It must be corrected at least once a year with a **physical inventory,** which is an actual physical count of all inventory the business owns. Physical inventories are often taken twice a year. The actual number of units of goods is counted manually and recorded on a list detailing every good and its size, color, and/or stock number. Figure 16-6 shows a physical inventory report.

Finding Inventory Suppliers

Entrepreneurs must find the best sources from which to buy inventory. Inventory suppliers, called *vendors,* must be carefully chosen. Entrepreneurs should seek out vendors who are dependable, stand behind their products, ship efficiently, and care about their customers. They should avoid purchasing from vendors who are out to make a quick profit.

Entrepreneurs actually begin to purchase inventory after they establish their purchase plan objective. Equipped with the purchase

---

perpetual inventory, an approximate written record of the amount of inventory available

physical inventory, an actual count of all inventory on hand

Chapter 16   Management Control Tools

Figure 16-6   Physical Inventory Report

Description	Quantity	Sizes	Colors	Wholesale Each	Retail Each	Wholesale Total	Retail Total
Bags, duffle, equipment, nylon	9	n/a	black, navy gray	3.50	7.00	31.50	63.00
Bags, duffle, equipment, canvas	9	n/a	same	4.50	9.00	40.50	81.00
Belts, stretch, cinch, women's	45	S, M, L	yellow, white, pink, gray, lt. blue	2.50	5.00	112.50	225.00
Gloves, Triangle, leather	24	n/a	gray, white	10.00	20.00	240.00	480.00
Jump rope, heavy rope, rubber	3	3½ lbs.	black	12.50	25.00	37.50	75.00
Jump rope, heavy rope, rubber	3	5 lbs.	black	15.00	30.00	45.00	90.00
Jump rope, aerobic	6	n/a	white	5.00	10.00	30.00	60.00
Legwarmers, Softouch	72	n/a	yellow, white, pink, orchid, gray, black, navy, lt. blue, off-white	7.00	14.00	504.00	1008.00

plan, entrepreneurs set forth into the marketplace in search of goods. Depending on the industry, goods might come from one or more of the sources discussed in the following paragraphs.

Trade Shows. Industry representatives frequently gather at central points in the marketplace and invite potential buyers to visit their exhibits. Trade shows can be as small as a few companies renting space at a local motel to show their goods, entertain customers, and make new contacts. A trade show is an opportunity for networking. Networking is the process of making business contacts by meeting people who can assist in business development. Trade shows can be exciting ventures whether entrepreneurs are shopping for goods or selling their own. For potential buyers, trade shows are an opportunity to discover what is new in their industry that can help increase profits. They can buy unique goods, compare prices of several vendors, or purchase merchandise that the competition is not offering.

Sales Calls. When not selling at trade shows, sales representatives are usually traveling through their assigned sales territories demonstrating their goods or services to customers—business owners, purchasing agents, and store managers, among others—at their places

Illus. 16-2 Trade shows allow entrepreneurs to market their goods, entertain customers, and make new contacts.

© *Loren Santow/Tony Stone Images, Inc.*

of business. Quite often, sales representatives make contacts and presentations at trade shows and then close sales deals with entrepreneurs at the business itself. Or, buyers may purchase a certain amount of inventory at a trade show and a certain percentage of it from sales representatives who visit their businesses.

Catalog Ordering. Just as people use mail order catalogs at home for convenient buying, business owners can also use them to purchase inventory. Vendors often spend considerable amounts of money on making catalog presentations of their products or services. By providing these catalogs to customers, they offer a convenient method of ordering inventory. Using a catalog allows entrepreneurs to order whenever it is convenient.

Telemarketing. Business owners may be contacted by some vendors over the phone. Obviously, when acquiring inventory, business owners cannot rely on telemarketers. However, the telephone is an excellent means for sales follow up and sometimes for a sales closing. However, it is not normally effective as an approach or presentation, since it does not allow the customer—in this case, the business owner—to see or touch the product.

INVENTORY AND SALES FLUCTUATIONS

Let's look at what happens when objectives are either not met or exceeded. Using the sales and inventory purchase plan in Figure 16-5, let's assume that August's total sales are a disappointing $10,000, as opposed to the $12,000 projected. The immediate result is that the cash flow projection is $2,000 less than planned and the inventory level is $2,000 higher. Unless there is reason to believe that lower sales are a long-term trend, simple short-term corrections should be made.

Cutting back on the planned inventory arrivals by $2,000 in the next 30 days will correct the inventory level by October 1. At the same time, the business owner could reduce planned inventory purchase expenditures by $2,000. In this way, the cash flow projection will also be back in line in 30 days.

If sales had exceeded the projection by $2,000, the business owner should increase the planned inventory arrivals. If he or she fails to do this, the $2,000 inventory shortage will cause a decrease in anticipated sales sometime in the near future. As you can see, fluctuations in sales can easily get out of hand when they are not closely monitored. If immediate corrections are not made, a string of three or four months with sales revenue objectives not being met will seriously disrupt the entire operation. This is why control reports must be kept up to date.

Scheduling Inventory Arrival

Because sales projections never exactly match actual sales, the business owner must build flexibility into the purchase plan. Most businesses will make planned purchases well in advance of the planned period of sales. For example, a retail store might place orders for the Christmas selling season six to nine months beforehand to ensure receipt of the best selection of merchandise from vendors. In doing this, entrepreneurs must recognize that numerous conditions might change that could cause them to alter a sales projection made that far in advance. For this reason, the entire amount of planned purchases should not be ordered at one time.

Astute business owners place orders in advance for the sales about which they feel most confident. Cash should be set aside in a reserve fund from which additional purchases may be made depending on sales performance. Money that is allocated for inventory purchases, but is not yet spent, is called the business's **open to buy.** Open-to-buy money is used to place orders for immediate delivery during the planned sales period. As an example, a business owner operating with the purchase plan in Figure 16-5 might place orders totaling $70,000 at a trade show at the beginning of the sales period and keep $45,000 available as an open to buy. If sales are higher than expected, more than $45,000 in inventory should be purchased. If sales are lower, some amount less than $45,000 will be used.

open to buy, money that is available for the purchase of inventory

Terms of Sale

It is very important to buy from sources that offer fair terms. Payment terms on goods sold vary from industry to industry. However, in most industries, vendors give discounts to those buyers who pay most promptly and order the largest quantities. The terms of sale are shown on the invoice, a statement the seller gives to the buyer that lists the contents of a shipment or delivery, the terms of sale, the number of units or items delivered, the unit price, and the total cost. Some examples of the more common terms of sale are as follows:

- C.O.D. (cash on delivery)—Amount of invoice is collected upon delivery of goods.

- 2/10/n30, R.O.G.—Buyer receives a two-percent discount if the invoice amount is paid within ten days of receipt of delivery. The net (*n*) amount is due on the thirtieth day from the date the entrepreneur receives the goods. R.O.G. represents *receipt of goods*.
- 2/10/n30, E.O.M.—Buyer receives a two-percent discount if the invoice amount is paid within ten days from the end of the month in which delivery is received. The net amount is due by the thirtieth day from the end of the month. E.O.M. stands for *end of month*.
- 3/10, 1/15, n60—Buyer receives a three percent discount if the invoice amount is paid within ten days of delivery, or one percent if it is paid within 15 days. The net amount is due in 60 days.
- E.O.M.—The amount billed is due at the end of the month; no discounts apply.

The terms of the sale will have an important impact on the cash flow projections. Business owners wish to have as much time as possible before paying for inventory purchases. Ideally, they would prefer not to pay the vendor until after there has been ample time to sell the inventory. For cash in advance (C.I.A.) or C.O.D. purchases, the money for the inventory is invested immediately and taken out of cash flow. If generous terms such as n/60 are granted to the buyer, the total sales price, including the profit, might be collected before taking the money out of cash flow. This can make quite a difference to a business that makes a high percentage of its annual sales during the holiday season. Paying in January for merchandise sold in November and December, instead of paying in September when the merchandise was delivered, can be a big help. If merchandise must be paid for before it has had a chance to sell, business owners often find it necessary to borrow money from the bank until the merchandise sells. This requires paying interest on the borrowed money, thereby decreasing the potential net profit. On the other hand, the benefit of discounts on invoices means additional profit for the business.

Since entrepreneurs wish to tie up money in inventory for the shortest time possible, they must devise an inventory system that allows the most efficient possible use of money. Many businesses use an inventory system called *just-in-time inventory control*. By working closely with vendors and operating a very tight inventory control system, business owners schedule inventory to arrive "just in time" to fill empty shelves or manufacturing parts bins. This allows business owners to avoid having money tied up in inventory that simply sits in a stockroom. The key to this system is knowing the capability and dependability of suppliers and closely monitoring inventory levels.

Most businesses assign a reorder point for inventory used on an everyday basis. When the stock of an item falls to this level—the reorder point—the item is automatically reordered. The reorder point is influenced by the delivery time of the replacement inventory. Some businesses use a computerized cashiering system to alert management that it is time to reorder a product. Others use a manual system to check stock levels of inventory daily or weekly.

EFFECTS OF INVENTORY AND SALES FLUCTUATIONS ON OTHER BUSINESS OPERATIONS

Poorly planned and controlled sales and inventory purchase objectives can have a ripple effect throughout the entire operation. In addition to cash flow problems, the business will experience disruptions in personnel scheduling, insurance expenditures, and promotional efforts.

Personnel Scheduling

The organization chart and personnel needs are designed to accommodate the projected sales objectives. In the event that these projections get out of line, the business owner will have to adjust personnel schedules. If sales are too low, there will be employees with not enough work to do. Some may have to be laid off, or their hours may need to be decreased. Some companies will reduce the pay rate of employees. All of these measures have a negative impact on employee morale. Poor morale could, in turn, cause excessive personnel turnover, which could result in the expensive task of employee recruiting and training.

If sales exceed the objectives, the owner may have to hire extra personnel to handle the added volume. If the business is understaffed, customers may not receive the quick, efficient assistance to which they are accustomed, and they might go to the competition instead.

Personnel schedules, like inventory purchase plans, should be designed with flexibility. Successful business owners have a plan of action to handle excess or decreased sales periods. They should also cross-train employees so that they can handle additional responsibilities. Names of people who can work on a part-time, temporary basis should be on hand.

Business owners should warn employees in advance of possible courses of action the company will take to handle periods of high or low

Illus. 16-3 High-sales periods, such as Christmas, require flexible personnel scheduling.

sales. For example, there might be times when they are asked to work overtime, or circumstances in which their working hours are cut back. Entrepreneurs and their families should be prepared to work extra hours when needed. In the event it is necessary to lay off employees because of poor sales, owners should provide as much notice as possible to the affected personnel to give them time to search for other jobs.

Insurance

Unexpected changes in sales and inventory plans will also have an impact on the insurance requirements of the business. Entrepreneurs must carry insurance to protect them from losing their investments as a result of fire, accidents, or other unexpected occurrences. Owners pay insurance premiums based on the value of the business. The more property that is insured, the higher the premiums. Additional inventory increases the value of the business, which means the entrepreneur should purchase additional insurance coverage. If the value of inventory increases by $25,000, the amount of insurance coverage should increase by the same amount. Entrepreneurs must inform their insurance company of changes in the value of the business or coverage will not be sufficient. Many businesses carry a "peak season" coverage that automatically increases insurance coverage during times of the year when inventory increases are anticipated. In case of a fire or other emergency, the owner will not receive reimbursement for lost property that has not been reported to the insurance company.

Promotional Events

Promotional events and advertising campaigns are planned in advance. If there is a change in sales and inventory levels prior to a promotional event, it might have an effect on the event. A business should not spend money advertising a product if it does not have sufficient stock to satisfy customer demand. If inventory levels are not sufficiently monitored and controlled, the business runs the risk of being embarrassed by advertising a product or service that it cannot provide. Customers may lose their trust in the business, and its reputation could suffer. Advertising plans, budgets, and schedules must also be flexible to accommodate circumstantial changes. If the business owner is able to buy something unusual on short notice and wishes to inform the public, there should be a method available to allow him or her to do so.

Security Controls

Unfortunately, it is a fact of life that some people steal. Businesses are often victims of theft from customers and employees. If business owners do not take proper security measures, inventory theft can have a serious impact on a business's inventory control system—and its profits.

The best method of controlling inventory theft is through prevention techniques. Some techniques for preventing customer theft include the following:

- Train the staff to watch all customers closely, but not in an annoying manner. If potential thieves know they are being watched, they generally will not steal. In a retail environment, all customers should be acknowledged as they enter. It is not only polite, but also gives notice to shoplifters that the employees are aware of their presence.
- Teach employees the procedures to follow in the event that they witness a theft. Call your local police department to learn about procedures or training for business owners. If a shoplifter is apprehended and arrested, it serves as notice to others that the business does not tolerate shoplifting.

- Invest in security prevention devices. Alarm systems, hidden cameras, and security tags on merchandise are commonly used methods. The cost of some security systems might be partially offset by reduced insurance premiums. As a prevention tool, it is usually a good idea to publically post the security measures being used.

Businesses must also establish prevention measures against employee theft, which is actually far more common in many industries than customer theft. Common methods to utilize include the following:

- Check or search all articles taken out of the business at closing time or employee work shift changes. Articles that may be searched include purses, tote bags, briefcases, and lunch bags.
- Administer periodic lie detector tests on a random basis.
- Devise a system of checking inventory levels against sales results. If an item is not accounted for, compare sales receipts with physical inventory to determine whether it may have been stolen.

The best method of ensuring employee honesty is through creating an open working relationship between employees and management. Employees who work as a team and take pride in their work are less likely to be tempted to steal from the business.

Illus. 16-4 Hidden cameras, security tags on merchandise, and alarm systems are commonly used as loss-prevention devices.

The amount of stolen inventory can be calculated at the time the physical inventory is taken. Business owners can presume that merchandise, products, or parts not accounted for by sales, use, or damage have been stolen. If there is a significant amount of theft, it will reduce inventory levels, causing problems in achieving objectives.

USING COMPUTERS AS A CONTROL

Personal computers have become great tools for small business owners. There are many choices to make concerning the type of equipment to purchase for a business's computer system. The most important consideration is choosing the software that best fits the particular business. Computer software refers to programs that instruct the computer how to operate. There are many software packages available. Some are suited for manufacturing, while others are designed with a service business or retail establishment in mind. For example, one type of software can compute long columns of numbers, while another is designed to arrange graphic symbols on a page to produce signs.

Entrepreneurs must shop carefully for the system that best fits their own business, then find the computer hardware that accommodates the chosen system. Computer hardware is the actual equipment and accessories needed to run the software. Small-business owners typically begin by purchasing a central processing unit (CPU), a monitor or screen, a keyboard, and a printer. Generally speaking, entrepreneurs can expect to spend $1,500 to $5,000 on computer hardware and software. They may upgrade and add to their initial investments as the business grows and/or changes. Courses are available through local colleges, community centers, and retail computer stores to learn computer applications. New-business owners should take whatever educational courses necessary to become proficient in the use of a computer.

With proper training, entrepreneurs have the ability to keep records as efficiently as large businesses do. What was once a tool for only large businesses because of the expense has become affordable to all business operations. Businesses can use computers for the following functions:

- Financial statements—Updated income statements and balance sheets can be easily maintained and reproduced when needed.

- Inventory control—Perpetual inventory totals can be tracked by product line as well as business total. Some businesses have computer systems tied into sales terminals that automatically subtract the item sold from its product classification.
- Personnel payroll records—It is possible to maintain year-to-date records showing all tax deductions per employee. An employee payroll program also automatically calculates all tax and other deductions for each pay period. This can save considerable time for the person preparing the payroll checks.
- Accounts payable and receivable—By recording all incoming or outgoing invoices, the business is able to keep current and convenient records of all monies owed by vendors and customers.
- Correspondence—Word processing software programs make writing and keeping records of all business correspondence simple. These programs also can be very helpful for designing advertisements or brochures for promotional activities.

Illus. 16-5 Portable computers allow entrepreneurs to maintain records as efficiently as large businesses do.

Photo by Alan Brown/Photonics

THE FASHION ATTIC

Laura needed to design a purchase plan for the Fashion Attic's first six months. Since she planned her opening for July, Laura would have to display summer and early-fall fashions on opening day. She would have on order late-fall and winter holiday merchandise. Laura decided to purchase $38,000 of initial inventory and hoped to increase her inventory by $3000 at the end of the six-month period. Since she knew that her sales projection was $100,000 for the first six months, Laura was able to plug these numbers into the purchase formula.

(beginning inventory)	(purchase)	(sales)	(markdowns)	(ending inventory)
$38,000	+ ??	− $100,000	− $10,000	= $41,000

Laura's calculation of the formula produced a total open to buy of $113,000. She went to work devising the purchase plan for each month, keeping in mind that she had to build the inventory to accommodate the busy fall and Christmas selling season. Laura's completed purchase plan is shown in Figure 16-7.

Satisfied with the plan, Laura attended the fashion trade show in New York City. She spent a good deal of time at the show getting to know the representatives of the various fashion design companies. When she felt convinced that they were sincere and reliable in their offers of assistance, she began to place orders for both immediate and future deliveries of merchandise. Laura ordered all her opening inventory—$38,000—and over one half of what she needed for the upcoming seasons—$60,000 worth. This left her with an open to buy of $53,000 to order new styles during the six-month period. She could order these at local shows or from sales representatives when they visited. Laura's plan also allowed her a reserve of cash to use if sales conditions changed or if she wanted to reorder particularly popular designs.

Since the Fashion Attic was a new account for vendors, Laura was not able to receive trade credit for the opening inventory orders, but she did receive as high as 8/10/n30 credit terms on many of her follow-up orders.

The buying trip had been exciting. Laura looked forward to unpacking and displaying her selections for her new customers.

Figure 16-7 Six-Month Purchase Plan for the Fashion Attic

Inventory Fluctuations (in dollars)

	July	August	September	October	November	December	Total
Beginning Inventory	38,000	38,900	39,600	40,100	45,500	47,500	
(+) Purchases	13,000	15,000	17,000	23,000	24,000	21,000	113,000
(−) Sales	11,000	13,000	15,000	16,000	20,000	25,000	100,000
(−) Markdowns	1,100	1,300	1,500	1,600	2,000	2,500	10,000
= Ending Inventory	38,900	39,600	40,100	45,500	47,500	41,000	

SUMMARY

Small-business owners must control all aspects of business operations if they are to reach their objectives. Management by objectives clearly states the goals of the business and meshes them with the goals of the employees to ensure that everyone is involved. Objectives are stated for all operational aspects of the business.

Once sales objectives are set, sales results are monitored on a daily, weekly, and monthly basis to make sure everything is operating as planned. If sales objectives are off the mark, there will be a ripple effect throughout the operation. Missed sales objectives force changes in inventory levels, personnel and scheduling needs, insurance requirements, and promotional plans.

Entrepreneurs should carefully design their inventory purchase plans and choose suppliers. The purchase plan must be flexible to accommodate changes in sales revenue forecasts.

Personal computers have become valuable control tools for small-business owners. By using a computer and various reporting procedures, entrepreneurs can control business operations quickly and efficiently.

VOCABULARY BUILDER

On a separate sheet of paper, write a brief definition of each word or phrase based on your reading of the chapter.

1. Management by objectives
2. Inventory
3. Return on investment
4. Perpetual inventory
5. Physical inventory
6. Open to buy
7. Invoice
8. C.O.D.
9. R.O.G.
10. E.O.M.
11. Just-in-time inventory planning

REVIEW QUESTIONS

1. Why is the management-by-objectives technique both a planning and a control tool?
2. Why is it necessary to monitor sales results daily, weekly, and monthly?
3. What happens to inventory if sales exceed projections?
4. What is the starting point for designing a purchase plan?
5. What is the difference between a perpetual and a physical inventory?
6. In what four ways can small-business owners acquire inventory?
7. Why should inventory arrivals be scheduled over a period of time instead of all at once?
8. What do the following notations mean: 2/10/n30 and 3/10, 1/15, n60?
9. What is the advantage of a just-in-time inventory control system?
10. In what five ways can small-business owners make use of computers?

DISCUSSION QUESTIONS

1. How can you use a management-by-objectives method in doing your homework assignments?
2. What happens to your personal budget when you receive less money than you expect? How is a business affected when sales are lower than projected?
3. What do you usually do if a store is sold out of an item that you need? Why?
4. What do you think is management's responsibility to employees when poor sales force a reduction in payroll?
5. What are the advantages of using a computer in a small business?

CRITICAL THINKING

The business that you manage has experienced sales far in excess of what was projected. After the first month of operation, sales are twice what you had expected. Do you think the sales forecast and the inventory purchase plan should be doubled for the entire first year? If so, what risks might you incur? What other plan of action could you take that would be less risky?

SHORT CASE: TOO MANY SUPPLIERS

Carlotta needed help. She sat in front of a desk stacked with invoices and folders discussing her situation with Henry Carson, a consultant with the local Small Business Development Center. "I can't keep up with all these bills. I am totally confused about which ones to pay and which ones I can hold off on until later."

Henry was not surprised. Carlotta's business was a mess—a gift shop with shelves stuffed with miscellaneous gifts. There really was no theme or direction. "How many suppliers do you have, Carlotta?"

"I'm not really sure, Henry—maybe 50 or 60. When I go to trade shows I buy whatever looks good. I don't pay much attention to who the seller is."

Henry handed Carlotta a blank tablet. "Carlotta, let's get this place organized. A gift shop this size does not need that many suppliers. Make a list of all your suppliers by classification. Then we will determine what percentage of your total sales comes from each classification. We need to design a plan to control your buying procedures."

Carlotta presented the following list to Henry a week later.

Classification	Number of Suppliers	Percent of Sales
Greeting cards, paper products	14	31
Novelty gifts	21	38
All-occasion gifts	15	23
Fine gifts	4	8

"Carlotta, you have 54 suppliers! You can't operate a store with an average of 2 percent of sales per vendor (100% ÷ 54). By consolidating your buying, you will receive better service from the suppliers, have a better grip on your business, and make a more focused presentation to your customers. If you cut the list to 20 suppliers—5 percent of sales from each supplier—you will save on shipping costs, receive some discounts for buying larger quantities of merchandise, and cut down your administrative duties greatly."

Working together, Henry and Carlotta made a new list.

Classification	Number of Suppliers	Percent of Sales
Greeting cards, paper goods	5	31
Novelty gifts	7	38
All-occasion gifts	6	33
Fine gifts	2	8

"I recommend that you pay careful attention to your choice of vendors. Buy only from those you know you can depend on, and who will offer assistance when you need it. Choosing the best vendors will make your inventory selection better than ever. I believe you will also find that the more established the vendor, the better your payment terms will be. Design a purchase plan of needs and a budget before you go to the next trade show—and stick to it."

Questions

1. What do you think caused Carlotta to have an inventory problem in the first place?
2. What control tools should she implement now for the future?
3. Have you seen stores that seem to be overcrowded and do not seem to focus their offerings to their customers? What is your impression of such places?

PROJECT CHALLENGE

In your business plan notebook, prepare a six-month purchase plan for your hypothetical business. Start by stating your beginning inventory and your potential ending inventory. By inserting your six-month sales forecast and calculating a percentage for markdowns, you will be able to determine your initial open to buy. Use a table such as the one in Figure 16-5.

Then determine from which vendors you will purchase inventory. You can accomplish this by visiting would-be competitors in your community. Find out if there are trade shows for your hypothetical industry and where and when they are held.

17
Computer Applications

Entrepreneurs must fulfill many day-to-day responsibilities to ensure the success of their businesses. The average business day for entrepreneurs usually extends well into the evening, long after their employees have gone home. If they have no employees, the day might be even longer. Entrepreneurs often need to complete paperwork and other management chores after the traditional close of the business day. Business owners have to do most, if not all, of the work themselves. Their ultimate success is a direct result of hard work. The length of time that it takes to do much of this work, however, can be shortened by working "smart." Working smart means taking advantage of available technology. Successful entrepreneurs realize that technology can ease the management burden of entrepreneurship.

Illus. 17-1 Entrepreneurs shoulder a significant management burden.

Courtesy, International Business Machines Corporation

After mastering the information contained in this chapter, you should be able to:

17-1 Identify the basic parts of a computer and explain their functions.

17-2 Describe basic word processing applications, basic database applications, and basic spreadsheet applications.

17-3 Identify ways in which entrepreneurs can benefit from desktop publishing applications.

17-4 Identify basic telecommunications applications, and explain how they are useful to entrepreneurs.

COMPUTER BASICS

Technological understanding requires a basic knowledge of computers. Entrepreneurs who want to be successful must first become **computer literate.** They must be able to use common software programs and know the functions of the various computer hardware components.

Computer hardware simply refers to the various components of computer equipment. The most common components of computer hardware are the keyboard/mouse, central processing unit, monitor, and printer. These are the most visible parts of the computer. **Software,** on the other hand, is the program that translates the user's commands to the computer hardware.

A good analogy to the computer is the human body. The body's hardware consists of arms, legs, hands, fingers, and so on. The body's software is the brain. The body's hardware is useless until its software (the brain) tells the various parts what to do. A computer functions in much the same way: its software is its brain. Just as your brain tells your hand to turn the page in this text, the software in a computer tells the hardware to save a document, print a document, add a column of numbers, draw a picture, send a message, and so on.

COMPUTER HARDWARE

The hardware components of a computer consist of a system of interconnected electronic and mechanical devices. Any computing machine, be it a calculator carried in a pocket, a microcomputer sitting on a desk, or a large mainframe computer installed in a specially designed room, has the same parts.

Keyboard and Mouse

The **keyboard** is the piece of hardware that typically uses alphanumeric keys to input data into the computer. The medium through which the entrepreneur communicates with the computer is the keyboard.

Many hardware configurations allow the user to also use a mouse by which to communicate with the computer. The **mouse** is a pointing device used with a video display screen or monitor. A mouse controls cursor movements on the screen. A device known as a trackball is designed to perform the same functions as a mouse. A trackball can be thought of as a stationary mouse (or a mouse on its back). It

---

computer literacy, possessing basic competence in the use of common software programs and familiarity with the functions of computer hardware components

computer hardware, the various components of computer equipment

software, computer programs that tell the computer what to do

keyboard, the piece of hardware that typically uses alphanumeric keys to input data into the computer

mouse, controls cursor movement on the screen

Illus. 17-2 There are many different types of computers such as this laptop.

Photo by Alan Brown/Photonics

consists of a ball in a stationary housing. Some trackballs are designed as extensions of keyboards.

Central Processing Unit

The **central processing unit** (CPU) is the main component of a computer hardware system. It is made up of three subunits: the control unit, the arithmetic or logic unit, and the main memory unit. The control and arithmetic/logic units are known as the processor or microprocessors.

The *control unit* examines the instructions in a computer program and directs other parts of the CPU to carry out those instructions. For example, in response to an instruction to multiply 2 times 10, the control unit directs the arithmetic/logic unit to do the multiplication.

The *arithmetic/logic unit* contains the circuitry necessary to perform operations such as addition, subtraction, multiplication, and division. This unit is also capable of making logical comparisons, for example, comparing one number with another and determining whether it is larger, smaller, or equal to the other number.

central processing unit (CPU), contains the microprocessor that contains the logic and control units

The *main memory unit* stores data received from input devices such as the keyboard and mouse, and from storage devices such as floppy disks. The memory also stores the programs that control the computer and the data being processed.

Disks and Disk Drives

Data and software can be stored on both hard disks and floppy disks. **Disk drives** are the devices used to store and retrieve data and programs on disks. **Hard disks** are round metal plates coated with a magnetic surface. **Floppy disks** (frequently referred to as diskettes) are made from a round plastic sheet coated with a magnetic surface. The plastic sheet is inserted in a 5 $\frac{1}{4}$ inch jacket or a 3 $\frac{1}{2}$ inch plastic cartridge. A hard disk can usually store thousands of pages of information. Floppy disks provide less storage space than a hard disk and are sensitive to heat, magnets, and bending. Hard disks and floppy disks are sometimes called secondary storage. Secondary disk storage is needed because every software program and all the data needed to perform computer functions cannot be stored in the main memory unit of the CPU at one time.

disk drive, the device used to store and retrieve data and programs on disks

hard disks, round metal plates that store information and are coated with a magnetic surface

floppy disks, round plastic sheets that store information and are coated with a magnetic surface

Illus. 17-3

Pictured is a 2 gigabyte, 3.5 inch disk drive.

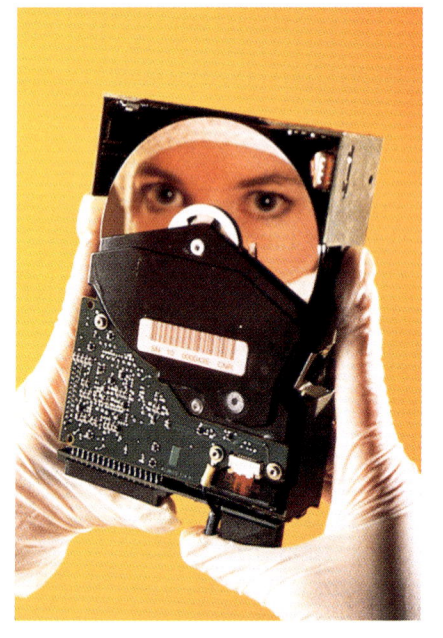

Courtesy International Business Machines Corporation

Monitor

The **monitor** is the part of the hardware that provides the video display of data. Monitors are available in models that display a variety of colors on the screen (color monitor), and in models that display only one color on the screen (monochrome).

monitor, the part of the hardware that provides a video display of data

Printer

The **printer** is the device that allows the user to generate a hard (paper) copy of information generated by or stored in the computer. Printers come in a variety of styles with a myriad of options. The choice of a printer will depend to a large extent on software options and the quality of printed material required.

printer, the device that allows the entrepreneur to generate a hard (paper) copy of information generated by or stored in the computer

COMPUTER SOFTWARE

Computer software comes in many forms to serve hundreds of needs. An entrepreneur could spend endless hours exploring the various options. The most practical approach, however, is probably to discuss software needs with friends, family, an accountant and entrepreneurs in similar businesses. Their suggestions can usually provide a reasonable starting point. As the entrepreneur begins to research the appropriate software, several categories of applications should be considered.

Word Processing Applications

Entrepreneurs need to maintain, and often increase, the efficiency and productivity of their offices. By accomplishing this objective, office expenses, which can account for up to 60 percent of business expenses, can be cut. Office expenses tend to increase yearly, so small business owners must utilize all the technology that is available to keep these costs down. One way to reduce costs is through the use of word processing. **Word processing** means creating, processing, printing, distributing, and filing a document through the use of computer technology.

word processing, creating, processing, printing, distributing, and filing a document through the use of technology

 The typical entrepreneur today wants to get paperwork done at the fastest possible rate, at the least cost, and with a high-quality appearance. Word processing can accomplish this task. The greatest contribution of word processing to office productivity occurs when it is used for repetitive documents, such as form letters. Word processing enables these documents to be produced time after time without rekeying. It also greatly increases office productivity when long letters with many revisions must be generated.

The basic features common to most word processing software programs are word wrap, insert, strikeover, center, boldface and underline, copy, search and replace, spell check, headers, and footers.

- *Word wrap* automatically runs the text to the next line.
- *Insert mode* allows new text to be entered between previously entered characters.
- *Strikeover mode* allows new text to be entered on top of previously existing characters.
- *Center command* is useful for positioning headings evenly between the left and right margins.
- *Boldface and underline commands* add special emphasis to certain words.
- *Copy command* is used to copy text in one part of a document onto another part.
- *Search and replace command* allows the user to search for all occurrences of one word and replace it with another.
- *Spell check* allows the user to check the spelling in a document.
- *Header command* is used to print the same information at the top of every page of the document.
- *Footer command* is used to print the same information at the bottom of every page of the document.

Database Applications

Almost all entrepreneurs need to develop list upon list of information. Many entrepreneurs compile lists of all their customers, as well as lists of all their vendors. Add to these lists of products and services available for sale, lists of customer requests, lists of potential customers, lists of employees, and lists of competitors and the result is a great deal of information that must be maintained and organized. How can the entrepreneur keep all these lists under control? One way is through the use of database software. A **database** is a collection of information that is normally kept in list form. **Database software** is a set of instructions used with a computer to set up and provide access to a listing of data.

A database stored in a computer makes it easy to organize information, keep the information up to date, and produce printed copies

database, a collection of information that is normally kept in list form

database software, a set of instructions used with a computer to set up and provide access to a listing of data of the information. A database is organized so that many people can retrieve information from it, use it for different reasons, and format it in different ways. Table 17-1 is an example of how information about customers can be stored in a database.

When creating a database such as the one in Table 17-1, the entrepreneur must first decide what information about customers is important to keep on file. The entrepreneur who developed the database in Table 17-1 wanted a list of all customers with the address and phone number of each as well as their year-to-date purchases. If the entrepreneur later decides that he or she wants to include additional information about each customer, then that information could be added to the database. For instance, if the entrepreneur wanted to know the year that each customer started purchasing from her or his business, that information could be added as a fifth category.

Information can be retrieved from the database and sorted on the basis of a particular characteristic that the entrepreneur chooses. For example, if the entrepreneur wants to know which customers are

Table 17-1 Customer Database

Name	Address	Phone	Purchases Year to Date
Sultan Manufacturing	2101 Industrial Rd.	303-243-1999	$25,389.89
Reed Manufacturing	104 Constitution Ave.	303-248-1010	18,296.54
Johnson Sales	802 South St.	303-245-9898	30,143.09
Wong Energy	567 Wales Ave.	303-248-0753	100,945.10
Stein Manufacturing	143 S. Hampton Rd.	303-245-7777	76,243.65
Dinges Works	341 Colfax Rd.	303-243-5436	10,365.89
Zu Welding	557 Colorado St.	303-245-9183	7,512.76

located in the area of town that has phone numbers with the prefix 243, the database could search for all phone numbers that begin with 243. The search would yield two customers: Sultan Manufacturing and Dinges Works. The entrepreneur could use this information to arrange to call on both customers when he or she is in that part of town. Or, perhaps the entrepreneur wants to reward all customers who have ordered at least $25,000 worth of merchandise year-to-date. The search based on this characteristic would yield four customers: Sultan Manufacturing, Johnson Sales, Wong Energy, and Stein Manufacturing. Searches based on many other characteristics can also be made.

A database can be used to create mailing labels, generate reports, and track inventory. The ability to store and organize information in different ways can be a very valuable tool to the business owner. By mastering the technology contained within a good database software package, the entrepreneur will become a much more efficient manager.

Spreadsheet Applications

As we discussed in Chapter 13, one of the major activities of an entrepreneur is to keep accurate accounting records. The most efficient way to keep these records is with spreadsheet software. A **spreadsheet** is an electronic replacement for an accountant's columnar ledger, pencil, and calculator. Entrepreneurs can use spreadsheets in their businesses to calculate budgets, prepare financial statements, and analyze financial problems. Spreadsheets can be used to compute almost any math problem that can be solved with a calculator.

spreadsheet, an electronic replacement for an accountant's columnar ledger, pencil, and calculator

As numbers are changed on a spreadsheet, totals are recalculated automatically. This feature of spreadsheet software facilitates planning different financial scenarios. For example, when you are completing the initial capitalization portion of your business plan, you will find it very useful to experiment with different figures to determine actual startup costs. If you wanted to see what your total costs would be with a building rent of $650 per month instead of the $800 per month that you had originally estimated, you could substitute the $800 figure with $650. The spreadsheet would then automatically recalculate your initial capitalization cost, as shown in Table 17-2. To recalculate all the figures by hand would be time-consuming, while the computer can calculate the substituted information for you instantly.

Table 17-2 Sample Spreadsheet of Business Startup Costs

First Estimate

	A	B	C	D
1	Telephone	100		
2	Equipment	10000		
3	Wages	4000		
4	Rent	800		
5	Utilities	350		
6	Advertising	400		
7	Merchandise	20000		
8	Total	35650		

Second Estimate with Rent Change

	A	B	C	D
1	Telephone	100		
2	Equipment	10000		
3	Wages	4000		
4	Rent	650		
5	Utilities	350		
6	Advertising	400		
7	Merchandise	20000		
8	Total	35500		

Desktop Publishing Applications

Remember the old saying, "A picture is worth a thousand words"? Well, desktop publishing can provide that picture and much more. **Desktop publishing** is the process of designing and producing a publication using a personal computer. The entrepreneur will find it a very useful and money-saving tool.

In the past, entrepreneurs relied solely on printing companies for documents to be designed, typeset, and printed. Now, more and more businesses hire employees to create documents within the company using desktop publishing software. Desktop publishing software can be used to develop newspapers, magazines, advertisements, brochures, and manuals, all of which look as though they had been professionally created.

Using desktop publishing software, entrepreneurs can electronically combine pictures or graphics on the same page with words. Both text and graphics can be seen on the computer screen at the same time. The screen shows the page much as it will look when it is printed.

Figures 17-1 and 17-2 are examples of how entrepreneurs can use desktop publishing to create professional-looking documents. Figure 17-1 is an advertisement, and 17-2 is the cover of a business brochure.

Entrepreneurs use desktop publishing because it gives them control over their document production. An original layout of a document can be created quickly. Entrepreneurs no longer have to deal with commercial printers who often have heavy workloads and require weeks of advance notice to complete an assignment. Because desktop publishing can be performed within the company by people who require less training than professional typesetters, there is a definite cost advantage to the entrepreneur once the software has been purchased. In-house desktop publishing also offers more flexibility. For example, changes to a publication can be made immediately and tight deadlines can more easily be met.

TELECOMMUNICATIONS

Telecommunications is the communication of information by computer via telephone lines, cables, or satellite. Telecommunications makes it possible to send and receive messages through the computer and to do research without ever having to leave your computer. Stock quotes can be accessed by the computer, games can be played

---

desktop publishing, the process of designing and producing a publication using a personal computer

telecommunications, the communication of information by computer via telephone lines, cables, or satellite

Figure 17-1   Desktop-Published Advertisement

with other people sitting at their own computers, and pictures and messages can be sent in a matter of minutes.

Telecommunications is indispensable to entrepreneurs. As you read the following definitions of various forms of this technology, think about which ones would be most useful to you in your future business.

Electronic Mail

Electronic mail involves the use of software that enables users to send and receive messages through the computer. Companies use electronic mail for interoffice communication as well as for the transmittal of information to outside sources. Electronic mail can transmit information more quickly and efficiently than sending mail through the U.S. Postal Service or a private carrier. Electronic mail makes it easy to create messages, send messages, and store messages for

electronic mail, the electronic delivery of correspondence

Figure 17-2 Desktop-Published Brochure Cover

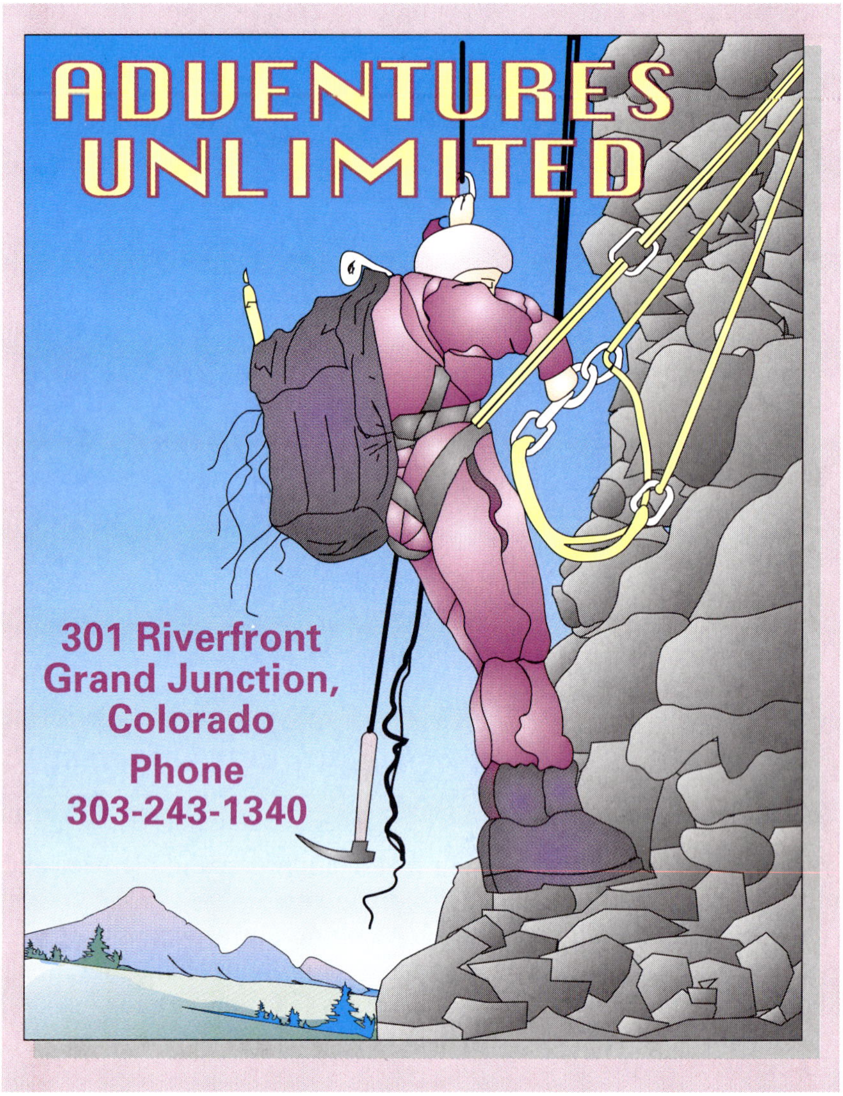

future reference. Electronic messages can be read on a visual display screen, or they can be printed as hard copy.

Facsimile (fax) Machine

A **facsimile machine** translates a printed page or graphics into electronic signals to be transmitted over telephone lines. The signals are

facsimile (fax), translation of a printed page or graphics into electronic signals to be transmitted over telephone lines then reproduced through a fax machine at the receiving end. A fax machine can transmit text, graphics, charts, drawings, photos, and signatures. Modern businesses would find it very difficult to function without fax machines. In today's small businesses, the fax is almost as indispensable as the telephone. The following is typical of the daily use of a fax machine.

8:00 A.M.	letter sent to vendor inquiring about rush order
10:00 A.M.	draft contract received from attorney
10:45 A.M.	order for additional merchandise sent to wholesaler
1:00 P.M.	customer request for merchandise
1:30 P.M.	vendor responds to inquiry about rush order
2:50 P.M.	draft contract with comments is sent back to attorney
3:40 P.M.	response sent to customer requesting merchandise

As you can readily discern, a fax machine is a part of daily business life. Almost all businesses today expect other businesses to either have a fax machine or have easy access to one.

Voice Mail

Voice mail, also called voice messaging or voice store and forward, refers to an electronic means of sending, retrieving, and saving voice

Illus. 17-4   Fax machines are an indispensable part of doing business today.

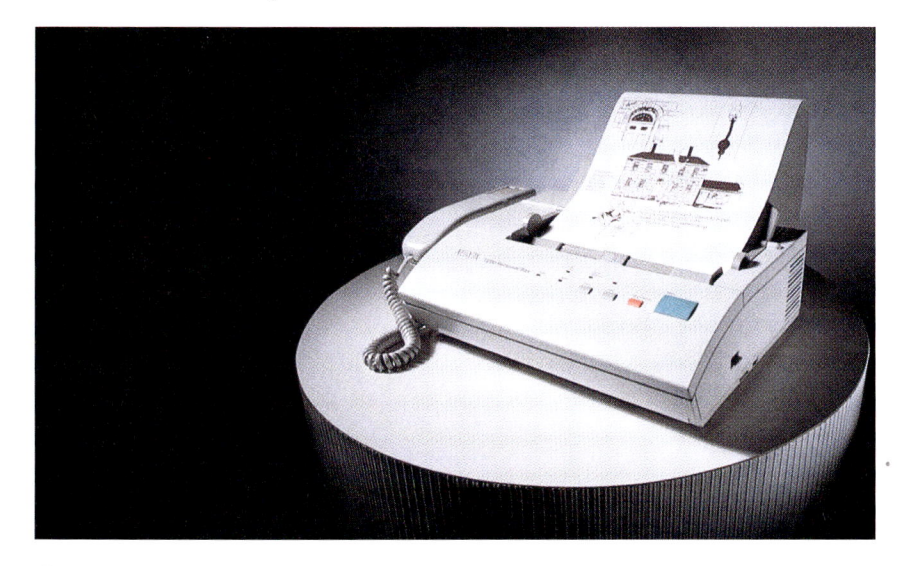

voice mail, also called messaging or voice store and forward, refers to an electronic means of sending, retrieving, and saving voice messages

Courtesy Xerox Corporation

messages. Voice mail differs from a telephone answering machine in several ways. Unlike answering machines, voice mail stores messages on a computer in digital form. Voice mail systems also allow the sender to transmit a message simultaneously to many people either within a company, within the local calling area, or long distance.

The technology of voice mail eliminates many communication problems in the workplace. Most telephone calls do not get through the first time because the recipient of the call is either out of the office or on another telephone line. With voice mail, however, the caller can leave a complete voice message that is stored in computer memory. If the individual who is being called is not available, the computer records the message onto *disk* where it is filed and retrieved later when needed. The ability to store messages at any time is particularly useful when different time zones are crossed or when messages must be left during non-working hours. Perhaps the most appealing aspect of voice messaging is the broadcast feature: one message can ultimately be transmitted to many users of the system simultaneously.

There are, however, some disadvantages to voice mail. The primary concern is that some people do not feel comfortable leaving a message on a machine whether it is sent to a computer or to an answering machine. Another concern is that the personal/social contact with clients might be lost.

THE FASHION ATTIC

Laura understood that basic computer knowledge coupled with appropriate hardware and software would help her run her business more efficiently and save money. Laura also understood that the word processing skills she used in college would no longer be sufficient for her needs. She decided to attend a 3-hour seminar, "Introduction to Computers," at the local Small Business Development Center to become familiar with what computer technology might offer.

At the seminar, Laura was relieved to see that she was not the only "computer illiterate" around! The instructor spent most of the evening explaining the many uses of a computer in a small business environment. Laura quickly learned it would take longer than three hours in this seminar to computerize her business.

Laura was already comfortable handling basic correspondence on a computer. She was, however, surprised to learn that a good word processing/desktop publishing program could create advertisements, flyers, and attractive announcements for direct mail purposes. Having already decided to rely heavily on personal correspondence with her customers, Laura quickly saw how useful a desktop publishing program would be in her business.

An accounting spreadsheet program was another option Laura knew would be useful. In addition to reducing accounting service fees, she could do payroll, create an income statement, maintain a balance sheet, reconcile her checking account statement, keep an accounts payable ledger and analyze the cash flow of her business. Tracking inventory was another business function that could be improved through the use of software.

It all sounded great but Laura was overwhelmed at the thought of trying to put it all together. At the conclusion of the seminar, she approached the instructor and asked for his recommendation as to what her first step should be.

"Laura, discuss your plans with your accountant. Coordinate your hardware and software needs with your accountant's. Then take advantage of courses offered privately or through an evening college that will teach you what you need to know to become proficient in the use of your hardware system and its accompanying software."

Following the advice of her instructor, Laura made an appointment with her accountant, Frank Duffy, the next day. Laura could now stay better informed on a daily basis as to how her business was doing if she understood the computerized bookkeeping and inventory tasks Frank handled for her. After Frank explained the systems that he used, Laura registered for a financial accounting software course and a desktop publishing course at a local college. At the conclusion of six weeks of classes she felt competent to handle many accounting operations presently handled by her accountant. She also felt capable of creating flyers and announcements that could be mailed directly to customers.

SUMMARY

Technology can be very valuable to the entrepreneur in the management of a small business. Entrepreneurs must become proficient in the use of several forms of technology. They must first become familiar with computer hardware, which consists of the keyboard, mouse, central processing unit (CPU), disks, the monitor, and the printer. Next, computer software must be mastered. Useful software for entrepreneurs includes word processing, database applications, spreadsheet applications, and desktop publishing.

The term "telecommunications" refers to the technique and technology of communication by electrical or electronic means. Telecommunications technology is also indispensable to entrepreneurs, especially electronic mail, fax machines, and voice mail.[1]

VOCABULARY BUILDER

On a separate sheet of paper, write a brief description of each word or phrase based on your reading of the chapter.

1. Computer literacy
2. Computer hardware
3. Software
4. Central processing unit
5. Keyboard
6. Mouse
7. Hard disks
8. Floppy disks
9. Disk drive
10. Monitor
11. Printer
12. Word processing
13. Database
14. Database software
15. Spreadsheet
16. Desktop publishing
17. Telecommunications
18. Electronic mail
19. Facsimile (fax)
20. Voice mail

REVIEW QUESTIONS

1. What are the three subunits of the central processing unit?
2. What are the two computer hardware components that are designed for the secondary storage of data?
3. What are the two basic types of disks?

---

[1]Much of the information in this chapter was adapted from *Computer Applications and Concepts*, by Groneman and Jaderstrom. For a more in-depth study of this content area, please refer to the aforementioned text.

4. What is a monochrome monitor?
5. If the computer is instructed to multiply 2 times 10, which part of the CPU directs the arithmetic/logic unit to do the multiplication?
6. In what area does word processing make the greatest contribution to office productivity?
7. If you want to effectively organize and manage lists, what type of software would you use?
8. What type of software would you use for accounting?
9. Why is in-house desktop publishing usually less expensive than sending the documents to a commercial printer?
10. What are three methods of telecommunication?
11. What are possible advantages of adding telecommunication capability to your business? What are two disadvantages?

DISCUSSION QUESTIONS

1. What is the difference between computer hardware and computer software?
2. What is the difference between database software and spreadsheet software?
3. Write a script for a voice mail announcement that would be user-friendly to nervous customers and also set a professional tone for the business. Find out what information must be included for the system to work.
4. What is the most practical approach to deciding what kind of software to buy?
5. You have $2,500 to spend on computer and telecommunications equipment as you start your new business. What are your priorities for spending this money and why?

CRITICAL THINKING

Jan Moller has been in business for about a year. Lately, her business has required that a large amount of correspondence be sent to customers. Much of the time, identical letters are sent to all of Jan's customers. So far, all of the correspondence has been produced on an electric typewriter. Jan thinks that there must be a better way.

1. If you were advising Jan, what would you suggest?
2. Assemble a list of businesses in your area that sell computer hardware and/or software.
3. After assembling your list, visit one of the businesses and collect some sales literature about computers and software.
4. Select the hardware components and the type of software (by brand name) that you would suggest Jan purchase.

SHORT CASE: BUSINESS IS BOOMING

Billie has been in the mail order business for three years. Since she first started the business, catalog sales have grown an average of 11.5 percent each month. As a result of this phenomenal growth, the management of the paperwork has become very time consuming and tedious.

The idea for starting the business originated when Billie had become aware of all the small cottage industries located in the valley where she lived. Most of these entrepreneurial ventures involved the manufacturing of inexpensive gift items. The majority of the items were manufactured in home garages or basements and sold at local art fairs and flea markets.

Billie had figured that if she could market these same items through the mail; she would accomplish two things. First, she would make a very nice living for herself, and second, she would add to the economic development of her valley.

Billie's success is almost more than she can manage. It is especially difficult for her to keep track of all her documents. She now has more than 200 people supplying 300 different gift items for sale. She also has a catalog mailing list of over 10,000 households. Until now, Billie had been doing all her paperwork, including making address labels, on an old electronic typewriter that she had bought at an auction at the local high school.

Not only is the paperwork almost overwhelming, but the cost of doing business is increasing. The printer who produces Billie's catalog just informed her that the cost of printing her catalog will be increasing by 7 percent because of increased paper costs. Success is starting to be burdensome. Billie is not only working 60 hours a week to get everything done, she is also starting to make less profit.

1. What technology would you recommend that Billie consider for managing the paperwork that her business involves? Why?
2. What are Billie's options concerning production of her catalog? What do you think is her best choice? Why?
3. Do you think that desktop publishing is a reasonable option for producing the sales catalog? Why or why not?

PROJECT CHALLENGE

As you continue the planning process for your new business, you must make a decision about the role of technology in your entrepreneurial venture. Using the information in this chapter and other sources, develop a technological plan for your business. You should consider the following:

1. Determine what computer hardware components will be necessary.
2. Decide on the type of word processing software that you will use.
3. Determine what type of database software you will use.
4. Determine what type of spreadsheet software you will use.
5. Determine whether or not you will need desktop publishing in your business.
6. Identify the telecommunications needs of your business.

18
Small Business Assistance

After mastering the information contained in this chapter, you should be able to:

18-1 List federal and state government agencies that small business owners may contact for assistance.

18-2 Understand the importance of Small Business Development Centers to business owners.

18-3 Identify sources of assistance in your community.

18-4 Identify the services that various professionals might provide to small businesses.

Because entrepreneurs are often the sole creators and/or directors of their enterprises, they sometimes work in isolated environments. As we have seen, entrepreneurs must become knowledgeable in many areas to successfully operate their businesses and compete in today's sophisticated marketplace. This chapter provides resources for entrepreneurs to gain the information necessary to establish and maintain their businesses.

FEDERAL AGENCIES

Many types of support and assistance are available to entrepreneurs, primarily through numerous government agencies and private professionals. Entrepreneurs can usually obtain most of the information, education, and direction they need through these sources.

Small Business Administration

The United States government recognizes the important role that small businesses play in our society. Congress authorized the formation of the Small Business Administration (SBA) in 1953 to encourage small business development and the important inventions and innovations that these businesses provide.

The SBA was created to assist in the development of small businesses. It helps small businesses secure government contracts and acts as a special advocate with other federal agencies and state and private agencies. The SBA helps small businesses increase their revenues and profits which increases tax revenue for the government and helps to maintain our standard of living. There are more than 100 SBA offices located throughout the United States. Assistance available through the SBA includes loans, counseling, and publications.

SBA Loan Assistance. The SBA provides assistance in financing thousands of businesses that would not qualify for conventional financing. It offers two basic types of business loans, guaranteed and direct, which were discussed in Chapter 12.

Counseling. One of the sources of SBA counseling services is the **Service Corps of Retired Executives (SCORE).** There is no cost for these services—SCORE is a volunteer organization. Members use their business experience to advise and guide small business owners. SCORE volunteers come from all areas of business, including commercial and industrial. They contribute their time to help others succeed. SCORE counselors can provide business owners with information about business basics, but they may not be able to answer questions specific to a particular business. SCORE also provides comprehensive workshops for prospective and new business owners (see Figure 18-1).

Another source of free counseling is the **Small Business Institute (SBI).** SBI counseling services are provided by student teams at many colleges. Contact the SBA office to obtain information about these services; they are available only during certain periods of a school's term.

Service Corps of Retired Executives (SCORE), a counseling service—staffed by volunteers who have business experience—for new and established small-business owners

Illus. 18-1 SCORE counselors are volunteers who use their business experience to advise and guide small business owners.

Figure 18-1 SCORE Workshop Announcement

STARTING RIGHT

PRESENTED BY SCORE
(614) 469-2357

Are you PROPERLY PREPARED to start your own business?

If you are thinking of starting your own business or if you are struggling with your current business, you will likely benefit from SCORE'S **"STARTING RIGHT"** workshop. Hundreds of entrepreneurs have.

STARTING RIGHT is an all-day workshop designed to increase your skills in the operation and management of your own business. STARTING RIGHT is held once a month at the Ohio State University Fawcett Center For Tomorrow, 2400 Olentangy River Road. Those who have attended this workshop have found it to be very informative.

Maybe **you** have a business concept that you have been dreaming about for years or maybe it is your life's ambition to have your own business, but don't know how to get started. Then this could be just the boost you need! This workshop may very well reinforce your plan, or cause you to rethink your plans or abandon your idea and remain in your current situation.

The STARTING RIGHT program consists of eight segments:

- PLANNING YOUR BUSINESS
- LEGAL STRUCTURES
- MARKETING OVERVIEW
- BUSINESS RECORDS
- BUSINESS INSURANCE
- FINANCIAL PLANNING
- SOURCES OF CAPITAL
- TAXES AND LICENSES

No matter in what stage your thoughts are, there is no time like **NOW** to go forward with your dreams to start your own business.

For further information please call the **SCORE Office at 469-2357**.

The Service Corps of Retired Executives is partially funded by the U.S. Small Business Administration. The support given by the U.S. Small Business Administration through such funding does not constitute an express or implied endorsement of the cosponsor(s) or participants' opinions, products or services.

SCORE

SBA/SCORE
85 MARCONI BLVD., ROOM 512 • COLUMBUS, OHIO 43215-2887

Publications. The SBA offers a number of publications and videotapes to provide information to small business owners. Most are available at a nominal cost and can be ordered through any SBA office (see Figure 18-2 on the next page).

Other Federal Agencies

Small business owners can also obtain assistance from numerous government offices. These offices are widely distributed throughout the United States and their services cover the full range of business needs.

United States Department of Commerce. The Department of Commerce encourages, serves, and promotes international trade, economic growth, and technological advancement. The Department provides a wide variety of programs that offer assistance and information, including social and economic statistics for business, and research and support for scientific, engineering, and technological development. It also grants patents, trademarks, and service marks, provides assistance to promote economic development, and assists in the growth of minority businesses. These functions are served through 12 different bureaus within the Department of Commerce, the most prominent of which are listed here.

- The Office of Business Liaison develops and promotes a cooperative working relationship between the Department of Commerce and the business community. This office keeps the business community aware of the Department of Commerce's administration, resources, policies, and programs, and keeps administration officials within the Department of Commerce aware of issues that concern businesses. It also promotes business involvement in departmental policymaking and program development, and provides technical assistance to businesses that need help in dealing with the government. The Office of Business Liaison is the focal point for all communication between the Department of Commerce and the business community.
- The Office of Small and Disadvantaged Business Utilization (OSDBU) works in conjunction with the SBA to assist some small and minority-owned businesses to secure contracts, both private and federal.
- The Bureau of the Census collects, tabulates, and publishes a wide variety of statistical data about the people and the economy of the United States. The principal means by which the Bureau

Figure 18-2 Partial Listing of SBA Publications

VIDEOTAPES

Each VHS videotape below comes complete with a workbook.

Marketing: Winning Customers With a Workable Plan

This program, developed by two of the country's leading small business marketing experts, offers a step-by-step approach on how to write the best possible marketing plan for your business. You'll also learn the best methods for determining customer needs, how to identify and develop a working profile for potential customers and much more. PLUS...the workbook that comes with each video provides easy-to-follow examples of how to use this information to meet your marketing goals.

VTI $30.00

The Business Plan: Your Roadmap To Success

This videotape teaches you the essentials of developing a business plan that will help lead you to capital, growth, and profitability. It tells you what to include, what to omit, and how to get free help from qualified consultants. You'll also find out what an SBA executive, a venture capitalist, and a banker will be looking for when reviewing your business plan. The workbook that comes with each video includes a checklist of information to include as well as samples of the income statement, balance sheet, and cash flow forecast.

VT2 $30.00

Promotion: Solving The Puzzle

Advertising, public relations, direct mail, and trade shows are the parts of the promotion puzzle. Each piece is important to the whole and each piece works to reinforce the others. This videotape and workbook package shows you how to put the pieces together to present a sound promotional plan aimed at targeting new customers, increasing sales and getting the most for your promotional dollar. Learn how to choose the best advertising medium for your needs, write a press release that grabs attention, and much more.

VT3 $30.00

PUBLICATIONS

PRODUCTS/IDEAS/INVENTIONS

Ideas Into Dollars

This publication identifies the main challenges in product development and provides a list of resources to help inventors and innovators take their ideas into the marketplace.

PI1 $2.00

Avoiding Patent, Trademark And Copyright Problems.

Learn how to avoid infringing the rights of others and the importance of protecting your own rights.

PI2 $1.00

Trademarks And Business Goodwill

Learn what trademarks are and are not and how to get the most protection for your commercial name.

PI3 $1.00

FINANCIAL MANAGEMENT

ABC'S Of Borrowing

This best-seller tells you what lenders look for and what to expect when borrowing money for your small business.

FM1 $1.00

Profit Costing And Pricing For Manufacturers

Uncover the latest techniques for pricing your products profitably.

FM2 $1.00

Basic Budgets For Profit Planning

This publication takes the worry out of putting together a comprehensive budgeting system to monitor your profits and assess your financial operations.

FM3 $1.00

Understanding Cash Flow

The owner/manager is shown how to plan for the movement of cash through the business and thus plan for future requirements.

FM4 $1.00

A Venture Capital Primer For Small Business

Learn what venture capital resources are available and how to develop a proposal for obtaining these funds.

FM5 $0.50

Accounting Services For Small Service Firms

Sample profit/loss statements are used to illustrate how accounting services can help expose and correct trouble spots in business financial records.

FM6 $0.50

Analyze Your Records To Reduce Costs

Understand the nature of expenses and how they interrelate with sales, inventories, and profit. Achieve greater profits through more efficient use of the dollar.

FM7 $0.50

Budgeting In A Small Service Firm

Learn how to set up and keep sound financial records. Study how to effectively use journals, ledgers, and charts to increase profits.

FM8 $0.50

Sound Cash Management And Borrowing

Avoid a "crash crisis" through proper use of cash budgets, cash flow projections and planned borrowing concepts.

FM9 $0.50

assists small businesses is through its provision of printed reports, computer tapes, and special tabulations.
- The Bureau of Economic Analysis (BEA) strives to provide a clear picture of the U.S. economy through analysis of national economic statistics, including personal income, business activity, and investment activity. Results of BEA analyses are published monthly in *Survey of Current Business* and *Business Conditions Digest.*
- The Economic Development Administration (EDA) was established to generate new jobs, protect existing jobs, and stimulate commercial and industrial growth in economically distressed areas. The EDA provides assistance to state and local governments, public and private nonprofit organizations, and industrial and commercial businesses. One of the ways in which the EDA provides assistance to businesses is by providing loan guarantees. Proceeds from EDA loans can be used for working capital, to maintain or expand operations, or for purchasing assets.

The remaining seven offices of the Department of Commerce provide technical information; assistance for international trade (both

Illus. 18-2 The EDA helps economically distressed areas generate new jobs, protect existing jobs, and stimulate commercial and industrial growth.

© *Martin Rogers/Tony Stone Images, Inc.*

import and export) and minority business development; extensive research for scientific and technological businesses; environmental monitoring; telecommunications development; incentives for invention, research and development, and commercialization; and information about travel and tourism.

Government Printing Office. The Government Printing Office (GPO) executes orders for printing and binding documents for all divisions of the federal government. Although government publications are not produced by this office, it does produce and distribute catalogs of all publications that are available and processes orders for these publications.

Federal Trade Commission. The primary purpose of the Federal Trade Commission (FTC) is to ensure that business practices in the United States are fair. Meeting this responsibility requires constant monitoring of all aspects of business to ensure accurate product representation, fair competition, fair pricing, accuracy in credit reporting, fair cost for credit, and fair export trade. The FTC has the authority to make and enforce rules to regulate trade and protect consumers. To protect their own interests, entrepreneurs may report competitors' unfair or illegal business practices to the FTC. (The FTC is discussed further in Chapter 19.)

Internal Revenue Service. An office of the Department of the Treasury, the Internal Revenue Service (IRS) is a division that all of us come in contact with on a regular basis. The IRS is responsible for collecting taxes and for ensuring compliance with tax laws. The IRS also provides services to taxpayers. It issues federal taxpayer identification numbers for businesses, distributes (upon request) publications that explain tax rules, and assists with tax-related questions, both by telephone and through IRS representatives at local IRS offices.

FEDERAL/STATE COOPERATIVES

Some sources of assistance are funded by both the federal government (through the SBA) and state governments. One such agency is the **Small Business Development Center (SBDC).** The SBDC program is a cooperative venture between the SBA and each state's business development department, with active participation by local chambers of commerce and colleges and universities. A typical SBDC consists of these three components:

Small Business Development Center (SBDC), an agency funded by both the federal government and state governments to provide counseling and training for small business owners

1. An administrative unit, which is generally housed with other departments of the state
2. Several subcenters, which provide small business information, in-depth counseling, referrals, and owner/manager education programs
3. Satellite offices, which offer some, but not all, of the services available through the subcenters

The programs and seminars offered (see Figure 18-3) cover all aspects of business operation. Entrepreneurs can obtain much valuable information by attending a "How to Start a Business" seminar. A wide variety of other seminars provide information about many of the phases of business development. Some sample seminar titles include "Legal Aspects of Operating a Business," and "Preparing Loan Proposals." Many of the seminars will also help established business owners.

A typical SBDC subcenter's staff includes a director and several consultants who have experience in operating small businesses. They act as advisors for preparing business plans, completing loan applications, developing marketing programs, and planning other business activities.

SBDC offices are excellent sources of help in designing a business plan. Since they often cooperate with the state's university system, they have access to information and research in almost every field. They are also backed by the SBDC Connection, a central library that provides information to all centers. Many states' SBDCs have specialists available in international trade, minority business development, and government procurement to provide information. There are 650 SBDCs in the United States.

STATE AGENCIES

Assistance is also available to small businesses at the state level.

State Departments of Development

Each of the 50 states has a **Department of Development (DOD).** This department administers federal community development programs, and is usually made up of several divisions, such as the following:

- The Division of Business Development coordinates the various business programs, including tax incentive and financial assistance

Department of Development (DOD), a state agency that works to advance economic growth and to encourage new and existing businesses to operate within the state

Unit 4 Managing the Small Business

Figure 18-3 SBDC Brochure Cover

Clayton State College
SBDC
Small Business Development Center

Non-Profit Org.
U.S. POSTAGE
PAID
PERMIT No. 27
Morrow, Ga.

COUNSELING AND CONTINUING EDUCATION ACTIVITIES AT CLAYTON STATE COLLEGE

Co-sponsored with: The Chambers of Commerce in Carroll, Clayton, Coweta, Fayette, Henry, Rockdale, South Fulton, and Spalding Counties: the Office of Community Services, Clayton State College; and The University of Georgia.

BUSINESS DEVELOPMENT SEMINARS

The Clayton State College Small Business Development Center continues its series of programs to help small business owners and managers meet the challenges of operating their businesses. The programs are led by expert resources from the College, the community and the University System of Georgia. The programs are co-sponsored by the Chambers of Commerce in Carroll, Clayton, Coweta, Fayette, Henry, South Fulton, Rockdale, and Spalding counties; the Office of Community Services, Clayton State College; and The University of Georgia.

!!! **NEW LOCATION** !!!
(See map on back.)
SMALL BUSINESS DEVELOPMENT CENTER
Continuing Education Center
Second Floor
(414) 961-3440

"Special arrangements for the handicapped will be made, if requested in advance, by contacting (404) 961-3515."

Clayton State College is committed to the principle of affirmative action and shall not discriminate against otherwise qualified persons on the basis of race, color, religion, national origin, sex, age, physical or mental handicap, disability, or veteran's status in its recruitment, admissions, employment, facility and program accessibility, or services.

SCHEDULE OF WORKSHOPS

Developing A
  Business Plan . . . . July 1

How To Start A New Business. . . . . . July 13

Legal Aspects Of Business . . . . July 16

Small Business Tax Workshop . . . . . July 18

Bookkeeping For Small
  Business . . . . July 30 & August 1

Business Use Of The Home . . . . . . August 6

Avoiding Small Business
  Mistakes . . . . August 8

How To Promote A Small
  Business . . . . August 13

Prepared Loan Proposals
  SBA And Conventional . . . . August 19

Financial Planning For The
  Small Business Owner . . . . August 15

How To Use Your Small
  Business Computer . . . . August 22

programs, that are designed to enhance the state's business climate. Subdivisions of this department promote the state to out-of-state industries and businesses, and encourage existing companies to maintain and/or expand their facilities. They also provide information about locations, markets, labor, taxes, and finances, and often provide customized job training programs.
- The Economic Development Financing Division administers various state economic development financing programs.

The DOD provides assistance to small and developing businesses through a Small Business Division and a Minority Business Development Division. The Small Business Division assists small businesses in the areas of licensing, business structure, taxes, and financing. It also serves as a liaison between the small business community and state government agencies. The Minority Business Development Division provides services to aid the growth of the state's minority-owned businesses and monitors state-administered loan and funding programs for minority businesses.

Other divisions of a state DOD include an International Trade Division, a Community Development Division, a Division of Energy,

Illus. 18-3 The Minority Business Development Division provides services to aid the growth of the state's minority-owned businesses.

© Steven Peters/Tony Stone Images, Inc.

a Marketing and Research Division, a Policy and Intergovernmental Relations Division, and an Administration Division. In addition, many state DODs have one department that is equipped to supply new business owners with all of the information, and sometimes the applications, they need regarding licensing and permit requirements for their particular businesses.

Other State Agencies

Further assistance is available to small business owners through a variety of other state agencies. The following six agencies exist in most states in the U.S.

The Worker's Compensation Board. All business owners who have employees must provide insurance that gives employees or their survivors benefits in the event of work-related injuries or deaths. The Board works with employers to provide this protection at a reasonable cost.

The State Department of Agriculture and The Consumer Protection Division. These departments issue permits for businesses involved with the processing, handling, storage, or distribution of food products. They also issue permits for businesses of public interest, such as daycare centers, schools, financial institutions, and employment agencies.

The State Sales and Use Tax Division. This agency issues identification numbers to retail businesses, which must collect and remit sales taxes. It also provides instructions for collecting, reporting, and remitting the sales taxes to the state.

The State Department of Labor. This department provides information regarding employer responsibilities in relation to unemployment insurance. All employers must contribute a specified percent of wages to the state's fund for compensation for displaced workers.

The Office of the Secretary of State. General business information as well as information and forms for incorporation are provided by this office, as are forms for registering state trademarks and business names.

COMMUNITY RESOURCES

Many communities offer their own assistance centers for small business owners. The principal community assistance center is often a chamber of commerce.

Chambers of Commerce

The purpose of a chamber of commerce, operated and funded by local municipalities and businesses, is to stimulate local economic growth. Economic growth is important to all communities. It ensures that there will be enough jobs and income to attract and keep residents. The chamber of commerce office is usually staffed by people who are very familiar with the commercial activities of the community. They are an excellent source of information for owners of both new and established businesses.

Local business owners and managers are elgible to be members of a chamber of commerce. Becoming a member of the chamber of commerce is an excellent way to make contact with other business owners.

Other Community Resources

Colleges, universities, and technical schools often offer community outreach services through educational training and research support. Entrepreneurs should take advantage of these resources, if they are available.

A trip to city hall or the county courthouse to determine what municipal and county government agencies exist in your community is worthwhile. Often included within municipal and county agencies are the following offices, with which entrepreneurs should become familiar.

- Licensing and Permit Offices—business licenses
- County Health Department—local health and safety regulations
- County Extension Services—resources for agricultural businesses

PROFESSIONAL SERVICES

Small business owners can also obtain assistance from individuals who make their living providing information and assistance. These services seldom come without a cost. Entrepreneurs usually need to plan ahead and include such services in their budgets.

Attorneys

Many business owners seek help from attorneys to be sure that they follow the proper procedures in all legal aspects of their business operation, such as drafting and/or signing lease agreements. Attorneys provide valuable information about business owners' rights, the best legal structure for a business, protecting assets, preventing legal action, obtaining patents and trademarks, and tax and business legislation. Business owners should establish a relationship with an attorney even if legal services are not needed on a regular basis.

Accountants

In addition to designing and maintaining bookkeeping systems, accountants can often provide planning and management advice. In particular, they may be able to make valuable recommendations for minimizing tax liability.

Insurance Agents

Certified insurance agents have extensive training related to insurance requirements and regulations. Entrepreneurs should discuss their insurance needs with a qualified agent. Good agents will help small business owners determine how to obtain the coverage they need at the lowest possible cost. They will also provide suggestions for changes that can be made to reduce insurance cost, such as certain safety and security precautions.

Illus. 18-4 In addition to bookkeeping services, accountants can provide financial planning and management advice as well as recommendations for minimizing business tax liability.

Photo by Alan Brown/Photonics

THE FASHION ATTIC

Laura was quite pleased about her business plan following her meeting with the loan officer at the bank. She decided that it would be a good idea to make a return visit to her SBDC advisor for a full analysis. She met with Lois Cartwright to see if there was anything she had omitted.

Lois reviewed the plan and was quite complimentary regarding its organization.

I. Description of the Business
II. The Market
III. The Competition
IV. Location of the Business
V. Management
VI. Personnel
VII. Financial Data
VIII. Application and Anticipated Effect of the Loan
IX. Executive Summary

"It looks good, Laura, but there are no details about your insurance program," said Lois. "How did you arrive at your estimated insurance cost?"

"I asked my father's friend. He told me how much he thought it would cost to protect my inventory," Laura replied.

"You need to talk to a professional insurance agent, Laura," Lois said. "There's a lot to learn about proper insurance coverage, and you must make sure that you are adequately protected. A good agent will be able to help you determine your insurance needs. If you put this off until the last minute you may be unpleasantly surprised by the cost. I don't believe your business is as complicated as some are, but please be sure to investigate this thoroughly before proceeding. After that, you'll be ready to start your business education."

"I've already signed up for two computer courses here at the college," Laura said.

"Good, but that should be just the beginning. I recommend you sign up for additional seminars and workshops on operating a small business. The seminars provided by the SBDC are inexpensive, and they will be very helpful to you. Also, you will meet other business owners. Let's look at the current schedule and see which programs will meet your needs."

Lois pointed out three seminars that she thought would help Laura. It was becoming clear to Laura that business education was to be an ongoing process throughout her entrepreneurial career.

SUMMARY

Entrepreneurs have a support system: they can obtain assistance from many outside sources. Various government agencies provide assistance, counseling, and information. These agencies function at federal, state, and local levels. Types of services include information packets and brochures, seminars and workshops, financial assistance, planning assistance, and one-on-one counseling. Professionals such as attorneys, accountants, and insurance agents also provide valuable services to business owners. It is important that entrepreneurs take advantage of the help that is available.

VOCABULARY BUILDER

On a separate sheet of paper, write a brief definition of each word or phrase based on your reading of the chapter.

1. Small Business Administration
2. Service Corps of Retired Executives
3. Small Business Development Center
4. Department of Development
5. attorney
6. insurance agent

REVIEW QUESTIONS

1. Why was the Small Business Administration created?
2. What services are available through the SBA?
3. What does the acronym SCORE stand for? What do SCORE volunteers do?
4. What agency should you contact for information regarding patents and trademarks?
5. What services are available through Small Business Development Centers?
6. What purpose do chambers of commerce serve?

7. What professional services might entrepreneurs use?
8. How can attorneys help small businesses?

DISCUSSION QUESTIONS

1. What roles do the various federal agencies play in assisting small businesses?
2. Why should small business owners attend SBDC seminars?
3. What impact does your local chamber of commerce have on the business community?
4. Do any of the professional services appeal to you as a career? Why or why not?

CRITICAL THINKING

The SBA's existence has been threatened during times of government budget reduction. However, it has always continued to receive congressional support. What makes this agency so important? What would happen if it were eliminated?

SHORT CASE: READY OR NOT

Janet Stalen had completed the preparations for opening her new candy and nut store. She was looking forward to her grand opening—it was only three days away.

Because she had enough capital to finance her business, Janet had decided that she did not need to write a business plan. She felt that her background as an employee in a small retail store had given her enough knowledge about operating a business that she did not need to attend any of the business development workshops her friend Rollin had recommended.

Rollin had opened a sporting goods store two years ago. The classes he had attended—and the business plan he had developed with the information he obtained—had been a big help to him. When he opened his door to the public for the first time, he felt confident that he was ready to serve his customers and that his business was likely to succeed.

Rollin decided to call Janet to wish her luck and to find out whether she needed any help with her final preparations.

"Hello, Janet. This is Rollin. I just called to wish you the best of luck and to see if you need anything."

"Thank you, Rollin! I'm ready to open my store *now*; I'm really looking forward to Monday. The store opens at 10:00, and one of my employees will be in at 10:30. I don't think we'll have any problems at all."

"I'm glad to hear that, Janet. Did you have any trouble getting your identification numbers or the licenses and permits you need?"

"What identification numbers? What licenses and permits? I have my vendor's license—what else do I need?"

"Didn't you get a checklist of the requirements for your business when you attended the workshops I suggested?"

"Well, I didn't go, Rollin. I was awfully busy, and I felt like I knew everything I needed to know to get started. What do I do now? Can I still open my store on Monday?"

"Call the SBA right away, Janet. They can tell you who to get in touch with to find out what you need and how to get it as quickly as possible. Good luck!"

After checking with the SBA, Janet called her state's One-Stop Business Permit Center. The representative she talked with suggested that she stop by the center and pick up the necessary forms, then contact the agencies involved to determine whether she would be able to open her store as planned.

Questions

1. What was Janet's big mistake?
2. Janet told Rollin she hadn't had time to attend the workshops that he had recommended. Were there other ways she could have found out what was required for her business?
3. What requirements did Janet fail to meet for her business?
4. Do you think Janet was able to open her store as planned? Why or why not? Contact the agencies that issue the permits you think she needed and verify your answer.

PROJECT CHALLENGE

Visit the nearest SBA office or SBDC subcenter for an informal review of your business plan. (If there is no SBA office or SBDC subcenter near you, take your business plan to the local chamber of commerce or the business education department of a college for review.) Review any changes or additions that are recommended and decide whether you will make these changes or additions. Give reasons for your decisions. Make a list of scheduled seminars and/or workshops that might be helpful to you.

PARTNERSHIP WITH A HANDSHAKE

Unit 4 Case

After working for a large corporation for ten years, Charlie Benison quickly accepted Tad Kelly's invitation to join him in his newly expanded auto parts distribution business. The thought of being a co-owner with his long-time friend appealed to him.

The first decision Tad and Charlie made together was whether their business relationship should be a partnership arrangement or a corporation. They discussed the question at length, and concluded that the easiest thing to do was to form a fifty-fifty partnership. A partnership would save legal and accounting costs and, since they were such good friends, Tad & Charlie felt positive they could discuss and resolve any problems that might arise. They sealed the agreement with a handshake.

◆

Business started out with a boom exceeding their expectations. Tad's job kept him out on the road selling parts to retail stores while Charlie remained in the office to coordinate all shipping and administrative matters. Charlie was surprised at the work pace he had to keep as he supervised a crew of four shipment packers. It was much different than his former corporate job.

◆

Charlie was using the shipping and scheduling control methods he had used at his previous job. To explain the daily and weekly objectives he had established, Charlie started each day by showing the employees elaborate computer print outs of shipping schedules and charts.

◆

In making his schedules Charlie did not take absenteeism into consideration. Therefore, when an employee was unable to come to work, Charlie had to fill in so the shipping schedule could be met. This frustrated Charlie because it disrupted his routine. Calling the personnel department for a substitute worker was not an option for Charlie as it had been before.

357

Regular communication between Tad and Charlie was difficult due to Tad's travel schedule. Management style, procedures, and business priorities did not receive the attention needed to help the business run smoothly. Consequently, serious problems developed.

◆

First, Tad had a disagreement with Charlie concerning buying another company's inventory. Because the price was greatly reduced, Tad wanted to hold off until he could research the market and make what he felt would be an informed decision.

◆

Next, the employees requested a confidential meeting with Tad to air their grievances about working with Charlie. They told him that the time Charlie spent creating, revising, and explaining his reports, charts, and schedules kept them from doing their jobs. The employees also pointed out that though Charlie made the unrealistic work schedules, he became angry when he had to fill in for an absent worker. The employees emphasized to Tad that they could not continue to work under these conditions.

◆

Tad knew these problems had to be resolved quickly when he discovered a number of late shipments and orders that had been cancelled because the shipment had not been made in a timely manner. He arranged a meeting with Charlie.

◆

"Charlie, this business isn't working. Your talents do not lend themselves to a small business environment. We should end this partnership before the business goes under. I'll return your investment and maybe you can go back to your old job."

◆

Charlie was furious. "You can't do that, Tad! I'm not sure I can get my old job back. If you want me out, you have to give me my investment back plus six months' pay. It's not my fault the employees don't understand shipping procedures and are absent so much. If you don't give me my money back, plus the six months' pay, I will sue and put you out of business for sure." He stalked out of Tad's office.

◆

Tad shook his head. "How did this happen?" he thought. "I'm in danger of losing both my business and my best friend. I wish I had listened to the advice of the attorney and the SBDC counselor about writing an article of partnership. If we had written out, in advance, an agreement as to what to do in the event of a dissolution of partnership, this wouldn't be happening. I'm stuck now. I can't afford to pay Charlie six months' salary and give back his initial investment besides. I would have to close the business. If it goes to court I can't afford the legal expenses. Where do I go for help now?"

(See the following page for case questions.)

Case Questions

1. How would a written partnership agreement have helped resolve this situation? Could a partnership agreement have helped avoid this situation? Give reasons to support your answers.
2. Is it possible to have too many control tools in a business?
3. Where would you suggest Tad turn for help?

UNIT 5
LEGAL AND ETHICAL CONSIDERATIONS

19 Special Regulations

20 Contracts and Agreements

21 Buying and Selling

22 Real Property and Insurance

23 Ethics and Social Responsibility in Entrepreneurship

19
Special Regulations

After mastering the information contained in this chapter, you should be able to:

19-1 Explain the Federal Trade Commission and the impact it has on advertising, consumer credit, product warranties, and competition.

19-2 Explain the Consumer Product Safety Act and its provisions.

19-3 Understand environmental protection legislation.

19-4 Understand the components of the Fair Credit Billing Act.

There is more to successfully operating a business than hanging a sign and opening the door. You have examined the importance of marketing, financing, and managing to the success of your entrepreneurial venture. Now it is time to take a look at some legal considerations.

As an entrepreneur, you will enjoy a considerable amount of freedom to operate your business as you see fit. This freedom may be somewhat restricted, however, by certain laws and regulations. To prevent costly lawsuits and other unpleasant encounters, you should understand certain basic laws that exist to regulate business activities. By becoming familiar with these regulations, you will have knowledge that will enable you to succeed.

FEDERAL TRADE COMMISSION

As was discussed in Chapter 18, the Federal Trade Commission (FTC) is a federal administrative agency charged with the responsibility of ensuring fair, free, and open business. In general, it is concerned with unfair business practices in interstate commerce. Its scope is very wide, affecting advertising, consumer credit, product safety, and business competition.

The FTC accomplishes its job in several ways. First, it interprets laws and creates regulations. It also advises businesses when requested to do so. If unfair business practices are suspected, the FTC will investigate. Its powers enable it to issue "cease and desist" orders to businesses, which can then voluntarily discontinue unfair, deceitful, or illegal business practices. If a business does not agree to stop such activities, the FTC may hold hearings to prosecute the firm. As you read about the FTC's four major areas of responsibility—advertising, consumer credit, product warranties, and competition—in the following paragraphs, think about which ones might apply to the business you would like to start.

When credit cards are used, the requirements of this law are shifted from the entrepreneur to the credit card company.

Offering credit card usage to customers is a marketing strategy. Consumers tend to spend more money on goods in a business where credit payments are allowed. If entrepreneurs permit payment with major credit cards, they are likely to see sales increase since it is easier for most customers to pay with credit than with cash.

Fair Credit Reporting Act. The **Fair Credit Reporting Act** allows consumers access to their personal credit information. Business owners use consumer credit agencies to determine whether or not to grant credit to particular consumers. If an individual is denied credit by a business owner, that business owner is required by law to provide the consumer with the name and address of the credit agency used. Business owners may also report delinquent credit customers to consumer credit agencies. For example, Mike Camp applied for a loan for a new car at a local car dealership. The car dealer ran a credit check on him. Mike failed the credit check and the dealer denied Mike the loan.

Under this act, Mike has a right to know what information is included in his credit history. If he feels that some of the information is incorrect, he may challenge it. If Mike challenges the information, the credit company must either provide documentation of the information or remove it from the record. This must be done in a reasonable time period.

In Mike's case, he contacted the credit company and requested a copy of his file. When he received and examined the file, he discovered the problem. Two years ago, Mike had joined a health club and signed a one-year contract. After six months, the club closed. Yet it continued to send Mike bills. He refused to pay. The club then reported this to the credit company. Mike challenged the part of the credit report dealing with the health club. The credit company tried to document the information, but could not. It therefore had to remove the information from Mike's report. Mike later went back to the car dealer. This time he was successful in his attempt to buy and finance a new vehicle.

Equal Credit Opportunity Act. The **Equal Credit Opportunity Act** states that any business offering credit must make it available to all creditworthy customers regardless of race, national origin, marital status, religion, sex, age, or receipt of public assistance. If you, the entrepreneur, decide to extend credit as a service to your customers, you must make it available to everyone.

Fair Credit Reporting Act, a law that allows consumers access to their personal credit information

Equal Credit Opportunity Act, a law that requires any business offering credit to make it available to all creditworthy customers regardless of race, national origin, marital status, religion, sex, age, or receipt of public assistance

Product Warranties

Generally speaking, a warranty is a guarantee of the integrity of a product. Entrepreneurs need to be aware of two types of warranties—express and implied.

Express Warranty. An **express warranty** is a clearly stated fact about the quality or performance of a product. The warranty often serves as an important factor in the buying decision. It may be either written or verbal. For example, a label on a sweater saying "100 percent cashmere" is an express warranty.

Entrepreneurs need to exercise caution when purchasing goods from suppliers. They need to judge whether or not products can deliver what their owners or their labels state they can. Furthermore, entrepreneurs or salespeople working for the business need to be careful what they say about product performance or quality when talking to customers. If they are not careful, sales talk may become an enforceable warranty.

As an example, consider Jeanne Ellis. She works at Mountain Products Limited, a sporting goods store. A customer, Mary, enters the store and wants to look at sleeping bags. During the course of the sales pitch, Jeanne says, "I guarantee that this bag will keep you warm even if the temperature drops to 30 degrees below zero." Whether the bag was designed for that temperature or not does not matter: Jeanne has issued an express warranty. The store can now be held liable for failure of the product to protect the buyer at –30 degrees. This bit of sales talk can ultimately be costly to the store if what is stated is not true. The salesperson should never warranty a product in any way that is not supported by the manufacturer.

Implied Warranty. An **implied warranty** is an unwritten warranty ensuring that a product will perform under normal use and circumstances. In other words, the consumer is entitled to certain minimum levels of quality when purchasing products.

As an example, assume a customer purchased a radio designed for use in the shower from your retail store. The first time the buyer used the radio, it stopped playing as soon as it got wet. Since the radio was designed to be used in the shower, getting it wet would be considered normal use. Therefore, based on the implied warranty, the customer is legally able to return the radio to your store and get a replacement.

FTC's Role in Warranties. The FTC is charged with enforcement of the **Magnuson-Moss Warranty Act**, which provides standards for

---

express warranty, a clearly stated fact about the quality or performance of a product

implied warranty, a warranty imposed by law ensuring that a product will perform under normal use and circumstances

Magnuson-Moss Warranty Act, a law that sets standards for companies that offer written express warranties on consumer products

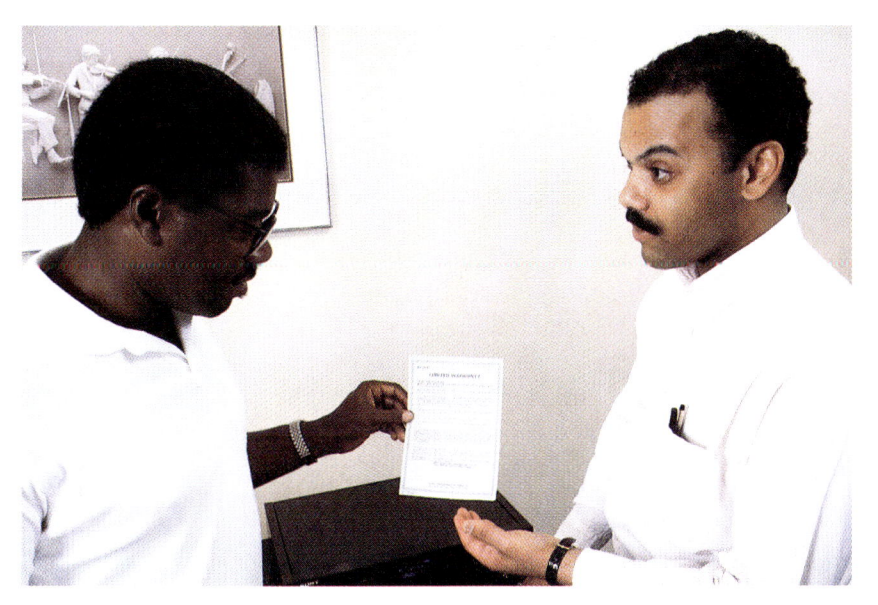

Illus. 19-3 Product warranties provide consumers with specific legal rights.

companies that choose to give written express warranties on consumer products. Specifically, the law requires the seller to include, in simple language and in a conspicuous fashion, the following information:

- the words "This warranty gives you specific legal rights and you may also have other rights which vary from state to state."
- which parts of the product are covered by the warranty
- a description of the product, including parts not included
- time limits of the warranty (such as 90 days or 2 years)
- instructions for obtaining repair or replacement
- the manufacturer's responsibilities in case of warranty breach

Competition

The FTC guarantees fair competition among U.S. businesses through the enforcement of the Sherman Antitrust Act, the Clayton Act, and the Robinson-Patman Act (see Chapter 6). Sometimes, however, a business may do something that does not violate one of these acts, but still interferes with fair competition. The FTC can step in if a valid complaint is filed. As an example of this kind of situation, consider a bank that wants to increase its deposits. As an incentive, it offers an interest rate that is a full percentage point higher than what other local banks are offering. For consumers to earn this higher rate, though, they must agree to do all of their banking business with this particular bank. The bank is not violating any antitrust laws, but it is still trying to interfere with fair competition. The FTC has the authority to step in and investigate the issue.

STATE AND LOCAL REGULATIONS

In addition to the federal regulations presented in this chapter, there are also many state and local regulations that restrict business activity. Many states have enacted their own versions of federal laws and some are more strict than the federal regulations. To learn about laws that affect you and your enterprise, talk to other small-business owners in your particular industry or join a trade association. As mentioned in Chapter 18, the SBA and SCORE may have detailed information regarding regulations affecting your business.

In addition, if you want to engage in certain types of business such as real estate or car sales, most states require that you have a license. Some licenses require testing or certification as well as the payment of fees.

Knowledge of rules and regulations is essential during the planning stages of a business. It is also very important to keep that knowledge current throughout the life of the firm. The risks of not knowing—fines, negative public relations, legal hassles, and even imprisonment—are simply too great to ignore.

CONSUMER PROTECTION

When planning the opening of a new small business, entrepreneurs must be aware that there is considerable legal protection available for consumers. Several areas of this protection have already been discussed. There are three additional areas of consumer protection: product safety, environmental protection, and fair credit billing. These issues are important to both retailers and manufacturers. Lack of knowledge about these areas can seriously impede entrepreneurial success.

Product Safety

With the growing realization that thousands of consumers were being injured or killed annually as a result of faulty products, Congress passed the **Consumer Product Safety Act** in 1972. This law was passed to protect the public from dangerous products and to provide for the evaluation of product safety hazards.

In addition to passing the act, Congress created the Consumer Product Safety Commission (CPSC) to administer it. The CPSC administers the act in many ways. It establishes and enforces product safety standards such as design, manufacture, quality, and labeling. Regarding labeling, the CPSC administers the federal **Hazardous Substances Labeling Act,** which states that labels must warn consumers of the hazards of using products that may cause illness or death if improperly used. The CPSC may also ban, seize, and prevent the sale of hazardous products. In addition, it establishes industry product safety standards and collects, records, and analyzes product injury data.

As an entrepreneur, think about all the trouble that could arise for your company if you were not aware of the Hazardous Substances Labeling Act. Take Marty Schmidt as an example. Marty developed a new chemical formula for killing garden insects. After extensive testing to make sure that the new formula worked, Marty decided to start a small chemical plant to produce the product. After he produced 50,000 five-pound bags of the product, he sold and distributed it in eight states. Then the CPSC informed Marty that his initial production would have to be recalled and relabeled. Why? Marty had

Consumer Product Safety Act, a law that protects the public from dangerous products by providing for the evaluation of product safety hazards

Hazardous Substances Labeling Act, a law stating that labels must warn consumers of the hazards of using products that may cause illness or death if used improperly

Illus. 19-4 Under the Hazardous Substances Labeling Act, labels must warn consumers of possible hazards in the use of a product.

not been aware of the Hazardous Substances Labeling Act and had not properly labeled his product and revealed the hazards of using it. Marty had to recall all 50,000 bags because they were not labeled correctly. The profit he would have made from the first batch of insecticide was lost because of the extra expense of the recall and relabeling process. Marty had not investigated all the legal requirements for starting his business.

Another federal act relating to safety is important to all employers. The Occupational Safety and Health Act (OSHA) requires that certain safety standards be maintained in the workplace. OSHA states that every worker in the United States should have a safe place to work. Entrepreneurs need to make sure that the physical place of work is free from hazards that may cause injuries to employees, customers, or clients.

Environmental Protection

In 1969 Congress passed the National Environmental Policy Act (NEPA). This Act set the stage for a series of laws designed to prevent air and water pollution and to reduce noise pollution.

NEPA, in turn, established the Environmental Protection Agency (EPA) in 1970 to coordinate all of the federal government's efforts to protect the environment. The EPA's primary role is to prevent pollution. It investigates charges of infractions of air, water, pesticides, radiation, land, and noise regulations.

During the business planning process, small business owners should determine whether any part of the proposed business venture has environmental implications. If there are concerns, they should be examined carefully and provisions should be made for dealing with them. Entrepreneurs with EPA concerns are typically those planning to start manufacturing operations. Retail and service businesses, as a general rule, have few serious concerns in this area. There are exceptions to this rule, however, so be careful to look at your individual business.

Fair Credit Billing

Fair Credit Billing Act, a law enacted in an attempt to protect consumers against unfair and incorrect billing activities

All entrepreneurs should be aware of the **Fair Credit Billing Act,** which was enacted in an attempt to protect consumers against unfair and incorrect billing activities. From an entrepreneurial perspective, the law has two kinds of application. First, it provides protection for consumers dealing with businesses. Second, it provides protection for businesses dealing with suppliers.

The Fair Credit Billing Act has several components. There are four areas of primary interest to entrepreneurs planning to extend credit to consumers. First, business owners must give consumers an address where billing questions can be sent. Second, business owners must observe certain billing timelines. Specifically, they must mail bills 14 days in advance of the due date. Consumers have 60 days to question a billing. Businesses must acknowledge billing questions within 30 days, and settle billing questions within 90 days. The act also addresses the issue of billing harassment. If a bill is not paid by a credit customer, a creditor may pursue collection, but is prohibited from making threatening phone calls or sending threatening letters. The law also allows businesses to offer discounts to customers paying with cash as opposed to paying with credit, and grants certain other rights to consumers who use a credit card to purchase merchandise which is later discovered to be defective.

THE FASHION ATTIC

Laura had arranged a meeting with an attorney to make sure she understood her legal responsibilities as a business owner. Although she had thought it would essentially be a get-acquainted meeting, Laura was surprised to learn that there were many legal regulations governing the operation of a small business. Realizing that she would have to devote some time to understanding these regulations, Laura got to work on her legal research.

Laura soon recognized that one of her biggest areas of concern was to make sure that any advertising she planned adhered to the law. She would have to make sure that none of her ads or promotions deceived customers in any way. This would involve checking and double-checking all published material, including in-store signs, to ensure honesty and integrity. Laura planned to train her salespeople thoroughly to make sure that there would be no appearance of bait and switch advertising or selling. She also decided to issue rain checks for any sold-out merchandise that had been advertised at special prices. This would allow customers to purchase out-of-stock merchandise at a later date for the advertised sale price. In the event that a particular style was discontinued, she would promise her customers that similar merchandise would be made available to them. Laura was also determined to offer only real sale merchandise and not phony promotional items that had never been offered at the original suggested price. She was familiar with stores that sometimes violated this principle; however, she was aware that this practice was unethical and, in fact, illegal.

Laura also resolved to make sure her salespeople understood the concept of express warranties. She did not want customers returning merchandise that had been sold through false promises. She was going to select only quality merchandise that her salespeople could confidently sell. Laura was also going to be very careful in her choice of vendors, so she would not be the victim of buying under false assumptions.

Laura requested a personal visit from the credit card company representatives that she planned to use. She was glad that these companies would be responsible for credit transactions; however, she wanted all the procedures explained in detail so neither she nor her staff would make errors involving credit regulations.

When Laura had completed her research about the legal responsibilities she would have as a small-business owner, she was relieved. Legal regulations were a concern, but as long as she was aware of them, they should not interfere with her ability to run a profitable business.

SUMMARY

The Federal Trade Commission is a federal administrative agency charged with responsibility for ensuring fair, free, and open business. It interprets laws and creates regulations, advises businesses when requested, and investigates when unfair practices are suspected. The FTC has several overall areas of responsibility, including advertising, consumer credit, product warranties, and competition.

In the area of advertising, entrepreneurs should be sensitive to false and deceptive advertising, bait and switch advertising, and deceptive pricing. In the area of consumer protection, several acts are important to remember: the Truth-in-Lending Act, the Fair Credit Reporting Act, and the Equal Credit Opportunity Act.

There are two types of warranties: express and implied. These are regulated by the FTC through enforcement of the Magnuson-Moss Warranty Act. Additionally, product safety is monitored through the Consumer Product Safety Act. Product safety is further supported by the Hazardous Substances Labeling Act. The Occupational Safety and Health Act monitors workplace safety.

The National Environmental Policy Act set the stage for a series of laws designed to prevent air, water, and noise pollution. It established the Environmental Protection Agency, which coordinates all of the federal government's efforts to protect the environment.

All entrepreneurs should be aware of the Fair Credit Billing Act, enacted to protect consumers against unfair and incorrect billing activities. It provides protection for consumers dealing with business owners as well as protection for business owners dealing with suppliers.

VOCABULARY BUILDER

On a separate sheet of paper, write a brief description of each word or phrase based on your reading of the chapter.

1. Federal Trade Commission
2. False and deceptive advertising
3. Bait and switch advertising
4. Fair Credit Reporting Act
5. Equal Credit Opportunity Act
6. Express warranty
7. Implied warranty
8. Magnuson-Moss Warranty Act
9. Consumer Product Safety Act
10. Hazardous Substances Labeling Act
11. National Environmental Policy Act
12. Environmental Protection Agency
13. Fair Credit Billing Act

REVIEW QUESTIONS

1. What are the four areas of responsibility of the Federal Trade Commission?
2. What are the names of three acts that deal with consumer credit?
3. What is the difference between the two major types of warranties?
4. What is the name of the agency that coordinates all of the federal government's efforts to protect the environment?

DISCUSSION QUESTIONS

1. What is false advertising? Deceptive advertising? Give examples of each.

2. What is deceptive pricing? Give an example.
3. Why is the Fair Credit Reporting Act important to consumers?
4. How could an express warranty hurt a business? An implied warranty?

CRITICAL THINKING

Charles Spitz owns a small car-rental agency. Recently, a customer came into the business inquiring about renting a car. The customer was considering a small economy model. When Charles's salesperson was asked about the car's gas mileage, she replied that the car in question averaged about 40 miles per gallon. The truth was that the car averaged only 25 miles per gallon. The salesperson was relatively new and did not know much about that particular model.

1. What type of warranty was issued on the car's gas mileage?
2. What recourse does the customer have if the car does not average 40 miles per gallon?
3. How could Charles avoid this type of problem in the future?

SHORT CASE: THE HABERDASHERY HOAX

Tom Flynn works for the Federal Trade Commission. His assignment is to investigate complaints about advertising in the Chicago metropolitan area. Recently, he has received several complaints concerning a clothing store located on Michigan Avenue.

The store, Wircenski's Haberdashery, has been in business for 10 years at the same location and has a good reputation. If he had received a single complaint, Tom would ordinarily consider the reputation of the store and then decide what to do. A store such as Wircenski's would probably not be investigated further. The complaint would simply be attributed to a disgruntled customer.

This time, however, after several complaints from different people, Tom decided to investigate. To begin, he went to the newspaper office and requested a copy of the most recent ad run by the store. The advertisement is shown on the facing page.

Assume that Tom has asked for your help. Evaluate the advertisement and answer the following questions as they apply to the complaint against Wircenski's Haberdashery.

> **WIRCENSKI'S HABERDASHERY**
>
> sale　　　　　　　**SAVE**　　　　　　　sale
>
> DRESS SHIRTS $10—POPULAR BRAND NAMES AVAILABLE
>
> MEN'S DESIGNER SUITS—LOWEST PRICES IN TOWN
>
> SHOES ON SALE—TRUCKLOAD JUST ARRIVED—SAVE $$$$
>
> sale　　　　　　　　　　　　　　　　　　sale

Questions

1. Do you think there are areas of concern? If so, what are they?
2. What questions should Tom ask Mr. Wircenski about the advertisement?

Now rewrite Wircenski's advertisement for shirts, suits, and shoes. Word the advertisement so that there is no question as to what the products are and the prices at which they are being offered.

PROJECT CHALLENGE

As you continue to plan your new business, consider any special regulations that might apply to you. In your business plan notebook, record the following information.

1. List any special regulations that may apply to your hypothetical business.
2. Rank the regulations on your list in order from the one that has the greatest impact on your business to the one that has the least.
3. Next to each item on your list, write at least one step that you can take to comply with that regulation.

20
Contracts and Agreements

After mastering the information contained in this chapter, you should be able to:

20-1 List and explain the components of a legally enforceable contract.

20-2 List and explain six types of contracts.

20-3 Explain breach of contract.

20-4 Understand assignment of contract.

contract, a legally enforceable agreement negotiated between two or more persons

offer, communication of a proposal

Entrepreneurs encounter contracts and agreements—both formal and informal—on a daily basis. These contracts take many forms and occur under many different circumstances. Each contract or agreement an entrepreneur establishes may be different from his or her other contracts. Because of the variety—and the potential complexity—of contracts, it is important for entrepreneurs to understand the basic principles by which contracts and agreements operate.

CONTRACTUAL REQUIREMENTS

A **contract** is a legally enforceable agreement negotiated between two or more persons. A "person" may be either a juristic person or a human being. A juristic person is an entity, such as a corporation, created by law. A legally enforceable contract fulfills requirements in five areas:

- agreement (offer and acceptance)
- legality
- consideration
- contractual capacity
- contractual form

Agreement (Offer and Acceptance)

A contract must provide for an offer by one party and an acceptance by another. This is not as simple as it sounds, however; certain requirements must be met for the offer and for the acceptance.

Offer. A contractual **offer** must be an offer that is intended to be legally binding. The intent is judged to be legally binding if a reasonable person would consider it binding.

Illus. 20-1 Entrepreneurs should understand the basic principles of contracts and agreements.

> Marty, a salesperson, is taking a client to lunch and her car won't start. She says, "I'd sell this thing for two cents. It's no good." Marty is angry; she wouldn't really sell her car for two cents.

This is not an offer in the legal sense.

> Marty calls her friend Bill and says, "I'm buying a new car; would you like to buy my old one for fifteen hundred dollars?" Marty really wants to sell her car.

An offer has been made in the legal sense.

The offer must also be in definite terms and communicated in some ordinary fashion. In the second example above, Marty made a definite offer—the sale of her car. Marty also communicated the offer to Bill in some ordinary fashion—verbally.

Once communicated, the offer does not remain open forever. It may be ended in several ways, as listed here.

1. The party making the offer retracts it prior to acceptance.
2. The party receiving the offer rejects it. Once the offer is rejected, the party that rejected it cannot later demand that the offer be honored.

3. The party receiving the offer makes a counteroffer—the original offer is ended and a new offer exists. In the second example above, Bill might tell Marty that he will give her $1,000 instead of $1,500. At that point, the original offer is ended and replaced by the second.
4. An offer ends after the passage of a reasonable length of time.
5. The death or mental incapacity of either party ends an offer.
6. Any change in a law, making an offer illegal, ends an offer.

> Hector offers to sell a three-wheeled recreational vehicle to Tom for his customers at the hotel to use. After the offer has been made, a law is passed that makes it illegal to drive a recreational vehicle with less than four wheels. The offer is now illegal and, therefore, ended.

acceptance, an offer is agreed to by the receiving party

Acceptance. An **acceptance** must be clear and positive. The party accepting an offer must agree to all of the terms of the offer unconditionally. The acceptance may be communicated to the party making the offer in any fashion unless a specific method of acceptance is designated. If, however, the acceptance is not communicated in a manner equal to or better than that of the communication of the offer, the acceptance is not effective until thus received.

Illus. 20-2 An acceptance must be clear and positive.

> Marty wrote Bill a letter to offer her car for sale. Bill wrote back accepting the offer. His acceptance was effective when he mailed the letter. Marty cannot change her mind, even if she has not yet received the letter.

Legality

A legally enforceable contract must have a lawful objective. If the satisfaction of a contract requires breaking the law or violating a statute or policy, it does not have a lawful objective.

> Jo told Ben she would use her employee discount from working at a retail computer-store to buy a computer for his new clothing store if he would sell her two new outfits at cost. Since the discount is intended for Jo's personal use and is not transferable, the contract does not have a lawful objective and is not enforceable.

Consideration

Each of the parties involved in a contract must receive value. The legal term for that value is **consideration.**

consideration, value given and value received as a result of contractual agreement

> If Bill accepts Marty's offer, the consideration (value) to Marty is Bill's $1,500 and the consideration to Bill is Marty's car.

Contract law does not require that the considerations be equal. Marty's car may be worth $2,000. That does not matter; as long as consideration is involved, the contract is binding.

Something that has already been done or something that a person has a legal duty to do is not consideration.

> If Mario comes back from his vacation and discovers that two of his employees were responsible for the apprehension of a would-be thief, he may be so happy that he promises to give each of them $100.

This is not a legal contract. Consideration is current or future value. Past actions are not part of a legally enforceable contract.

> Gloria agrees to purchase a certain percentage of the remote-controlled airplanes she sells from her competitor, the only other company that sells the planes, in exchange for the competitor's promise not to sell planes to consumers at prices below a certain level.

This is not consideration on the competitor's part—the competitor already has a legal obligation not to undersell Gloria because of the laws that prohibit monopoly. These laws also prohibit pricing policies that present price reductions to some customers and not others, unless they are justified by quantity discounts. NOTE: There are exceptions to the consideration requirement.

Contractual Capacity

All parties to a legally enforceable contract must meet the legal requirements for **capacity.** Among those who do not meet the legal requirements for capacity are minors (persons under age 21), persons who are under the influence of alcohol or drugs when the agreement is made, and persons who are mentally deficient.

Minors can choose to fulfill the terms of a contract, but since they do not meet the requirements for legal capacity, they are not *required* to do so. A party who enters into a contract with a minor, however, is obligated to fulfill the terms of the contract. Business owners take great risks if they enter into contracts with minors. A minor may void or enforce the contract. The business owner has no choice—the wishes of the minor must be honored.

If a minor chooses not to honor a contract, the other parties involved may try to recover any goods given to the minor as a part of the contractual agreement, but they cannot legally enforce any other aspects of the contract.

capacity, the ability to fully understand and comprehend the requirements of a contract as specified by law

> Billie Marcus, a 16-year-old high school junior, is an avid reader. She reads an average of three novels a week. With the price of books increasing steadily, Billie's reading is getting very expensive.
> Last month an offer to join a book club came to Billie's house in the mail. Billie could get 10 novels for 99 cents by joining the club. Billie would then have to purchase 10 novels at regular prices within 12 months. The offer stated that regular prices on the novels would be at least 25 percent less than the prices at a bookstore and that future selections could be made from a list of hundreds of books.
> Billie decided the offer was great. After all, the required 10 novels represented less than one month's purchases. What could go wrong if

the purchase requirement was 10 in one year? Billie signed the form and returned it with the 99 cents. The 10 novels would soon be on their way.

A few days later, Billie's mother noticed the book club information and asked what it was. Billie explained why accepting the club's offer had been a good decision. Billie's mother sat down and read the book club information very carefully.

After reading the information, Billie's mother said, "Buying 10 hardcover novels may be very expensive." Billie had not read the statement that said all novels except the first 10 would be in hardcover! Billie intended to pay for the books with earnings from a part-time job. Instead of being obligated to spend about $40, Billie was obligated to much more. Even with a 25 percent discount, the total would be more than $300.

Sending the signed form to the publisher meant that Billie had entered into a contract. Is there any help for Billie? Is there a way out of this mess?

Billie may either honor the contract and purchase at least 10 more novels, or she may return the 10 paperback novels as soon as they are received and void the contract.

A person who is under the influence of alcohol when a contract is negotiated may void the contract, but only if the other party can be restored to precontract condition.

Illus. 20-3   Mail solicitations should be carefully studied to avoid unwanted agreements.

> Lu-Yin was intoxicated at the time she told Carla she would buy 50 books of the coupons that Carla was selling in her store. Lu-Yin took the coupons and promised to pay Carla $150 the following week. Later that day, the coupons were stolen from Lu-Yin's car. She sought to void the contract on the grounds that she was intoxicated at the time the contract was made, but since she cannot restore Carla to her precontract condition (return her coupons), she must honor the contract and pay the $150.

A person who claims mental deficiency as a reason for voiding a contract must prove that the mental deficiency existed at the time the contract was made. The condition does not, however, have to be permanent. Lack of knowledge is not considered mental deficiency.

> Jamie is a business owner who can sign his name and read a little, but that's about all. Jamie signed a contract to purchase some expensive equipment from Walt. Afterwards, he explained the deal to his attorney and showed him the contract. After reading the contract, the attorney told Jamie that, according to the contract, Jamie's cost for the equipment would be about ten percent higher than the price Walt had quoted.
> Jamie sought to void the contract on the grounds that he could not read the contract and thus did not fully understand what was involved. Jamie must honor the terms of the contract, however, because lack of understanding is not the same as lack of legal capacity.

Contractual Form

Contracts may be verbal or written; both are legally enforceable. Some contracts are regulated by the Statute of Frauds and must be written and signed. The Statute of Frauds monitors several types of contracts.

Sale of Land. Any contract for transferring an interest in real property must be written. Real property includes land, buildings, and other things permanently attached to land.

Sale of Goods Exceeding $500. Most contracts for the sale of goods for $500 or more must be written. This will be discussed in Chapter 21.

Contract for Services That Cannot Be Performed within One Year. According to the Statute of Frauds, the expiration of the time limit for satisfaction of a contract is determined by the date of the contract.

Performance of the duties of the contract must be completed within one year from the date of the contract, not the date the performance begins. A contract for services that cannot be completed within one year from the date of the contract must be written.

> On January 1, Antonia hires Candy to paint a mural on the wall of the restaurant she is building. The wall will not be ready for Candy to work on until November. Candy knows she will need at least three months to complete the job.

Since the job will not be completed within one year from the date the agreement was made, a written contract that specifies the date of completion is required.

Promise to Assume the Debt or Legal Responsibility of Another. Any agreement to assume the debt or legal responsibility of another person must be written.

> Jon wants to buy a building for his new business. Because he has no credit history, either in his personal name or the business' name, the bank refuses to lend him the money he needs. Jon's father decides to help, and accompanies him back to the bank. Jon's father tells the banker that if the loan is made and Jon is not able to repay it, he will pay it himself. Jon's father's promise to assume Jon's debt is a contract with the bank: it must be written.

Promise by the Administrator or Executor of an Estate to Assume Responsibility. An administrator or executor is a person charged with the responsibility of handling the final distribution of a person's possessions and funds after death. The law does not require this person to assume personal responsibility for repayment of the debts of the deceased. If the administrator or executor chooses to assume this responsibility, a written contract must be drafted and signed.

> Luisa's business partner passed away, naming her as executor of his estate. He had cash and assets of $63,000 when he died, and his personal debts totalled $68,000. To protect the business, Luisa promised her partner's creditors that she would pay the debts personally. This agreement with the creditors must be written.

CONTRACT CLASSIFICATIONS

There are many different types of contracts. The most common contract classifications are unilateral or bilateral, express or implied, and formal or simple.

Unilateral or Bilateral

In a unilateral contract, an offer is accepted through performance of the requested act.

> Brian initiated a new program for his employees. He set up a suggestion box and posted a notice on the bulletin board stating that he would give a $10 reward to the employee who contributed the best suggestion for improving client relations or business operations each month. Brian is contractually obligated to pay one of the participating employees the reward.

In this unilateral contract, acceptance takes place when Brian actually chooses the monthly winner.

In a bilateral contract, two parties exchange promises.

> Phyllis asks Jennifer, "I'll complete all of the cash reports if you will finish stocking the shelves. Will you?" Jennifer says, "Yes."

They have established a bilateral contract.

Express or Implied

In an express contract, the terms of the agreement are stated, either verbally or in writing. In an implied contract, intent is shown by a party's conduct; the contract is established when a person performs a certain action.

> Yoriko and her date go to a restaurant and order dinner. By their conduct (ordering dinner), they have entered into an implied contract: They have a contractual obligation to pay for their dinner.

Formal or Simple

A formal contract must be prepared in a specific manner and must contain certain components. For example, a personal check is a formal contract. It is negotiable only if it meets certain requirements. The check must be made out to a specific person or company, the amount must be written in figures as well as spelled out, and the check-writer's signature must be included in a certain place.

A simple contract can be structured in any manner; there are no specific requirements as long as all components are included. All contracts are either formal or simple; most are simple.

BREACH OF CONTRACT

When a **breach of contract** occurs, the injured (nonbreaching) party has certain rights. Commonly referred to as remedies, these rights include rescission or cancellation, a lawsuit for monetary damages, a demand for specific performance, and restitution.

breach of contract, the failure of a party to a contract to perform his or her obligation(s) as specified in the agreement

Illus. 20-4 An injured party has certain rights, including filing a lawsuit for monetary damages.

© *Dawson Jones/Tony Stone Images, Inc.*

Rescission or Cancellation

The injured party in a breach of contract has a right to rescind or cancel the contract. If the contract is rescinded, all parties are returned to their precontract condition and no damages are claimed. If the contract is cancelled, the contract is voided but the injured party may seek damages.

The question of whether rescission or cancellation is appropriate is usually decided by determining what sort of damage the injured party suffered as a result of the breach. If the injured party suffered inconvenience but no monetary loss, the contract would be rescinded. If the injured party suffered monetary loss, the contract would be cancelled.

Suit for Monetary Damages

The injured party in a breach of contract may sue the noninjured party for monetary damages. The amount of money awarded to the injured party is usually the amount required for restoration to nonbreach position.

> The dance committee at West Wilson College agreed to pay the Live Wires, a rock-and-roll band, $5,000 for five hours' worth of music at a school dance. The band members later reconsidered and decided they did not want to play for the dance. The dance committee located another band at the last minute but had to pay $6,500. The committee could sue the Live Wires for the difference—$1,500—to restore the dance fund to nonbreach condition.

Demand for Specific Performance

In a demand for specific performance, the injured party forces the breaching party to comply with the original terms of the contract.

> Alternatively, the West Wilson dance committee could sue the Live Wires for specific performance. Instead of hiring the other band for $6,500, the committee could ask that a court force the Live Wires to honor their agreement because the school cannot obtain the same services elsewhere for $5,000. The only way the committee will be restored to nonbreach condition is if the Live Wires play for the dance.

Restitution

Restitution is required when the injured party has a right to request that something that was delivered as part of the contract be returned.

> Lois, a retired administrative assistant, started a small word processing pool to provide services to local businesses when they had overflow clerical work and word processing. She designated the den in her home as a working room. She purchased computer equipment, workstations, and comfortable chairs for the word processors who worked for her. Lois accepted delivery of the equipment and arranged to pay in five equal installments. After paying the first two installments, Lois stopped paying. Since Lois breached the contract by not paying, the equipment company could sue her for restitution. Lois would probably be required to return the equipment.

ASSIGNMENT OF CONTRACT

Assignment of a contract is the transfer of contractual rights to a party that was not part of the original agreement.

> Dennis bought a car from Gina and agreed to pay it off in monthly installments. Gina ran into some other expenses and needed cash immediately. She assigned her rights under the contract with Dennis to an acquaintance of hers, Karl, for a set amount of cash. Dennis must now pay Karl each month. If Dennis breaches the contract by not paying, Karl may sue for damages.

Any party to a contract can usually assign the rights of the contract unless the assignment is specifically prohibited by law. Circumstances in which rights may not be assignable include the following:

1. The contract specifically states that rights are nonassignable.
2. Risk is increased for the nonassigning party.

> Marla has a small fleet of freezer trucks, which she hires out to various frozen food vendors. Jackie agrees to pay Marla to transport frozen meat from Jackie's meat processing plant to a frozen-food distribution center. Marla overbooks her trucks and hires Bob to transport a load of Jackie's frozen meat. Bob does not have a freezer truck, but the trip is quite short and Marla feels it won't be a problem. This, however, increases the risk to Jackie—her product may be spoiled during transport.

3. Terms are personal in nature and cannot be delivered in the same fashion by another party.

Illus. 20-5   Terms of a contract are personal in nature.

Jerry is an interior designer. Sharon has agreed to pay Jerry a specific sum in exchange for his services in redecorating her store. Jerry cannot assign the contract to another designer—Sharon contracted for a personal service that can be delivered only by Jerry.

Legal restrictions concerning assignment vary. You should verify local laws before making a decision concerning assignment of rights.

THE FASHION ATTIC

Laura was surprised to learn that many contracts are entered into on an everyday basis by retailers. She had never given much thought to what makes a contract legally enforceable. As a sole proprietor who can not afford the risk of civil lawsuits, however, she was quickly discovering that she needed to know exactly what constitutes a legal contract.

Laura found that contracts are more complicated than she had thought. Her first indication of this came when she reviewed her lease with her attorney. It was a twenty-five page document that spelled out responsibilities and obligations in many different ways. In addition to the monetary terms for rent, there were clauses and subclauses, warranties and guarantees, and assurances and promises about everything from the type of insurance she must carry to the type of signs she could use. It was very complicated, and Laura was somewhat intimidated when she understood all that was expected of her as a tenant. She was glad to have an attorney take the time to thoroughly explain each and every clause, because she knew that once she put her signature to a document, she was legally bound to uphold the promises it contained.

Laura decided that once she was familiar with what constitutes a contract, she would have to make sure that her employees understood contracts as well, particularly implied contracts. Once merchandise had been priced and put out on the floor, there could be no changes at the time of purchase because a mistake had been made in marking the price when the display was being set up. Laura would also make sure that when she signed purchase orders from vendors, all terms were clearly stated and understood. She knew that this was particularly important in the fashion industry, since much of the merchandise was cut specifically by order from retailers and therefore no exchange or refund provisions could be made.

At this stage in planning for the Fashion Attic, Laura was beginning to realize that knowledge and preparation were going to be her best protection against future legal problems. She was going to make sure that all of her contractual agreements were properly structured, and she would know what to do if the terms of a contract were not fulfilled.

SUMMARY

A contract is a legally enforceable agreement that is negotiated between two or more persons. A contract must fulfill requirements in five areas:

- agreement
  (offer and acceptance)
- legality
- consideration
- legal capacity
- contractual form

Contract classifications include unilateral or bilateral, express or implied, and formal or simple. In a unilateral contract, an offer is accepted through performance of the requested act. In a bilateral contract, two parties exchange promises. In an express contact, the terms of the agreement are stated, either verbally or in writing. In an implied contract, intent is shown by a party's conduct. A formal contract must be in a specific form. A simple contract can be structured in any manner, provided all five components are included.

When a breach of contract occurs, the injured (nonbreaching) party has certain rights. Commonly referred to as remedies, these rights include rescission or cancellation, a lawsuit for damages, demand for specific performance, and restitution. Any party to a contract can usually assign the rights specified unless assignment is specifically prohibited by law.

VOCABULARY BUILDER

Write a brief description of each word or phrase based on your reading of the chapter.

1. Contract
2. Offer
3. Acceptance
4. Consideration
5. Legal capacity
6. Statute of Frauds
7. Unilateral contract
8. Bilateral contract
9. Express contract
10. Implied contract
11. Formal contract
12. Simple contract
13. Breach of contract
14. Rescission
15. Cancellation
16. Suit for damages
17. Demand for specific performance
18. Restitution
19. Assignment

REVIEW QUESTIONS

1. What five requirements must a legally enforceable contract fulfill?
2. What five types of contracts must be written?
3. What are the most common contract classifications?
4. What are four remedies for breach of contract?

DISCUSSION QUESTIONS

1. What are the differences between unilateral contracts and bilateral contracts? Give an example of each.
2. What are the differences between formal contracts and simple contracts?
3. What is the concept of "demand for specific performance" as it applies to breach of contract?
4. What two conditions dictate that a contract cannot be assigned?

CRITICAL THINKING

Marsha Lynch owns a small record store. Her store is very close to the local high school, so a large portion of her clientele is high school students. Many of the students are repeat customers—they buy from her on a regular basis. She lets several of the regulars take records home and pay for them later. She asks these students to sign agreements. Recently, a student refused to pay her. She told this student that a contract had been signed and she could require him to pay.

1. Does Marsha have a legally enforceable contract with the student? Why or why not?
2. What would you advise Marsha to do?
3. What is the student's responsibility in this situation?

SHORT CASE: ASSIGN AND BREACH— ARE THEY THE SAME?

Jim Arnold owns an unusual auto body shop in Pueblo, Colorado. He specializes in rebuilding antique automobiles. When Jim started his business 10 years ago, he had very few customers. However, the last five years have been very busy and very profitable.

Five years ago Jim rebuilt a classic Model A Ford for a customer from Detroit. Shortly after Jim delivered the car, a story featuring the car's owner was printed in a national magazine. The story included a description of the car and mentioned that a man named Jim Arnold in Pueblo, Colorado had rebuilt the car. As a result, Jim has been getting business from all over the country. Sometimes he has more than he can handle.

Jim recently agreed to rebuild a 1965 Corvair for a man from Florida. Although he was busy, he thought he could complete the car by the time the man wanted it. They signed an agreement specifying the charges and the delivery date, and Jim scheduled his time so that he could start the Corvair job on June 3.

Jim encountered an unusual problem while working on another project and had to spend a lot of time taking care of it. He knew he was taking more time than he had planned, and there was no way he could get to the Corvair on time. That meant he would never finish it on schedule.

Jim called his cousin Blaine, who was also in the auto body business, and asked him to do the work on the Corvair. Blaine agreed and started immediately. When he finished, Jim checked the work. He was a bit disappointed. Blaine had done a good job on the car, but not as good as Jim might have done. However, it would have to do.

When the man from Florida came for his car, Jim told him what he had done and gave him the bill. The man was very angry and refused to pay. He claimed that Jim had breached the contract.

Questions

1. Did Jim have the right to assign this contract to his cousin? Why or why not?
2. Did Jim breach the contract? Why or why not?
3. If Jim did breach the contract, what remedy or remedies can the car owner seek?

PROJECT CHALLENGE

Make a list of the contracts you think you will require for your hypothetical business. Consider any particular specifications the contracts should include and what form they should take. Make sure that all of the contracts meet the requirements covered in this chapter.

21
Buying and Selling

Buying and selling is at the heart of any entrepreneur's dream business. It does not really matter if the entrepreneur sells a product or a service; regardless of what entrepreneurs sell, they must buy products to support the business and sell products or services to ensure business success.

The skill and knowledge with which entrepreneurs approach buying and selling is a key element to business success. Entrepreneurs can learn the hard way or the easy way. The hard way consists of learning it on the job through considerable trial and error. The easy

Illus. 21-1   A mastery of the principles of buying and selling is essential for the entrepreneur.

Photo by Alan Brown/Photonics

After mastering the information contained in this chapter, you should be able to:

21-1 Understand the sale of goods.

21-2 Describe sales contracts as they relate to other contracts.

21-3 Explain the nature of sales contracts.

21-4 Explain transfer of ownership and risk of loss.

21-5 Understand the rights and responsibilities of vendors and purchasers in sales contracts.

way consists of a fair amount of reading and study and/or consultation with an attorney before the business opens.

Aside from the entrepreneurial aspects of buying and selling, these concepts are also important in every person's daily life. Hardly a day passes when the average American does not buy something. Whether it is a can of sodapop or a new car, the laws of sales apply. Mastery of the principles contained within this chapter will make you not only a better entrepreneur but also a better consumer.

SALE OF GOODS

sale, the immediate transfer of ownership of goods for a price

goods, items of tangible personal property other than money

Uniform Commercial Code, a group of uniform business rules adopted by most states

A **sale** is defined as the immediate transfer of ownership of goods for a price. **Goods** are defined as items of tangible personal property other than money. In a sales transaction, the seller is known as the vendor and the buyer is known as the purchaser (also called vendee).

Laws about the sale of goods are included under Article 2 of the **Uniform Commercial Code** (UCC). The UCC unifies state laws pertaining to the sale of goods and makes them simpler to understand. Entrepreneurs should be familiar with the legal aspects of buying and selling so that the rights of their businesses are protected.

SALES CONTRACTS

In Chapter 20, you learned about contracts and the components needed to form them. In general, when a contract is not for the sale of goods, common-law contract principles apply. What you learned about contracts holds true for the sale of goods as well. The UCC simply takes those same components and applies them to the sale of goods.

Sales contracts, like other contracts, have certain legal requirements. An offer must be made and accepted, and there must be **consideration** in the sale. The requirements vary depending on the type of seller involved. Certain terms are required; others are optional, or permissible, terms. There are special requirements concerning written sales contracts as well as exceptions to those requirements.

Types of Sellers

merchant, sells a particular good or goods on a regular basis and claims special knowledge

There are two types of *sellers*. The first, a **merchant,** sells a particular good or goods on a regular basis and claims special knowledge. The second, a **casual seller,** only sells occasionally and claims no special knowledge. The UCC makes a distinction between these two types of sellers. Since merchants are supposedly knowledgeable about the products or services they sell, they are usually held to a higher standard and may have to be licensed or abide by other special regulations. As examples, let's look at the distinction between Mark and Kay.

casual seller, a person who offers a good or goods for sale but is not in the business of selling

> Mark has a shotgun with which he shoots skeet. Because he has given up the hobby, he wants to sell the gun. Mark sells the gun to Susie for $200. Mark, according to the UCC, is a casual seller. He does not have to abide by any special regulations.
>
> Kay sells shotguns for skeet shooting at the store she owns. These shotguns are the store's main product line; she sells guns on a daily basis. The UCC considers Kay a merchant. She must abide by special regulations, such as possessing a Federal Firearms License, and keeping very detailed sales records.

Consideration in Sales Contracts

In a sales contract, consideration is required. It usually takes one of two forms. The first is price. *Price* is the amount of money agreed to by the parties to the sale. Once agreed upon, price becomes the consideration. The second form of consideration is that of **barter,** the term used for a sale involving only the exchange of goods, no money changes hands. In the case of barter, the UCC considers both parties to the sale as vendors of the goods they have transferred. Once agreed upon, the bartered goods become the consideration.

barter, a sale involving only the exchange of goods; no money changes hands

Offer and Acceptance

There are some exceptions to common law when dealing with the offer and acceptance of sales contracts. Entrepreneurs should know and understand these exceptions.

The Offer. The first exception has to do with the offer. Remember that in a contract, an offer can be revoked. That is also true of sales contracts, unless the offer is a firm offer. A **firm offer** is a written, signed sales offer in which the merchant expresses the intention that it cannot be revoked. The merchant may also express a time period of up to three months for the contract to be irrevocable. In addition, no consideration is required for a firm offer. In other words, the merchant is held to the sales contract for the period of irrevocability even though no consideration has been received.

firm offer, a written, signed sales offer in which the merchant expresses the intention that it cannot be revoked

> Ricardo owns a small manufacturing plant. He makes an offer to Gerald to sell him a machine made in the plant. The written offer includes a price for the machine, indicates that the offer will not be revoked for 60 days, and has Ricardo's signature on it. This is a firm offer and cannot be revoked by Ricardo. Note that Gerald has not given Ricardo any consideration to hold the offer open. Gerald may accept the offer or not. He has up to 60 days to decide.

Acceptance. The second exception in a sales contract deals with the counteroffer. According to common law, if an offer is not accepted as is, the counteroffer becomes a rejection of the original offer. In relation to a sales contract, this is not true. The counteroffer may become part of the original offer unless specifically forbidden in the original offer.

> Marcie, a merchant, made a firm offer to Roger of a new Ford Bronco with a six-cylinder engine for $20,000. Roger responded that he would accept if Marcie would substitute a CD player for the regular radio. Since the offer does not alter the original offer significantly, it can become part of the contract if Marcie does not object.

Illus. 21-2 Once an offer is accepted, consideration must be present for a legally binding sales contract to exist.

Once the offer is accepted, consideration must be present for a legally binding sales contract to exist. However, the exact amount of that consideration does not have to be included in the sales contract.

Required Terms

In relation to the required terms of the sales contract, the UCC is much less strict than common law. Three things are required by law in a sales contract. First, the contract must include the names of the people involved in the contract. Second, the contract must specify the monetary value of the goods involved. Third, the signature of the person responsible for breach or nonperformance must be included.

Permissible Terms

In addition to the required terms of a sales contract, certain other terms are permissible. They include price, time and place, the purchaser's right to inspection, risk-of-loss terms, and transfer of ownership.

Price. The price may be included in the contract but is not required. If the price is not included, it will be assumed to be a reasonable and customary price that is charged in the industry.

Time and Place. The time and place for the performance of the contract may or may not be included in the contract. If the time and place for things such as delivery of goods are not specified, it is assumed that such performance will be reasonable.

Purchaser's Right of Inspection. The sales contract may include the purchaser's right of inspection prior to payment. If this term is included in the contract, the purchaser may check goods for damages before accepting and paying for them.

Risk of Loss. The sales contract may also include terms dealing with **risk of loss.** In other words, the contract may specify which party—the vendor or the purchaser—will assume the financial responsibility if the goods are damaged while being shipped or transported.

risk of loss, the financial responsibility assumed by a party in a sales contract for damaged or destroyed goods

Transfer of Ownership. Terms in a contract that deal with the actual transfer of title of the goods may also be included. This, along with risk of loss, will be discussed in more detail later in the chapter.

Legal Restrictions

Just as a regular contract is not enforceable if it pertains to an illegal product or service, neither is a sales contract. Parties involved in illegal sales activities are subject to prosecution and there is no legal recourse for persons involved in illegal sales contracts.

> Joel wanted to buy some fireworks to sell to a few of his best customers, who had been asking about them. Fireworks are illegal in the state in which Joel lives. He paid Charlie $200 to buy some for him out of state. What he asked Charlie to do is illegal. Charlie never bought or delivered the fireworks, but kept the money instead. Joel cannot go to court to get his $200 back from Charlie since he was party to an illegal sales contract.

Exceptions to Written Contract Requirements

As with common-law contracts, sales contracts may be either verbal, written, or implied. If the amount of goods involved in the sale is $500 or more, then the contract must be in writing. There are exceptions to this requirement, however. The exceptions are discussed in the following sections.

1. If a verbal contract for $500 or more is confirmed in writing and signed by one party, it is then enforceable. The receiving party must have knowledge of the confirmation and not object to it within ten days. If the receiving party does object within ten days, the contract is void.

   > Sumio agreed verbally to buy $800 worth of fresh fish from Chris. Chris later wrote to Sumio to confirm the verbal contract, and Chris signed the confirmation. If Sumio knows of the confirmation and does not object within ten days, the verbal agreement becomes enforceable.

2. If a person admits, in writing, that a verbal contract for $500 or more exists, the verbal contract becomes enforceable. Using the previous example, let us see how this works.

   > Sumio changes his mind about buying the fish. He writes to Chris saying that the verbal contract to purchase the $800 worth of fresh fish is not enforceable because it is for goods totalling $500 or more. By admitting in writing that the contract exists, it is now enforceable.

3. When the goods in question have been received and accepted by the buyer, the verbal contract becomes enforceable.

> Millie enters into a verbal contract with Regina to sell her $600 worth of lawn furniture. Millie delivers it and Regina accepts possession of the furniture. Because Regina accepted delivery, she is bound by the verbal contract.

4. When the goods have been paid for in full and the seller has accepted payment, the verbal contract becomes enforceable.

> Suppose Regina paid Millie the $600 for the lawn furniture before it was delivered, and Millie accepted the payment. Once Millie accepted the payment, the verbal contract became enforceable.

5. When the goods involved are of special manufacture and not suitable for other uses, a verbal contract is enforceable if the manufacturer has made a substantial beginning in either the manufacture or purchase of goods.

Illus. 21-3 When the goods in question have been received and accepted by the buyer, the verbal contract becomes enforceable.

Courtesy of Phelps Dodge

> Leah owns a specialty advertising company. Chou contracts verbally for $1,000 worth of matchbooks bearing the name and logo of his Chinese restaurant. One month later Chou changes his mind and tries to get out of the contract by arguing that it was not in writing. Leah has already contracted with a printing company to have the work done. Since a substantial beginning has been made by Leah, Chou is bound by the verbal contract.

TRANSFER OF OWNERSHIP AND RISK OF LOSS

Entrepreneurs should be aware at what point the transfer of ownership occurs and when the risk of loss shifts from the vendor to the purchaser.

> James, who owns a video arcade, enters into a sales contract with Gene, who manufactures video game machines. Gene agrees to sell James five new machines for a total of $10,000. Gene ships the machines by train to James. While in transit, the machines are destroyed in a train accident. Who is responsible for the loss?

Usually, the risk of loss is associated with the holding of title. Knowing the law pertaining to these issues can be very important in business situations that involve damaged or lost goods.

Ownership

It is best if the transfer of ownership/title is specifically addressed in the sales contract. If it is not, then a court must decide to which party merchandise belonged at the time of damage. To have goods or the title to goods tied up in court proceedings can become very expensive. It is also possible to alienate good customers and honest suppliers when you enter into legal proceedings. The possible costs of collecting damages may be greater than the potential compensation received from the other party.

The concern over transfer of ownership usually has to do with who bears risk of loss. The following are examples of common situations involving such transfers between vendors and purchasers.

When Vendors Deliver Merchandise. Generally speaking, when the vendor is to deliver the merchandise to the purchaser, ownership/title transfers upon the agreed-to delivery and notification.

> Jennifer, the vendor, agrees to deliver to Julio, the purchaser, ten dozen dresses for the fall season. Julio's receiving department takes delivery from Jennifer's truck driver. Ownership transfers at that point. Jennifer's driver could not just unload the cartons of dresses onto Julio's receiving dock, however, and drive off. The driver needs to notify Julio or one of his employees of the delivery.

When Vendors Ship Merchandise. The sales contract may authorize the vendor to ship the merchandise by a third party, such as a trucking or railroad company, to the purchaser. If it does, then ownership transfers once the merchandise is delivered to the third-party shipper.

> Suppose instead that Julio authorizes Jennifer to ship the dresses via ABC Trucking, Inc. Jennifer then delivers the dresses to the trucking company. Once the goods are delivered to the trucking company, ownership passes to Julio. If the goods are damaged while in ABC's possession, Jennifer has no responsibility.

When Purchasers Pick up Merchandise. If the purchaser picks up the merchandise at the vendor's location, ownership passes at the time of the pick-up.

> Jennifer offers Julio a ten percent discount if he will pick up the dresses. Julio agrees and sends one of his trucks to Jennifer's manufacturing plant. Once Julio's driver takes possession of the dresses, ownership passes to Julio. Jennifer has no further responsibility for the goods.

Ownership in Retail Sales

The following terms pertaining to transfer of ownership are common to retail sales and those handled over the phone or through the mail.

Cash and Carry. When a buyer goes into a store and purchases merchandise with cash, ownership passes when the transaction is complete—that is, with payment to the store.

> Jackie goes into an auto parts store and purchases windshield-wiper blades. Once Jackie pays the clerk and the transaction is complete, ownership of the wiper blades passes from the auto parts store to Jackie.

Credit. Ownership passes in a credit sale in the same way as in a cash sale. The only difference is that payment is mutually agreed upon at a later date.

> If, in the above example, Jackie went to the auto parts store and purchased the wiper blades on credit, ownership would pass once the sales transaction was complete—in this case, when the purchaser signs the charge slip.

C.O.D. Ownership in a C.O.D. transaction passes once the cash is paid to the delivering party. This is different from other cash transactions, however, because the buyer is not permitted to inspect the merchandise prior to acceptance.

Sale on Approval. Sometimes goods are sold to a customer as a **sale on approval.** Even though the buyer has actual possession of the merchandise, ownership does not transfer until the buyer approves the merchandise.

sale on approval, a sales transaction in which the buyer has a right to approve the merchandise prior to the transfer of ownership

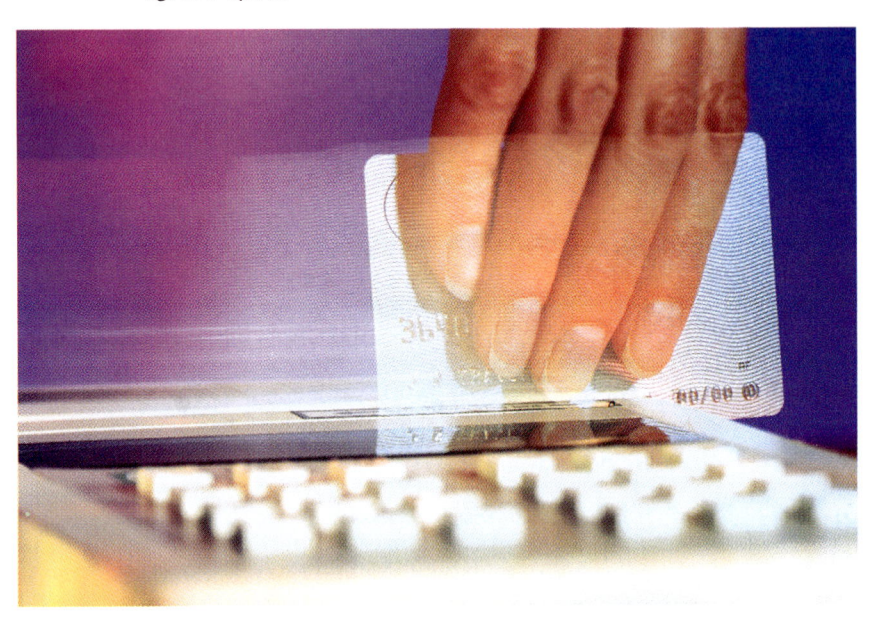

Illus. 21-4 In a credit sale, payment at a later date is mutually agreed upon.

© *Shaun Egan/Tony Stone Images, Inc.*

> Sandi received an offer in the mail for a new type of windshield-wiper blade with three sides. The offer said that the blades would be sent to the buyer for a ten-day trial without obligation. At the end of ten days, either payment or the blades must be returned to the manufacturer. If after ten days, Sandi returns the blades, ownership remains with the manufacturer. If Sandi sends payment, ownership transfers to her.

OBLIGATIONS AND PERFORMANCE

Sales contracts, like all other contracts, can be breached. If there is a sales contract breach, or nonperformance, the injured party has certain rights. The obligations and performance agreed to in the contract can be enforced in certain circumstances which are described in the following paragraphs.

Vendor Rights When the Vendor Is at Fault

Even though a vendor is at fault in a contract nonperformance, he or she still has certain rights. If sufficient time (according to the agreement) remains, the vendor is allowed to correct the error and fulfill the contract.

> Woody owns a small sporting goods store. He orders 25 Brand X fishing reels from Reels, Inc. Reels, Inc. substitutes Brand Y by mistake in Woody's order. Woody informs Reels, Inc. that the contract has been violated because he received the wrong merchandise. If time remains according to the original agreement, Reels, Inc. can still honor the contract by sending the correct merchandise. If they are able to do this, Woody is still obligated to the contract.

Vendor Rights When the Purchaser Is at Fault

The purchaser may be at fault by doing such things as refusing to accept merchandise or refusing to pay. If such is the case, the vendor has certain rights, including the right to sue the purchaser for either payment or damages, or to cancel the contract.

Purchaser Rights When the Vendor Is at Fault

The vendor may be at fault for such things as failing to deliver goods or delivering incorrect merchandise. If such is the case, the purchaser has certain rights. These include the right to sue for specific performance, such as requiring the vendor to deliver the contracted merchandise; to sue for recovery of any money paid to the vendor; to sue for damages due to lost profit or due to excess cost in obtaining substitute merchandise; and to cancel the contract.

THE FASHION ATTIC

Laura was quickly learning that there was much more to buying and selling than she could possibly remember. It all seemed more complicated than the other aspects of entrepreneurship that she had encountered.

Laura decided that the best course of action would be for her to write out some basic buying and selling policies for the Fashion Attic. These would serve as guidelines for her and her employees. She would add to them as she encountered new situations.

1. All prices for merchandise for sale will be clearly posted.
2. Procedures for exchanges and returns will be posted at each point of purchase and included on the customers' sales receipts.
3. Merchandise will not be allowed to leave the premises on approval.
4. Layaway policies will be written out and signed by the customer before the transaction is considered final.
5. All purchase orders for inventory will be signed.
6. All sales contracts for capital asset sale or purchase must be written.
7. No C.O.D. orders will be made by the Fashion Attic.
8. No delivery receipts will be signed without inspection for completeness of shipment.
9. Transfer of ownership information will be included in sales contracts.
10. Damages discovered in shipments will be reported to the vendor within 24 hours of receipt of goods.

Laura knew that other policies would have to be added to her list.

SUMMARY

A sale is defined as the immediate transfer of ownership of goods for a price. Goods are defined as items of tangible personal property other than money. The sale of goods is covered under Article 2 of the Uniform Commercial Code. In a sales transaction, the seller is known as the vendor and the buyer is known as the purchaser (also called vendee).

Sales contracts have required components for legality. Sales contracts are affected by type of seller. They require an offer and acceptance, consideration, and three required terms for the sale. Sales contracts permit some other terms as well. Legal sales contracts must pertain to legal goods and legal transactions. Entrepreneurs should also be aware of the requirement that contracts worth more than $500 must be written, and the exceptions to that requirement.

Entrepreneurs should be aware at what point the transfer of ownership occurs and the risk of loss shifts from the vendor to the purchaser. Risk of loss refers to the financial responsibility assumed by a party to a sales contract if something happens to damage or destroy the goods or merchandise in question. Usually, the risk of loss is associated with the holder of title. It is best if the transfer of ownership/title is specifically addressed in the sales contract.

Sales contracts, like all other contracts, can be breached. If there is a sales contract breach or nonperformance, the injured party has certain rights. The obligations and performance agreed to in the contract can be enforced in certain circumstances.

VOCABULARY BUILDER

Write a brief description of each word or phrase based on your reading of the chapter.

1. Sale
2. Goods
3. Uniform Commercial Code
4. Vendor
5. Purchaser
6. Vendee
7. Seller
8. Merchant
9. Casual seller
10. Price
11. Barter
12. Firm offer
13. Risk of loss
14. Sale on approval

REVIEW QUESTIONS

1. What set of rules governs the sale of goods in most states?
2. What are the two types of sellers in day-to-day sales?
3. What are the two common types of consideration used in sales contracts?
4. What are the three required terms in sales contracts?

DISCUSSION QUESTIONS

1. What terms are permissible, but not required, in a sales contract?
2. What are two exceptions to the requirement that a written contract is necessary for the sale of goods totalling $500 or more?
3. Why is it important for entrepreneurs to know when the transfer of ownership of merchandise takes place?
4. When does transfer of ownership occur in a credit sale?

CRITICAL THINKING

Marla Grubbs owns a plant that manufactures office furniture. Recently she received an order from Clarksdale High School for 25 red office chairs. The purchaser specified in the contract that the chairs should be delivered by September 1. On June 30, Marla shipped the chairs. Since she had no red chairs in inventory, she sent black ones. Upon receipt of the chairs on July 20, the principal of the school called Marla and informed her that she had breached the written contract by sending the wrong color of chairs.

1. Did Marla violate the sales contract?
2. What are Marla's rights in this situation?
3. Can Marla still enforce the terms of the contract against Clarksdale High School?

SHORT CASE: MINI-GOLF, ANYONE?

Gabe DeGabrial lives in Key West, Florida. After working for other people around town for several years, Gabe has decided to open his own business. After much thought and research, he chose to open a miniature golf course. That was about a year ago. Since then he has been developing his business plan and moving forward with the project.

Designing the various holes for his miniature golf course was one of the first things Gabe did. Using an Everglades theme, he created what he considered to be eighteen challenging and fun holes. After he completed the design, Gabe contacted a local contractor and discussed the fixtures he would need for each golf hole. Upon reaching a verbal agreement concerning what was needed, the two shook hands and parted.

The contractor agreed to deliver the fixtures five weeks before the scheduled opening, so that there would be ample time to install them. With the scheduled opening six months away, the contractor felt that he had enough time to complete the $12,000 job.

Three months later, Gabe was talking with a friend about the new miniature golf course. When the friend, who was a carpenter, heard how much the fixtures were going to cost, he told Gabe that $12,000 was too much money for the work. He told Gabe that he could build the whole thing for $8,000.

After thinking about it for a couple of days, Gabe decided to let his friend do the work. After all, he had no written sales contract with the contractor. Gabe then entered into a written contract with his friend to do the work. Upon calling the contractor, Gabe was told that he was breaching the sales contract. Gabe told the contractor that since the contract was not in writing, it was not enforceable.

Questions

1. Is Gabe correct about the contract not being enforceable? Why or why not?
2. What rights does the contractor have?
3. If the contract is enforceable, how does that affect the new contract with the carpenter? What are the carpenter's rights?

PROJECT CHALLENGE

As you continue your business planning process, it is time to develop a set of policies regarding sales contracts. Develop policies in the following areas:

1. Sales contracts for which your business is the purchaser
2. Sales contracts for which your business is the vendor

22

Real Property and Insurance

After mastering the information contained in this chapter, you should be able to:

22-1 Classify property and explain the reason for its classification.

22-2 List the ways that real property can be acquired.

22-3 Explain the options for real property ownership.

22-4 Explain easements.

22-5 Describe the types of real property leases that are available to business owners.

22-6 Explain the rights that tenants and landlords have or may have in a real property lease situation.

22-7 Explain insurable interest.

property, something that is owned or can be owned

PROPERTY OWNERSHIP

Entrepreneurs choose their life-style because they want the independence of being the boss. Their ultimate goal is freedom. To have this freedom requires properly managing a business in an independent fashion, and making the decisions that guide the business.

One of the primary goals of many entrepreneurs is property ownership. Without this ownership, a small part of the freedom they want may be missing. Entrepreneurs should give property ownership serious consideration during the business planning process to determine whether it is a realistic expectation. It may be something that occurs later—lease or rental may make more sense during the start-up phase. Property ownership is not required, and leasing or renting may give the entrepreneur adequate control of the property at a lower cost.

A certain level of knowledge is required whether the entrepreneur chooses to buy property or rent it. Real property is an expensive part of any entrepreneur's dream, and its acquisition must be carefully planned.

Property Classification

Property is usually classified as either real property or personal property. The distinction is made for legal purposes.

Real Property. Real property includes land, buildings, and fixtures. Land usually consists of the earth's surface, a reasonable airspace above the land, and anything that is located below the ground. Growing things, such as trees and crops, are usually considered real property until they are removed (that is, harvested). They then become personal property. In certain circumstances, however, things

Illus. 22-1   Real property includes land, buildings, and fixtures; personal property is unattached.

that are below-ground may be a separate concern. Entrepreneurs who are planning to purchase land should be sure to verify their rights and responsibilities for what cannot be seen.

Buildings, as they relate to real property, are structures that are permanently attached to land. Movable structures, such as sheds, that are on skids or other foundations are usually not considered buildings.

Fixtures are items of personal property that are permanently attached to real property. As a rule, once it is attached, a fixture becomes a part of the real property.

> Phyllis is planning to open a store that sells antique dolls. To protect the dolls, Phyllis hires Misty, a carpenter, to build several display units with glass doors. Misty delivers the units and Phyllis has them permanently attached to the walls of the store she is renting.

When Misty delivers the units to Phyllis, they become Phyllis's personal property. Once Phyllis attaches the units permanently to the walls, they become fixtures and may become the landlord's property. When Phyllis moves or closes her business, the provisions concerning leasehold improvements as stated in the lease contract determine the disposition of the fixtures—that is, whether they will remain or be removed.

Personal Property. The distinction between real and personal property is important. Personal property is any property that is unattached and, therefore, not classified as real property. Personal property includes items such as clothing, furniture, jewelry, and automobiles.

Acquiring Real Property

Entrepreneurs may acquire real property in one of the following three ways:

- through purchase or receipt as a gift
- by inheritance
- by adverse possession

Purchase or Gift. Most owners of real property purchase their property. A written contract is required for the purchase of real property, and the contract must detail all terms of the transfer.

Real property may also be received as a gift. A gift is the transfer of property without charge. The gift is valid only if the person who gives does so unconditionally. The gift must take place in the present, not at some future time (such as after the giver's death), and the gift must be accepted.

The actual transfer of title, after purchase or receipt by gift, is accomplished through the use of a **deed.** There are two main types of deeds: warranty deeds and quitclaim deeds.

A warranty deed is a deed that transfers a seller's interest in real property with certain warranties. These warranties ensure that the item to be transferred is free from defects and from any claims. The following provisions are usually warranted.

1. The seller owns the property or has authority to transfer it.
2. No undisclosed claims, such as unpaid taxes, exist against the property.
3. The purchaser's right to possession will not be disturbed. This means no person or company will, at a later date, make a claim against the property based on circumstances that existed at the time of purchase.
4. The seller will do whatever is necessary to ensure that the title to the property is valid.

A quitclaim deed transfers whatever ownership interest the seller has, including liabilities, to the buyer. There are no warranties made concerning validity of the title. Accepting a quitclaim deed to real property is generally not a good idea.

Margin note: **deed,** a written document by which an individual conveys title and other rights of ownership of real property to another individual

The deed for the property should be recorded, or legally documented, as soon as it is received. This is usually done in the courthouse of the county in which the property is located. Once recorded, the deed provides a public record of ownership, which protects the new owner. Recording the deed will prevent possible loss in any dispute over ownership of the property.

Inheritance. Real property may be inherited. In this situation, title does not pass by deed but by distribution from an estate. This transaction must also be recorded at the county courthouse.

Adverse Possession. An individual can take real property from the legal owner without paying for it through **adverse possession.** If a property is to be taken in this manner, however, several requirements must be met. They are as follows:

adverse possession, the acquisition of another's land by occupation, without the owner's permission and without payment

1. The adverse possessor (person trying to take the property) must be occupying and using the property.
2. The adverse possessor's use of the property must be clearly evident.
3. The adverse possessor must be using the property without permission.
4. The adverse possessor must openly claim ownership to the property.
5. The adverse possessor's occupation and use of the property must meet the duration requirement established by the laws of the state in which the property is located (usually 5 to 20 years).

> Mary Sherman purchased a 35-acre parcel of land in a mountain resort area as an investment. She visited the undeveloped land prior to purchase, then returned home. Since the land was undeveloped, Mary did not feel it would be necessary to visit the property on a regular basis. Six years after purchasing the property, Mary decided to visit it while in the area on vacation. Much to her surprise, the land was fenced and had cattle grazing on it. A sign identified the property as part of the Lazy S Ranch. Mary learned that the fence and sign had been in place for more than five years and that the owner of the Lazy S Ranch had been continually using the land for cattle grazing. The adverse possession period for the state in which the property was located was five years. As unfair as it seemed, Mary had lost her land.

If all of the requirements for adverse possession are met, the original owner will probably lose title. However, the circumstances are not usually as extreme as those in Mary's situation.

Illus. 22-2

A survey can help determine property rights.

© *Don Spiro/Tony Stone Images, Inc.*

> Jim and Katie own adjacent pieces of property in the downtown section of their city. Katie recently built a restaurant on her property. The construction company erroneously extended Katie's parking lot five feet onto Jim's property. Neither Jim nor Katie is aware of the error. If Jim does not discover the error before the lapse of the adverse possession period in his state, Katie will gain title to the portion of his property she is using.

Owning Real Property

If an entrepreneur decides that purchasing, rather than leasing, property is the best course, then the form of ownership becomes an issue. Joint tenancy, tenancy by entirety, or tenancy in common are the forms of real property ownership to consider. Entrepreneurs should weigh these choices carefully; a decision made now will determine the future disposition of the property.

Joint Tenancy. Entrepreneurs who are co-owners of a business may choose **joint tenancy** as the form of ownership to ensure that the other owner or owners will acquire ownership interests upon their deaths.

joint tenancy, ownership by more than one person, with rights of survivorship

> Bill and his friend Charles started a business together, and they bought a building to house the business. They chose to own the building in joint tenancy. If Bill dies, the building becomes Charles's property—Bill's heirs have no claim on the property. The same is true for Charles's heirs if he dies.

A joint tenancy may be dissolved if one of the parties to the agreement sells his or her interest. The buyer does not automatically become a joint tenant.

Tenancy by Entirety. The **tenancy by entirety** form of ownership is available only to entrepreneurs who are married to each other at the time the property is acquired.

tenancy by entirety, ownership by husband and wife, with rights of survivorship

> Susie and Jon are husband and wife. They purchase a building for their business and choose tenancy by entirety as the form of ownership. If one of them dies, the other becomes the sole owner of the property.

A tenancy by entirety can be dissolved only if both parties agree to sell the property.

Tenancy in Common. In the **tenancy in common** form of ownership, if one of the parties to the agreement dies, that person's interest in the property passes to his or her heirs.

tenancy in common, ownership by more than one person, without rights of survivorship

> Maria, Chin, and Shaun started a small business together. They purchased a building as tenants in common. One year after the business opened, Shaun died. His interest in the building passed to his heirs.

In this example, any of the three parties is free to sell his or her interest in the building. This type of ownership is the most common when the entrepreneurs involved are not related.

Community Property. Several states have **community property** laws. Under these laws, all property acquired during marriage automatically becomes community property and is owned jointly by the husband and wife. If either spouse dies, his or her interest is distributed as dictated by the will, or if no will exists, as dictated by state law.

community property, property acquired during marriage

> Christi and two friends formed a partnership and started a catering business, working from their homes in La Jolla, California. The business

Illus. 22-3

Under community property laws, all property acquired during a marriage is automatically owned jointly by the husband and wife.

© Steve Leonard/Tony Stone Images, Inc.

> did well, and after two years the three partners decided to purchase a building to house their business. After much discussion, they chose to purchase the building in their own names. A year later Christi died, and her husband of four years claimed ownership of one sixth of the building—half of Christi's interest. Christi's partners argued that, since Christi's husband was not involved in the business and had not invested in it in any way, he was not entitled to the ownership he claimed.

The property in question is governed by community property laws, because California is one of the states that recognizes such laws. Therefore, Christi's husband does own one-sixth of the building.

easement, a nonpossessory right to use land owned by another party

An **easement** allows one person to cross another person's property to gain access to his or her own property. The party that is granted the easement must maintain the property involved in the easement. The other party may not interfere with the easement.

Jabar bought 50 acres of land that is completely surrounded by land owned by Gene (see Figure 22-1). An easement must be granted if Jabar is to have access to his property.

LEASING REAL PROPERTY

Many entrepreneurs find that leasing a facility is more sensible than buying. This is especially true during business start-up, when entrepreneurs have so many expenses to cover.

Types of Leases

Leases for business properties usually fall into one of four categories—tenancy for years, periodic tenancy, tenancy at sufferance, or tenancy at will. The terms of a lease are what determine which type of lease it is.

Tenancy for Years. The fixed term for a **tenancy for years** lease may be any specified period of weeks, months, or years. This type of lease often includes an option for renewal or an option for purchase. Entrepreneurs may choose this type of lease, with an option to purchase, if the facility is a good candidate for a permanent place of business.

tenancy for years, a lease for a fixed period of time

Periodic Tenancy. The most common type of **periodic tenancy** lease is a month-to-month lease. A designated period of notice is usually required for cancellation of a lease of this type.

periodic tenancy, a lease for a set period of time that will continue for similar periods of time until terminated

Figure 22-1 Map of Jabar's Property

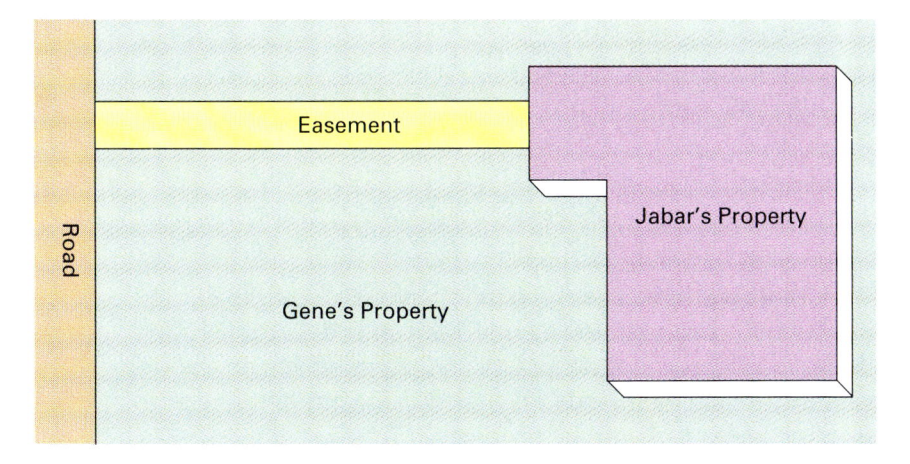

tenancy at sufferance, a lease in which a tenant may remain in the facility after termination of the lease

Tenancy at Sufferance. When a **tenancy at sufferance** lease expires, the landlord can choose to evict the tenant or allow the tenant to remain by continuing to accept lease payments. If payment is accepted, a new periodic tenancy is created. The length of the new lease will be tied to the length of the old one. If the old lease was for one year, the new one will also be a one-year lease.

tenancy at will, the possession of real property without benefit of an agreement that documents terms

Tenancy at Will. If the lease is a **tenancy at will** lease, neither the duration of the tenancy nor the amount of the rent is documented. This type of lease allows change or termination at any time, by either party.

Rights and Duties

Both landlords and tenants have certain rights and duties under ordinary lease agreements. Tenants are given the right to possess and use property in return for the duties of paying rent and taking care of the property. In some leases, the tenant is also given the right to sublet (lease all or part of the leased property to a third party) or assign (transfer the entire interest in the property to a third party) the property. In a sublease, the person with the original lease remains responsible to the landlord. In an assignment, the third party becomes primarily responsible to the landlord.

The right to sublet or assign is governed by the lease agreement. It is very important to be sure these rights are included in a business lease. Their absence could be very costly in the event that a business is dissolved.

> Millie signed a two-year lease on a small building in which she opened a manufacturing business. After six months she had to close the business because of poor health. A clause in the lease allowed her to assign her tenancy, so she was able to transfer the lease to a competitor who needed additional space.

If Millie's lease had prohibited assignment, she would have had to pay rent on the facility for 18 months after she closed the business. This would have been a financial disaster.

Landlords have the right to receive rent and, in some cases, to keep any fixtures that are added to the property in return for the duties of maintaining the facility and paying taxes on the property. If rent is not paid, landlords may sue for the amount due and/or evict (remove) tenants from the property.

INSURANCE

There are many risks involved in operating a business in modern-day America. Successful entrepreneurs are aware of probable risks and plan for them. The most important form of protection against the hazards of operating a business is insurance. Entrepreneurs must procure several types of business insurance if they are to be properly protected.

Obtaining the proper insurance coverage for a business begins with determining what the business's insurance needs are. Entrepreneurs must be sure that they provide for coverage of all aspects of the business. The types of coverage most commonly needed to ensure proper protection include the following.

1. Property insurance: provides protection against loss or damage for any property that would need to be replaced (e.g., business facility, equipment, inventory).
2. Liability insurance: provides protection against losses that result from customer claims of bodily or monetary injury. These claims often result in lawsuits and usually in a legal responsibility for payment of damages. The liability can be a result of an injury that is incurred while the customer is at the place of business or an injury that results from use of the product or service purchased.

Illus. 22-4 Property insurance provides protection against loss or damage for any real or personal property that might need to be replaced.

3. Business interruption insurance: provides protection against loss of revenue that results from an unexpected temporary shutdown.
4. Key person insurance: provides protection against potential loss of revenue that results from loss of personnel whose services are critical to the successful operation of the business.
5. Life insurance: provides the surviving owner(s) with sufficient capital to purchase a deceased owner's interest in the business.

Certain relationships must exist if insurance on people or property is purchased. Those relationships are referred to as *insurable interest*. The concept of insurable interest was established by law to prevent profit from a situation in which there is no real involvement.

> Abby knows that Viana likes to drive her car very fast and take risks. Abby buys a one-million dollar life insurance policy on Viana. She figures she will be a million dollars richer if Viana happens to get killed.

Under the concept of insurable interest, situations such as the one in this example are illegal. Insurable interest must exist at the time personal or property insurance is purchased.

Insurable Interest in People

Entrepreneurs may discover that other people—partners or employees—are critical to the success of a business. Without them, the business might suffer tremendous financial loss. If this is the case, an entrepreneur has an insurable interest in them and may purchase insurance, called key person insurance, to protect against such a loss.

> Blaine, an electrical engineer, and Wylie, a chemical engineer, form a partnership to manufacture small electronic components for the defense industry. The skills of both men are essential to the success of the business. To protect themselves against potential loss, Blaine and Wylie take out a life insurance policy on each other.

Blaine and Wylie have a legitimate insurable interest in each other's lives.

Insurable Interest in Property

Generally speaking, a person with a legitimate insurable interest in property is one who owns, rents, or holds the property as security for another debt. It is essential to insure any property associated with the business that is critical to its success. Do not overlook rental property—it can be as essential to success as owned property. Its destruction or damage could hinder or even prevent the continuation of business.

THE FASHION ATTIC

Laura was astounded to learn of the many types of insurance coverage available. She had known that she would have to have property and liability coverage for both peace of mind and to comply with her lease. The shopping mall lease required that she protect her assets in case of fire and also that she carry considerable liability protection in case a customer was accidentally hurt while on the property. What she wasn't prepared for were the decisions to be made concerning protection in case of vandalism, water-sprinkler leakage, burglary, and sign and exterior glass breakage—just to mention a few. By the time her insurance agent had listed all possible forms of coverage, the total premium payments were out of line with her projected budget.

Laura felt better when her agent took the time to explain that some forms of coverage might not be necessary if she were willing to take some limited risk. He explained that many business owners were willing to take risks in areas for which they could afford to cover possible damage themselves. Since the risk of accidents was not high in some areas, Laura omitted those for which she could provide a replacement if the worst happened. She knew that it was possible to be insurance rich and cash poor if she paid premiums on every possible accidental occurrence. Her final policy covered all catastrophic occurrences and had a comfortable allowance for liability factors.

Laura's inventory and fixtures were well insured against fire. Since she was leasing space, real property coverage was necessary only to cover the carpeting and fixtures that were attached to the landlord's building. Her insurance agent recommended that she insure her assets for their replacement costs as opposed to their book values since inflation could dramatically increase the cost to replace the items.

Laura was relieved to have the insurance issue settled. She had chosen an agent who had been highly recommended and had many years of experience in writing commercial insurance policies. She was satisfied with the suggestions he had made, and she was confident that she would be protected under all possible circumstances.

SUMMARY

One of the primary goals of many entrepreneurs is property ownership. Entrepreneurs must consider carefully whether to buy property or rent it. Real property is an expensive part of any entrepreneur's dream, and its acquisition must be carefully planned.

Property is usually classified as real property or personal property. Real property includes land, buildings, and fixtures. Personal property is any property that is unattached and therefore not classified as real property. Personal property includes such items as clothing, furniture, jewelry, and automobiles.

Real property is usually acquired in one of three ways: purchase or gift, inheritance, or adverse possession. The actual transfer of title, after purchase or receipt by gift, is accomplished through the use of a deed. There are two major types of deeds: warranty and quitclaim.

When the decision to purchase property is made, a form of ownership must be selected: joint tenancy, tenancy by entirety, or tenancy in common. Property ownership may involve an easement. The nonpossessory right provided by an easement allows a person to cross another person's property.

Many entrepreneurs find that leasing a facility is more sensible than buying. A lease for business property is usually one of four types: tenancy for years, periodic tenancy, tenancy at sufferance, or tenancy at will. The terms of the lease determine which type of lease it is.

Both tenants and landlords have certain rights and duties under ordinary lease agreements. Tenants have the right to possess, use, and possibly sublet or assign the property. Landlords have the right to receive rent and to keep any fixtures added to the property.

Insurance is very important to entrepreneurs. They should purchase insurance to protect against potential losses. To purchase personal or property insurance, certain relationships must exist. Those relationships are referred to as insurable interest. The concept of insurable interest was established by law to prevent profit from a situation in which there is no real involvement.

VOCABULARY BUILDER

Write a brief description of each word or phrase based on your reading of the chapter.

1. Property
2. Real property
3. Land
4. Buildings
5. Fixtures
6. Personal property
7. Deed
8. Warranty deed
9. Quitclaim deed
10. Adverse possession
11. Joint tenancy
12. Tenancy by entirety
13. Tenancy in common
14. Community property
15. Easement
16. Tenancy for years
17. Periodic tenancy
18. Tenancy at sufferance
19. Tenancy at will

REVIEW QUESTIONS

1. What items are classified as real property?
2. What are some examples of personal property?
3. What are the three ways in which real property is usually acquired?
4. What are the two main types of deeds?

DISCUSSION QUESTIONS

1. What is adverse possession? What five conditions must be met to claim adverse possession?
2. What are the characteristics of two types of real property ownership?
3. What is an easement? Why are easements sometimes necessary?
4. What does insurable interest mean?

CRITICAL THINKING

Trip's apartment is owned by a friend of his father. He has lived there for two years and pays $250 per month in rent. He has no written lease that documents the terms of the lease. When he moved in, the friend told him he could stay in the apartment and pay what he could afford. Last week the friend told him that he would have to move at the end of the month.

1. What type of lease does Trip have?
2. Does Trip have to move? Why or why not?

SHORT CASE: INSURANCE INFORMATION WANTED

Sheila is planning to start a new business with three friends—Barry, Ruth, and Charlton. They are currently finalizing their business plan.

Sheila has five years of experience as a licensed and certified architect. She specializes in custom designing private homes. Barry is a real estate agent. He specializes in new home sales. Ruth is an interior designer and is considered the best in the business by many of the builders in town. The majority of her work is in new home interior design. Charlton's specialty is residential construction. He has been running his own business successfully for three years.

Sheila, Barry, Ruth, and Charlton are planning to start a real estate development company. Their dream is to purchase land, design and build houses, and market these houses. All functions would be performed by their company—no subcontractors would be involved.

The four are currently planning for their insurance needs. They are considering their life and property insurance needs, including coverage for the small office space they plan to lease.

Questions

1. Which of the four people involved should be insured? Why?
2. Should the partners purchase insurance for the new office space? Why or why not?

PROJECT CHALLENGE

It is now time to make your final decision about your facility. In your business plan notebook, answer the following questions.

1. Are you going to lease or purchase? Why?
2. If you lease, what type of lease will you choose? Why?
3. If you purchase, what type of ownership will you choose? Why?
4. What types of insurance will you need for the new business?

23
Ethics and Social Responsibility in Entrepreneurship

Most people, when asked whether they are ethical, respond that they are ethical. But what does being ethical really mean? **Ethics** can be defined as moral standards or rules of conduct. *Business ethics* are rules about how businesses and their employees ought to behave.

Almost everyone has a set of moral standards. At issue, however, is whether or not those standards are appropriate in a business setting. If the entrepreneur does not have a high standard of ethics regarding his or her business, then it is very likely that the business will ultimately suffer as a result.

Ethics in the workplace are often dictated by the work environment. What are acceptable ethics to management are usually adhered to by the employees. As an entrepreneur, you will be the manager. Your ethics will become your employees' ethics. You should act accordingly by creating a code of ethics for your business and demanding strict adherence to it. Good ethics mean good business.

A CODE OF ETHICS

A *code of ethics* is a list of principles of appropriate behavior. Codes of ethics generally address topics such as professional conduct, confidentiality of information, conflicts of interest, political contributions, and the like. If a code of ethics is to make a real difference, it must be carefully designed and implemented. Employees are more likely to accept a code if managers and others affected by it are involved in its development.

Members of the American Marketing Association (AMA) are committed to ethical professional conduct. They have joined together in subscribing to a code of ethics that guides many areas of business behavior. The code is shown in Figure 23-1. Any AMA member found to be in violation of any provision of this code may have his or her Association membership suspended or revoked.

After mastering the information contained in this chapter, you should be able to:

23-1 Describe marketers' responsibilities under the Code of Ethics of the American Marketing Association.

23-2 Explain the importance of ethics as they relate to consumers, competition, and employees.

23-3 Understand the importance of social responsibility in relation to the environment.

23-4 Identify ethical issues that are related to the use of computers.

ethics, moral standards or a system of morals

Figure 23-1 Code of Ethics of the American Marketing Association

Responsibilities of the Marketer

Marketers must accept responsibility for the consequences of their activities. They must make every effort to ensure that their decisions, recommendations, and actions function to identify, serve, and satisfy all relevant publics: consumers, organizations and society. Marketers' professional conduct must be guided by the following:

1. The basic rule of professional ethics: not knowingly to do harm
2. The adherence to all applicable laws and regulations
3. The accurate representation of their education, training, and experience
4. The active support, practice, and promotion of their Code of Ethics

Honesty and Fairness

Marketers shall uphold and advance the integrity, honor, and dignity of the marketing profession by observing the following:

1. Being honest in serving consumers, clients, employees, suppliers, distributors and the public
2. Not knowingly participating in conflict of interest without prior notice to all parties involved
3. Establishing equitable fee schedules including the payment or receipt of usual, customary, or legal compensation for marketing exchanges.

Rights and Duties of Parties

Participants in the marketing exchange process should be able to expect the following:

1. That products and services offered are safe and fit for their intended purposes
2. That communications about offered products and services are not deceptive
3. That all parties intend to discharge their obligations, financial and otherwise, in good faith
4. That appropriate internal methods exist for equitable adjustment and/or redress of grievances concerning purchases

It is understood that the above includes, but is not limited to, responsibilities in the areas outlined in the following paragraphs.

Product development and management. Marketers must disclose all substantial risks associated with a product or service. They must also identify any product component substitution that might materially change the product or influence the buyer's purchase decision.

Extra-cost added features must be identified as well.

Promotions. Marketers must avoid false and misleading advertising. They must reject high-pressure manipulations, misleading sales tactics, and avoid sales promotions that use deception or manipulation.

Figure 23-1   (continued)

> **Distribution.**   Marketers must not manipulate the availability of a product for the purpose of exploitation, not use coercion in the marketing channel, and not exert undue influence over resellers' choice to handle a product.
>
> **Pricing.**   Marketers must not engage in price fixing or predatory pricing, and they must disclose the full price associated with any purchase.
>
> **Marketing.**   Selling or fund raising under the guise of conducting research is prohibited. Marketers should maintain research integrity by avoiding misrepresentation and omission of pertinent research data. They should also treat outside clients and suppliers fairly.
>
> **Organizational Relationships**
>
> Marketers should be aware of how their behavior may influence the behavior of others in organizational relationships. They should not encourage unethical behavior in others, such as employees, suppliers, or customers. Their relationships should be guided by the following behavior:
>
> 1. Confidentiality and anonymity should be maintained in professional relationships with regard to privileged information.
> 2. Obligations and responsibilities in contracts and mutual agreements should be met in a timely manner.
> 3. Taking the work of others, in whole, or in part, and representing this work as their own or directly benefiting from it without compensation or consent of the originator or owner should be avoided.
> 4. Manipulation to take advantage of situations to maximize personal welfare in a way that unfairly deprives or damages the organization of others should be avoided.

Source: American Marketing Association

TREATMENT OF CONSUMERS

Ethical behavior toward consumers is of paramount importance to any entrepreneur's success formula. The only exception is the business that does not need repeat customers, and very few such businesses exist.

Regardless of the type of business, customers rely on the honesty and integrity of the business with which they are dealing. If customers feel that they have been dealt with in an unethical fashion, they will usually not come back with repeat business. All entrepreneurs should therefore develop a code of ethics governing their treatment of consumers. Areas to be included are pricing, advertising, selling, and warranties.

Illus. 23-1   Ethical behavior is often dictated by work environment.

Photo by Alan Brown/Photonics

Pricing

As was discussed in Chapter 9, the proper pricing of a product or service addresses two objectives. The first objective is for the price to serve as a public relations tool. A fair price tells the customer that the business offers good value, thus encouraging a demand for the product or service. The second objective is for the price to ensure profit to the seller, thereby allowing the business to continue serving the market. The ethical entrepreneur will strive to set a fair price that accomplishes both objectives.

Advertising

Ethical advertising means not engaging in false advertising, deceptive advertising, or bait and switch advertising. False advertising contains information that is not true or would cause the average consumer to reach a false conclusion about a particular product or service. Deceptive advertising contains information that would cause the average consumer to be misled about a particular product or service. Bait and switch advertising is the practice of advertising a low priced item as a means of luring customers into the store for the real purpose of selling them a higher priced item. Entrepreneurs who want to develop their customers' trust should make sure that their advertising is honest and accurate.

Warranties

In Chapter 20, warranties were discussed in some detail. The two major types of warranties are express and implied. An express warranty is a clearly stated fact about the quality or performance of a product. An implied warranty is a warranty imposed by law ensuring that a product will perform under normal uses and circumstances. Maintaining ethical behavior in relation to warranties is imperative to the successful entrepreneur.

Ethical behavior regarding warranties is more than simply honoring the letter of the warranty (what it actually says). Often, it also involves honoring the intent of the warranty (what it actually means). A good rule of thumb for the entrepreneur is to ask the question, "If I were the customer in this situation, would I think that I was treated fairly?" The answer to that question can go a long way in helping entrepreneurs to decide what is ethical.

Illus. 23-2   Ethical behavior is important in all aspects of customer relations.

Photo by Alan Brown/Photonics

TREATMENT OF THE COMPETITION

Just as ethical treatment of consumers is important to entrepreneurial success, so too is ethical treatment of competitors. You have already learned that competition is a critical component of private enterprise, but private enterprise can be effective only if fair competition is guaranteed. Only the entrepreneurs themselves can truly make that guarantee.

The Federal Trade Commission has as its purpose the enforcement and monitoring of fair competition. The Sherman Antitrust Act, the Clayton Act, and the Robinson-Patman Act have as their purpose the prevention of monopolies. However, the real force in ensuring fair competition comes from the entrepreneur, through high moral standards that manifest themselves in the ethical treatment of all competitors.

Ethical treatment of competitors may involve abstaining from the use of proprietary information that was gained from a competitor in an unethical fashion. For example, a disgruntled employee of one of your major competitors gives you a copy of your competitor's promotion calendar. To use this information would be unethical. It may also involve being honest in all pricing, advertising, and selling practices. In general, ethical treatment means that entrepreneurs treat their competition in the same fair and honest manner they would hope to be treated themselves.

TREATMENT OF EMPLOYEES

Just as important as the ethical treatment of consumers and the competition is the ethical treatment of one's own employees. Such treatment should cover all aspects of employment, including hiring and firing, compensation, and overall working conditions.

Hiring and Firing

Various laws prevent discrimination in the hiring process based on sex, race, color, religion, national origin, disability, or age. If all entrepreneurs maintained high ethical standards throughout the employment process, these laws would not be necessary.

Entrepreneurs should develop hiring policies based on the fair treatment of all applicants. The result will be a quality work force of employees who respect the business for its fairness and integrity. A secondary result will be the pride of the entrepreneur in knowing that his or her hiring practices are fair, not because it is the law, but because it is the right thing to do.

Compensation

The compensation of employees is an ethical decision as well as a management decision. It is part of the overall strategy of doing business. Salaries that are too low may discourage productivity and lower employee morale. Salaries that are too high may create unreasonable expectations from employees and at the same time, dangerously erode the business's profit margin. The ethical entrepreneur will establish a compensation plan that maximizes the earning potential of employees yet ensures a reasonable profit and return on investment.

Working Conditions

As was discussed in Chapter 15, the Occupational Safety and Health Act (OSHA) assures workers in the United States a healthy and safe working environment by regulating exposure to hazardous substances and setting requirements for safety equipment. The truly ethical entrepreneur will not have to be forced by law to provide safe and comfortable working conditions; she or he will do so out of a genuine concern for the health and safety of employees.

By demonstrating a genuine concern for employees, the entrepreneur will, in all likelihood, receive a high level of professionalism

Illus. 23-3   The ethical entrepreneur will provide safe working conditions out of genuine concern for employees.

Courtesy of Western Electric

Illus. 23-4

Employees' personal information should be treated with respect.

and loyalty in return. The ethical treatment of employees is imperative for success in any business venture.

TREATMENT OF THE ENVIRONMENT

social responsibility, the responsibility of businesses to pursue policies that benefit society

Social responsibility is the responsibility of business to pursue policies that benefit society. Social responsibility and ethics go hand-in-hand. Have you noticed the trend among fast-food restaurants to eliminate take-out food containers that harm the environment? Styrofoam containers that were once commonplace are slowly but surely being replaced by containers that are more biodegradable. The fast-food industry is making an effort to be more responsive to the environment.

The makers of disposable diapers have developed technology that allows them to manufacture a diaper that keeps babies drier and at the same time uses less material. The result is a diaper that takes up about half as much space in a landfill. Again, this is the result of an industry trying to be more responsible in relation to the environment.

The time is long gone when an entrepreneur could ignore the impact of the entrepreneurial venture on the environment. Social responsibility dictates that all entrepreneurs should try to minimize the negative impact of their business ventures on the environment. As with the fast-food and disposable diaper industries, concern for the environment, not requirements of the law, should drive these decisions. Business decisions should fulfill broad social needs and expectations as well as those of the business.

USE OF COMPUTER TECHNOLOGY

Questions about the ethical use of computers have the added confusion of being associated with a new technological field. Along with genetic engineering for example, computer technology has no clearly defined history of ethical values, as do more established areas of business such as marketing and management.

Some areas are already clear. For example, in the early 1980s, an employee at a Fortune 500 company, with the aid of an accounts payable clerk, used the computer to create bogus invoices for personal gain. The employee was fired and forced to pay back the stolen money. This is clearly an unethical practice as well as an illegal one. Other areas aren't as clear.

Copying computer software is one area of great concern. Is it ethical for an employee to copy software purchased by the company and take it home for personal use? What about the viewing of other people's electronic mail? Or, what about an employee securing access to another employee's personnel file? Although such actions are not always illegal, they may not be ethical. Through a focus on the ethics related to computers and other technologies in both schools and the workplace, guidelines can be established that will make ethics in these areas clearer for the next generation. Ethical standards related to computer use are evolving as various issues are encountered. The following are possible solutions to the problem of unethical use of computers.

- The U.S. Supreme Court recently ruled that the compiling of data is not eligible for copyright. A possible solution to protecting such data and their accompanying software programs is for the company to clearly identify the information as a trade secret, limit

access to that information and maintain a security policy to control the access.[1]
- Most businesses operate under the mistaken assumption that electronic mail is protected in the same way as mail sent through the U.S. Postal Service, and that it is a felony to tamper with or intercept others' electronic mail. A solution to the unethical use of electronic mail is for a company to establish and share rules with all employees. Additionally, managers should set a positive example by properly using electronic mail themselves, and by using viewing privileges sparingly.[2]

Figure 23-2 is the Code of Ethics of the Association of Computing Machinery.

Figure 23-2 Code of Ethics of the Association of Computing Machinery

1. General Moral Imperatives

As an ACM member I will . . .

    1.1 Contribute to society and human well-being,
    1.2 Avoid harm to others,
    1.3 Be honest and trustworthy,
    1.4 Be fair and take action not to discriminate,
    1.5 Honor property rights including copyrights and patents,
    1.6 Give proper credit for intellectual property,
    1.7 Access computing and communication resources only when authorized to do so,
    1.8 Respect the privacy of others,
    1.9 Honor confidentiality.

2. More Specific Professional Responsibilities

As an ACM computing professional I will . . .

    2.1 Strive to achieve the highest quality in both the process and products of professional work,
    2.2 Acquire and maintain professional competence,
    2.3 Know and respect existing laws pertaining to professional work,
    2.4 Accept and provide appropriate professional review,
    2.5 Give comprehensive and thorough evaluations of computer systems and their impacts, with special emphasis on possible risks,
    2.6 Honor contracts, agreements, and assigned responsibilities,
    2.7 Improve public understandings of computing and its consequences.

---

[1] Mills, Jerry W. "Copyright Won't Work? Call It a Trade Secret." *Computerworld,* 24 February 1992: 104.
[2] Kolstad, Rob. "Demons and Dragons: Mail Privacy." *UNIX Review* , August 1992: 79-81.

Figure 23-2 (continued)

> 3. Organizational Leadership Imperatives
>
> *As an ACM member and organizational leader, I will . . .*
>
> 3.1 Articulate social responsibilities of members of an organizational unit and encourage full acceptance of those responsibilities,
> 3.2 Manage personnel and resources to design and build information systems that enhance the quality of working life,
> 3.3 Acknowledge and support proper and authorized uses of an organization's computing and communication resources,
> 3.4 Ensure that users and those who will be affected by a system have their needs clearly articulated during the assessment and design of requirements; later the system must be validated to meet requirements,
> 3.5 Articulate and support policies that protect the dignity of users and others affected by a computing system,
> 3.6 Create opportunities for members of the organization to learn the principles and limitations of computer systems.
>
> 4. Compliance with the code
>
> *As a member, I will . . .*
>
> 4.1 Uphold and promote the principles of this Code,
> 4.2 Agree to take appropriate action leading to a remedy if the Code is violated,
> 4.3 Treat violations of this code as inconsistent with membership in the ACM.

Source: Reprinted courtesy of the Association for Computing Machinery (ACM) (Bylaw 17, Constitution of the ACM, revised October, 1992). From "ACM Code of Ethics and Professional Conduct," *Communications of the ACM,* May 1992: 94–99.

ESTABLISHING A CODE OF ETHICS

Who is responsible for employee ethics? Is it the business owner's responsibility to develop ethics among employees, or should employees come to work with a system of ethics already in place? Whether employees behave ethically depends largely on the actions and attitudes of management. A standard code of ethics should be set by businesses so that employees have general guidelines to follow.[3] Although ethics are generally personal in nature, they can be strengthened through an increased emphasis on teaching business ethics in schools. It also helps when employers establish guidelines of expected ethical behavior for their employees.

---

[3] McPartlin, John P. "Ethics." *Information Week*, 13 July 1992: 30-36, 40.

Entrepreneurs who decide to establish their own code of ethics should take the following points into consideration.

- Ethics is a behavior, and businesses are dependent upon their employees' behaviors. Therefore, guidelines for ethics should be provided.
- If employees are to place proper value on the use of information, it must be regarded as an asset and equated to tangible assets. It should be reinforced that information is generally personal in nature. It should be treated with respect.
- Ethics should guide people, not trap them. Ethics should also follow generally established societal values.
- When goals are established for ethics programs, they should be realistic and in the realm of achieveability.
- A code of ethics specific to the business can be made, with employees encouraged to see their participation as vital.
- Employees and other managers can be tested on the code of ethics' procedures prior to actual implementation.[4]

Although ethics are generally personal in nature, they can be strengthened through an increased emphasis on teaching business ethics in schools. Ethics training is a part of some management development programs. Employers should also establish guidelines of expected ethical behavior for their employees. With a focus on ethics in both schools and the workplace, businesses and professional groups have principles governing appropriate behavior.

THE FASHION ATTIC

Since the very beginning, Laura had known that her goal was to operate the finest retail store imaginable. She would always put customers first, treat her employees fairly, and maintain a reputation of integrity throughout the community. As she got closer to the opening of the Fashion Attic, Laura decided to write a manual that would demonstrate her commitment to these values. A copy of the manual would be given to each employee, and a code of ethics would be posted in the store where all the customers could read it.

---

[4]DeMaio, Harry B. "Your Organization Needs an Information Ethics Program!" *Management Accounting*, November 1991: 22-23.

Laura began by creating a list of twelve values:

1. All merchandise offered for sale will be of the finest quality available for the price requested.
2. All statements, written or spoken, which represent the store and its merchandise will be honest, with no intent to deceive.
3. All terms of sale will be clearly stated.
4. The store will support in entirety any express or implied warranties offered with the merchandise.
5. Employees will respond to both customer requests for assistance and customer concerns in a timely and polite manner.
6. The store will treat competition in a fair and ethical manner and will not attempt to sabotage any competitors' transactions.
7. Employees will be hired, paid, and promoted in a non-discriminatory manner.
8. Employees will be given a safe and comfortable working environment.
9. Employees will work under a compensation plan that maximizes their earning potential.
10. Employees will have an open invitation to discuss concerns, ambitions, or personal considerations with the owner at all times.
11. The Fashion Attic will act in compliance with all environmental concerns.
12. The Fashion Attic will act in a manner to ensure the beneficial development of the community at all times.

As she reviewed her list, Laura realized that her manual would be quite lengthy once all the points were properly clarified. It would take some time to write—time she didn't feel she had—but she would do it because she felt that it was one of her most important responsibilities.

SUMMARY

All entrepreneurs should create a code of ethics for their business and demand strict adherence to it. Good ethics means good business. Examples of good codes of ethics are available from organizations such as the American Marketing Association and the Association of Computing Machinery. All codes of ethics for today's businesses should cover the following major areas: consumers, competition, employees, the environment, and use of computers.

VOCABULARY BUILDER

On a separate sheet of paper, write a brief definition of each word or phrase based on your reading of the chapter.

1. Ethics
2. Business ethics
3. Social responsibility

REVIEW QUESTIONS

1. What usually dictates work place ethics?
2. What is a code of ethics?
3. In the development of a code of ethics for consumers, what areas should be considered?
4. What is ethical advertising?
5. What is the difference between an express warranty and an implied warranty?
6. What is a good rule of thumb to use in determining ethical treatment of customers concerning warranties?
7. What does the ethical treatment of competitors involve?
8. On what basis is discrimination forbidden in the hiring process.
9. Who is responsible for employee ethics in the area of computers?
10. What are possible solutions to the problem of unethical use of computers?

DISCUSSION QUESTIONS

1. Why do ethics dictate that entrepreneurs should try to minimize the negative impact of their business ventures on the environment?
2. How would you as an entrepreneur benefit from having a code of ethics? How are you affected by others' ethics or lack of ethics?
3. Some corporations and businesses demand certain behaviors from their employees even when they're not at work. What would you as an entrepreneur and employer demand from your employees when not at work? What would you do if their off-duty behavior interfered with their job performance?
4. Why is ethical treatment of competitors important to businesses?
5. Why is it important to develop hiring policies based on the fair treatment of all applicants?
6. What are the general ethical responsibilities of the marketer?

CRITICAL THINKING

Leslie Martinez owns a business specializing in the wholesale distribution of gasoline. Her business has grown to the extent that she needs to hire several new employees. Currently, there is a need for a truck driver, a clerical employee, and a person to coordinate and schedule the deliveries of gasoline to retailers. After placing an ad in the paper, Leslie received 35 applications. Of these, ten were qualified for the various jobs. Among those qualified were two women, three ethnic minorities, and a disabled person. All present employees of the business are white men.

1. Do you think Leslie has an ethical obligation to hire any of the female, ethnic minority, or disabled applicants? Why or why not?
2. Assume that you were asked to give Leslie some advice about hiring the disabled applicant. Research the Americans with Disabilities Act (ADA). What obligation does Leslie have?
3. Contact a local company that has written hiring policies. Bring a copy of the policies to class and discuss the major components.

SHORT CASE—KEMP COMPUTER SERVICES

After ten years as an employee of a major international computer company, Belinda Kemp decided to leave her high-paying management position at the company's headquarters in Atlanta and start her own business.

That was eighteen months ago. Today her new business, Kemp Computer Services, is doing quite well. For the past six months, the company has been realizing a steadily increasing profit margin. This month she added two new salespeople and one systems analyst, bringing her total number of employees to eleven. Belinda feels that her business has gotten off to a good start and that the future is bright.

Kemp Computer Services is a business that sells a service. It specializes in providing this service to medium-to-medium-large independent businesses. Based on considerable market research and her own experience, Belinda has identified a target market for her services. The market consists of companies that have experienced enough growth to justify the computerization of their businesses.

After one of her sales representatives sells the service to a client, other staff members go into the company and create an individualized computer system based on the business' needs. The complete package usually involves the purchase of computer hardware plus the development and/or purchase of software. The majority of Belinda's profit to date has come from the systems design and software development components of the business. Typically, the cost of hardware has been a pass-through, with no profit taken by Belinda.

On Monday morning, Gene Cook came by to see Belinda. He was one of the new salespeople and had been on the job less than a month. He told her that his previous employer, a computer hardware manufacturer, had approached him with a business proposition. They proposed that Belinda install only their hardware in companies for which they worked. In return, Belinda would receive a 15 percent commission on all equipment sold. Belinda told Gene that she would think about the proposal and get back to him.

Billie Matthews, the first salesperson hired by Belinda, was waiting to see her when Gene left. MLB Manufacturing, one of Belinda's first clients, was having a problem with some of the software that her company had created for them. The software seemed to have a minor problem that until now had gone undetected. At issue was how much money to charge to correct the problem, since the warranty for the work had expired three months ago.

Belinda thought to herself, "It's definitely Monday; there are already two problems to deal with, plus the word processing software issue." When she started the business, Belinda had purchased a word processing software package with a license for ten users. With the new employees she now had eleven people who would need to use the software. Should she buy additional software or just install a copy of what she had on the extra machine? After all, who would ever know? And she had purchased it, hadn't she?

1. Should Belinda accept the offer from the computer hardware manufacturer? Why or why not? What are the ethical implications of the decision?
2. What would you suggest Belinda do about MLB and their software problem? Are there any ethical issues concerned? If so, what are they?
3. What would you do about the word processing software and why?

PROJECT CHALLENGE

As you continue the planning process for your new business, you will need to give careful thought to the ethics involved. By using the information in this chapter and other sources, develop a basic code of ethics for your new company. The following areas should be included:

1. Ethical treatment of consumers, competition, and employees.
2. Responsibility for the environment.
3. Ethical use of computer technology.

SALVAGING THE SALVAGE COMPANY

Unit 5 Case

Elton Perez lives and works in the large metropolitan area of Los Angeles. He has been running his own business—a salvage company—for the past three years.

Elton operates his business in a simple and straightforward manner. When a natural disaster occurs somewhere in the United States, Elton goes to the disaster site and buys damaged merchandise to sell in Los Angeles. For example, as soon as Elton could get into San Francisco after the earthquake of 1989, he contacted the companies that insured the businesses that had damaged goods. He offered to purchase the goods, paying ten cents on the dollar. He then arranged to have his company trucks pick up his purchases. When the merchandise arrived, he placed a large advertisement in the local newspapers to offer it for sale. His advertisement mentioned the disaster involved and promised "huge savings."

Elton recently visited the site of a devastating tornado in Kansas. He verbally contracted with an insurance company to purchase damaged sporting goods for $10,000, again paying 10 cents on the dollar. He was sure he could resell the merchandise very quickly, and at a considerable profit. He was so sure that he wrote a $10,000 check and gave it to the insurance company's representative before leaving Kansas. The check had been cashed by the time he returned home. During Elton's absence, his assistant placed an unauthorized advertisement in the local newspapers in eager anticipation of the arrival of the sporting goods. The advertisement promised name-brand sporting goods at the lowest prices in town.

Also during Elton's absence, his real estate agent had found a building for Elton's business. Business was going so well that Elton needed more space to house his merchandise. His current facility was leased; Elton wanted to buy his next facility. When Elton visited the building, he knew it was perfect. He signed a contract for its purchase immediately.

Elton contacted his landlord to notify him that he would be moving his business. The landlord reminded Elton that his lease bound him to the current building for another two years. If Elton did not continue to make the lease payments, the landlord would sue for breach of contract.

◆

Elton looked at his copy of the lease and found that it specified a term of five years and a monthly rent of $4,000. There was no provision for early cancellation.

◆

A few days after Elton returned to Los Angeles, the insurance company representative from Kansas called to say that the company had decided not to sell the merchandise. The sporting goods were not damaged badly enough to accept 10 cents on the dollar for them. There was a $10,000 check already on the way to Elton in Los Angeles.

◆

Elton did not think that life was treating him very well. He decided to sleep on his problems. If he didn't come up with any solutions overnight, he would call his attorney in the morning.

Case Questions

What advice would you give Elton if you were his attorney? Consider the questions that follow.

1. The advertisement Elton's assistant placed in the newspapers promised name-brand sporting goods at the lowest prices in town. Was this advertisement legal? Would Elton be at risk in selling the merchandise?
2. Is the verbal contract between Elton and the insurance company legally enforceable? Why or why not?
3. Will Elton have to continue making lease payments on his current facility after he moves his business? Why or why not?

UNIT 6

CAREERS IN ENTREPRENEURSHIP

24 International Entrepreneurship

25 Environmental Entrepreneurship

24
International Entrepreneurship

After mastering the information contained in this chapter, you should be able to:

24-1 Explain the role of the International Trade Administration in developing international trade.

24-2 Understand the various options available in the overseas marketing of goods.

24-3 Understand the various methods of overseas financing.

24-4 Explain economic integration, trade pacts, and opportunities in international trade.

24-5 Explain how to get started as an international entrepreneur.

export, goods and services made in one country and sold to others

import, goods and services that are bought from other countries

The most rapidly changing area of entrepreneurship today is the international market. As a result of the tremendous improvements in telecommunications and computer technology over the past twenty years, the world truly has become a global marketplace. Until recently, only large businesses had the resources necessary to enter the global marketplace. With the affordability of present-day computers, fax machines, and overseas telephone service, small businesses are finding that they too can take advantage of international opportunities and now businesses of all sizes can compete. The international marketplace is ever-changing, and entrepreneurs thrive on the opportunities created by change. For an entrepreneur who is willing to take the time to learn the intricacies of trading goods and services with consumers or businesses in other countries, exciting and rewarding opportunities lie ahead.

THE INTERNATIONAL MARKET

Any goods or services made in one country and sold to other countries are **exports.**

Imports are goods or services that are bought from sources in other countries. When a country imports more goods than it exports, a **trade deficit** results.

When total exports are greater than total imports, the difference is called a **trade surplus.** The United States has endured a trade deficit with other countries for over two decades. The trade deficit hurts our economy because it results in fewer opportunities for our workers. The United States would much prefer that our workers create products for overseas shipment, rather than have other countries' workers manufacture the goods that we commonly use in our everyday lives. The trade deficit also makes the United States dependent on other countries for goods and services, some of which are critical to our national well-being, such as oil. Because of this ongoing trade deficit and the problems associated with it, the U.S. government has implemented various incentives and assistance resources for businesses engaging in international trade, particularly those that export goods and services. One such assistance resource is the International Trade Administration of the U.S. Department of Commerce.

trade deficit, total imports are greater than total exports

trade surplus, total exports are greater than total imports

THE INTERNATIONAL TRADE ADMINISTRATION

The **International Trade Administration (ITA)** acts as an information source for entrepreneurs interested in exploring international trade possibilities. This group has 47 district offices and 21 branch offices throughout the United States. These offices receive information from the U.S. Foreign Service, which has offices located in 125 foreign countries. The areas of information available through the ITA include the following:

International Trade Administration (ITA), information source for international trade possibilities

Illus. 24-1   The United States has had a trade deficit with other countries for over two decades.

Photo by Jeff Greenberg

- Growing and changing foreign markets
- Policies and product standards of various countries
- Tariff and nontariff barriers. International trade is carried out by both businesses and governments as long as no one puts up trade barriers. A **tariff** is a tax imposed on imported goods as a barrier to trade. Protective tariffs make imports less attractive to buyers than domestic products. For example, to protect its automobile industry, the United States has in the past increased tariffs and placed restrictions on the number of Japanese automobiles permitted to enter our country. Limits on the quantity of certain goods imported is a **nontariff barrier.** The goal of setting **import quotas** is to limit the number of units that may be imported into a country.
- Domestic and foreign competition
- Products and services that foreign markets are buying, and what they seek that is in short supply
- Advertising media available in various foreign markets
- Distribution possibilities in foreign countries, including lists of possible wholesalers and retailers for particular industries and how to contact them
- Sales trends and pricing information for specific products
- Assistance in providing credit checks and ratings on overseas companies, as well as opinions about their reliability and dependability
- Assistance in contacting foreign customers through seminars and trade shows. The ITA also helps to arrange company visits for foreign visitors interested in exploring trade possibilities in the United States.

The U.S. Department of Commerce also produces a number of publications designed to assist entrepreneurs in the investigation of foreign market distribution. These publications contain information about economic trends in foreign markets, foreign government procurement procedures, statistical data on various commodities traded throughout the world, and current trade regulations.[1] An example of the information available is shown in Figure 24-1.

tariff, a fee imposed on imported goods to protect the country's domestic industries from being undersold

nontariff barrier, limit on the quantity of certain goods imported

import quota, a published specific number of units of a particular product allowed to enter the importing country

---

[1] Specific information can be obtained by writing to: International Trade Administration, U.S. Department of Commerce, 14th & Constitution, Room 3850, Washington, D.C. 20230.

Figure 24-1 Information From U.S. Department of Commerce Publications

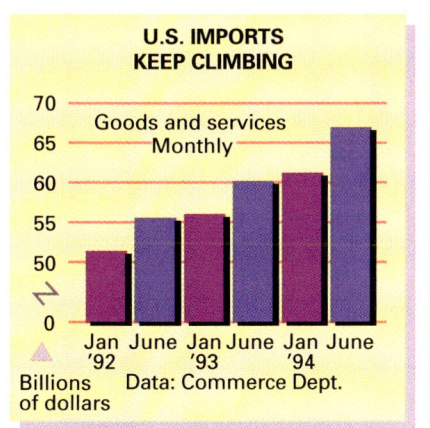

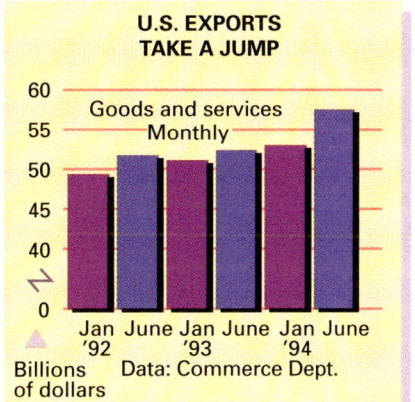

OVERSEAS MARKETING

There are two ways to export: **directly** and **indirectly.** A company that exports directly must find a foreign buyer and make all the arrangements necessary to ship its products overseas. A manufacturer's representative stationed in the foreign country or a foreign distributor can be used for direct marketing. The representative is either a commissioned agent or an employee of the company and usually has full authority to make commitments on the company's behalf. A foreign distributor purchases the product directly from the company for resale overseas. The profit potential of selling directly to an overseas market is greater than what can be obtained using an indirect marketing system; so too are the risks and the investment required.

Indirect exporting is accomplished through an export intermediary. Entrepreneurs who are thinking about using an export intermediary should consider several types and the functions of each. The various types of intermediaries are explained in the following paragraphs.

direct export, company finds foreign buyer and makes all necessary arrangements to ship product

indirect export, company uses an export intermediary to arrange transactions

Commissioned Agents

Commissioned agents act as brokers for a product. They are usually foreign nationals who find buyers within their country for specific products. As agents, they rarely accept the title to goods (ownership); however, they often perform all the steps necessary

commissioned agents, product brokers who usually find buyers within their country to arrange shipping and export documentation. They are paid a commission for their efforts.

Export Management Companies

export management companies, act as marketing agents for domestic companies in international markets

Export management companies (EMCs) represent products from numerous companies. They act as marketing agents for domestic companies in international markets. EMC's find buyers and perform many functions for the companies they represent. Some of the services that EMCs commonly provide are the following.

1. Attend trade shows and promote products in foreign countries.
2. Perform market research in order to discover the best markets for specific products.
3. Locate distributors and determine advantageous channels of distribution.
4. Arrange financing.
5. Make export shipping arrangements, including invoice preparation, insurance arrangements, and filing the necessary documentation.
6. Advise about legal and cultural aspects of the foreign country in which marketing activities are being performed.

Illus. 24-2 Export management companies (EMCs) can make export shipping arrangements, including filing the necessary documentation.

© *Don Smetzer/Tony Stone Images, Inc.*

While EMCs usually operate on a commission basis, some do accept the title to goods and resell the products themselves.

Export Trading Companies (ETC)

Trading companies, both domestic and foreign, are a risk-free way for entrepreneurs to do business overseas. They perform the same functions as EMCs; however, they routinely accept the title to goods. The ETC would then resell the goods internationally, adding a markup for itself. They operate on a transaction-driven basis, in which they first procure orders and then find companies to supply the orders.

export trading companies, perform the same function as export management companies, usually accepting title to goods

Piggyback Exporting

Another indirect marketing option for the entrepreneur is to allow another company that is already in the export distribution system to sell the entrepreneur's products in addition to its own. This option is a quick and easy way of entering a foreign market, although it can be more expensive as there will be additonal commissions to be paid. **Piggyback exporting** is often the preferred way of getting started in overseas marketing.

piggyback exporting, another company in the export distribution system sells the entrepreneur's products in addition to their own

Strategic Alliances

Many entrepreneurs decide to avoid making marketing decisions and instead opt to create a strategic alliance with a foreign partner. This type of arrangement is often accomplished through either a licensing agreement or the creation of a joint venture.

Licensing is a contractual arrangement in which a firm (licensee) buys or rents the right to use the patent, trademark, production process, brand name, product, or company name of another firm (licensor). The licensee agrees to pay the licensor either royalties on sales or a fixed fee. Licensing can reduce a firm's risk while increasing its revenue. Financial risk is less because the domestic company does not have to make an investment abroad. However, since countries differ in regard to patent, trademark, and copyright protection, there is a risk to the licensing company of losing control of this intellectual property. An attorney specializing in licensing agreements should always be consulted when creating such an agreement.

licensing agreement, a contractual arrangement in which a firm buys or rents the right to use the patent, trademark, production process, brand name, product, or company name of another firm

Joint ventures allow two or more firms (including governments) to share ownership of a business. A foreign manufacturing joint venture creates a partnership between a company and a foreign

joint venture, two or more firms (including governments) share ownership of a business

manufacturer. Joint management is incorporated into the production and marketing of the product in the foreign country. These ventures normally require substantial investment in both equipment and management. Many joint ventures come about when no single firm will assume the financial risk for an enterprise. Entrepreneurs who engage in joint ventures gain immediate inside knowledge of a country's culture, legal environment, and marketing and distribution systems. Developing countries often insist on joint ventures in order to have access to technology or proven manufacturing procedures.

Entrepreneurs who want to enter into a licensing agreement or joint ventures should give careful consideration to potential partners. The selection of the right partner is essential to success. Some government-sponsored agencies can assist in the selection process.

OVERSEAS FINANCING SOURCES

Problems associated with receiving payment and arranging financing in international trade are considerably eased by government and private sector assistance. Resources available to assist entrepreneurs doing business overseas include the following.

Eximbank

One valuable financial resource for international entrepreneurs is the **Export-Import Bank (Eximbank)** of the United States. Eximbank is a government agency responsible for facilitating the export of goods and services from the United States. Its primary role is to provide guaranteed loans to banks that, in turn, extend loans to U.S. exporters. Entrepreneurs can receive short-term loans to complete a specific export order. Eximbank loans allow small businesses to obtain additional inventory, carry accounts receivable, and meet essential operating expenses. This organization, however, is not a source of start-up funds for new businesses. Government financing assistance for exporters is also available through the Small Business Administration (SBA) and Small Business Investment Companies (SBICs). Exporters can sometimes obtain help from foreign government assistance resources, depending on a country's need for a specific product.

Eximbank, a government agency responsible for facilitating the export of goods and services from the United States

Commercial Banks

Large commercial banks have international departments that handle financing for import and export businesses. Commercial banks can make pre-export loans and help process letters of credit (see page 452) and other methods of payment. Commercial banks often handle government-guaranteed loans for exporters.

Factors

Another form of short term financing using accounts receivable is **factoring.** A firm's accounts receivable are sold outright to a factor. Factors (usually a commercial bank or other financial institution) purchase receivables at a discount or at a percentage below their actual value. Factoring houses provide the exporter with immediate cash for goods and eliminate the burden of handling foreign accounts receivable. Factors allow a firm to turn its accounts receivable from exports into cash without the worries of collecting. Although the easiest method to receive payment, it is also the most expensive.

factor, a form of short term financing using accounts receivables

Illus. 24-3   Commercial banks often handle government-guaranteed loans for exporters.

METHODS OF PAYMENT

The international entrepreneur must decide on the most efficient and profitable method to receive payment from foreign customers. An inefficient method will result in long delays in receiving cash or, in some instances, in not receiving payment at all. Options for collecting payment include the following.

1. **Payment in advance.** The most secure method is to receive payment before shipment; however, a request for payment in advance of shipment is often an obstacle to making a sale in a competitive situation.
2. **Letter of credit.** Letters of credit are internationally recognized instruments of payment. A letter of credit is issued by a bank on behalf of the purchaser (see Figure 24-2 for an example). Essentially, a **letter of credit** is a guarantee from the purchaser's bank that payment will be made on behalf of its client. The seller (or exporter) is assured that payment will be made by a bank, rather than the purchaser. Payment is guaranteed as long as the bank is secure. Once all conditions of delivery have been satisfied, the purchaser's (importer's) bank transfers the funds to the seller's (exporter's) bank.
3. **Draft.** A **draft** is a collection notice requiring the buyer (importer) to pay the face amount either on sight (sight draft) or on a specified date in the future (time draft). The title to goods does not change hands until the draft is paid or accepted.
4. **Open account.** An **open account** functions in the same way as many domestic accounts. With an open account (accounts receivable), payment is not due until a specified time after the goods have been received by the buyer. An example of an invoice is provided in Figure 24-3 on page 254. The firm's collection policy will determine what steps to follow if the customer's payment falls behind schedule.

ECONOMIC INTEGRATION AND TRADE AGREEMENTS

Nations that frequently trade together may decide to formalize their relationship. The governments involved meet and work out an agreement for a common economic policy. The result is **economic integration.**

---

letter of credit, a guarantee from the purchaser's bank that payment will be made on behalf of the client

draft, notice requiring the buyer to pay the face amount either on sight or on a specified date

open account, payment is not due until a specified time after the goods have been received

economic integration, nations that trade together work out an agreement for a common economic policy

Figure 24-2 Sample Confirmed Irrevocable Letter of Credit

INTERNATIONAL BANKING GROUP
C&S/Sovran Corporation
P.O. BOX 4899, ATLANTA, GEORGIA 30302-4899
CABLE ADDRESS:CITSOUTH
TELEX NO. 3737650
SWIFT NO. CSBKUS 33

OUR ADVICE NUMBER: EA00000091
ADVICE DATE: 08MAR91
ISSUE BANK REF: 3312/HBI/22341
EXPIRY DATE: 23JUN91

****AMOUNT****
USD****25,000.00

BENEFICIARY:
THE WALTON BUILDING SUPPLIES CO.
2356 SOUTH BELK STREET
ATLANTA, GEORGIA 30345

APPLICANT:
BBH HONG KONG
34 INDUSTRIAL DRIVE
CENTRAL, HONG KONG

WE HAVE BEEN REQUESTED TO ADVISE TO YOU THE FOLLOWING LETTER OF CREDIT AS ISSUED BY:
FIRST HONG KONG BANK
1 CENTRAL TOWER
HONG KONG

PLEASE BE GUIDED BY ITS TERMS AND CONDITIONS AND BY THE FOLLOWING: CREDIT IS AVAILABLE BY NEGOTIATION OF YOUR DRAFT(S) IN DUPLICATE AT SIGHT FOR 100 PERCENT OF INVOICE VALUE DRAWN ON US ACCOMPANIED BY THE FOLLOWING DOCUMENTS.

1. SIGNED COMMERCIAL INVOICE IN 1 ORIGINAL AND 3 COPIES.

2. FULL SET 3/3 OCEAN BILLS OF LADING CONSIGNED TO THE ORDER OF FIRST HONG KONG BANK, HONG KONG NOTIFY APPLICANT AND MARKED FREIGHT COLLECT.

3. PACKING LIST IN 2 COPIES.

EVIDENCING SHIPMENT OF: 5000 PINE LOGS—WHOLE—8 TO 12 FEET
                        FOB SAVANNAH, GEORGIA

SHIPMENT FROM: SAVANNAH, GEORGIA   TO: HONG KONG
LATEST SHIPPING DATE: 02JUN91

PARTIAL SHIPMENTS NOT ALLOWED   TRANSHIPMENT NOT ALLOWED

ALL BANKING CHARGES OUTSIDE HONG KONG ARE FOR BENEFICIARY'S ACCOUNT. DOCUMENTS MUST BE PRESENTED WITHIN 21 DAYS FROM B/L DATE.

AT THE REQUEST OF OUR CORRESPONDENT, WE CONFIRM THIS CREDIT AND ALSO ENGAGE WITH YOU THAT ALL DRAFTS DRAWN UNDER AND IN COMPLIANCE WITH THE TERMS OF THIS CREDIT WILL BE DULY HONORED BY US.

PLEASE EXAMINE THIS INSTRUMENT CAREFULLY. IF YOU ARE UNABLE TO COMPLY WITH THE TERMS AND CONDITIONS, PLEASE COMMUNICATE WITH YOUR BUYER TO ARRANGE FOR AN AMENDMENT.

Figure 24-3 *Sample Pro Forma Invoice*

Tech International
1000 J Street, N.W.
Washington, DC 20005

Telephone 202-555-1212   Fax 202-555-1111

PRO FORMA INVOICE

Date: Jan. 12, 19—

To: Gomez Y. Cartagena
Aptdo. Postal 77
Bogota, Colombia

Your Reference: Ltr., Jan. 6, 19—
Our Reference: Col. 91-14

We hereby quote as follows:

Terms of Payment: Letter of Credit
Terms of Sale: CIF Buenaventura

Quantity	Model	Description	Unit	Extension
3	2-50	Separators in accordance with attached specifications	$14,750.00	$44,250.00
3	14-40	First stage Filter Assemblies per attached specifications	$1,200.00	$3,600.00
3	custom	Drive Units—30 hp each (for operation on 3-phase 440 v., 50 cy. current) complete with remote controls	$4,235.00	$12,705.00

TOTAL FOB Washington, D.C. domestic packed $60,555.00
Export processing, packaging, prepaid inland freight
to Dulles International Airport & forwarder's
handling charges FOB Dulles Airport, Virginia. $63,670.00
Estimated air freight and insurance .... $ 2,960.00
Est. CIF Buenaventura, Colombia $66,630.00

Estimated gross weight 9,630 lbs.   Estimated cube 520 cu. ft.
Export packed 4,212 kg.   Export packed 15.6 cu. meters

PLEASE NOTE

1. All prices quoted herein are U.S. dollars.
2. Prices quoted herein for merchandise only are valid for 60 days from this date.
3. Any changes in shipping costs or insurance rates are for account of the buyer.
4. We estimate ex-factory shipment approximately 60 days from receipt here of purchase order and letter of credit.

NAFTA

The passage of **NAFTA** (North American Free Trade Agreement) in November of 1993 was hotly debated. Its approval eliminates tariffs and eases trade barriers between the United States, Canada, and Mexico. By eliminating tariffs between our neighbors to the north and south, many small businesses will find that doing business with a customer in Ontario, Canada or Mexico City, Mexico is as easy as completing a transaction in Indianapolis. A supplier wishing to sell to a producer in Mexico or Canada can now do so with a minimum of bureaucracy, which has not been the case in the past. Manufacturers can now ship freely across national borders. The creation of a free trade market is expected to stimulate business expansion across borders, increase business revenues and create job growth for all three countries. **NAFTA** is considered by many to be a boon to smaller businesses through making entry into these markets easier. Small businesses should be able to compete on a level field with large businesses.

NAFTA, agreement that eliminated tariffs and trade barriers between the U.S., Canada, and Mexico

Illus. 24-4 The North American Free Trade Agreement (NAFTA) eliminates tariffs and eases trade barriers between the United States, Canada, and Mexico.

© Chris Thomaidis/Tony Stone Images, Inc.

GATT

GATT, the largest free trade agreement ever passed

After eight years of negotiation and debate, the U.S. Congress ratified GATT on December 1, 1994. The **General Agreement on Tariffs and Trade** is the largest free trade agreement ever passed. The first GATT was passed in 1947 and included 23 nations. This expanded version involves over 90 member countries. The agreement cuts tariffs by 40 percent, expands protection for intellectual properties (patents, copyrights, tradenames, etc.) and establishes rules for international investment and conducting trade among service businesses.

The organization established by GATT is headquartered in Geneva, Switzerland, and is supported by contributions from the member nations. Many of the participating countries have previously used restrictive tariffs to protect their economies against a high volume of imports. Although this new version will not be fully implemented for ten years, GATT continues to pave the way for a new world order of free trade. GATT should also prove to be of particular benefit to small businesses wishing to compete in the international market.

The U.S.-Canada Free Trade Agreement

U.S.-Canada Free Trade Agreement, the first of the many free trade agreements of the current era

Implementation of the **U.S.-Canada Free Trade Agreement** began on January 1, 1989 as tarrifs, or duties, were totally removed from one-third of the products and services traded between the countries and the duties were reduced on the other two-thirds. On Jan. 1, 1994 the second group was totally tariff-free and on January 1, 1999 trade between the United States and Canada will be completely barrier-free. As these nations are each other's biggest customer, the agreement is expected to benefit both economies in the long-run.

Economic Communities (European Union or EU— the Common Market)

economic community, a group of nations agree to cooperate in terms of tariffs, import quotas, and other trade concerns

Economic communities, also known as **common markets,** form when a group of nations agree formally to cooperate in terms of tariffs, import quotas and other trade concerns.

The European Union (EU) is an alliance of twelve European countries whose purpose is to integrate its member nations' economies. In 1992 the "Internal Market," known as Europe 92, was formed. Its long-term plan is to remove all barriers, including those on investment and immigration along with products and services, to create one European economic community.

OPPORTUNITIES IN INTERNATIONAL TRADE

As a result of the tremendous political changes that began in eastern Europe in the late 1980s, new markets have continued to emerge. The unification of Germany and the easing of trade barriers and restrictions in the countries that were once the Soviet Union have resulted in booming sales, particularly in computers and telecommunications equipment, energy related equipment, chemicals, and medical equipment. Trade experts forecast continued growth of sales opportunities to these markets.

Other forecasts include that sales to western European countries, which already comprise the biggest market overseas for American-made products, are expected to keep growing, as restrictions decrease on the movement of goods and services due to the beginning of the "Internal Market" in 1992. Also opportunities and markets have developed quickly in the Middle East since the 1991 Gulf War with Iraq. Construction materials continue to be in demand as a result of war damage. At the same time Japanese businesses will continue to be highly competitive with American exporters, although the Japanese recession of 1994 has opened some doors of opportunity for imports to Japan. The implementation of trade agreements, including the GATT, NAFTA and the U.S.-Canada Free Trade Agreement, open up foreign markets to U.S. entrepreneurs and also provide domestic competition as foreign firms export their products to the United States.

Many firms earn large profits without ever operating abroad. However, more and more U.S. firms recognize how profitable foreign markets can be. Generally the level of profit from these markets depends on the level of investment. However, if an overseas operation falls apart, a firm can suffer a big loss. The firm is also vulnerable to political actions by foreign governments, such as expropriation (making private assets property of the government). The decision to enter the international market is one that an entrepreneur should make only after a thorough analysis of all factors.

GETTING STARTED

Entrepreneurs who are interested in exporting goods to foreign markets or importing goods from foreign suppliers should first consider the following steps. These steps apply both to entrepreneurs who already own a business and to those who are interested in acquiring one.

1. Research the export or import potential of your company. Analyze the financial capabilities of the business, industry trends, and the effect the decision to export or import will have on the domestic operations of the business.
2. Get professional advice. Contact the U.S. Department of Commerce, state development agencies, and any other resources that are available. Ask questions and try to obtain factual answers and sound advice from professional business people with overseas experience.
3. Conduct thorough market research to find the one or two best markets for the company's products. Use expert resources for advice and assistance.
4. Develop an export or import strategy that is workable for the particular business. Set objectives, plan marketing activities, and allocate financial resources. Visit trade fairs and make contacts with foreign representatives and agents.
5. Decide how to sell the product or service. Decide whether you will sell directly or indirectly to your markets.
6. Arrange financing through Eximbank or commercial international banks.
7. Learn how payments are to be made by foreign buyers or to foreign sellers. The U.S. Small Business Association publication, *Market Overseas with U.S. Government Help,* is a good resource for learning about how payments can be made.

For most entrepreneurs, importing is easier than exporting, since they are usually more familiar with the domestic market than with foreign markets. Nevertheless, before an entrepreneur decides to import a product for sale in the domestic market or export a product for sale in the foreign market, he or she should consult with an experienced international trade authority and write a business plan with heavy emphasis on market research and analysis of the country under consideration.

THE FASHION ATTIC

The Fashion Attic opened with great success. Laura's efforts to plan her business were paying off. Six months after the opening, sales were running 25 percent above projections, and a profitable level of operation had already been achieved. Laura knew that to continue on an upward path she must always be on the lookout for new opportunities.

One such opportunity arose in connection with a line of blouses that Laura had been buying from a friend who operated a limited design-and-production facility from her basement. The unique design appealed to Laura's customers, who were buying them at a rapid turnover rate.

One day a sales representative and buyer for a large fashion house in New York City noticed the unique tropical look of the blouses. The buyer asked Laura from whom had she purchased them. When Laura explained that she bought them from a friend, she was astounded at the buyer's response.

"My company markets merchandise to Florida, Southern California, and Mexico," the buyer said. "I'm sure that the tropical look of these blouses would be very popular in those areas. Do you think your friend would be interested in having us act as a commissioned agent for her product? We would handle all the specifics, including all the documentation needed to ship to Mexico, if she could produce enough blouses to lower the price so that we would make a fair commission."

Laura knew that her friend could not increase production without additional help and money. She wondered whether she should consider investing the needed money and labor to help her friend.

"International marketing?" she thought. "I guess anything is possible for an entrepreneur. It might be worthwhile to write a business plan to investigate the possibility." Laura called her friend to set up a meeting for the next day.

SUMMARY

Technological developments in the computer and telecommunications industries have opened the door for small businesses to engage in international trade. There are numerous government and private sector assistance resources to help entrepreneurs get started, particularly in exporting. The International Trade Administration has offices throughout the United States and in various other parts of the world to assist with overseas marketing, financing, and networking. The international entrepreneur must make important decisions regarding whether to market directly or indirectly through foreign intermediaries. He or she can choose to enter into a strategic alliance with a foreign company through the formation of a joint venture or a licensing agreement. Entrepreneurs must also become familiar with financing resources and determine the best method of collecting revenues. The constantly changing international marketplace carries great risk, but it also represents opportunities for realizing great profits. The opportunities have been enhanced with the easing of many former trading barriers through such agreements as NAFTA and the GATT.

VOCABULARY BUILDER

On a separate sheet of paper, write a description of each word or phrase based on your reading of the chapter.

1. Trade deficit
2. Trade surplus
3. International Trade Administration
4. Tariff
5. Nontariff barrier
6. Indirect overseas marketing
7. Direct overseas marketing
8. Licensing agreement
9. Joint venture
10. Eximbank
11. Letter of credit
12. Draft
13. Open account
14. Economic integration
15. NAFTA
16. GATT

REVIEW QUESTIONS

1. Why is a trade deficit harmful to our economy?
2. What federal agency offers assistance to United States exporters?
3. What is the greatest advantage to using an indirect overseas marketing system?
4. What are the functions of export management and trading companies?
5. What is piggyback exporting?
6. What is the difference between a licensing agreement and a joint venture?
7. How does the Export-Import Bank of the United States assist international entrepreneurs?
8. How do factors work with international entrepreneurs?
9. Why is a letter of credit the preferred method of receiving payment from foreign buyers?
10. What is the biggest overseas market for American products?

DISCUSSION QUESTIONS

1. Give possible reasons for choosing one marketing method over the others in order to export a product to Syria? to England? to Canada?
2. Discuss the advantages and disadvantages of direct versus indirect overseas marketing and describe methods of each.
3. Give an example of a United States company that is licensing its product to overseas investors.
4. What are the benefits of government involvement in trade among countries? What might be some drawbacks?
5. If you were a congressional representative, would you have voted in favor of NAFTA? How would you explain your vote to your constituency?

CRITICAL THINKING

The United States has experienced a trade deficit in its balance of trade for many years. How do you think the deficit could be reduced or eliminated? What sacrifices would have to be made to accomplish your objective? What benefits would result?

SHORT CASE: DON'T BE AFRAID TO ASK

Greg Harris was having lunch with an American friend, Ross Evans, at an outdoor café in Berlin. Ross, a banker, was visiting Germany for the first time to attend an international banking convention. Greg visited Germany annually to buy cuckoo clocks made in Germany's Black Forest for his United States wholesale business. Their lunch conversation was about international trade. Ross asked Greg how he went about making contacts and finding products to import to the United States.

"I am not afraid to ask questions," said Greg. "It seems to me that the only way to find something out quickly is to ask until you find out. People are usually quite helpful. Here's an example. Do you see that truck over there? It is loaded with what seem to be fine-quality canoes. If I thought there was a need in the United States for those well-built canoes, I would go directly to the truck driver and ask him where he was taking that shipment and where it was coming from. If he works for the manufacturer, I bet he can tell me a lot about those canoes including their price. If, after talking to him, I still thought the canoes would sell well in the United States, I would call the manufacturer and arrange to visit with him to see if he would be interested in shipping canoes to the U.S. If we agreed on my commission, I would return home and look for businesses that would like to sell those types of canoes. Once I found buyers for the canoes, I would place the orders with my new-found German canoe manufacturer in exchange for a fee. Making business contacts is not as difficult as many people think. The common objective of making profits helps us overcome language, cultural, and financial obstacles."

Questions

1. What marketing role is Greg playing in the conversation?
2. Do you think that you could approach situations as boldly as Greg does? Discuss how being inquisitive is a requirement for being a successful entrepreneur.

PROJECT CHALLENGE

Create a scenario for the future that allows you to take the business idea you are planning into the international market. How would you research the market, how would you market your product, and how would you finance such an idea?

25
Environmental Entrepreneurship

In recent decades the deterioration of the environment has become a matter of widespread public concern. One source of pollution has been business firms that discharge waste into streams, contaminants into the air, and noise into the areas surrounding their operations. Efforts to preserve and redeem the environment have captured the interests of environmentalists and entrepreneurs.

Although environmentalists will probably never agree with each other on which environmental concerns are the most threatening, the general consensus is that we are not doing nearly enough to combat the environmental degradation of our planet. New technology for dealing with environmental problems must be developed, and more people must become involved in the battle. Many entrepreneurs are attempting to do just that. They are seeking new ways to help the environment and, at the same time, develop promising business opportunities.

Illus. 25-1

The average American family of four generates over 2,500 pounds of solid waste in a year.

After mastering the information contained in this chapter, you should be able to:

25-1 Describe the major environmental issues facing the United States today.

25-2 Explain the impact of environmental legislation on the operation of a business.

25-3 Identify entrepreneurial opportunities related to the environment.

25-4 Explain the need for entrepreneurs to start environmentally friendly businesses.

ENVIRONMENTAL ISSUES

When it comes to polluting the earth, no one is without blame. At one time or another, all of us have contributed to pollution. Even little things like throwing a piece of paper on the ground or not recycling a sodapop can exacerbate environmental problems. Actions such as not properly disposing of the spent oil after changing the motor oil in an automobile can create even more damage. When individual transgressions are combined with automobile emissions, pesticide pollution from agricultural ventures, government and big-business pollution, and waste disposal problems of both large and small communities, the result is a problem of monumental proportions. All five billion-plus inhabitants of Earth share in this crisis. As entrepreneurs, however, we should look at problems and see opportunities.

Solid Waste

solid waste, trash that cannot easily be recycled

Solid waste is trash, or garbage, that normally cannot be recycled in an economical fashion. The average American family of four generates more than 2,500 pounds of solid waste in a year. Estimate the number of families in your community and multiply that number by 2,500 pounds. What does your city currently do with its trash and garbage? Is your community growing? If so, then your solid waste problem is also growing.

Air Pollution

air pollution, the contamination of air by combusting or burning fuels

Air pollution is the contamination of air by combusting or burning fuels. Much of this pollution is caused by power plants, car exhausts, or factory smoke. If you have ever visited a big city or live in one, you already know about air pollution: you can usually smell it and you can often see it as well. The air is so polluted in many major metropolitan areas that the news reports include reports on air quality. Often, there are even warnings for those with respiratory problems to stay inside.

Water Pollution

water pollution, the invasion of chemicals or other harmful substances in water supplies or underground water reserves

Water pollution occurs when chemicals or other hazardous substances are allowed to invade our water supplies or seep into underground water reserves. Significant increases in manufacturing operations and the increased use of chemicals in the production of agricultural products are two major causes of water pollution. Other

Illus. 25-2

Manufacturing operations and agricultural products are two major causes of water pollution.

Courtesy of the USDA

contributing factors are the improper storage of hazardous waste, hazardous waste spills, the failure to dispose properly of the by-products of mining, and inadequate means of sewage disposal. Individual carelessness also adds to water pollution, as do countless other sources. The earth's water supply is threatened both by pollutants and by the squandering of this precious resource which is reducing our available supply of fresh water.

Hazardous Waste

Hazardous waste can be generically defined as any waste product that poses a substantial threat to human health or the environment when it is improperly treated, stored, transported, disposed of, or otherwise managed. All one has to do is turn on the television or pick up the daily newspaper to understand the magnitude of the hazardous waste problem. Hazardous waste spills are becoming so common that almost every fire department in the country now has a hazardous materials control unit, and all department personnel are specially trained in handling such waste.

hazardous waste, any waste product that threatens human health or the environment

ENVIRONMENTAL LEGISLATION

Not only are there innumerable environmental issues facing would-be entrepreneurs today, but there are also numerous laws concerning those issues. Entrepreneurs must be familiar with such laws and comply with them. Adherence to environmental laws will ensure that the business does not become involved in litigation as a result of violations, and it will also ensure that the business is an environmentally friendly one.

The Impact of Legislation on Business

Environmental protection legislation, at the federal, state, and local levels, deal with air pollution, water pollution, solid waste disposal, and toxic substances.

There are several major pieces of national legislation that govern the production of toxic or hazardous waste. Anyone planning an entrepreneurial venture that may be affected by such laws should be familiar with them. Would-be entrepreneurs should also consult an attorney about these laws during the planning phase, or prior to the actual start-up of a business.

- **The Federal Water Pollution Control Act of 1952 and the Air Pollution Control Act of 1955.** These were the first two major statutes to regulate emissions of hazardous substances in the air and water—the most likely channels for human exposure to hazardous waste. Congress significantly strengthened these laws with the passage of the Clean Air Act Amendments of 1970 and the Federal Water Pollution Control Act Amendments of 1972.
- **The Atomic Energy Act of 1954.** This act still regulates the handling and storage of radioactive wastes that are generated primarily at nuclear power reactors and at federal nuclear weapons plants. Hazardous waste sites contaminated with radioactive waste are regulated under the Comprehensive Environmental Response, Compensation, and Liability Act of 1980.
- **The Federal Environmental Pesticide Control Act of 1972.** Amended by the Insecticide, Fungicide, and Rodenticide Act of 1975, this act regulates the manufacture and use of pesticide products to ensure safety according to directions on their labels.

Illus. 25-3 The Atomic Energy Act of 1954 regulates the handling and storage of radioactive wastes.

Courtesy of the American Petroleum Institute

- **The Safe Drinking Water Act of 1974.** This act was aimed at protecting the public from various contaminants in drinking water supplies.
- **The Toxic Substances Control Act of 1976.** This gave the Environmental Protection Agency broader regulatory authority to identify and control chemical products that may threaten human health through their manufacture, commercial distribution, or disposal.
- **The Resource Conservation and Recovery Act of 1976 (RCRA).** The RCRA made provisions for the overall management of hazardous wastes. Appropriate techniques and regulations for handling all hazardous waste, from generation to disposal, were established by this act.
- **The Comprehensive Environmental Response, Compensation, and Liability Act of 1980 (CERCLA).** This act addressed the problem of what to do about hazardous waste contamination from past disposal activities. It established a federal program, commonly known as

Superfund, to finance the cleanup of the nation's most contaminated waste sites. CERCLA set detailed guidelines for cleaning up these sites and established a system of legal liability in which those responsible for the waste would be forced to pay for the cleanup.

- **The Hazardous and Solid Waste Amendments of 1984 (HSWA).** These amendments significantly strengthened RCRA, primarily in response to the Environmental Protection Agency's slow progress in implementing RCRA. They also required the cleanup of contamination from leaking underground storage tanks, which CERCLA did not address.
- **The Superfund Amendments and Reauthorization Act of 1986 (SARA).** SARA strengthened CERCLA and significantly increased its fund from $1.6 billion to $8.5 billion to clean up the nation's most contaminated hazardous waste sites. It provided the Environmental Protection Agency with the means to implement permanent solutions, rather than merely remove and relocate hazardous waste. This legislation also mandated that federal agencies identify, investigate, and clean up all hazardous waste sites at their facilities.
- **The Clean Air Amendments of 1990.** Also known as the Clean Air Act of 1990, these amendments have substantially changed the federal regulation of emissions. They increased the Environmental Protection Agency's mandate to impose much stricter control over a variety of air pollutants and set a goal to reduce acid rain by ten million tons by the year 2000. A goal was also set to cut industrial emissions of 189 toxic substances by 90 percent by the year 2003. The 1990 Clean Air Amendments also created a policy whereby companies can use credit for reduced sulfur dioxide emissions to buy and sell pollution rights as though they were economic commodities. The SO_2 reduction would entitle the company to a permit which they could sell to another company so it could have the credit for one of their factories or the original company could keep the permit and use the earned credit to build a less "clean" plant.

ENTREPRENEURIAL OPPORTUNITIES

The only limit to entrepreneurial opportunities relating to the environment is the imagination of individual entrepreneurs. Just as small-business people have helped to solve many of the past problems of this country, so too shall they help to solve the problem of how to maintain a cleaner and healthier environment. Since most true innovation has come from small entrepreneurs looking for a solution to a problem, these entrepreneurs are likely to provide long-term solutions to many of the problems that plague our environment. Because our economy is market driven, profit will provide the incentive necessary to clean up the environment, just as profit was a major contributor to the creation of the problem.

Recycling of Solid Waste

Probably the easiest environmentally conscious business to start is one involving some form of recycling. **Recycling** is the process of transforming used and obsolete goods into useable and saleable goods. The goal of recycling is to reduce the volume of trash we produce by, first, reducing the amount we use and, second, reusing whatever we can. Small businesses are leading the way in this high-growth industry; they are finding profitable ways to collect paper, glass, aluminum cans, automobiles, building materials, tires, motor oil, plastics, and many other products and get them to the proper locations for recycling.

recycling, the transformation of used and obsolete goods into useable and saleable goods

Paper Recycling. The substance taking up the most space in our overloaded landfills is paper, which accounts for more than 40 percent of landfill waste. Approximately 71 million tons of paper are used in the United States each year. Of that amount, it is estimated that less than one-third is currently being recycled. This presents a potentially profitable opportunity for entrepreneurs who can develop cost-effective methods for the collection and reprocessing of the other two-thirds of used paper.

Glass Recycling. There is a particular need for more glass recycling programs. Glass is an undesirable addition to landfills because it does not deteriorate as do many other waste products. Glass essentially remains inert. If you unearth the contents of an old landfill twenty years after its burial, paper will have deteriorated, while glass will be in the same form as it was the day it was buried. The American public throws away over ten million tons of glass a year, and only about 13 percent of this is recycled. Given this low level of recycling, there are many opportunities for entrepreneurs who are interested in developing new programs to recycle glass.

Illus. 25-4 This paper recycling plant helps eliminate the disposal of paper in landfills.

Aluminum Can Recycling. Aluminum cans are probably the most recycled products. Many of us have been recycling aluminum cans for years. However, the market for recycling aluminum cans is still not saturated. While the estimated usage of aluminum cans is four and one–half million tons a year, less than half that amount is being recycled. There are still plenty of opportunities for entrepreneurs with new ideas for collecting and reprocessing aluminum cans.

Automobile Recycling. Most of us never considered starting our own junk yard, even though we have been familiar with this type of recycling for much of our lives. Yet there are profitable entrepreneurial opportunities in this area of recycling. Each year in the United States, approximately seven million cars are recycled. This estimate does not even include the many buses and trucks that also end up in junk yards. The Automotive Dismantlers and Recyclers Association reports that over 15 million tons of cast iron and steel are recycled each year. When the many other salvageable components of automobiles are also considered, it becomes clear that automobile recycling can be a highly profitable business.

Building Materials Recycling. How many buildings have you seen being demolished during the past year? Did you ever ask yourself what happens to all the debris? Given the high cost of constructing new buildings, it would seem that salvaged material would be of value. The materials do have value, but there is a dilemma as to how to salvage the material in a cost-effective manner so that it can be recycled. Building materials recycling is an area greatly in need of an innovative approach. There are tremendous opportunities for the entrepreneurs who can develop efficient ways to recycle the materials.

Tire Recycling. Over 250 million tires are discarded each year in this country. Adding this 250 million to the approximately two billion that are already in existence creates a staggering total. With the current recycling rate hovering around 18% percent, the problem of what to do with used tires is becoming a major issue in many local communities. To reduce the growing mounds of discarded tires, entrepreneurs must find new uses for the tires or cost-effective ways to reprocess the rubber, steel, and fabric they contain.

Motor Oil Recycling. Although it is known that the quantity of motor oil used every year in this country is enormous, exact figures are not available. It is estimated, however, that somewhere in the neighborhood of one and one–half billion gallons of motor oil per year are required to keep America's cars and trucks on the road. Currently, only about 800 million gallons are recycled each year. This means that only a little over half of the oil used is actually recovered and recycled. Clearly, there are opportunities for enterprising entrepreneurs to find ways of recycling the other 700 million gallons.

Plastic Recycling. The business potential of recycling plastic is probably higher than any other areas because an efficient, cost–effective method of recycling plastic has not yet been developed. The estimated use of plastic in this country is well in excess of 25,000,000 tons per year. With less than 1 percent of that tonnage currently being recycled, the potential profit is enormous for the entrepreneur with the right solution to this growing problem.

Starting a Recycling Business

Entrepreneurs who are thinking about starting a recycling business should begin by checking with people in their neighborhood to find out what method is currently being used to discard recyclable trash. If there is no program—or an inadequate one—in place, the entrepreneur should contact local households and offer to pick up their recyclables on a regular basis. The residents should save their recyclable items—paper, glass, aluminum, and plastics—in separate containers. Businesses located nearby, such as laundromats, travel agencies, restaurants, insurance companies, and gas stations, should also be contacted. Businesses that generate a lot of garbage in the form of sodapop cans, excess paper, or glass bottles often are willing to pay a nominal fee for a pick–up service.

After a pick-up method has been determined, all recyclables should be returned to a central point, possibly a garage. When a sufficient amount of recyclables has been accumulated, the entrepreneur should contact a recycling cartage service to arrange a pick–up or drop–off plan. Recycling cartage companies pay by the pound for items that have been collected. Once the recycling plan is complete, the entrepreneur should check with municipal and county agencies to see if any financial assistance is available. Whether the success of the recycling business is modest or great, the entrepreneur will be earning money and, at the same time, helping to save our environment.

There are other recycling-related opportunities in addition to the collection of discarded materials. Many entrepreneurs convert the waste into marketable products. For example, some businesses use paper shredders to convert trash paper into saleable confetti. The same shredded paper can also be used as packaging material for shipping purposes. Other businesses recycle used furniture by refinishing it into like–new condition. Many printing establishments use recycled paper. Other enterprises that are related to recycling include hazardous waste removal companies, and retail stores and franchises selling recyclable paper products or furniture made of recycled materials.

Before entering the recycling market, the entrepreneur should research the subject through periodicals and government publications. Copies of *Inc.* and *Entrepreneur* magazines are available at public libraries. The Environmental Protection Agency is also a good source of information. Environmental groups such as the Sierra Club and the Nature Conservancy support environmental efforts and provide information about many environmental issues. Many of these groups have local chapters.

Illus. 25-5 Less than half of the overall usage of aluminum cans is being recycled, creating potential opportunities for entepreneurs.

THE NEED FOR ENVIRONMENTALLY FRIENDLY BUSINESSES

How can future entrepreneurs treat the environment as a trusted and valued friend? First of all, entrepreneurs can choose ventures with an environmental theme. They can start recycling businesses or businesses that provide services for waste disposal and reduction, environmental testing and analysis, regulatory compliance, and many other areas. Secondly, entrepreneurs whose new businesses are not directly related to the environment can make sure that their businesses have a minimum negative impact on their natural surroundings. As the business planning process is completed, entrepreneurs should be sure to consider the environmental impact of their new business ventures. If a negative impact is possible, ways to minimize or eliminate it must be determined. Planning that takes the environment into account can prevent or minimize future problems.

THE FASHION ATTIC

Laura had every reason to be proud of her business. She had followed her plan closely and was enjoying each day of work more than she thought possible. The challenges were great, the responsibilities sometimes very difficult, and the hours sometimes seemed never ending, but it was her own business and that made it all worthwhile. She was providing jobs, her products were in demand, and the store was a business the community was proud to support.

Although the business was exceeding expectations, Laura continued to seek assistance and explore new opportunities at every opportunity. She knew that she could not stand still. She attended seminars at the local SBDC and subscribed to several monthly magazines written for entrepreneurs. She was already wrestling with the idea of an expansion so she kept her business plan nearby and up to date.

Laura also began to help others get started in business. She began to do volunteer counseling work for the SBDC and taught a seminar on "How to Write A Successful Business Plan." She felt an obligation to help others just as she had been helped. It was fun to learn about the many opportunities others were exploring. There were several interested in exploring opportunities related to environmental concerns. Recycling businesses were becoming popular. It was surprising to learn of the many types of recycling that are possible. It was also apparent that these entrepreneurs would have to stay on top of the numerous environmental laws that affected their industry.

Laura looked back on her decision to leave her job to become an entrepreneur with great satisfaction. The opportunities were indeed great for a person with her determination, resources, confidence, creativity and desire.

SUMMARY

There are a number of environmental problems for which solutions are needed. Many business opportunities related to environmental problems are open to entrepreneurs today. Areas of both concern and opportunity include solid waste disposal, air pollution, water pollution, and hazardous waste disposal.

The easiest environment-related business to start is one involving some form of recycling. There are many opportunities for entrepreneurs to develop programs to recycle paper, glass, aluminum cans, automobiles, building materials, tires, motor oil, plastic, and many other products. Whether or not a business is directly related to environmental issues, entrepreneurs must make sure that their businesses do not have a negative impact on the environment.

VOCABULARY BUILDER

On a separate sheet of paper, write a brief definition of each word or phrase based on your reading of the chapter.

1. Solid waste
2. Air pollution
3. Water pollution
4. Hazardous waste
5. Recycling

REVIEW QUESTIONS

1. When it comes to polluting Earth, who is to blame?
2. How is trash, or garbage, defined?
3. How much garbage is generated each year by an average American family of four?

4. What causes most air pollution?
5. What were the first two major statutes regulating emissions of hazardous substances in the air and water?
6. What are the two most likely channels of human exposure to hazardous waste?
7. What legislative act still regulates the handling and storage of radioactive wastes?
8. What are some provisions of the Clean Air Amendments of 1990?
9. What is the only limit to entrepreneurial opportunities relating to the environment?
10. What product accounts for more than 40 percent of landfill waste?

DISCUSSION QUESTIONS

1. How has Earth's environmental crisis come about?
2. If you could tackle only one form of pollution, which would it be and why?
3. Why is an understanding of and compliance with environmental law important to would-be entrepreneurs?
4. Why is the profit motive such a powerful influence on the environment?
5. Your partner wants to make as much profit as possible and is trying to convince you to follow only the letter of the environmental laws and certainly not do anything more than legally necessary. "After all," he says, "we didn't cause this mess, why should we have to clean it up?" What do *you* say?

CRITICAL THINKING

Obviously, businesses have caused many of the environmental problems plaguing our country. Do you think that businesses do not care about the environment? Should business be more concerned, even at the expense of reduced profits? Why?

SHORT CASE: PICK UP AND RECYCLE

Linda Cowan became upset after watching a television documentary about America's dangerously full landfills. She decided that it was time for her to get serious about recycling. Linda called City Hall to inquire about recycling services available in her area. She was told that although there were some suggested recycling methods for residents to follow, there was no regular recycling pick–up service available, and only one recycling drop–off center existed in her city.

"Someone has to provide a pick–up service," Linda thought, "and it might as well be me." This led her to a series of activities that included getting referral support from municipal and county agencies, arranging a method of and schedule for residential pick–up service, and establishing a suitable financial agreement with the recycling processing center. The center would pay her by the pound for aluminum, glass (clear, brown, and green), certain types of plastic, and newspaper.

Two months later, Linda was operating a thriving business. She had bought a used pick–up truck and was providing pick–up service for more than 200 homes. Residents were responsible for sorting glass, plastics, aluminum cans, and newspaper into separate containers. Linda picked up individual containers and took them to a small warehouse space that she had rented. She further sorted the items, and when a sufficient weight had been collected, she arranged for the recycling processing center to pick up the bundles and pay her. Linda charged a small annual fee to her customers for her service. Business was so good that she was thinking about adding another truck and hiring an employee to help. Some day she hoped to have her own processing center.

1. How was Linda acting as an entrepreneur?
2. Should Linda consider expanding her operation? Why or why not?

PROJECT CHALLENGE

The plans for your hypothetical business should be nearly complete. In your business plan notebook, record the following information.

1. Consider and describe any environmental concerns that might relate to your business.
2. In marketing your product or service, you will be faced with uncontrollable environmental factors. The factors affect the way your business markets its products or services, including demographic changes, competition, economics, social trends, and technological changes. Identify the uncontrollable environmental

factors that affect your business, analyze them and adjust your firm's marketing strategy accordingly. Record your findings in the form of a report.

Complete your Project Challenge by writing down your personal conclusions about the possibility of someday starting your own business. Do you think that you are a future entrepreneur? What are your strengths and weaknesses that would affect your success as an entrepreneur?

THE SEARCH

Unit 6 Case

The time was right for James Barron to explore new career opportunities. He was completing his Bachelor of Arts degree in business administration and his job with a large west coast defense contractor was probably going to be eliminated due to industry-wide downsizing. With a degree, experience as a purchasing agent, and the knowledge that he wanted to be his own boss, James was ready to identify the employment options available to him.

James decided to start by creating a list of jobs he felt would interest him. He first evaluated his past work experiences to determine which responsibilities and tasks he enjoyed most. Working with people, accepting increased responsibilities, and initiating new projects headed this list. Personal choice criteria indicated a desire to serve the community, maintain professional satisfaction, and earn respect from clients and peers. Skills James identified included his management style, computer expertise, and the ability to negotiate contractual agreements. From this information James compiled the following list of industries that he found appealing:

food services	recycling
wholesale, manufacturing parts	delivery services
restaurant supply	retail, sporting goods

The next step for James was to acquire information from various local agencies. The Los Angeles Chamber of Commerce provided statistics concerning the economic health and growth projection of surrounding communities. The Small Business Development Center offered James leads as to where to go for specific industry information. The Los Angeles Economic Development Agency was able to provide a list of industries which they considered to be under represented in southern California. James ended up with a small library of information to study and analyze from more than a dozen agencies. After more than a month of research, telephone calls, and personal visits, James narrowed his findings to three primary markets.

1) Restaurant supply. The Los Angeles area appeared to have a need for a restaurant supply business specializing in gourmet produce. Many restaurateurs were dissatisfied with the service they received from the few available suppliers. The deliveries arrived late in the day and the produce frequently did not look fresh.
2) Recycling. Small communities on the metropolitan fringe areas of Los Angeles did not have adequate recycling services. There were not enough municipal or private recycling companies to fill this growing need.
3) Exporting manufacturing parts. Requests and orders for manufacturing parts from Pacific rim companies were being ignored. At the same time, there appeared to be a surplus of inventory from many smaller local parts manufacturers.

◆

Having gotten this far, James was ready for the next step. All three opportunities interested him. How would he find the one with the most potential?

Case Questions

1. Give James a course of action to follow for each alternative.
2. Given what you know about James, what would appear to be the opportunity of greatest potential interest to him and why?

GLOSSARY

absentee management   when a business owner oversees the business but is not present at the location
acceptance   an offer is agreed to by the receiving party
accountant   an individual trained in the methods and procedures used in assimilating and maintaining financial records
adverse possession   acquisition of another's land by occupation, without the owner's permission and without payment
advertising   paid nonpersonal public notice that draws attention to the benefits of a product or service
air pollution   the contamination of air by combusting or burning fuels
anchor store   a store large and popular enough to attract customers by itself
Articles of Incorporation   an application asking the state for permission to form a corporation
autonomy anchor   trait that allows individuals to be satisfied by being free thinkers and individualists

bait and switch advertising   the practice of advertising a low-priced item as a means of luring customers into the store for the real purpose of selling them a higher priced item
balance of trade   the difference between the amount of goods and services a country imports and how much it exports
balance sheet   a financial statement that shows the worth or value of a business
barter   a sale involving only the exchange of goods; no money changes hands
bond   certificate that verifies a debt owed to an individual by a corporation or government agency
breach of contract   failure of a party to a contract to perform its obligation(s) as specified in the agreement
break-even point   the price at which the costs of producing and/or selling a product or service are covered
business broker   agent who brings business buyers and sellers together
business plan   a written description of all steps necessary to ensure success in owning and operating a business

capacity   ability to fully understand and comprehend the requirements of a contract as specified by law
capitalization   obtaining the necessary capital assets needed to operate a business
career anchor   essential satisfiers we wish to achieve from our work

cash flow   how money comes in and goes out of a business operation during a specific period of time
casual seller   a person who offers a good or goods for sale but is not in the business of selling
central processing unit (CPU)   contains the microprocessor that contains the logic and control units of the computer
certificate of deposit (CD)   certificate that shows evidence of money being held by a financial institution for a specified period of time bearing a specified interest rate
chain of command   the reporting relationship of positions depicted on the organization chart
charter   document that allows a new corporation to do business in that state
Clayton Act   a follow-up to the Sherman Antitrust Act that further prohibits monopolies from forming and makes tying agreements illegal
collateral   assets used as security for the payment of a debt
column inch   formula for calculating the cost for newspaper advertising
commercial lease   a signed legal agreement that specifies the terms (length of time, cost, conditions to be met) for use of a business property by someone other than its owner
commissioned agents   product brokers for imported goods who usually find buyers within their country
community property   property acquired during marriage
community shopping center   shopping center large enough to provide convenience goods and shopping goods to several neighborhoods
competition   a rivalry between companies that sell similar products or services
competitive analysis   identifying and examining the characteristics of a competing firm
competitive impact   competing effectively with other businesses
competitor   an individual or business that sells the same products or services as another business and appeals to the same types of customers
computer hardware   the various components of computer equipment
computer literacy   possessing basic competence in the use of common software programs and familiarity with the functions of computer hardware components
consideration   value given and value received as a result of contractual agreement
Consumer Product Safety Act   law that protects the public from dangerous products by providing for the evaluation of product safety hazards
contract   a legally enforceable agreement negotiated between two or more persons
convenience goods   products that people purchase regularly
corporation   a legal entity created by law
creativity anchor   trait that allows individuals to derive satisfaction from coming up with unique ideas
current asset   property that is easily converted into cash
current liability   debt that is to be paid within 12 months
customer   an individual who has the means to satisfy his or her needs
customer profile   a recorded and complete description of the ideal customer for a business

database   a collection of information that is normally kept in list form
database software   a set of instructions used with a computer to set up and provide access to a listing of data

debt capital money loaned to a business with the stipulation that the original amount borrowed, plus interest, will be paid to the lender within a certain time period

deceptive advertising advertising that contains information that would cause the average consumer to be misled about a particular product or service

deed a written document by which an individual conveys title and other rights of ownership of real property to another individual

demographic study a study of the statistics for the population in the proposed market

Department of Development (DOD) a state agency that works to advance economic growth and to encourage new and existing businesses to operate within the state

desktop publishing the process of designing and producing a publication using a personal computer

direct competition competition by businesses that derive the majority of their profits from the sale of products or services that are the same or similar to those sold by another business

direct export company finds foreign buyer and makes all necessary arrangements to ship product

disk drive the computer component that stores and retrieves data and programs

draft notice requiring the buyer to pay the face amount due either on sight or on a specified date

earnings approach the method of determining the value of a business by calculating its potential profit and return on investment

easement a nonpossessory right to use land owned by another party

economic stability an economy's ability to withstand changes

economic community a group of nations that agree to cooperate in terms of tariffs, import quotas, and other trade concerns

economic integration nations that trade together work out an agreement for a common economic policy

economics the study of how the resources of a society are allocated

electronic mail the electronic delivery of correspondence

entrepreneur an individual who is willing to take the risk of investing time and money in a business that has the potential to make a profit or incur a loss

entrepreneurship the act of managing an enterprise that has the potential to make a profit or incur a loss

Equal Credit Opportunity Act law that requires any business offering credit to make it available to all creditworthy customers regardless of race, national origin, marital status, religion, sex, age, or receipt of public assistance

equity capital money invested in a business in return for a share in ownership and, therefore, in the profits of the business

ethics moral standards or a system of morals

ethnic ratio the proportion of a particular ethnic group to total population

Eximbank a government agency responsible for facilitating the export of goods and services from the United States

export goods and services made in one country and sold to others

export management companies act as marketing agents for domestic companies in international markets

export trading companies   perform the same function as export management companies, usually accepting title to goods

express warranty   a clearly stated fact about the quality or performance of a product

facsimile (fax) machine   translates a printed page or graphics into electronic signals to be transmitted over telephone lines

factor   a form of short term financing using accounts receivables

Fair Credit Billing Act   law enacted in an attempt to protect consumers against unfair and incorrect billing activities

Fair Credit Reporting Act   law that allows consumers access to their personal credit information

false advertising   advertising that contains information that is not true or would cause the average consumer to reach a false conclusion about a particular product or service

Federal Trade Commission   a regulatory agency that enforces and monitors fair competition and other business practices

financial plan   portion of the business plan that projects start-up costs, income, operating expenses, and cash flow

firm offer   a written, signed sales offer in which the merchant expresses the intention that it cannot be revoked

fixed asset   property that normally takes a longer time to convert into cash

fixed cost   a cost that does not vary even though there are changes in production and/or sales volume

floppy disks   round plastic sheets that store information and are coated with a magnetic surface for use with the disk drive

franchise   a right or privilege to conduct a particular business using a specified trade name

franchise broker   a person who obtains the right from a franchisor to sell franchises within a certain territory—the franchisee pays royalties to the franchise broker, who pays royalties to the franchisor

franchisee   the person who buys a franchise from a franchisor

franchising   method of doing business by which a franchisee is granted the right to engage in offering, selling, or distributing products or services under a specified marketing format

franchisor   the person or company that offers the franchise to others

GATT   the largest free trade agreement ever passed

gender ratio   the proportion of each gender to total population

general partner   a partner who actively engages in the day-to-day management of the business and is fully liable for any actions for, by, and against the business

goods   items of tangible personal property other than money

goodwill   the value of a business' image and community relations

government security   certificate that bears evidence of money on deposit with a government agency

hard disks   round metal plates that store information and are coated with a magnetic surface

Hazardous Substances Labeling Act   law stating that labels must warn consumers of the hazards of using products that may cause illness or death if improperly used

hazardous waste   any waste product that threatens human health or the environment

home-based business   a business conducted from the owner's residence
home equity   the difference between the appraised value of a house and the amount owed on it
hygiene factor   a work environment characteristic needed to ensure job satisfaction

implied warranty   a warranty imposed by law ensuring that a product will perform under normal use and circumstances
import   goods and services that are bought from other countries
import quota   a published specific number of units of a particular product allowed to enter the importing country
income statement   financial report that shows a business' revenues collected and expenses paid out over a specified period of time
incubator   a facility that houses a number of small businesses, usually fewer than ten, which share certain operating expenses
indirect competition   competition by businesses that derive only a small percentage of their profits from the sale of products or services that are the same or similar to those sold by another business
indirect export   company uses an export intermediary to arrange transactions
industrial park   a section of land allocated for use by industrial businesses
institutional advertising   advertising that promotes the advantages of doing business with a particular business or organization
International Trade Administration (ITA)   information source for international trade possibilities
inventory   the number of units and the value of the units a business has available for sale or manufacture
inventory turnover   the number of times a business sells the amount of its base inventory in a year
investor   a financial source that provides capital in return for partial ownership of the business

joint tenancy   ownership by more than one person, with rights of survivorship
joint venture   two or more firms (including governments) share ownership of a business

keyboard   the piece of hardware that typically uses alphanumeric keys to input data into the computer

leasehold improvement   the fix-up performed on a store or business to enhance its appeal to customers
lessee   the person who promises to pay a specified sum of money for the use of space
lessor   the person who allows someone to use his or her property under certain terms
letter of credit   a guarantee from the purchaser's bank that payment will be made on behalf of the client
licensing agreement   a contractual arrangement in which a firm buys or rents the right to use the patent, trademark, production process, brand name, product, or company name of another firm
limited partner   a partner who does not actively engage in the day-to-day management of the business and has liability limited to the extent of his or her investment in the business

line and staff organization an organization that has staff positions to assist the line functions
line organization an organization in which all members are involved in performing duties directly related to creating and/or selling products or services
liquidation value the value of assets if liquidated or sold immediately
long-term liability debt that becomes due after 12 months, usually associated with the purchase of fixed assets

Magnuson-Moss Warranty Act law that sets standards for companies that offer written express warranties on consumer products
mall an enclosed shopping center with a controlled climate
management by objectives (MBO) a management technique that clearly states the goals of the business and meshes them with the goals of the employees
managerial anchor trait that allows individuals to be satisfied by working with and through people and by assuming many duties and responsibilities
markdown the difference between the original selling price and the price at which an item is actually sold
market a group of consumers who have an unsatisfied need for a particular product or service
market potential total potential sales dollars for a particular market
market research systematic gathering, recording, and analyzing of information concerning the market for goods and services
market segmentation process of dividing the market into groups of similar consumers
market share the portion of a particular market that uses a particular product or service
market value the value of similar goods, homes, properties, businesses, etc., in similar markets
marketing concept the belief that consumer wants and needs are the driving force behind any product development or marketing effort
marketing mix four variables—product, place, price, and promotion—that must be manipulated to ensure success in marketing
marketing plan defines and quantifies consumers, demand, competition, geographic market, and pricing policy for a specific small business
marketing research the systematic gathering, recording, and analyzing of data relating to the marketing of goods or services
market segmentation process of dividing the market into groups of similar consumers
marketing strategy planned activity designed to increase the sale of a business' products or services
markup amount added to the cost of an item to arrive at a selling price
maturity date the predetermined time that a bond becomes payable to the bondholder
merchant sells a particular good or goods on a regular basis and claims special knowledge
merchant association an organization of merchants who work together to promote shopping at their shopping area

monitor   the part of the computer hardware that provides a video display of data
monopoly   a business agreement whereby a single company controls a specific supply of products or services
motivator   a work environment factor that provides workers with satisfaction and motivation
mouse   controls cursor movement on the computer screen

NAFTA   agreement that eliminated tariffs and trade barriers between the U.S., Canada, and Mexico
neighborhood shopping center   small shopping center, usually with fewer than 20 stores, that serves its immediate neighborhood
nontariff barrier   limit on the quantity of certain goods imported

offer   communication of a proposal
open account   payment is not due until a specified time after the goods have been received
open to buy   money that is available for the purchase of inventory
organization chart   illustration of an organization's distribution of its human resources

partners   individuals who voluntarily agree to conduct a partnership
partnership   a voluntary association of two or more persons to carry on as co-owners of a business for profit
partnership agreement   the official document forming the contract between partners
per capita income   average amount of money made or received, per person, on an annual basis
periodic tenancy   lease for a set period of time that will continue for similar periods of time until terminated
perpetual inventory   an approximate written record of the amount of inventory available
personal selling   face-to-face communication between the buyer and the seller
physical inventory   an actual count of all inventory on hand
piggyback exporting   another company in the export distribution system sells the entrepreneur's products in addition to its own
price discrimination   charging different prices to different customers for the same goods
price fixing   the agreement between competitors to establish and maintain prices of their goods and services
primary data   information collected for the first time for a specific project
prime rate of interest   the publicly stated rate that major commercial banks charge their most creditworthy business customers for short-term loans
printer   the device that allows the entrepreneur to generate a hard (paper) copy of information generated by or stored in the computer
pro forma financial statement   projected statistical report used to illustrate the expected financial status of a business at a future date

product advertising advertising that draws attention to the features, advantages and benefits of a particular product or service
profit margin (markup) the difference between what the seller and the consumer pay for a product
promoter a person who starts the process to create a corporation
promotional event a planned activity that is designed to promote goodwill for the business that is conducting the event
property something that is owned or can be owned
psychographics psychological variables (personality, attitude, beliefs, self-concept) and life-style values
publicity advertising that does not incur cost to a seller

recycling process of transforming used and obsolete goods into useable and saleable products
regional shopping center shopping center that usually has three or four anchor stores and more than 40 other stores
replacement value the cost of purchasing new assets at current market value
retained earnings profits that remain in a business for future use
return on investment the payback of the money invested in a business operation
risk of loss the financial responsibility assumed by a party in a sales contract for damaged or destroyed goods
Robinson-Patman Act adds to the Clayton Act by outlawing price discrimination
royalty an ongoing fee paid to a franchisor at specific intervals—usually a percent of gross revenue or net sales

sale the immediate transfer of ownership of goods for a price
sale on approval a sales transaction in which the buyer has a right to approve the merchandise prior to the transfer of ownership
sales approach the part of the selling process that is intended to attract the potential buyer's attention and stimulate interest
sales close the part of the selling process that requests an action, such as an order or purchase
sales plan any planned attempt to stimulate a potential customer's attention, interest, and desire
sales presentation the part of the selling process that emphasizes the features, advantages, and benefits of a product or service
sales promotion things other than advertising and personal selling that will have a positive impact on the purchasing decision
sales training planned education techniques which demonstrate selling techniques and motivate sales personnel
secondary data information already published and available
security anchor trait that allows individuals to be satisfied by working in a large organization with the assurance of long-term employment

seller a person who offers a good or goods for sale
Service Corps of Retired Executives (SCORE) a counseling service—staffed by volunteers who have business experience—for new and established small-business owners
Sherman Antitrust Act makes any business deal illegal that unreasonably restricts trade or commerce among states, and outlaws price fixing
shopping goods products that people purchase occasionally
Small Business Administration a federal agency created to assist the development of the country's small business sector
Small Business Development Center (SBDC) an agency funded by both the federal government and state governments to provide counseling and training for small business owners
social responsibility the responsibility of businesses to pursue policies that benefit society
software computer programs that tell the computer what to do
sole proprietorship a business established, owned, and controlled by one person
solid waste trash that cannot easily be recycled
spreadsheet an electronic replacement for an accountant's columnar ledger, pencil, and calculator
specialty goods products that people purchase infrequently
staffing the recruitment and selection of employees
stand-alone store a store that is not located in a shopping area
stock certificate representing ownership in a corporation
super regional shopping center a colossal shopping mall made up of many anchor stores and sometimes hundreds of smaller stores

target marketing marketing to a selected group of consumers
tariff a fee imposed by a government on imported goods to protect the country's domestic industries from being undersold
technical anchor trait that allows individuals to derive satisfaction from doing a specific job correctly
telecommunications the communication of information by computer via telephone lines, cables, or satellite
telemarketing using the telephone as a vehicle to sell or introduce a product or service to potential customers
tenancy at sufferance lease in which a tenant may remain in the facility after termination of the lease
tenancy at will possession of real property without benefit of an agreement that documents terms
tenancy by entirety ownership by husband and wife, with rights of survivorship
tenancy for years lease for a fixed period of time
tenancy in common ownership by more than one person, without rights of survivorship
Theory X manager a manager who directs with little consideration for human relations

Theory Y manager a manager who is very concerned with human relations
total pricing concept prices are set to compete successfully, build good customer relations, and ensure the long-term success of a business
trade credit a type of financing that allows delayed payment for merchandise
trade deficit a country's total imports are greater than total exports
trade show a gathering of many producers in the same industry to display products to customers
trade surplus a country's total exports are greater than total imports
tying agreements the practice of a seller requiring a customer to buy one type of product in order to be permitted to buy another type

undercapitalize failure of a business owner to obtain the needed resources to meet operating expenses in early stages of business
Uniform Commercial Code a group of uniform business rules adopted by most states
U.S.-Canada Free Trade Agreement the first of the many free trade agreements of the current era
utility satisfaction using one's money (utility) for the product or service that will bring the greatest need satisfaction

VANE acronym for values, attitudes, needs, expectations
variable cost a cost that fluctuates with changes in production and/or sales volume
venture capitalist an investor who specializes in funding high-risk business proposals that are not acceptable to banks
visual merchandising creative display of merchandise for attracting customers' attention and creating a desire to purchase
voice mail also called messaging or voice store and forward, refers to an electronic means of sending, retrieving, and saving voice messages

water pollution the invasion of chemicals or other harmful substances into water supplies or underground water reserves
whole life insurance an investment that yields cash value from premium payments that are invested
word processing creating, processing, printing, distributing, and filing a document through the use of technology

zoned editions sections of newspapers or magazines that are printed for and circulated only to specific areas of the total readership

INDEX

A

Absentee management, **13–14**
Acceptances, **380–381**
Accountants, **35, 352**
Accounts payable ledger, **235**
Accounts receivable financing, **211**
Accounts receivable ledger, **235**
Adverse possession, **413–414**
Advertising:
    bait and switch, **365**
    billboard, **172**
    budget for, **140–141**
    creating copy for, **174–175**
    deceptive, **363–365**
    definition of, **167–168**
    direct mail, **173–174**
    ethics and, **428–429**
    evaluating results of, **175–176**
    false, **363**
    guidelines for, **168**
    institutional, **169**
    in the marketing mix, **136–137**
    newspaper, **169–170**
    product, **169**
    for prospective employees, **279–281**
    radio, **170–171**
    television, **172**
    yellow pages, **172–173**
Age Discrimination in Employment Act of 1967, **290**
Agreements. *See* Contracts and agreements
Air Pollution Control Act of 1955, **466**
Air pollution, **464**
American Marketing Association (AMA), **425**

Analysis:
    competitive, **102–103, 105**
    data, **82, 85–87, 134**
Anchor stores, **116**
Articles of Incorporation, **266**
Assets, **231–232**
Assignment, contract, **389–390**
Atomic Energy Act of 1954, **466**
Attorneys, **35, 61, 351**
Autonomy anchor, **9**

B

Balance sheets, **231–232**
Banks:
    business plan and, **33**
    commercial, **208–212**
    investment, **216**
    references for, **34**
    savings and loans, **212**
Barron's magazine, **58**
Barter, **397**
Bilateral contract, **386**
Bonds, **198**
Bookkeeping, **235, 241.** *See also* Record keeping
Breach of contract, **387–389**
Break-even point, **151**
Business:
    brokers, **41**
    home based, **119–120**
    industrial, **118–119**
    stages, **168–169**
Business opportunities:
    advantages of purchasing an existing business, **43**
    business brokers and, **41**
    classified advertising and, **40–41**

    disadvantages of purchasing an existing business, **44–45**
    evaluation considerations, **49–52**
    finding existing business for sale, **40–43**
    franchising, **56–67**
    how to purchase a business, **45–47**
    market value and, **40**
    through industry sources, **41–42**
    types of, **48–49**
    using goodwill to evaluate, **48**
    using liquidation value to evaluate, **51**
    using replacement value to evaluate, **51**
    using the earnings approach to evaluate, **49**
Business plans:
    concept history and background, **27–29**
    description of, **25–26**
    financial plan and, **33**
    and forms of ownership, **32**
    formulating a, **26–27**
    goals and objectives, **29,** 30
    and legal requirements, **31–32**
    marketing plan and the, **30–31**
    organization, management, and staffing plan, **33–34**
    short-term and long-term goals, **29–30**

C

Capacity, **382**
Capital. *See* Financing
Capitalization, **224**

491

492
Index

Career anchors:
   autonomy anchor, **9**
   creative anchor, **9**
   managerial anchor, **9**
   security anchor, **9**
   technical anchor, **8–9**
Cash and carry, **403**
Cash flow statements, **232–233**
Cash in advance (C.I.A.), **309**
Cash on delivery (C.O.D.), **309**
Cash on hand, **196–197**
Casual seller, **396–397**
Catalog sales, **307**
Central processing unit (CPU), **323–324**
Certificate of deposit (CD), **201**
Chain of command, **278**
Chambers of commerce, **351**
Charters, **266**
Civil Rights Act of 1964, **290**
Classified advertising, **40–41**
Clayton Act, **97**
Clean Air Amendments of 1990, **468**
Collateral, **199–201**
College placement services, **280**
Commercial banks, **208–212**
Commercial leases, **120**
Commissioned agents, **447–448**
Common markets. *See* Economic communities, **456**
Community colleges, planning assistance, **35**
Community property, **415–416**
Competition:
   competitive analysis, **102–103, 105**
   direct, **98–99**
   freedom to enter or exit business, **97**
   FTC and, **369–370**
   the guarantee of fair competition, **97–98**
   impact of, **96**
   indirect, **99–100**
   and the marketing plan, **30–31**
   multiple buyers and sellers, **96–97**
   and private enterprise, **96–98**
   similar products and services, **96**
Competitors, **95**
Comprehensive Environmental Response, Compensation, and Liability Act of 1980 (CERCLA), **467–468**
Computers:
   basic description of, **322**
   central processing unit (CPU), **323–324**
   disks and disk drives, **324**
   hardware, **322–323**
   as a management control tool, **314–315**
   software, **325–330**
   telecommunications, **330–334**
Consideration, **381–382**
Consumer credit, **366–367**
Consumer goods, **112–113**
Consumer Product Safety Act, **371**
Consumer protection, **370–372**
Consumer Protection Division, **350**
Consumers, and the marketing plan, **30**
Contracts and agreements:
   acceptance, **380–381**
   agreement, **378**
   assignment of, **389–390**
   bilateral, **386**
   breach of, **387–389**
   capacity, **382–384**
   consideration, **381–382**
   contract, **378**
   contractual form, **384–385**
   express or implied, **386**
   formal or simple, **387**
   legality of, **381**
   offer, **379–380**
   rescission, **388**
   sales, **211–212**
   simple, **387**
   unilateral, **386**
Controlling. *See* Human resources management
Convenience, **111–112**
Convenience goods, **112–113**
Corporations, **32**
   advantages of, **268–269**
   disadvantages of, **269–270**
   domestic or foreign, **267**
   ownership and management of, **266–267**
   starting, **266**
Creative anchor, **9**
Credit, ownership by, **404**
Current assets, **231–232**
Current liabilities, **232**
Customers. *See also* Consumers
   analyzing strengths and weaknesses of, **102–103, 105**
   and market research, **79–90**
   description of, **78–79**
   geographic distribution and, **100–102**
   profiles of, **130**

D

Data:
   analysis of, **82, 85–87, 134**
   collection of, **80–82, 134**
   implementation of, **87, 134**
   primary, **81, 134**
   secondary, **81–82, 134**
Database, **326–328**
Debt capital. *See* Financing, debt capital
Deeds, **412**
Demand for specific performance, **388**
Demographics, **80**
Department of Development (DOD), **347, 349–350**
Desktop publishing, **330**
Direct competition, **98–99**
Direct export, **447**
Disbursement journal, **235**
Discrimination, **430**
Disk, computer, **324**
Draft, **452**

E

Earnings approach, **49–50**
Easements, **416–417**
Economic communities, **456**

Index

Economic integration, **452**
Economics, **148**
Economic stability, **80**
Electronic mail, **331–332**
Employment agencies, **280**
Employment applications, **281**
End of month (E.O.M.), **309**
Entrepreneur magazine, **58**
Entrepreneurs:
    capabilities of, **14**
    and career anchors, **8–10**
    characteristics of, **4–6**
    choosing to be an, **4**
    definition of, **2–4**
    life-style of, **14**
    and setting personal goals, **10–19**
    success as, **7–8**
    VANE and, **10**
Entrepreneurship, **2**
    environmental, **463–473**
    international, **444–458**
Environment:
    air pollution, **464**
    entrepreneurial opportunities in, **469–473**
    hazardous waste, **465**
    legislation, **466–468**
    solid waste, **464**
    water pollution, **464–465**
Environmental Protection Agency (EPA), **372**
Equal Credit Opportunity Act, **367**
Equal Employment Opportunity Commission (EEOC), **291**
Equipment vendors, **212–213**
Equity capital. *See* Financing, equity capital
Ethics:
    and American Marketing Association (AMA), **425**
    and social responsibility, **425**
    and the environment, **432–433**
    and treatment of consumers, **427–429**
    and treatment of the competition, **430**
    business, **425**
    computer technology and, **433–435**
    definition of, **425**
    establishing a code of ethics, **435–436**
    in treatment of employees, **430–432**
Ethnic ratio, **80**
European Union (EU), **456**
Eximbank, **450**
Export management companies (EMCs), **448–449**
Export Trading Companies (ETC), **449**
Exports, **444**
Express contract, **386**
Express warranty, **368**

F

FAB (features, advantages, benefits), **156**
Facilities, **103**
    evaluating, **121–122**
    and home-based businesses, **119–120**
    incubators, **119**
    leasing, **120–121**
    professional office space, **120**
Facsimile machine, **332–333**
Factoring, **451**
Fair Credit Billing Act, **372–373**
Fair Credit Reporting Act, **367**
Fair Labor Standards Act of 1938, **290**
False advertising, **363**
Federal Environmental Pesticide Control Act of 1972, **466**
Federal Trade Commission (FTC):
    advertising, **363–365**
    competition, **97, 98, 369–370**
    consumer credit, **366–367**
    deceptive pricing, **365–366**
    Equal Credit Opportunity Act, **367**
    Fair Credit Reporting Act, **367**
    franchises and, **61**
    Magnuson-Moss Warranty Act, **368–369**
    product warranties, **368–369**
    Truth-in-Lending Act, **366–367**
Federal Water Pollution Control Act of 1952, **466**
Financial plan, **33**
Financing:
    balance sheets, **231–232**
    borrowing against collateral, **199–202**
    calculating personal net worth, **196**
    cash flow statements, **232–233**
    commercial banks, **208–212**
    computing initial capital needs, **225–227**
    debt capital, **207–208**
    determining available cash, **196–199**
    equipment vendors, **212–213**
    equity capital, **215–217**
    financial plan and, **224–225**
    financial statements and, **227–233**
    income statements, **228–230**
    maintaining financial records, **235–246**
    matching resources to needs, **217–218**
    methods of payment, **452**
    overseas sources, **450–452**
    personal financial statement, **34**
    pro forma financial statements, **227–228**
    savings and loans, **212**
    Small Business Administration, **214**
    state and local business development funds, **213**
    supply vendors, **212**
Firm offer, **397**
Fixed assets, **232**
Fixed costs, **151**
Fixtures, **410**
Forbes magazine, **58**
Formal contract, **387**
"Franchise Annual, The," 58
Franchise brokers, **61**
Franchisee, **57, 67**
Franchise Opportunities Handbook, **58**

Franchises:
  advantages of purchasing, 58–60
  classifications of, 57–58
  definition of, 56–57
  definition of franchising, 57
  disadvantages of purchasing, 60
  and the franchise agreement, 61, 63–65
  legal aspects of owning, 60–65
  questions to ask before purchasing, 66–67
  sources for finding, 58
  and the Uniform Franchise Offering Circular (UFOC), 61
"Franchise Yearbook," 58
"Franchising for Free," 58
Franchisors, 57, 66–67
Furniture, fixture, and equipment ledger, 235

G

GATT (General Agreement on Tariffs and Trade), 456
Gender ratio, 80
General partner, 264
Geography, customer distribution and, 100–101
Goals, 29–30
Goods, 396
Goodwill, 48
Government Printing Office, 346
Government securities, 197–198

H

Hazardous and Solid Waste Amendments of 1984 (HSWA), 468
Hazardous Substances Labeling Act, 371–372
Hazardous waste, 465
Herzberg, Frederick, 284–285
Home-based businesses, 119–120
Home equity, 199–200
Human resources management:
  controlling, 286–289
  effects of inventory and sales fluctuations on, 310–311
  employee theft, 313–314
  interviewing, 281–283
  job applications, 281
  labor laws, 289–291
  managing, 283–286
  recruiting, 279–281
  staffing, 276–279
Hygiene factors, 285–286

I

Immigration Reform and Control Act of 1986, 290
Implied contracts, 386
Implied warranties, 368
Import quotas, 446
Imports, 444
Income:
  retained earnings, 11
  return on investment, 11–12
  statements, 228–230
Incubators, 119
Indirect competition, 99–100
Indirect export, 447
Industrial parks, 119
Info Franchise Newsletter, 58
Inheritance, 418
Installment loans, 210
Insurance, 199, 311–312, 419–421
Insurance agents, 352
Internal Revenue Service (IRS), 346
International Trade Association (ITA), 445–446
International trade, 444–458
Interviewing, employee, 281–283
Inventory, 211, 225, 299–307
  cash in advance (C.I.A.), 309
  cash on delivery (C.O.D.), 308–309
  end of month (E.O.M.), 309
  financing, 211
  finding suppliers, 304, 307
  just-in-time inventory control, 309
  open to buy, 308
  perpetual, 304
  physical, 304
  purchase plan, 302–304
  receipt of goods (R.O.G.), 309
  theft, 312–314
  turnover, 225
Investment banks, 216
Investments, as collateral, 200–201
Investors, 215
Invoice, 308

J

Joint tenancy, 414–415
Joint ventures, 449–450
Just-in-time inventory, 309

K

Keyboard, computer, 322

L

Labor laws, 290–291
Leasehold improvements, 226
Leasing, 120–121
  periodic tenancy, 417
  rights and duties in, 418
  tenancy at sufferance, 418
  tenancy at will, 418
  tenancy for years, 417
Legislation, 466–468
Lessee, 120
Lessor, 120–121
Letter of credit, 452
Liability, 232
Licensing, 449
Limited partner, 264
Line and staff organizations, 278
Line of credit, 209–210
Line organizations, 278
Liquidation value, 51
Loans:
  assistance with, 341
  installment, 210
  mortgage, 210
Location, 103
  choosing, 113

Index

downtown shopping districts, **114–115**
for industrial businesses, **118–119**
shopping centers, **115–118**
stand-alone stores, **118**
Long-term liabilities, **232**

M

Magnuson-Moss Warranty Act, **368–369**
Mailing lists, **174**
Mail order. *See* Catalog sales
Malls, **116**
Management:
 absentee, **13–14**
 controlling revenues, **299**
 human resources, **286–289**
 inventory, **299–307**
 of inventory and sales fluctuations, **307–314**
 Management by Objectives (MBO), **297–299**
 motivating, **284**
 Theory X managers, **284**
 Theory Y managers, **284–285**
 using computers as a control, **314–315**
Management by objectives (MBO), **297–299**
Managerial anchor, **9**
Markdowns, **153–154**
Marketing mix:
 place, **135–136**
 price, **136**
 product, **135**
 promotion, **136–140**
Marketing plan, **30–31**
 marketing concept and, **129**
 market segmentation, **129**
 target marketing, **129–130**
Marketing strategies, **140–142**
Market research:
 analyzing data, **82–87, 134**
 collecting data, **80–82, 133–134**
 defining the question, **80, 133**
 definition of, **131–132**
 determining community need, **87–90**
 evaluating action, **87, 134–135**
 implementing data, **87, 134**
Markets:
 customers and, **78**
 franchises and, **67**
 geographic, **31**
Market share, **155**
Market value, **40**
Markups. *See* Profit margin
Maturity date, **198**
Merchant associations, **118**
Merchants, **396**
Monitor, computer, **325**
Monopoly, **97**
Mortgage loans, **210**
Motivators, **285**
Mouse, computer, **322**

N

NAFTA (North American Free Trade Agreement), **455**
National Environmental Policy Act (NEPA), **372**
Networking, **306**
Nontariff barriers, **446**
North American Securities Administrators' Association, **61**
Notes payable ledger, **241**

O

Occupational Safety and Health Act (OSHA), **290, 372**
Offers, **378–380**
Office of the Secretary of State, **350**
Open account, **452**
Open to buy, **308**
Organization charts, **33, 277–279**
Ownership:
 comparing forms of, **270**
 corporations, **32, 265–270**
 partnerships, **32, 216, 261–265**
 property, **410–421**
 sole proprietorships, **32, 258–261**

P

Partnerships:
 advantages and disadvantages, **265**
 closely held, **268**
 definition of, **32, 261**
 financing, **216**
 general partners, **264**
 limited partners, **264**
 and partnership agreements, **261–263**
 public or private, **267**
 termination of, **264–265**
Pensions, **199**
Per capita income, **80**
Periodic tenancy, **417**
Personal financial statements, **34**
Personal property, **412**
Personal satisfaction, **12**
Personal selling, **139,** 141
Personnel. *See* Human resources management
Piggyback exporting, **449**
Place, **135**
Planning:
 the business plan and, **25–35**
 sources for assistance in, **35**
Price, **102–103, 136, 397**
 determining, **150–156**
 discrimination, **98**
 fixing, **97–98**
 and pricing strategies, **154–156**
 and supply and demand, **148–150**
Pricing:
 deceptive, **365**
 ethics and, **428**
 marketing plan and, **31**
Primary data, **81, 134**
Prime rate of interest, **209**
Printer, computer, **325**
Products:
 demonstrations of, **179**
 description in business plan, **27–28**
 development of, **89**
 and the marketing mix, **135**

safety, **370–372**
warranties, **368–369**
Profit margin, **116, 152–153**
Profit sharing, **199**
Pro forma financial statements, **227–228**
Promoters, **266**
Promotion. *See also* Marketing mix, promotion
  advertising, **167–176**
  cold calling, **178**
  product demonstrations, **179**
  and promotional events, **176–177, 312**
  retailing, **178**
  and sales training, **180**
  telemarketing, **179**
  trade shows, **179**
Property:
  acquiring, **412–414**
  community, **415–416**
  definition of, **410**
  easements, **416–417**
  insurance, **419–421**
  joint tenancy, **414–415**
  leasing, **417–418**
  personal, **412**
  real, **410–411**
  tenancy by entirety, **415**
  tenancy in common, **415**
Psychographics, **80–81**
Publicity, **159**

Q

Quitclaim deeds, **412–413**

R

Real property, **410–412**
Receipt of goods (R.O.G.), **309**
Receipts journal. *See* Sales journal
Record keeping, **48**
Recruiting, **279–281**
Recycling, **469–472**
References, **34, 195–196**
Referrals, employee, **281**
Regulations, **362–373**
Replacement value, **51**

Rescission, contract, **388**
Resource Conservation and Recovery Act of 1976 (RCRA), **467**
Restitution, **388–389**
Resumés:
  bank financing and, **34**
  personal, **192–196**
Retained earnings, **11**
Return on investment, **11–12, 301**
Risk of loss, **399**
Robinson-Patman Act, **97, 98**
Royalty, **57**

S

Safe Drinking Water Act of 1974, **467**
Sale on approval, **404–405**
Sales:
  approach, **157**
  calls, **306–307**
  close, **157–158**
  contracts, **211–212**. *See also* Contracts and agreements
  definition of, **396**
  fluctuations, **307–314**
  journal, **235**
  of goods, **396**
  ownership, **402–405**
  plan, **156–159**
  presentation, **157**
  promotion, **137–138, 141**
  strategies, **158–159**
  telemarketing, **178–179, 307**
  trade shows, **179, 307**
  training, **180**
Savings and loans, **212**
Secondary, **81–82,** 134
Security. *See* Inventory, theft
Security anchor, **9**
Sellers, **396**
Service Corps of Retired Executives (SCORE), **341**
Sherman Antitrust Act, **97–98**
Shopping areas, **114–115**
Shopping centers:
  community, **115–116**
  neighborhood, **115**
  regional, **116**

super regional, **116–117**
Shopping goods, **113**
Simple contract, **387**
Small Business Administration (SBA):
  definition of, **4–5**
  financial assistance from, **214**
  loan assistance from, **341**
  planning assistance from, **35**
  publications, **343**
  Service Corps of Retired Executives (SCORE), **341**
  Small Business Institute (SBI), **341**
Small business assistance:
  community resources, **350–351**
  federal/state cooperatives, **346–347**
  federal agencies, **340–346**
  professional services, **351–352**
  state level, **347–350**
Small Business Development Center (SBDC), **346–347**
Small Business Innovation Research (SBIR), **217**
Small Business Institute (SBI), **341**
Small Business Investment Company (SBIC), **217**
Social responsibility, **425, 432–433**
Software, **325–330**
Sole proprietorships, **32**
  advantages of, **260–261**
  disadvantages of, **261**
  formation of, **259–260**
  operation of, **260**
Solid waste, **464**
Specialty goods, **113**
Spreadsheets, **328**
Staffing, **33–34, 276–283**
Stand-alone stores, **118**
State Department of Agriculture, **350**
State Department of Labor, **350**
State Sales and Tax Division, **350**
Status, **12**
Statute of Frauds, **384–385**
Stocks, **198, 216**
Suit for damages, **388**

Superfund Amendments and Reauthorization Act of 1986 (SARA), **468**
Supply vendors, **212**

T

Target marketing, **129–130**
Tariffs, **446**
Technical anchor, **8–9**
Telecommunications, **330–331**
Telemarketing, **178–179**, **307**
Tenancy at sufferance, **418**
Tenancy at will, **418**
Tenancy by entirety, **415**
Tenancy for years, **417**
Tenancy in common, **415**
Theory X managers, **284**
Theory Y managers, **284–285**
Thomas Register of American Manufacturers, **88**
Total pricing concept, **162**
Toxic Substances Control Act of 1976, **467**
Trackball, computer, **322–323**
Trade agreements:
    European Union (EU), **456**
    GATT, **456**
    NAFTA, **455**
    U.S.-Canada Free Trade Agreement, **456**
Trade credit, **212**
Trade deficit, **444**
Trade shows, **179**, **306**
Trade surplus, **444–445**
Truth-in-Lending Act, **366–367**
Tying agreements, **98**

U

Undercapitalization, **225**
Uniform Commercial Code (UCC), **396**
Uniform Partnership Act (UPA), **261**
Unilateral contract, **386**
United State-Canada Free Trade Agreement, **456**
United States Department of Commerce, **343**, **345–346**
Utility satisfaction, **149–150**

V

VANE (values, attitudes, needs, and expectations), **10**
Variable costs, **151**
Vendors, **304**
Venture capitalists, **215**
Venture magazine, **58**
Visual merchandising, **139–140**, **141**
Voice mail, **333–334**

W

Wall Street Journal, **58**
Warranties, **429**
Warranty deeds, **412**
Water pollution, **464–465**
Whole life insurance, **199**
Word of mouth, **158**
Word processing, **325–326**
Worker's Compensation Board, **350**
Working conditions, **481**

Z

Zoned editions, **170**